DESIGNING UBIQUITOUS INFORMATION ENVIRONMENTS: SOCIO-TECHNICAL ISSUES AND CHALLENGES

IFIP – The International Federation for Information Processing

IFIP was founded in 1960 under the auspices of UNESCO, following the First World Computer Congress held in Paris the previous year. An umbrella organization for societies working in information processing, IFIP's aim is two-fold: to support information processing within its member countries and to encourage technology transfer to developing nations. As its mission statement clearly states,

> IFIP's mission is to be the leading, truly international, apolitical organization which encourages and assists in the development, exploitation and application of information technology for the benefit of all people.

IFIP is a non-profitmaking organization, run almost solely by 2500 volunteers. It operates through a number of technical committees, which organize events and publications. IFIP's events range from an international congress to local seminars, but the most important are:

• The IFIP World Computer Congress, held every second year;
• Open conferences;
• Working conferences.

The flagship event is the IFIP World Computer Congress, at which both invited and contributed papers are presented. Contributed papers are rigorously refereed and the rejection rate is high.

As with the Congress, participation in the open conferences is open to all and papers may be invited or submitted. Again, submitted papers are stringently refereed.

The working conferences are structured differently. They are usually run by a working group and attendance is small and by invitation only. Their purpose is to create an atmosphere conducive to innovation and development. Refereeing is less rigorous and papers are subjected to extensive group discussion.

Publications arising from IFIP events vary. The papers presented at the IFIP World Computer Congress and at open conferences are published as conference proceedings, while the results of the working conferences are often published as collections of selected and edited papers.

Any national society whose primary activity is in information may apply to become a full member of IFIP, although full membership is restricted to one society per country. Full members are entitled to vote at the annual General Assembly, National societies preferring a less committed involvement may apply for associate or corresponding membership. Associate members enjoy the same benefits as full members, but without voting rights. Corresponding members are not represented in IFIP bodies. Affiliated membership is open to non-national societies, and individual and honorary membership schemes are also offered.

DESIGNING UBIQUITOUS INFORMATION ENVIRONMENTS: SOCIO-TECHNICAL ISSUES AND CHALLENGES

IFIP TC8 WG 8.2 International Working Conference,
August 1-3, 2005, Cleveland, Ohio, U.S.A.

Edited by

Carsten Sørensen
The London School of Economics and Political Science
United Kingdom

Youngjin Yoo
Case Western Reserve University
United States

Kalle Lyytinen
Case Western Reserve University
United States

Janice I. DeGross
University of Minnesota
United States

 Springer

Library of Congress Cataloging-in-Publication Data

A C.I.P. Catalogue record for this book is available from the Library of Congress.

Designing Ubiquitous Information Environments: Socio-Technical Issues and Challenges, Edited by Carsten Sørensen, Youngjin Yoo, Kalle Lyytinen and Janice I.DeGross

p.cm. (The International Federation for Information Processing)

Printed on acid-free paper.

ISBN 978-1-4419-3900-5
e-ISBN 978-0-387-28918-2

Printed in the United States of America.

9 8 7 6 5 4 3 2 1
springeronline.com

CONTENTS

Part 3: Organizational Impact

Part 4: Development Issues

Part 5: Innovation and Diffusion of Ubiquitous Information Environments

Part 6: Position Papers

Part 7: Panels

PREFACE

This book records one of the continuous attempts of the IFIP Working Group 8.2, studying the interaction of information systems and the organization, to explore and understand the shifting boundaries and dependencies between organizational activities and their computer support. The book marks the result of the IFIP WG 8.2 conference on "Designing Ubiquitous Information Environments: Socio-Technical Issues and Challenges." Since its inception in the late 1970s, IFIP WG 8.2 has sought to understand how computer-based information systems interact and must be designed as an integrated part of the organizational design. At that time, information systems handled repetitive and remote back-office functions and the main concern was work task design for repetitive input tasks and the potential impact of improved information support on organizational decision-making and structure. The focus of the information system design shifted in the 1980s when computers became part of the furniture and moved into the office. Reflecting this significant change, IFIP WG 8.2 in 1989 organized a conference dedicated to the design and impact of desktop technology in order to examine how organizational processes and the locus of action changed when the computer was moved into the office. Sixteen years later, we are experiencing another significant change. Computers are now becoming part of our body and sensory system and will move out of the traditional office locations and into the wilderness. Again, IFIP WG 8.2 must address the research challenge and explore how principles of organizing and organizational activity will become transformed when computing becomes pervasive, invisible, and embodied in our bodily experience. We wish that this conference will match the intellectual standards of inquiring interactions between organization form, activity, process, and computer support set by previous IFIP WG 8.2 conferences and that it will pave the way for a deeper examination of how complex socio-technical systems are designed and evaluated when they rely on or draw upon ubiquitous computer support.

Staging a conference and producing a book such as this one is never possible without the commitment and hard work of many individuals and organizations. We want to thank IFIP and the sponsors of the conference for providing the support and funding for its implementation. The sponsors are IFIP, Case Western Reserve University, London School of Economics, and Accenture.

The organizing committee has been responsible for the implementation of the program and for setting up the environment for the conference that facilitates interaction. The conference committee members are

- Kalle Lyytinen
- Youngjin Yoo
- Carsten Sørensen

- Colleen Gepperth
- Matt Germonprez
- Michel Avital

We wish to thank the following for contributing with reviews:

Mikko Ahonen
David Allen
Steven Alter
Michel Avital
Richard Baskerville
Nicholas Berente
Avi Bernstein
Kirsti Elisabeth Berntsen
Richard Boland
Laurence Brooks
Ann Brown
Silvia Calderwood
Bongsug Chae
Panos Constantinides
Karlene Cousins
Kevin Crowston
Jan Damsgaard
Gordon Euchler
Vladislav Fomin
Matt Germonprez
Majorkumar Govindaraju
Ole Hanseth
Jukka Heikkila
Ola Henfridsson
Rudy Hirschheim
Yisong Jiang
Juhani Iivari

Petteri Kaitovaara
Masao Kakihara
Helena Karsten
Jeffrey Kim
Jan Kietzmann
Helmut Krcmar
Steinar Kristoffersen
Kuldeep Kumar
Lynette Kvasny
Karl Reiner Lang
Eric Laurier
Heejin Lee
Jonathan Liebenau
Ben Light
Jan Ljungberg
Paul Luff
Scott Mainwaring
Lynne Markus
Lars Mathiassen
Catherine Middleton
Ramiro Montealegre
Eric Monteiro
Peter Nielsen
Petter Nielsen
Urban Nulden
Rosalie Ocker
Carsten Osterlund

Brian Pentland
Mark Perry
Daniele Pica
Alain Pinsonneault
Sandeep Purao
Anand Ramchand
Julie Rennecker
Dan Robey
Nancy Russo
Amarolinda Saccol
Steve Sawyer
Ulrike Schultze
Zixing Shen
Miro Siwczyk
Sean Smith
Adel Taitoon
David Tilson
Joe Valacich
John Venable
Katerina Voutsina
Joel West
Edgar Whitley
Mikael Wiberg
Gamel Wiredu
Eleanor Wynn
Heng Xu

We also want to thank Brian Warner, Yisong Jiang, and Nikhil Srinivasan who developed and managed the Web site for the on-line review process. Finally we want to thank the publisher, Springer, and in particular the longstanding friend of IFIP WG 8.2 Janice DeGross. Without her professional guidance and dedicated work for manuscript management and copyediting, it would have been impossible to produce the book in time and in this quality.
We welcome everybody to join the conference and to enjoy the book.

Cleveland and London, May 9, 2005

Kalle Lyytinen, General Chair
Carsten Sørensen and Youngjin Yoo, Program Cochairs

1 SOCIO-TECHNICAL STUDIES OF MOBILITY AND UBIQUITY

Carsten Sørensen
London School of Economics and Political Science
London, United Kingdom

Youngjin Yoo
Case Western Reserve University
Cleveland, OH U.S.A.

1 INTRODUCTION

This proceedings on *socio-technical issues and challenges in designing ubiquitous information environments* represents the first IFIP Working Group 8.2 conference dedicated to mobile and ubiquitous computing. It is, furthermore, only the third time an IFIP 8.2 Working Conference has been organized around an emerging information technology. In 1989, the working conference was dedicated to the technology of that time: desktop information technology. In 1992, the conference investigated the practices of using computer-aided software engineering (CASE) tools for software development. The 2005 conference is related to the 1989 conference in that the maturity of ubiquitous computing today is at about the same level as desktop computing technology was in 1989.

In 2004, IFIP Working Group 8.2 marked the 20th anniversary of the Manchester Conference, the landmark for research methods in information systems. Perhaps it is fitting that we dedicate the entire 2005 conference to the emerging technology of our time, thereby marking the first conference in the third decade of IFIP Working Group 8.2's history. In the first decade, IFIP Working Group 8.2 welcomed computers into our offices and onto our desks in 1989; in the second, we let them out into the world.

The rapid developments in mobile and wireless communication technologies and the continuing miniaturization of computing devices makes ubiquitous information environments more a technical reality than a distant vision. Ubiquitous computing as the next wave of organizational computing offers new possibilities and opportunities for organizations to improve their productivity and effectiveness. Companies such as FedEx and UPS are investing millions of dollars to upgrade their wireless network infrastructure, bringing information about packages, trucks, and couriers ever closer to their customers. Retail giant Wal-Mart is actively exploring the various mobile technologies such global positioning systems (GPS) and radio frequency identification (RFID) tags to improve its operations. Millions of customers in countries such as Japan and Korea have signed up for broadband cellular phone services to exchange video clips and download their favorite music. Companies in those countries are experimenting with the tight integration of mobile technologies into their core products and services. Scandinavian and European countries provide extensive mobile services supporting users in mobile banking, payments, and other business and personal services. Progressive Insurance, an American auto insurance company, has experimented with GPS in order to implement a usage-based premium system, and GM's OnStar service provides service support and other online services for automobile drivers. For the majority of workers, a mobile phone is now a natural part of their daily work. For an increasing proportion, the mobile phone is accompanied by a laptop.

However, the emergence of ubiquitous information environments not only signals opportunities, but also fundamentally challenges many of the traditional assumptions about organizations, management, computing, communication, and work. The increased mobility in ubiquitous information environments will bring about new socially defined meanings of issues such as the temporal and spatial aspects of organizational behavior. The unprecedented scale of deployment of wireless tools and sensors embedded in the environment challenges our understanding of technology acceptance and scale of operation in organizations. Technologies such as GPS and RFID are examples of increased attempts to bridge the gap between the physical and representations of the physical. The personalization and the pervasive nature of these tools and their linking of worlds will blur the boundaries between social and technical aspects of organizational computing.

While organizations are rapidly adopting various types of ubiquitous computing applications, there is a dearth of careful scholarly work examining the social dimensions related to the design and implementation of such computing environments. There is a range of research of a more technical nature exploring technical possibilities or evaluating the usability of various systems and prototypes. Given that ubiquitous information environments are relatively recent phenomena in terms of general adoption outside experimental settings, the relative lack of published work is perhaps not surprising. However, it is a unique opportunity for the IFIP Working Group 8.2 community of scholars to take active part in the development and use of technology in society at large. The development of ubiquitous computing not only opens up new research issues and topics to the Information Systems research community; it also invites us to revisit the classical concerns studied by the Group since its inception (Lyytinen and Yoo 2002; Lyytinen et al. 2004). The papers included in this volume cover investigations of both these endeavors.

A set of emerging information and communication technologies (ICTs) will interactively inspire and demand new social arrangements, just as social innovation will spark technological innovation. This does not, however, necessarily signal radical changes across the board. Although the emergence of PC technology signaled farewell to some old organizational roles and the emergence of new ones, it did not change all social aspects. The desktop information technology provided a vehicle for individual information and communication management in the office—or at home. It created a closer link between the individual and computer, personalizing the relationship. The best examples of this are spreadsheet and word processing applications. Ubiquitous information environments heralds an even closer bond between technical artifacts and social actions. This calls for a fundamental understanding of the social consequences of the technological properties as well as the technical opportunities and challenges of emerging social practices. The ubiquitous information environment not only links the individual and ICTs more tightly together in specific contexts, it seeks to transcend contexts as well as to actively employ computational awareness of these contexts.

2   BACKGROUND TO TOPIC

It could be argued that Lars Magnus Ericsson building a telephone for his wife Hilda's car in 1910 marked the beginning of a new era, even if its use required Hilda stopping the car and connecting the phone to telephone wires (Agar 2003, p. 8). It was, however, two-way closed radio systems sharing frequencies for the military and police forces during the 1930s and 1940s that marked the first significant implementation. Development of LCD displays, small powerful batteries, integrated circuits, and the reuse of frequencies through dividing areas into cells paved the way for the mobile phone—or the cell phone as it is called in the United States (Agar 2003). In the late 1960s and early 1970s, at the time of large, monolithic mainframes, Alan Kay and others from Xerox Parc formulated the conceptual design of the Dynabook, which in essence was a notebook or tablet computer. The Dynabook represented a conceptual leap in the understanding of how computers ought to support human activities. Another Xerox Parc researcher, Mark Weiser, was the first to properly formulate a vision of ubiquitous information environments in his *Scientific American* article from 1991 (see also Weiser 1999). Ubiquitous information environments imply the social embedding of mobile and pervasive technologies. Mobile technologies such as laptops, notebooks, mobile phones, personal digital assistants (PDAs), and smart-phones enable the user to access people and information sources while on the move. Pervasive technologies denote embedding computers in the environment beyond general purpose computing devices, as well as utilizing environmental and contextual information in the services offered.

　　Ubiquitous information environments signal the further development of computing and networking technologies where the computer has been subjected to miniaturization from the large mainframe to the PC to the laptop, tablet PC, PDA and smart-phone. Networking technology has evolved from the era of unconnected computers, through local area networks and wide area networks, to our current situation where several complementing and competing networking standards span the globe. Personal area networks (PANs) such as Bluetooth, Ultra Wide Band, and Zigbee offer device interconnectivity in close proximity. Local area network standards such as WiFi (IEEE 822.11.a/b/g/) provide medium-range wireless connectivity, and standards such as GSM, 3G, and WiMAX provide wide area wireless connectivity. Such rapid development of network technology has expanded the reach of computers around the globe, while at the same time bringing it ever more intimately into our everyday experience.

　　Simultaneously, with the emergence of smaller and increasingly pervasive computing technologies sporting a variety of wireless networking possibilities, day-to-day social activities have undergone significant change. The emergence of large geographically distributed organizations such as railway or oil companies from 1850 to 1920 led to the birth of scientific management (Yates 1989). The organization and management of work and the use of various technologies supporting this coevolved and formed the foundation for the introduction of mechanical and electronic computing equipment (Caminer et al. 1998; Yates 1989). Organizational changes during the 1980s aimed at meeting market demands for innovation led to phenomena such as internal markets, matrix organizations, concurrent engineering, and process reengineering (Kunda, 1992; Malone, 2004). These new ways of working attempted to alter previous organizational arrangements in order to support more direct connections among participants. Individual offices in many cases turned into cubicles and open-plan offices in order to support more fluid and *ad hoc* interaction. This has led to a significant amount of research into work, and indeed society as a whole, on networking (Castells 1996; Hinds and Kiesler 2002; Sproull and Kiesler 1993). One particular aspect of this is the understanding of remote and mobile working enabled and supported by ubiquitous information environments, for example by repair engineers or professionals (Barley and Kunda 2004; Kakihara 2003; Ljungberg 1997; Orr 1996; Wiberg 2001).

New working arrangements such as flexible working with home offices or hot-desking, remote working across branches or between continents, and mobile individuals working in the field are all examples of intricate configurations of working practices and ICT. New configurations of working practices and technologies have raised many challenging issues, including how to design appropriate working environments combining the two (Bjerrum and Nielsen 2003; Duffy et al. 1993; Laing et al. 1998; Schultze and Orlikowski 2004), how to maintain social relationships (Jarvenpaa and Leidner, 1999), provide leadership (Yoo and Alavi 2004), exercise remote control (Wiredu 2005), support for cognition (Boland et al. 1994), and how to engage and disengage mobile technologies (Sørensen and Pica 2005). The consequences of these emerging practices are still far from clear, but there are strong signs of increasing pressures on people to be constantly available and efficient (Bunting 2004). Understanding ubiquitous information environments in the context of modern working practices is critical in order to grasp the complex interactions between individual, organizational, and infrastructural issues. Human-computer interaction in collaborative work has been investigated by the HCI and CSCW communities (Dix and Beale 1996; Dourish 2001; Heath and Luff 2000; Lasen and Hamill 2005), as well as several academic journals such as *Personal and Ubiquitous Computing*. However, much of this research does not reconnect the debate to a concern for organizational performance.

In a broader context, it is equally important to understand the possibilities and consequences of ubiquitous information environments in everyday life beyond the confined boundary of work. The technologies and their use in the context of work have precisely contributed to the softening of barriers between working life and home life and emphasized an established trend (Brown et al. 2001; Bunting 2004; Hochschild 1997). It is in this area in particular that we find a significant body of research exploring the impact of, primarily, the mobile phone on social relations in general (Brown et al. 2001; Rheingold 2002). Much of this is broadly sociologically informed inquiries where the specific technical characteristics as well as the organizational consequences play a minor role compared to the overall social consequences (Cooper et al. 2002; Katz and Aakhus 2002; Kopomaa 2000; Ling 2004; Ling and Pedersen 2005). This strand of research will, as opposed to CSCW and IS research, often consider consequences broader than in the context of work, and theorize the much broader social issues such as a sociology of the mobile (Urry 2000, 2003).

Aside from those already mentioned, a broad range of disciplines have addressed the socio-technical developments related to ubiquitous information environments in general and the global diffusion of mobile phones in particular. These range from the obvious strictly technical or engineering concerns for devising the technical services and infrastructures (Baresi et al. 2004; Schiller and Voisard 2004; Umar 2004), to the study of the role of global infrastructure standards (Brunsson et al. 2000; Funk 2002), to architecture, arts, and aesthetics perspectives on ubiquitous information environments (Hoete 2003; Lovink and Gerritzen 2002; McCollough 2004)

Given the significance of the development and use of ubiquitous information environments, the wide range of issues raised must be met by a variety of perspectives and inquiry approaches. The IFIP Working Group 8.2 community is clearly able to provide a valuable contribution to this debate, both in terms of understanding the general socio-technical opportunities and impact, but perhaps more specifically in terms of addressing the issues of embedding these technologies in the context of organizational life.

3   THE REVIEW PROCESS

A total of 46 papers were submitted to the conference organizers. The papers were submitted from all over the globe, with 15 papers from AIS region 1 (the Americas), 25 from AIS region 2 (Europe, Middle East, and Africa), and 6 from AIS region 3 (Asia and the Pacific). Both program chairs managed all 46 papers together. In the few cases of past or previous shared affiliation between an author and one of the chairs, the other program chair was responsible for that particular paper. Each paper was allocated two reviewers recruited from the program committee, authors and selected members of the IFIP Working Group 8.2 community at large. The members of the program committee reviewed up to two papers each. We wish to express our gratitude to Matt Germonprez, University of Wisconsin, who at the time was at Case Western Reserve, and his graduate student, Brian Warner. They installed and managed an open source system enabling us to manage the entire submission and review process electronically over the Web. After minor issues of enrolling reviewers, the system worked remarkably well and it allowed us to accept the submissions, track reviews, and prepare final letters to the authors. After considering all of the reviews by the members of the Program Committee and the reviewers, we accepted 20 full papers and 3 position papers. We also invited four panels. The final selection of papers represents diverse theoretical and empirical perspectives on ubiquitous information environments.

4   OVERVIEW OF THE PAPERS

4.1 Keynotes

This volume includes extended abstracts of the keynotes by Thomas W. Malone (MIT), Lee Green (IBM), and Paul Durish (University of California, Irvine). We have chosen these three keynote speakers in part to emphasize the rich and diverse perspectives that can enrich our discourse on ubiquitous information environments. Picking up the theme of his recent book, in his talk "The Future of Work," Malone puts forward his view on how the development of information and communication technologies and the subsequent reduction of communication cost fundamentally alter the conditions for how we organize work. Although ubiquitous information environments have yet not reached their full potential, his views certainly invite us to ponder the impact of ubiquitous information environments on the organization of work. Green is responsible for IBM's worldwide product and identity design strategy. In his talk, "Its the Experience, Not the Price," Green discusses how IBM shifts its attention from hardware to *experiences* in dealing with customers' ubiquitous information environment needs. Building on IBM's recent projects with the Mayo Clinic and the New York Stock Exchange, Green illustrates how a *design* perspective can be a powerful lens for much more dynamic and complex requirements in ubiquitous information environments. Finally, Dourish's presentation, "The Culture of Information: Ubiquitous Computing and Representations of Reality," begins with the premise that movement toward ubiquitous information environments is more than mere changes in the computing platforms. Instead, he argues, the shift represents a fundamental transformation of our everyday experiences into "embodied interactions" that draws on physical, social, and cultural practices (Dourish 2001).

4.2 Papers

The accepted papers cover a wide range of topics drawing on an extremely rich set of theoretical perspectives. They are grouped into four categories: (1) papers exploring the use and consequences of ubiquitous information environments at the individual level; (2) research into the organizational consequences of ubiquitous information environments; (3) papers focusing on the development and integration of ubiquitous information environments; and (4) investigations of the challenges related to macro-level and institutional issues in the innovation and diffusion of ubiquitous information environments.

4.2.1   Individual Consequences

This section includes four papers exploring individual use of and experiences with ubiquitous information environments. The section begins with two papers examining the relationship between technology use and social life from two different perspectives. In their paper, "Friend or Foe? The Ambivalent Relationship between Mobile Technology and its Users," Sirkka L. Jarvenpaa, Karl Reiner Lang, and Virpi Kristiina Tuunainen explore how the use of mobile technologies create not only opportunities but also tensions in individuals. Through 33 focus group sessions in Finland, Japan, Hong Kong, and the United States, they explore various aspects of this paradox and offer a useful framework outlining the individual paradoxes in mobile technology use. Jeria L. Quesenberry and Eileen M. Trauth examine in their paper, "The Role of Ubiquitous Computing in Maintaining Work–Life Balance: Perspectives from Women in the IT

Workforce," the potential of ubiquitous computing to address the work-life balance from the perspective of women in the IT workforce. The empirical evidence for identifying the three key themes related to the potential benefit of ubiquitous information environments in addressing work-life balance issues for women is provided by 45 interviews. These themes are asynchronous communication, social networks, and personal life benefits.

The final two papers in this section extend user technology acceptance, one of the best-explored topics in the IS field, into the study of ubiquitous information environments. In their paper, "Reflexivity, the Social Actor, and M-Service Domestication: Linking the Human, Technological, and Contextual," Jennifer Blechar, Lars Knutsen, and Jan Damsgaard explore, based on an on-going field-study, how individual actors' own reflexivity and how on-going self-monitoring influences the adoption and domestication of mobile commerce services. In their paper, "Privacy Considerations in Location-Based Advertising," Heng Xu and Hock-Hai Teo also explore the adoption of mobile commerce services, but from a privacy perspective. They conducted an experimental study to test their hypotheses.

4.2.2 Organizational Impact

The eight papers in this section explore various challenges and consequences of ubiquitous information environments at the organizational level. The first four papers report experiences from different organizations that have adopted different ubiquitous information environments. The paper by Henrique M. G. Martins and Matthew R. Jones, "Mobility in the Round: Use of Wireless Laptop PCs in Clinical Ward Rounds," explores why a significant portion of doctors had never used the technology five years after the initial introduction. Their paper reveals how ubiquitous information environments need to adapt to the local and situated needs of individual users. Andrea Tapia and Steve Sawyer draw on their field study of mobile computing in the criminal justice system in their paper "Beliefs about Computing: Contrary Evidence from a Study of Mobile Computing Use among Criminal Justice Personnel." The paper explores how technology determinism can act as a belief system for individual users. The authors were struck by the persistent positive beliefs of the vision of mobile computing among the users in the trial, even though the device, applications, and network systems never worked as originally intended. The paper by Magnus Andersson, Rikard Lindgren, and Ola Henfridsson, entitled "Assessing the Mobile–Stationary Divide in Ubiquitous Transport Systems," focuses on the division between stationary office systems and mobile applications. The two technological systems have evolved from different innovation regimes and this is argued as a primary challenge in deploying enterprise-wide ubiquitous information environments. Anand Ramchand, Paul Raj Devadoss, and Shan L. Pan report from a case study of RFID implementation at Singapore's National Library Board. Their paper, "The Impacts of Ubiquitous Computing Technologies on Business Process Change and Management: The Case of Singapore's National Library Board," provides valuable insight into the social and organizational consequences of RFID deployment in organizations.

This section also includes two papers that explore the possibility of creating distributed socio-technical networks of distributed resources through ubiquitous information environments. Katrin Jonsson and Jonny Holmström in their paper, "Ubiquitous Computing and the Double Immutability of Remote Diagnostics Technology: An Exploration into Six Cases of Remote Diagnostics Technology Use," explore this using actor-network theory. They report from a case study of the use of remote diagnostic technology to create a distributed socio-technical network of knowledge resources. The paper, "Wireless Grids: Assessing a New Technology from a User Perspective," by Lee W. McKnight, Raed M Sharif, and Lidwien van de Wijngaert discusses the potential efficacy of wireless grids as a way of creating *ad hoc* networks for sharing resources. They do so through content analysis of the results of two focus group meetings.

The final two papers focus on the impact of mobility on work practices and activities. Masao Kakihara's paper, "Fluid Organizing of Work in the Ubiquitous Information Environment," explores structural changes in organizing work practices in the context of mobile professional work. He presents the notion of "fluid organizing" based on his field work in Japan. Gamel Wiredu, in "The Reconstruction of Portable Computers: On the Flexibility of Mobile Computing in Mobile Activities," draws on activity theory in his discussion of how work activities can be transformed through the use of mobile devices. Based on a field study of a mobile application for computer-mediated learning, he argues that the transformative capability of mobile devices is determined by affordances, motives, and modalities of mobility.

4.2.3   Development Issues

This section includes four papers dealing with various social issues related to the development of ubiquitous information environments. The first paper by Jens Henrik Hosbond and Peter Axel Nielsen, "Mobile Systems Development: A Literature Review," provides an extensive review of the mobile systems development literature. Hosbond and Nielsen suggest, that in order to provide a useful basis for mobile systems development, traditional systems development research needs expanding both in terms of its technology perspective (from stationary to mobile) as well as in terms of its organizational perspectives (from project based to interorganizational). The paper by Carl Magnus Olsson and Ola Henfridsson, entitled "Designing Context-Aware Inter-action: An Action Research Study," reports the results from an action research study on the design of context-aware computing environments. Conceptualizing a car as a platform for ubiquitous information environments, the project developed and tested design principles for context-aware applications. The paper illustrates new challenges of designing applications for ubiquitous information environments.

The final two papers in this section focus on the design and development of information infrastructure necessary in order to facilitate effective ubiquitous information environments. Panos Constantinides and Michael Barrett, in their paper, "Approaching Information Infrastructure as an Ecology of Ubiquitous Sociotechnical Relations," develop an analytical framework of information infrastructure as an ecology of ubiquitous socio-technical relations with seven layers. Their framework illustrates the complex social reality of designing, developing, and maintaining ubiquitous informa-tion environments and how configurations among different social actors in organizations can shape and influence the ways in which technical infrastructure and tools necessary for ubiquitous information environments are interrelated with each other. The paper by Gunnar Ellingsen and Eric Monteiro, "The Slight Surprise of Integration," reports from a case study of the implementation of a new information infrastructure at a university hospital in Northern Norway. Their discussion on the unintended consequences of integrating new technological infrastructures help us understand the social and organization challenges of creating ubiquitous information environments providing "seamless" integration of diverse computing resources.

4.2.4   Innovation and Diffusion of Ubiquitous Information Environments

This section includes four papers that broadly deal with innovation and diffusion of ubiquitous information environments. The first three papers explore institutional and interorganizational issues affecting the diffusion of ubiquitous information environments. In the paper "Scaling the Wall: Factors Influencing the Conditions of Market Entry in the Mobile Data Market," Annemijn F. van Gorp, Carleen F. Maitland, and Brian H. Cameron investigate the relationships between information providers and the powerful mobile service operators and discuss how such a relationship affects the diversity of information services. Shirley Chan, Heejin Lee, and Sangjo Oh explore the diffusion of innovations in China through the lens of disputes over standards. Their paper, "An International Mobile Security Standard Dispute: From the Actor–Network Perspective," examines the diffusion of how the innovation of a mobile security standard is being shaped and negotiated among social actors that represent national interests as well as different technological regimes. Steinar Kristoffersen, Petter Nielsen, Jennifer Blechar, and Ole Hanseth explore the coordination among different actors in the mobile services value network in the paper, "Ordinary Innovation of Mobile Services." Drawing on three case studies, they argue that existing theories cannot fully explain the innovation of mobile services.

Finally, Melanie Wilson's paper, "The Ubiquity and Utility of Resistance: Codesign and Personalization of Information Systems," puts forward the view that user resistance provides a site for personalization and local adaptation. She critically analyzes the term *ubiquity* and seeks to offer an alternative theoretical perspective to examine the role of users in the innovation of ubiquitous information environments.

4.3 Position Papers

The three accepted position papers explore various aspects of ubiquitous information environments. In the paper, "CrackBerries: The Social Implications of Ubiquitous Wireless E-Mail Devices," Melissa A. Mazmanian, Wanda J. Orlikowski, and JoAnne Yates outline a research agenda for studying how mobile e-mail devices find a place in the lives of mobile professionals. Mikko Ahonen's paper, "Building a Ubiquitous Artifact That Integrates Problem-Solving and Learning Processes to Support Creativity," reports from a doctoral project aimed at designing a prototypical ubiquitous information environment supporting learning and creativity. Finally, Majorkumar Govindaraju and David Sward in their paper, "Effects of Wireless Mobile Technology on Employee

Work Behavior and Productivity: An Intel Case Study," present a case study on the practical experiences with the use of wireless connected notebooks, for example, in terms of the flexibility of employees and the increasing ubiquity of the notebooks.

4.4 Panels

The conference includes four panels on issues related to ubiquitous information environments. The first panel on ubiquitous computing for health and medicine by Chris Atkinson, Bonnie Kaplan, Kent Larson, Henrique M. G. Martins, Jay Lundell, and Martin Harris explores the nature and transformative capacity of ubiquitous computing in healthcare. The telematics panel by Ola Henfridsson, John King, Glenn Mercer, Dave Pavlich, and Walt Scacchi debates the emergence of ubiquitous vehicle information environments. In the third panel, Scott A. Shamp, Lev Gonick, Sirkka L. Jarvenpaa, and Pouline Middleton, discuss community-based wireless networks as a novel form of social innovation around the world. The panel focuses on the opportunities and challenges faced by social actors participating in this type of ubiquitous information environment. The fourth and final panel consists of practitioners from industry including Richard Braley (Fed Ex), Andy Fano (Accenture Technology Labs), John Light (Intel), and Ora Lassila (Nokia). Matt Germonprez joins these panelists in exploring the challenges and opportunities for ubiquitous information environments from their own vantage point.

5   CONCLUSIONS

The selected papers, invited keynote presentations, and panels provide a rich canvas for intense debate of the social aspects of ubiquitous information environments. In terms of technologies, the selection of papers presented here covers a diverse set of technologies such as mobile phones, remote diagnostics, RFID, and m-learning. Assuming that ubiquitous information environments spell strengthening of the ties between social action and technological properties, it is important to keep a sharp eye on both in order to fully grasp the issues.

In terms of coverage of possible research issues, the selected papers discuss the individual, the organizational, and to some extent the interorganizational levels (Lyytinen and Yoo 2002). One interesting observation that can be made, based on the research in the area of ubiquitous information environments in general and the papers in this collection in particular, is the relative lack of team level research. Perhaps the substantial body of research on teamwork and technology from organizational science, decision support systems, and CSCW can inform the discourse further. Both individual and organizational level studies seem to focus on unexpected consequences or paradoxes. One way of moving further could be to combine a deeper understanding of how classical research concerns play out in ubiquitous information environments with further development of novel theoretical elements explaining truly unique charac-teristics. The proceedings contain a rich set of papers exploring innovation and the role of standards and institutional arrangements in a broader context than the individual organization. Also, in terms of the distinction between the design, use, adoption, and impact of services, there is a fairly broad representation of issues, perhaps with less discussion of design issues (Lyytinen and Yoo 2002). This is, however, the primary focal point for much HCI and CSCW related research. There are, in this collection, no adoption studies across industries. As IFIP Working Group 8.2 mostly adopts qualitative research approaches, this is probably not unexpected. Regarding the enabling capabilities of infrastructures as well as their governance and control, the collection of papers represents research on both, but there is still a need to further reconnect research on privacy, trust, and awareness to this debate (Bellotti and Sellen 1993; Heath and Luff 2000; Lyytinen and Yoo 2002).

In the case of desktop information technology, much of the debate was constructed along the way jointly between theoretical considerations and innovative experimentation in practice. We would of course expect a similar coevolution of the debate into ubiquitous information environments. The primary aim of the conference is to forward the mobilization of core IFIP Working Group 8.2 expertise in this debate contributing to the analysis of turbulent socio-technical phenomena associated with wide-ranging adoption of mobile and wireless ICTs. As program chairs, we are very pleased with the variety and quality of submissions to this conference despite the relatively recent academic debate of ubiquitous information environments within our field. It is our hope that the conference and this conference proceedings will contribute actively to furthering the debate. We are certain that the debate will be enriched but also that the IFIP Working Group 8.2 community will shape the debate in its own unique way.

REFERENCES

Agar, J. *Constant Touch: A Global History of the Mobile Phone*, Cambridge: Icon Books, 2003.

Baresi, L., Dustdar, S., Gall, H., and Matera, M. (Eds.). *Ubiquitous Mobile Information and Collaboration Systems: Second CAiSE Workshop,* Berlin: Springer-Verlag, 2004.

Barley, S. R., and Kunda, G. *Gurus, Hired Guns, and Warm Bodies: Itinerant Experts in a Knowledge Economy*, Princeton, NJ: Princeton University Press, 2004.

Bellotti, V., and Sellen, A. "Design for Privacy in Ubiquitous Computing Environments," in *Proceedings of the Third European Conference on Computer-Supported Cooperative Work*, G. DeMichelis, C. Simone, and K. Schmidt (Eds.), Dordrecht: Kluwer Academic Publishers, 1993, pp. 77-92.

Bjerrum, E., and Nielsen, O. *Bliver man lidt småsær af at have sit eget kontor? Nye arbejdsformer til debat (Does one become a bit odd by having one's own office? Debating new ways of working up)*, Copenhagen: JPBøger/Jyllands-Postens Erhvervsbogklub, 2003.

Boland, R., Tenkasi, R. V., and Te'eni, D. "Designing Information Technology to Support Distributed Cognition," *Organization Science* (5:3), 1994, pp. 456-475.

Brown, B., Green, N., and Harper, R. (Eds.). *Wireless World*, London: Springer-Verlag, 2001.

Brunsson, N., Jacobsson, B., and Associates. *A World of Standards*, Oxford, UK: Oxford University Press, 2000.

Bunting, M. *Willing Slaves: How the Overwork Culture Is Ruling Our Lives*, London: Harper Collins Publishers, 2004.

Caminer, D., Aris, J., Hermon, P., and Land, F. *L.E.O.—The Incredible Story of the World's First Business Computer*, London: McGraw-Hill Education, 1998.

Castells, M. *The Rise of the Network Society*, Oxford, UK: Blackwell, 1996.

Cooper, G., Green, N., Murtagh, G. M., and Harper, R. "Mobile Society? Technology, Distance, and Precence," in *Virtual Society? Technology, Cyberbole, Reality*, S. Woolgar (Ed.), Oxford, UK: Oxford University Press, 2002, pp. 286-301.

Dix, A., and Beale, R. (Ed.). *Remote Cooperation: CSCW Issues for Mobile and Teleworkers*, London: Springer-Verlag, 1996.

Dourish, P. *Where the Action Is: The Foundations of Embodied Interaction*, Cambridge, MA: MIT Press, 2001.

Duffy, F., Laing, A., and Crisp, V. *The Responsible Workplace: The Redesign of Work and Offices*, Oxford, UK: Butterworth Architecture in association with Estates Gazette, 1993.

Funk, J. L. *Global Competition Between and Within Standards: The Case of Mobile Phones*, Chippenham, UK: Palgrave, 2002.

Heath, C., and Luff, P. *Technology in Action*, Cambridge, UK: Cambridge University Press, 2000.

Hinds, P., and Kiesler, S. (Ed.). *Distributed Work*, Cambridge, MA: MIT Press., 2002.

Hochschild, A. R. *The Time Bind: When Work Becomes Home and Home Becomes Work*, New York: Owl Books, 1997.

Hoete, A. (Ed.). *ROAM: Reader on the Aesthetics of Mobility*, London: Black Dog Publishing, 2003.

Jarvenpaa, S. L., and Leidner, D. E. "Communication and Trust in Global Virtual Teams," *Organization Science* (10:6), Special Issue: Communication Processes for Virtual Organizations, 1999, pp. 791-815.

Kakihara, M. *Emerging Work Practices of ICT-Enabled Mobile Professionals*, unpublished Ph.D. Thesis, The London School of Economics and Political Science, 2003 (available online at http://is.lse.ac.uk/research/theses/).

Katz, J. E., and Aakhus, M. (Eds.). *Perpetual Contact*, Cambridge, UK: Cambridge University Press, 2002.

Kopomaa, T. *The City in Your Pocket: Birth of the Mobile Information Society* (translated by T. Snellman), Helsinki: Gaudeamus, 2000.

Kunda, G. *Engineering Culture. Control and Commitment in a High-Tech Corporation*, Philadelphia: Temple University Press, 1992.

Laing, A., Duffy, F., and Jaunzens, D. *New Environments for Working: The Re-design of Offices and Environmental Systems for New Ways of Working*, Watford, UK: Construction Research Communications Ltd., 1998

Lasen, A., and Hamill, L. (Eds.), *Mobile World: Past, Present and Future*, London: Springer-Verlag, 2005.

Ling, R. *The Mobile Connection: The Cell Phone's Impact on Society*, Amsterdam: Morgan Kaufmann, 2004.

Ling, R. R., and Pedersen, P. E. (Eds.). *Mobile Communications: Re-negotiation of the Social Sphere*, London: Springer-Verlag, 2005.

Ljungberg, F. *Networking*, unpublished Ph.D. thesis, Göteborg University, 1997.

Lovink, G., and Gerritzen, M. (Eds.). *Mobile Minded*, Amsterdam: BIS Publishers. 2002.

Lyytinen, K., and Yoo, Y. "The Next Wave of Nomadic Computing: A Research Agenda for Information Systems Research," *Information Systems Research* (13:4), 2002, pp. 377-388.

Lyytinen, K., Yoo, Y., Varshney, U., Ackerman, M. S., Davis, G. B. Avital, M., Robey, D., Sawyer, S., and Sørensen, C. "Surfing the Next Wave: Design and Implementation Challenges of Ubiquitous Computing Environments," *Communications of the AIS* (13), 2004, pp. 697-716.

Malone, T. W. *The Future of Work: How the New Order of Business Will Shape Your Organization, Your Management Style, and Your Life*, Boston: Harvard Business School Press, 2004.

McCollough, M. *Digital Ground: Architecture, Pervasive Computing, and Environmental Knowing*, Cambridge, MA: MIT Press, 2004.

Orr, J. E. *Talking About Machines: An Ethnography of a Modern Job*, Ithaca, NY: Cornell University Press, 1996.

Rheingold, H. *Smart Mobs*, New York: Perseus Books, 2002.

Schiller, J., and Voisard, A. *Location-Based Services*, San Francisco: Morgan Kaufmann, 2004.

Schultze, U., and Orlikowski, W. "A Practice Perspective on Technology-Mediated Network Relations: The Use of Internet-Based Self-Serve Technologies," *Information Systems Research* (15:1), 2004, pp. 87-106.

Sørensen, C., and Pica, D. "Tales from the Police: Mobile Technologies and Contexts of Work." *Information and Organization* (15:3), 2005 (forthcoming).

Sproull, L., and Kiesler, S. *Connections: New Ways of Working in the Networked Organization*, Cambridge, MA: MIT Press, 1993.

Umar, A. *Mobile Computing and Wireless Communications: Applications, Networks, Platforms, Architectures, and Security*, NGE Solutions, 2000 (http://www.ngesolutions.com).

Urry, J. *Global Complexity*, Cambridge, UK: Polity, 2003

Urry, J. "Mobile Sociology," *British Journal of Sociology* (51:1), 2000, pp. 185-203.

Weiser, M. "The Computer for the 21ˢᵗ Century," *Scientific American*, 1991, pp. 94-110.

Weiser, M. "Ubiquitous Computing," 1999 (available online at http://www.ubiq.com/hypertext/weiser/UbiHome.html).

Wiberg, M. *In Between Mobile Meetings: Exploring Seamless Ongoing Interaction Support for Mobile CSCW*, unpublished Ph.D. Dissertation, Department for Informatics, Umeå University, 2001.

Wiredu, G. *Mobile Computing in Work-Integrated Learning: Problems of Remotely Distributed Activities and Technology Use*, unpublished Ph.D. dissertation, London School of Economics, 2005 (available online at http://is.lse.ac.uk/research/theses/).

Yates, J. *Control through Communication: The Rise of System in American Management*, Baltimore: The Johns Hopkins University Press, 1989.

Yoo, Y., and Alavi, M. "Emergent Leadership in Virtual Teams: What Do Emergent Leaders Do?," *Information and Organization* (14:1), 2004, pp. 27-58.

ABOUT THE AUTHORS

Carsten Sørensen is a senior lecturer in Information Systems at The London School of Economics and Political Science, United Kingdom. He holds a B.Sc. in mathematics, an M.Sc in computer science, and a Ph.D. in information systems from Aalborg University, Denmark. Carsten has, through the past 16 years, been affiliated with a number of Danish, Swedish, and British institutions. He has also been actively engaged with executive education and has consulted for a range of organizations, including Microsoft, Orange, Caja Madrid, Kommunedata, and Netonomy. Carsten is studying how ICT shapes and is shaped by emerging working practices and organizational forms and, most recently, mobile technologies for organizational efficiency. He has been involved in research on mobile computing since the mid-1990s and is was one of the founding members of the Internet Project. In 2001, Carsten initiated the mobility@lse research network in mobile interaction (http://mobility.lse.ac.uk/), with the goal of drawing together academics and practitioners. Carsten has extensive EU and international project experience. Since 1997, he has been Research Director of Laboratorium for Interaction Technology (http://laboratorium.htu.se) at Trollhättan Uddevalla University, Sweden. He is on the editorial board for *Information and Organization* and *The e-Service Journal*. Carsten has served as organizer, chair, associate editor, track chair, and track co-coordinator for a number of international conferences, including the International Conference on Information Systems, the Hawaii International Conference on System Sciences, the European Conference on Information

Systems, and the Information Systems Research Seminar in Scandinavia. Carsten can be reached by e-mail at c.sorensen@lse.ac.uk.

Youngjin Yoo is an associate professor in Information Systems and the Lewis-Progressive Chair in Management at the Weatherhead School of Management, Case Western Reserve University. He holds a Ph.D. in information systems from the University of Maryland. He received his MBA and B.S. in Business Administration from Seoul National University in Seoul, Korea. His research interests include ubiquitous computing, knowledge management, the role of information technology for virtual teams, and IT-based new organizational forms. His work has been published in leading academic journals including *Information Systems Research, MIS Quarterly, Academy of Management Journal, Journal of Strategic Information Systems, Communications of the ACM, Information and Organizations,* and *International Journal of Organizational Analysis.* He has published several book chapters and presented his work at national and international research conferences, including International Conference on Information Systems, Americas Conference on Information Systems, and Hawaiian International Conference on Systems Sciences. Youngjin has researched leading companies including NASA, Andersen Consulting, Ernst and Young Center for Business Knowledge, IDEO, Gehry and Partners, University Hospitals in Cleveland, Lotus, Parker Hannifin, Poly One, and the Department of Housing and Urban Development. He was the first nonengineering faculty member to be selected as summer research fellow at the NASA Glenn Research Center in 2001. He has received research grants from the National Science Foundation and NASA. He is an associate editor of *Information Systems Research* and on the editorial board of *Organization Science, Journal of AIS,* and *Information and Organization.* Youngjin can be reached by e-mail at yyoo@case.edu.

Part 1

Keynotes

2   THE FUTURE OF WORK[1]

Thomas W. Malone
Patrick J. McGovern Professor of Management
MIT Sloan School of Management
Cambridge, MA U.S.A.

Imagine organizations where bosses give employees enormous freedom to decide what to do and when to do it. Imagine that workers are allowed to elect their own bosses and vote directly on important company decisions. Imagine organizations where most workers aren't employees at all, but electronically connected freelancers living wherever they want to. And imagine that all this freedom in business lets people get more of whatever they really want in life—money, interesting work, helping other people, or time with their families. These things are already happening today and—if we choose—they can happen even more in the future.

We are now in the early stages of a profound increase in human freedom in business that may, in the long run, be as important for businesses as the change to democracies was for governments. The key enabler for this remarkable change is information technology. By reducing the costs of communication, these technologies now make it possible for many more people, even in huge organizations, to have the information they need to make decisions for themselves, instead of just following orders from above. And so, for the first time in human history, we can now have the best of both worlds—the economic and scale efficiencies of large organizations, and the human benefits of small ones: freedom, motivation, creativity, and flexibility.

---

1   WHAT WILL THESE NEW WAYS OF ORGANIZING WORK LOOK LIKE?

There are three basic ways to make decisions in large groups while still giving individuals substantial freedom: *loose hierarchies, democracies,* and *markets.*

Some companies today, for example, already have *loose hierarchies* in which bosses still exist but considerable decision-making authority is delegated to very low organizational levels. Many management consulting firms, for instance, let the individual partners and consultants assigned to a project make almost all the operational decisions about it. And AES Corp., one of the world's largest electric power producers, lets low-level workers make critical multimillion-dollar decisions about things like acquiring new subsidiaries. In an even more extreme example, one of the most important computer operating systems in the world today—Linux—was written by a loosely coordinated hierarchy of thousands of volunteer programmers all over the world.

Going further, some businesses today already act like miniature *democracies* where decisions are made by voting. Many good managers, for instance, informally poll their employees about key decisions, and some companies have made the formal polling of workers a routine part of their management. In a few cases, such as the Mondragon Cooperative Corporation in Spain, the workers own the company and, therefore, can elect the equivalent of a board of directors and vote on other key issues.

The most extreme kind of business freedom occurs in *markets.* For example, many companies today outsource activities they used to perform inside—from manufacturing, to sales, to human resource management. In some cases, flexible webs of electronically connected free-lancers—"e-lancers"—can even do the same things big companies used to do but more effectively. In other cases, large companies can get many of the benefits of markets *inside* their own boundaries. For example, Intel is looking at letting individual salespeople and plant managers buy and sell products among themselves in an internal electronic market. This could give the plants immediate and dynamic feedback about which products to make each day, and help the salespeople continually fine-tune the prices they offer their customers.

To understand why such decentralized approaches to management are likely to happen more often in the future, we need to understand what leads to centralization and decentralization in the first place.

2   WHY IS THIS HAPPENING?

Dozens of factors affect how and where decisions are made in a business. But there is one crucial factor that is changing dramatically in the same direction almost everywhere today. In fact, when we look back carefully at the history of humanity, we can see that this very same factor has been implicated, time after time, in some of the most important changes in how entire societies were structured.

What is this factor?

It's the *cost of communication.*

Back when the only form of communication was face-to-face conversation, our distant hunting-and-gathering ancestors organized themselves in small, egalitarian, decentralized groups called bands. Over many millennia, as our ancestors learned to communicate over long distances—by writing—they were able to form larger and larger societies ruled by kings, emperors, and other centralized rulers. Then, only a few hundred years ago, our ancestors invented a new communication technology, the printing press, which reduced even further the costs of communicating to large numbers of people. This breakthrough allowed people to reverse their millennia-long march toward greater centralization. Soon after the printing press came into wide use, the democratic revolution began. Ordinary people—now much better informed about political matters—came to have more say in their own government than they had had since the hunting-and-gathering days.

Remarkably, this very same three-stage pattern appears to be repeating itself now—at a much faster rate—in the history of business organizations.

Throughout most of human history, up until the 1800s, most businesses were organized as small, local, often family affairs—farmers, shopkeepers, craftspeople—similar in many ways to the early bands of hunters and gatherers. But by the 1900s, new communication technologies like the telegraph and the telephone finally provided enough communication capacity to allow businesses to grow and centralize on a large scale, as governments had begun to do many millennia earlier. Because these "kingdoms" of the business world were so successful, many of us still unconsciously associate success in business with bigness and centralization.

But now, just as new technologies helped spur the rise of democracies, today's technological advances are beginning to spur a similar change in business. With new communication technologies like e-mail, instant messaging, and the Internet, it's becoming economically feasible—for the first time in history—to give huge numbers of workers the information they need to make more choices for themselves. That means that many more people can have the kinds of freedom in business that used to be common only in small organizations. And that can be very good news for both productivity and quality of life. When people are making their own decisions, for instance, rather than just following orders, they often work harder and show more dedication and more creativity.

Of course, reduced communication costs won't always lead to this kind of decentralization. In places where the benefits of economies of scale are overwhelmingly important—like some kinds of semiconductor manufacturing—we will probably see even more centralization. But in our increasingly knowledge- and innovation-based economy, the benefits of decentralization—flexibility, freedom, creativity, and motivation—are becoming important in more and more places. And in all those places, we should expect to see information technology leading to more and more decentralization.

3 WHAT DOES THIS MEAN FOR YOU?

If decentralization becomes increasingly desirable in business, then we'll need to manage in new ways. But most of us still have—deep in our minds—models of management based on the classic centralized philosophy of "command and control." To be successful in the world we're entering, we'll need a new set of mental models. We need to shift our thinking from "command-and-control" to "coordinate-and-cultivate." Coordinating and cultivating are not the opposites of commanding and controlling; they are the supersets. That is, they include the whole range of possibilities for management, from the completely top-down and centralized to the completely bottom-up and decentralized. To be an effective manager in the world we're entering, you can't be stuck in a centralized mindset. You need to be able to move flexibly back and forth on the centralization continuum as the situation demands.

If more people have more freedom in business, this also means they will naturally seek the things they value. Of course, one thing people value is money and the things you can buy with it, but most people value other things, too: time with their families, a feeling of achievement, a sense of meaning in their lives. That means companies will increasingly need to compete for workers, investors, and customers, not just in the marketplace for products and prices, but also in the marketplace for values.

And as individuals, we need to think more deeply than we usually do about what we really want from our lives and how our business choices can help us get those things. Because you will have more choices in this world, you'll be able to bring a broader range of your values, not just the economic ones, into your thinking about business. And that means, you can—if you choose—use your work to help create a world that is not just richer, but better.

3 ITS THE EXPERIENCE, NOT THE PRICE[1]

Lee Green
Director
IBM Corporate Identity & Design
Somers, NY U.S.A.

IBM has a long history of focusing on design and usability as a core competency and key differentiator for its branded products. From wearable and hand-held devices to super computers, design plays a key role in the development of advanced technology solutions. IBM has also utilized design for years to work in conjunction with IBM Research on advanced prototypes of the future. Some, like Blue Gene L, are now being developed for Lawrence Livermore Labs; others, such as our electronic newspaper concepts, or voice and video recognition headsets, are visions of the future and demonstrations of emerging IBM innovation.

In the last several years, IBM Corporate Design has teamed with IBM Engineering and Technology Services (E&TS) to extend Design Services as part of IBM's offering to customers.[2] Recently they have also begun to extend these services in conjunction with IBM Business Consulting Services. We are engaging with IBM clients around the world to provide our expertise in product design, human factors, and engineering. We are also now offering design consulting services to help IBM clients consider how they can envision and extend new experiences to their customers and leverage design to differentiate their offerings from their competition. This is a new offering being extended to IBM clients that no other IT company provides.

Design Services works with clients to understand marketplace context, create new user scenarios, model these scenarios, validate them and then implement solutions. Often this involves observation research to uncover new technology and service opportunities.

We have designed medical solutions for the Mayo Clinic, wireless floor trader solutions for the New York Stock Exchange,[3] and have many other projects in development.[4]   These include consumer electronics, medical monitoring concepts, and home entertainment concepts. We are also supporting IBM's engagement with Culturecom in China and their eTown initiative to extend network computing access throughout rural cities in China. This information access will provide educational information and support local economic growth. The first of these eTowns was jointly announced July 15, 2004 in Yun An, Guang Dong province.

ABOUT THE AUTHOR

Lee Green is the WW Director of Corporate Identity and Design for IBM Corporation. He has responsibility for IBM's worldwide product industrial design, advanced technology design, brand experience initiatives, and IBM's recently launched Design Services offering for IBM clients. Mr. Green has played a pivotal role in IBM's re-branding efforts over the last 12 years, which have included the redesign of all IBM products. He also leads the corporation's efforts in the area of "advanced concept design."

In his 25-year career with IBM he has held numerous design and management positions. Recently, he has launched IBM's Design Services working in conjunction with IBM's Engineering and Technology Group and with IBM Business Consulting Services. This capability provides Design Services Consulting as an IBM offering to customers. In addition to industrial design and human factors, it provides Design Consulting services to help IBM customers consider how they can extend new experiences to their customers, utilize design to differentiate their offerings from their competition, and leverage innovative IBM technology to enable these solutions.

Mr. Green has an undergraduate degree in design from Temple University and a Master's degree in communications design from Rochester Institute of Technology. He has published numerous articles and case studies on a variety of design and identity topics. He has also taught design courses and lectured on design at Stanford University, Harvard, MIT, and RIT, and was recently named Rochester Institute of Technology 2004 Distinguished Alumni of the Year. He currently serves on the Board of Directors and Advisory Board for the Design Management Institute.

---

[4]For an example, see http://www-03.ibm.com/technology/designconsulting/cs_orange.html.

4 THE CULTURE OF INFORMATION: Ubiquitous Computing and Representations of Reality[1]

Paul Dourish
University of California, Irvine
Irvine, CA U.S.A.

Weiser's original discussion of the emerging age of ubiquitous computing was formulated largely in technological terms, as an extrapolation of continuing trends in the design and capabilities of computer hardware, software, and infrastructure. Implicit in this transformation of computational platforms, though, lies a transformation of the ways in which we encounter, engage with, and experience interactive information systems. As computation becomes increasingly embedded in the everyday world, our experience of information systems increasingly draws upon our experience of the real world itself, in all its physical, social, and cultural manifestations. The nature of what, in my own work, I term "embodied interaction" is not merely a physical embodiment, but an experiential embodiment that draws as much on the social as the physical in the ways in which we encounter the world and find it meaningful.

The idea at work here is that our experience of the world is richer, more natural, more nuanced and in some ways more effective than our interaction with the disembodied information in conventional computer systems. So, in his classic article, Weiser (1991) makes the telling remark that there is more information available to us in a walk in the woods than there is when we sit in front of a computer, our quintessential information processing system. By this, he wants to draw attention to the complexity and clumsiness of traditional computer interfaces, and the obstacles that they put in the way of the tasks that they are designed to support. However, his analogy raises a separate question, which he does not explore but I wish to here: why should we think of a walk in the woods as an information exercise, and what happens when we do?

The use of "information" as a mass noun is a relatively new phenomenon (Day 2001). Information had previously referred to the process or activity of informing or of being informed; to "receive information" was to participate in a process, much as one

---

might "receive confirmation." More recently, though, and particularly since the development of electronic information systems, our idea of information has changed, and we start to think of information as a thing in itself (Buckland 1991). So, in casting the embodied experience of the physical world in information terms, Weiser isn't breaking new ground; rather, he is following in a distinctly twentieth century tradition of searching for mathematical models of everyday life. In particular, the notion of information as a fundamental coin of the realm is part of a broader movement from the analog world to the digital, a movement that also involves a radical conceptual shift. When digital information processing machines were first introduced, they were dubbed "electronic computers." Although it is difficult to remember now, this was not a new term; "computers" was a term in common use, referring to the people (largely women) who performed rote calculations for the production of, for example, artillery targeting tables. The new machines, then, were electronic computers in the sense that they were electronic equivalents of (human) computers. Indeed, these new machines were generally understood and thought of as equivalent or similar to organic entities; they were, as so many newspaper headlines declared, "giant electronic brains."

In the subsequent years, and in particular with the emergence of cognitive science in the 1960s and 1970s, a fascinating conceptual shift took place. The fundamental perspective of cognitive science was that the mind could be understood in computational terms; that information flow, information processing, and information storage were the terms in which human cognitive activity could be modeled and understood. In other words, where previously we had understood computer systems to be derivative of human behavior, this model was now inverted; humans were now to be understood as a form of computer. Where once the computer was a giant electronic brain, now the brain was a biological computer. Accordingly, the rhetoric of information processing that was part and parcel of the world of electronic computation became the model by which human experience was to be understood; memory could be understood in terms of storage capacity, and rationality in terms of operations performed per second.

As analog devices have increasingly been replaced with digital counterparts, this information rhetoric has continued to spread. Recent developments in ubiquitous computing—the same set of trends that Weiser was discussing—have been part of this shift. Ubiquitous computing sees the movement of computation away from traditional computer systems and into the everyday world, through the development of networked embedded and wearable technologies. So, the world becomes a site of computation and an object of informational representation. We start to understand and model the world in information terms, as suggested by Weiser's remark that even a walk in the woods can be thought of it terms of its information content.

This seemingly innocuous statement is actually a quite radical one. It equates information with experience (or, rather, suggests that experience is founded upon information.) It is a way of using the concept of information that is both practiced and culturally bound. Information, in other words, is a cultural category; an element of a broad cultural understanding of reality. We can see this best, perhaps, by looking for the boundaries. If a walk in the woods can be thought of in information terms, how about a loving relationship? How about a performance of Beethoven? How about an insult, or a physical exchange of blows? The very fact that we would inherently resist a suggestion that these experiences can be modeled and understood in terms of information flows, storage, and processing highlights the way in which information is a cultural category, one that reflects the ways in which we understand and think about the world and our place within it.

So, ubiquitous computing, as a research program, arises within this broader context which sees information as an object that can be uncovered, moved around, and processed, rather than as a reflection of social and cultural relations.

We can see this at work in the notion of "ambience," such as the explorations of ambient information displays originated at MIT and the European "ambient intelligence" program. Ambience draws our attention to distinctions between focus and periphery (Brown and Duguid 1994) and the different ways in which information can be incorporated into an environment. But at the same time, it retains this same focus on information as an object while obscuring other ways in which environments might be informative. For example, return to Weiser's question of the experience of space, but think about it from different points of view. Aboriginal Australians, for example, have an experience of their landscape that is quite different from Western traditions (Stanner 1958). They experience the landscape in terms of a series of ritual responsibilities, not just for its upkeep, but for its very existence. The link between the Dreaming and the everyday world, the link that connects the land to the processes that brought it into existence and continue to shape it, must be actively maintained. The land is experienced, too, in terms of clans and lineage groups; the very features of the land link it to the Dreamtime actions of totemic creatures whose continuance is marked by patterns of land occupancy and responsibility. Finally, the land is experienced in terms of historical events; the actions of humans leave their marks, both physically and spiritually, on the land. Any movement through the landscape, and any experience of it, is cast in these terms. There is much more to be "read" in the land than purely physical form, but this is an aspect of daily experience, not an information experience to be thought of as looking it up in a dictionary. Indeed, the land may be experienced first in terms of its symbolic meaning and only secondly in terms of its physical form. The landscape is experienced as meaningful, not read or processed as information.

If we think of information as a cultural category, then, and of *informating*—that is, the process of reading aspects of everyday life in information terms—then it is sensible to ask what is being done by that process. Arguably, the process of describing aspects of the world in information terms makes them amenable to information-based processes; to the forms of representation, transformation, and processing associated with a variety of technical disciplines. In recent discourse, though, the informating of everyday life brings it particularly into the domain of computer scientists and of commercial information systems providers. If your problem can be conceived of as an information problem, then it is a problem that Microsoft and IBM can help to solve. If your problem can be conceived of as an information problem, then it is a problem that a computer scientist can address. If your problem can be conceived of as an information problem, then it is one on which Moore's Law will naturally have its effect. What is at stake, then, is the right to create, define, and lay claim to both problems and solutions.

More broadly, this alternative view suggests some important research challenges for ambient intelligence. Recent shifts in how we think about technology and experience as embodied phenomena (Dourish 2001) mark not only an increasing concern with the physical aspect of interaction design, although that has clearly been an important issue and a significant element of the ubiquitous computing program, but a quite different reading of interaction beyond the information processing approach. Research in ubiquitous computing has often made use of social science methods as ways of understanding settings into which technology might be introduced; our considerations here suggest that we might fruitfully also use these approaches to investigate how these settings are understood by the people who populate and enact them. If information, ubiquity, and intelligence are cultural categories, then how can the relationship between technology and social and cultural practice be reimagined?

REFERENCES

Brown, J. S., and Duguid, P. "Borderline Issues: Social and Material Aspects of Design," *Human-Computer Interaction* (9), 1994, pp. 3-36.

Buckland, M. "Information as Thing," *Journal of the American Society of Information Science* (42:5), 1991, pp. 351-260.

Day, R. *The Modern Invention of Information: Discourse, History, and Power*, Carbondale, IL: Southern Illinois University Press, 2001.

Dourish, P. *Where the Action Is: The Foundations of Embodied Interaction*, Cambridge, MA: MIT Press, 2001.

Stanner, W. "The Dreaming," in *Reader in Comparative Religion: An Anthropological Approach*, W. A. Lessa and E. Z. Zohn (Eds.), Evanston, IL: Row, Peterson, 1958, pp. 513-523

Weiser, M. "The Computer for the 21st Century," *Scientific American* (265:3), 1991, pp. 94-104.

ABOUT THE AUTHOR

Paul Dourish is an associate professor in the Donald Bren School of Information and Computer Sciences at the University of California, Irvine, and associate director of the Irvine Division of the California Institute for Telecommunications and Information Technology. His primary research interests are in the areas of ubiquitous computing, computer-supported cooperative work, and human-computer interaction. He is especially interested in the foundational relationships between social scientific analysis and technological design. His book, *Where the Action Is: The Foundations of Embodied Interaction*, was published by MIT Press in 2001; it explores how phenomenological accounts of action can provide an alternative to traditional cognitive analysis for understanding the embodied experience of interactive and computational systems.

Before coming to UCI, he was a senior member of research staff in the Computer Science Laboratory of Xerox PARC; he has also held research positions at Apple Computer and at Rank Xerox EuroPARC. He holds a Ph.D. in Computer Science from University College, London, and a B.Sc. (Hons) in Artificial Intelligence and Computer Science from the University of Edinburgh.

Part 2

Individual Consequences

5   FRIEND OR FOE? The Ambivalent Relationship between Mobile Technology and its Users

Sirkka L. Jarvenpaa
McCombs School of Business
The University of Texas at Austin
Austin, TX U.S.A.

Karl Reiner Lang
Zicklin School of Business
Baruch College, City University of New York
New York, NY U.S.A.

Virpi Kristiina Tuunainen
Helsinki School of Economics
Helsinki, Finland

Abstract   *This paper reports on an empirical study that examined the total user experience of mobile technology users. We held a total of 33 focus group sessions comprised of 222 active mobile device users in four highly developed countries (Finland, Japan, Hong Kong, and the United States) with high penetration of mobile technology. We are specifically focusing on manifestations of paradoxes with regard to mobile technology. We identify eight major technology paradoxes that play a central role in the mobile technology usage experience: (1) empowerment–enslavement, (2) independence– dependence, (3) fulfills needs–creates needs, (4) competence–incompetence, (5) planning– improvisation, (6) engaging–disengaging, (7) public–private, and (8) illusion– disillusion. Our findings suggest conceptualizing the phenomenon of mobile technology usage experience from a context-based and process-oriented perspective where paradoxes of technology shape user experience and determine coping strategies.*

1   INTRODUCTION

Consumers and professionals alike struggle with the complexities of the fast-changing possibilities and limitations of the newly emerging mobile communication and computing technologies (Balasubramanian et al. 2002; Jarvenpaa et al. 2003). Mobility, ubiquity, and personalization are salient characteristics that differentiate mobile technologies from other information technologies. They mean *AAA* capability, that is, the ability to do anything, anywhere, at anytime. Mobile technology promises total computing and communication support for people on the go, the tool of choice for the modern nomad, moving between professional and social environments while seamlessly connected and engaged with business talk, family affairs, and social matters (Lyytinen and Yoo 2002). This technology-enabled augmentation of human powers has undoubtedly made a positive impact on many people's lives. This is the bright side of the technology coin. But this same coin has another, darker side, one that implies negative consequences for the users of mobile technologies. The very same technology that allows users to reach out at will and communicate and transact with others in turn allows these others to uncontrollably reach in from the outside and infiltrate personal space. In other words, mobile technology also means if *I can see you, you can see me* and that you cannot have one without the other. A personal mobile device establishes a place in itself, a location that provides a fixed contact point where the physical and the virtual space meet, where the individual self and the Net interact. This ambivalence is specific to mobile technologies. The positive and the negative impacts are conceptually inseparable. They create tension and paradoxes.

This paper presents an empirical study that examines the total usage experience of mobile technology users. We were interested in the manifestations of paradoxes with regard to this particular technology, if and in what form and to what extend they occurred, how they occurred, why they occurred, what impact they had on users, and how users responded to ensuing paradoxical situations. Besides providing a descriptive account of the various user experiences, we also aim to present a useful theoretical framework that helps us to anticipate, explain, and evaluate the different user experiences and consequences that result from the adoption and use of mobile technologies.

In order to better understand the contradictory and ambiguous reality of mobile technology use, we conducted a qualitative research study whose findings suggest conceptualizing the phenomenon of mobile technology usage experience from a context-based and process-oriented perspective. This view is in accordance with Orlikowski (1993), who argues that in order to account for the experiences and implications associated with the usage of IT one has to consider the specific contexts in which IT is being used as well as how the user experience unfolds over time. Similarly, the user-technology interaction process shapes total user experience, but the dynamics of the interaction process depend not only on the user's own responses to the technology but also, to a large degree, on the other users and their uses of the service as well. We identify eight major technology paradoxes that play a central role in the specific case of mobile technology usage: (1) empowerment–enslavement, (2) independence– dependence, (3) fulfills needs–creates needs, (4) competence–incompetence, (5) planning–improvisation, (6) engaging–disengaging, (7) public–private, and (8) illusion–disillusion. Coping with technology paradoxes emerged as the central theme from our data. While users almost universally acknowledged that mobile technology had made some improvements to their lives in terms of convenience, flexibility, connectedness, and new freedoms of choice, it became apparent that their overall experience was, to a large extent, determined by conflict situations they had encountered.

2   RESEARCH METHODOLOGY

Focus group research is an appropriate qualitative methodology to gain insights to causes and consequences of frequently occurring phenomena that may be experienced differently by different groups of people. Focus group data may also be used for uncovering theoretical concepts and their relationships between concepts in order to develop new theory. While it cannot scientifically test theory, it is a valid method for deriving scientific knowledge and theory building (Fern 2001).

This research followed the commonly accepted guidelines of focus group research (Fern 2001; Krueger 1994). We held a total of 33 focus group sessions comprised of 222 active mobile device users in four countries (Finland, Japan, Hong Kong, and the United States) with a high penetration of mobile technology devices. While all 33 focus groups were urban-based, the groups varied in age, gender, culture, and economic standing (see Table 1). Data were collected over a 9-month period in 2001. The focus group discussion questions, shown in Table 2, were kept as broad as possible to ensure open forums. Each focus group lasted about 90 minutes to 2 hours and was conducted by a moderator in the local language. The session protocol transcripts were translated and then content analyzed using the principles of the grounded theory approach (Auerbach and Silverstein 2003; Strauss and Corbin 1998).

For the purpose of this paper, we define mobile technology as an information technology artifact that is represented as a service bundle combining a device with its interface, network services, and software applications. Because these are so intertwined it does not make sense to disentangle device, interface, and applications when studying how mobile services create value for the users. This definition includes mobile phones, portable digital assistants, and integrated wireless enterprise solutions like the popular handheld BlackBerry™.

3   RESEARCH RESULTS

Among our focus group participants, voice communication clearly dominates the usage profile, followed by data services like e-mail, Web browsing, and text messaging. Other informational and transactional services were only moderately used on a regular basis. The process of experiencing mobile technology from a user's perspective is depicted in Figure 1, which shows the main themes and concepts that emerged from our data and the relationships that indicate significant interactions between them. This process model is proposed as an initial theoretical framework for anticipating, explaining, and evaluating the experiences and behavioral responses associated with the use of mobile technology.

Table 1. Focus Group Participants

Location	Focus Group Participants (Group Size)
Helsinki, Finland	Airline Maintenance staff (8) Adult hobby group (7) Late Teens (6) Boys, 11–12 years old (12) Girls, 11–12 years old (8) Mothers (8) Software Consultants (6) Entrepreneurs (8) Students (6) Researchers, all female (7)
Hong Kong	Undergraduate Students I (7) University Maintenance Workers, all male (5) Kitchen/Restaurant Staff (6) Undergraduate Students II (8) Rock Band (4) IT Professionals (4)
Tokyo, Japan	High School Students, all female (6) Vocational School Students, all female (6) Housewives (6) IT Sales Representatives (7) MBA Students (9)
Austin, USA	Real Estate Agents (7) Church Group (8) Engineers, all male (6) Lawyers, (7) Graduate Students (7) IT Professionals (6) Women's Group (5) Professionals (7)

Table 2. Focus Group Discussion Questions

1. How do you feel when you have to turn your device off? 2. Why are you using mobile services? 3. What kinds of services are missing? Why do you need them? 4. Why do you use a mobile device rather than a wired device to access a particular service? 5. How do other technologies support your use of mobile services? 6. What is the value of mobile services to you? What is the most valuable thing? 7. What problems and risks are associated with the use of mobile devices? 8. How have/are mobile phones changing your life and affecting the quality of your life?

The model in Figure 1 does not explain why or how consumers decided to acquire mobile technology. That is, the adoption decision is treated as an exogenous prior event. The actions and experiences of mobile technology users depend on situational and contextual factors. The given technology, social (personal or organizational), and cultural contexts influence user's motivations, goals, and usage patterns when using mobile technology for a particular purpose (arrow 1). Decisions to use mobile technology in different situations for different purposes provide accumulative context-feedback over time, which can change or reinforce those contexts (arrow 2). But no matter what the specific purpose might be, eventually and recurrently, technology use will create conflict situations for the user, although the specific nature of the conflict may differ between, for example, maintaining social relationships and performing business tasks (arrow 3). Again, context-dependent (arrow 4) conflict situations will arise from paradoxes that are inherently and systemically linked to technology use.

The repeated confrontation with paradoxically behaving technology impacts users on an emotional level. This has a significant effect on the total user experience. The continuous conflict with paradoxes and emotional responses leads, for many long-term users, to a search for identity as they keep participating in multiple realities, moving simultaneously in loosely connected virtual spaces and the physical space, a search that is typically accompanied by attempts of reconstructing the meaning of traditional social values and concepts. Reinforcing or modifying context-feedback is generated as users experience conflict (arrow 5).

A direct response to the challenges presented is the development of behavioral strategies that help users better cope with these conflict situations (arrow 6). Broadly speaking, users work out and adopt mechanisms that help them avoid or minimize conflict (avoidance strategies) or guide them in confronting and perhaps managing conflict (confrontative strategies). The particular reactions of users and their ability to manage conflict and to cope with the technology challenge are once more influenced by situational context factors (arrow 7). Context-feedback is generated as users gain experience with coping strategies (arrow 8).

4   MOBILE TECHNOLOGY PARADOXES AND CONFLICT SITUATIONS IN THE USER'S EXPERIENCE

This section describes in more detail, based on the data collected from our focus group sessions, the various manifestations of technology paradoxes (depicted in Figure 1) in the specific context of mobile technology. It discusses why paradoxes occur, how they occur, and how users respond to them. Eight central paradoxes emerged from our data. They are presented in order, starting out with paradoxes that occur primarily due to individual behavior and following with those that are increasingly determined by group behavior. The described paradoxes don't happen in isolation, they may overlap and interact with each other.

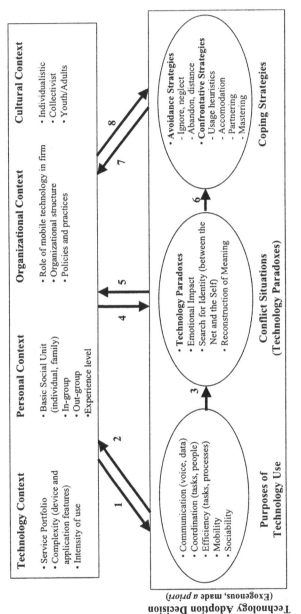

Figure 1. Total User Experience

4.1 The Empowerment–Enslavement Paradox

New freedoms of choice surfaced as the perhaps most salient issue from mobile technology use across all types of users. Nearly everyone praised some new possibilities that were related to the ubiquitous, 24/7, "always on" nature of mobile technology. Permanent connectivity allows people to take charge anytime wherever they are, whether it concerns business, family, or friends. This newly found freedom empowers users, but the very same connectivity also prevents users from creating and maintaining distance from others. *"The fact that you have to interact with these devices is bad,"* explained one user. Aside from concerns about increased surveillance by government and corporate institutions using GPS, it has generally become difficult to get away from people you would rather not communicate with. An older woman reminisced old times, *"when we did not have any of these technologies. Doing any kind of job was really hard back then. I can tell you that the cell phone really is a tremendous safety and access device. But I should be controlling it, not it controlling me."* The unpredictability and uncertainty if and when a call may come and demand unwanted attention counteracts the power that users derive from the technology. *"I am in a dilemma that I cannot leave my cell phone at home, but just the fact that I am always connected is stressful,"* remarked one person. And someone else added, *"Availability all the time! This is not what we humans were made for."* Some users had a pretty good sense of the power they could exert but also anticipated that it could backfire in just the same way. One participant observed, *"The mobile is great for controlling other people like your wife and kids, for example. That would be pretty good if I had the choice to decide who knows where I am and where I have been."* Many users reported great pressures and felt forced to respond to the technology, whether they wanted to or not. Some feared that they had become slaves to the machine.

The workplace was another area where the empowerment–enslavement paradox manifested itself on a regular basis. Most professionals welcomed the introduction of mobile technologies in their companies. They appreciated increased productivity, more flexibility, and more efficient ways to coordinate tasks and people. But again, the same tools that empowered them on their job in so many ways also took away long-cherished freedoms. Increased work pressure, closer monitoring and supervision, and the inability to separate and keep distance from work were cited frequently. Participants expressed displeasure having to play multiple roles at all times, especially having to constantly switch between family and work roles.

4.2 The Independence–Dependence Paradox

"My cell phone does everything," said one of our focus group members. More independence through mobility was one of the most important freedoms enjoyed by the participants of our study. But it also became clear that the power to connect independent of space and time created a new form of dependency that invariably coexists with independency. Or as one of our participants described, *"Always being available results in lack of independence. It is like having an electronic ankle chain."* While the result-ant *independence–dependence* paradox could be considered just a special case of the

above described *empowerment–enslavement* paradox, it warrants its own category because this particular aspect was almost universally acknowledged as an issue with which users were struggling. Some denied technology dependency or at least qualified it, but most found it quite difficult to break the always-on habit they had acquired and admitted quite bluntly that they had become dependent on total connectivity. Although *"there was life before these gadgets,"* for most users mobile technology has become part of their lives, for better or worse. Many agreed that *"life without a cell would be terrible"* and that *"once you get one you don't know how to live without it."*

Being cut off from her usual mobile services, one participant experienced withdrawal-like symptoms. *"Once I went on a trip to [nearby] Macau without my cell phone. Whenever I heard a ring tone I thought someone is calling me. I got so tense and thought it was my phone."* Once people get used to being always on it causes them great discomfort when they need to disconnect, even if it is only temporarily. Most users loathe turning off their devices for fear they may miss an important call. Missed calls attain a more meaningful status than most answered calls. The mere chance that someone may have tried to communicate something significant is given substantial consideration despite the fact that most turn out to be noncritical or outright trivial. This leaves users in a state of constant anticipation for some elusive messages that may or may not ever be send. The possibility of failing to immediately respond to either a great opportunity or some emergency is perceived as a great threat, although it is understood, from a rational perspective, that the odds are rather small that an event with significant consequences would be passed over because of a missed call.

4.3 The Fulfills Needs–Creates Needs Paradox

Mobile technology has *"taken simplicity out of our lives,"* commented one of our participants. Our data shows clearly that technology really is providing a solution to many problems that benefit from mobile connectivity, but at the same time it has also caused a whole range of new problems, problems that users didn't have before or didn't perceive having. This can be as trivial as the new need of always *"having to carry a bag that holds the mobile"* or that *"the battery runs down quickly,"* but often it creates much more intricate needs. The irony that solutions create problems did not go unnoticed. As one person urgently expressed, *"it is very important that users think about what specific need a particular service is really satisfying,"* while someone else wondered *"if adding more services is really productive? Every time they add something, people have problems."* Paradoxically, the same feature that fulfills one user need creates another. For example, mobility fulfills the need for more security because it allows people to stay in touch (e.g., parents with their children when they are out, wives with their husbands when they go on road trips, or elderly with caretakers if they encounter difficulties at home and can't reach the regular phone), but ironically this newly found security also seems to create a new sense of vulnerability as a number of people fear *"What if I lose it?"*

A new need for privacy was recognized by a number of participants. This need only arose because mobility and *AAA* capability had fulfilled user's need to be able to talk in public places. But once users experienced situations where they had a conversation in public that they really didn't mean sharing with anyone, and certainly not with random bystanders, or were involuntarily made to listen to some stranger talking on a mobile phone, they realized that going public with mobile communication creates a new need for privacy. Most prevalent, however, were cases where users had taken an active step to fulfill a perceived need just to find out that this same action created a new need.

4.4 The Competence–Incompetence Paradox

The ability to do anything, anytime, anywhere gives mobile technology users a whole set of new competencies. It allows them to do things they couldn't do before. It enables them to do things more efficiently and effectively than in the past. But as people are using their newly acquired, technology-enabled competencies to perform new tasks or try to perform tasks better, they soon experience a new sense of incompetence. Seemingly simple services turn out to be hard to use and newly gained efficiencies tend to be limited in scope and actually cause inefficiency at some higher level. The idea that a newly obtained competence lowers another, directly related competence or makes users experience incompetence, whether real or just perceived, emerged from our data in several different contexts. The most apparent relates to situations where users explore new device functions or try out new application services with the expectation of becoming a more competent user only to be confronted with unexpected difficulties that leave them feeling less competent than before. Such "less for more" bargains were reported frequently across groups.

Other examples illustrated how the use of one new competence can compromise another. The new competence of talking on the phone while driving can make you a bad and possibly dangerous driver. The new competence of using mobile text communication methods can have a negative effect on your written language competence. Relying on electronic memory may be detrimental to your own memory. Using mobile technologies in meetings may give you better information but may be distractive and actually weaken your performance and thus make you a less competent participant in the meeting.

In many ways, some particular mobile services themselves turn out to be much less competent than expected when applied in varying situations and often outright incompetent when used in ways that are only slightly different from the prescribed guidelines. In either case, mobile technology competencies are too often too narrow in scope and incapable of adapting to specific user environments to be of much value. This leaves the user with the impression that the technology itself is incompetent, or worse, it makes the users themselves feel incompetent as they struggle to make effective use of it.

Poor design or technical limitations like small screen size, tiny input keys, or some network constraints can render a service ineffective and make it look incompetent. On the other hand, complicated usage logic or incomprehensible behavior of a service diminishes self-efficacy and tends to create a sense of user incompetence.

4.5 The Planning–Improvisation Paradox

Mobile technologies can certainly be employed as effective planning tools allowing people to better coordinate meetings and plan work and social activities. One user, for example, said, "*I use the mobile to be polite and call to tell when I am five minutes late or I may check if the other person is really there where I am supposed to pick him up.*"

Taking advantage of *AAA* capabilities, users can prepare schedules in advance and then update and refine them independent of time and location and provide involved parties with additional information as they go along. This should, in theory, result in more efficient planning and less unproductive time. In practice, however, the opposite takes place all too often. People tend to spend less time and effort on working out schedules and instead rely more on the technology that allows them to make up for lack of preparation with continuous improvisation. Some users welcomed this new flexibility that makes *"life more unplanned because you can plan on the spot"* and found it liberating that *"you don't have to make arrangements in advance anymore."* Several participants described situations where vague planning of a meeting lead to numerous changes and improvisations that resulted in extra coordination efforts, modified agendas, and, in the end, increased lateness and actually less time spent together. To some extend, technology substitutes for planning rather than augmenting it.

Technology has been changing people's behavior. It used to be socially unaccept-able to be late, without a reasonable excuse, but now being late is almost expected; it has become the norm. As long as you update your party on your whereabouts and report on your progress toward the meeting, being late is acceptable. What is unacceptable, however, is not having a mobile phone and being out of reach. Forgetting the mobile at home or running out of battery have become inexcusable *faux pas* that can easily result in social exclusion. Another consequence of this emerging improvisation culture is the erosion of social conventions regarding acceptable calling times. In the absence of any preplanning, *"It has [for example] become easier to get a hold of a married friend. Since he answers his cell phone, I can call him in the middle of the night without giving any consideration to his family members."*

Too much improvisation causes disorganization. While mobile technologies are designed as instruments to support control, they create chaos if improperly used. Technology can facilitate not just planning but also controlling information access and input, but if people don't exercise discipline in their usage, chaos is bound to ensue. Too much communication creates chaotic disturbances in people's physical space; receiving too much information leads to information overload; messages are send and ignored, which triggers more messages and corrupts social communication protocols. Senders no longer know which of their messages have been received and recipients lose messages in an uncontrolled fashion.

4.6 The Engaging–Disengaging Paradox

One promise that comes with *AAA* capability is that mobile technology would enable users to choose when to engage in a discourse and when to disengage, promising tools that help users achieve a balance between involvement and retreat. This desire to retreat from stressful environments while at the same time staying involved surfaced in several of our focus group discussions. For example, one participant expressed that *"people want to know what is going on, but on the other hand, they also want to be in the middle of a forest."* Unfortunately, most people find it difficult to simultaneously engage in parallel activities, to engage in something new without disengaging from something else. When calls interrupt a conversation in the physical space, the person receiving the call will typically abruptly disengage from the current conversation and engage in a new one, often leaving others stranded. When driving, people make calls and engage in conversation while disengaging from their driving activity.

The realization that mobile technologies "*might be a detriment to other kinds of communication*" was widely acknowledged. Communication patterns in the family home have been altered since the fixed-line family phone has lost its role as the communication hub in the home. "*The phone at home does not ring that much anymore since everybody has their own cell phone. When it does ring, it usually is somebody trying to sell us something. No one else calls our home phone anymore.*" While family members develop their own personal mobile communication channels, they are prone to disengage from family life, especially teenage children. "*I would be even less home, if I didn't need to go home to read my e-mail [on the desktop computer]*," conceded a young daughter. And parents generally thought that heavy use of mobile technology among teenage kids was detrimental to family life and social interaction.

Generally, there was concern that engaging with mobile communication technologies may lead users to disengage from face-to-face social activities.

4.7 The Public–Private Paradox

Mobile technology devices are usually considered personal tools for private communication. In the past, personal communication (voice or data) only took place in personal physical spaces like the office or the home where it was by and large possible to set and control an adequate level of privacy. Now, freed from spatial and temporal constraints, people are increasingly taking private conversations into the public space, which creates friction and interferes with other people's activities and privacy. When exchanging messages or talking, the conversing parties create virtual communication spaces. But while technology can support users in managing multiple virtual communication spaces, it cannot eliminate interference with activities in the surrounding physical space. It is not just the noise and chatter that disturbs people, it is also the fact that they overhear only one half of a nearby conversation, wondering about the missing pieces and the absent person, involuntarily drawn into an interpersonal exchange that should be private but is happening in public. At the same time, people assume different roles as they switch between physical and virtual space, displaying behaviors, gestures, and emotional states that may befit an ongoing virtual interaction but may appear out of place in the context of the present physical space.

4.8 The Illusion–Disillusion Paradox

When our users acquired their first mobile devices or upgraded to new models they did so with certain expectations of partaking in joys that would come with *AAA* capability features that were promised and promoted. Whether these were reasonable or unrealistic, people were anticipating that their new gadgets would make their lives easier and enable them to do things they couldn't before. But soon they learned that true *AAA* capability represents an ideal that remains an illusion in people's reality and that available technology in many regards delivers merely a crude approximation to their initial expectations. Many users recounted frustration and disillusion as they discovered that *anywhere* communication really means in some places and areas only, while limited coverage and dead spots are really constraining connectivity. *"When I tried to send data from the Shinkansen [Japanese bullet train], the transmission was interrupted every time the train went thorough the tunnel,"* lamented a respondent. Likewise, *anytime* communication is severely compromised by short battery runtimes. And of course, anytime also requires that the intended communication partners are available and willing to communicate. Finally, *anything* barely covers voice communication as many connections are unstable or of poor quality while hardware and bandwidth limitations render access to Web sites and delivery of multimedia content inadequate. For example, one user thought *"it is a great idea to make comics available over cell phones, but the screen is too tiny. It takes the fun away."*

When adopting new mobile services, users were under the impression that they would get to enjoy an upgrade in service level or quality, but after using the new services they often felt that the services were inadequate for the task. They actually perceived a service downgrade. For example, the ability to access the Web with mobile phones promises a service upgrade, but the actual experience of struggling with small keypads and screens and slow connections creates the perception of a downgrade, especially when contrasted with the easily available wired Internet or wireless WiFi networks. *"I feel this Internet and mobile thing is like skis that are designed for classical style Nordic skiing and free style Nordic skiing. The middle way may not be the best—some services belong to the Internet and others will be mobile,"* stated one user. Difficult to use interfaces and cryptic command syntaxes were also significant factors contributing to disappointment about new services. A few people pointed out that more communication does not necessarily mean better communication, and that the ease of communicating with mobile technologies may have increased the quantity of communication but, at the same time, decreased its quality.

5   DISCUSSION AND CONCLUSION

The idea that technology is and behaves intrinsically paradoxically or ironically is, of course, not entirely new. For example, Arnold (2003), Castells (2000), and Easter-brook (2003) all argue, from a purely theoretical point of view, that technologies that bring us progress also create economic and social paradoxes that increasingly challenge people in their individual and social lives. Tradeoffs between privacy and awareness and between awareness and disturbance have been recognized as fundamental in the technology design space and are unlikely to be eliminated (Hudson and Smith 1996). In a more business-oriented discourse, Handy (1995) makes the case that the ability to manage paradoxes is key to corporate success in today's high-tech world. Mick and Fournier (1998) describe a post-modernist consumer society in which consumers are confronted with multiple and conflicting consequences from the consumption of consumer electronic products.

Among the information systems researchers, Orlikowski (1991) and Chinn (2001) discuss the paradoxical nature of information technology in general, while Howcroft and Wilson (2003) and Schultze and Orlikowski (2004) specifically examine paradoxes of participatory information systems development, which they see as a consequence of inherently conflicting organizational relations. Depending on situational context factors and the particular purposes, mobile technology users are invariably confronted with a set of technology paradoxes that affect their relationship with the technology ambiguously in terms of both emotional impact and behavioral response. In a recursive process, users interact with the properties of mobile technology and come up with their own set of rules that shape how they make use of the technology (Orlikowski 2000).

This research contributes to the understanding of technology paradoxes, and in particular why and how they occur in mobile environments. As indicated in Figure 1, we identify a number of coping mechanisms that can be broadly classified into two groups: avoidance and confrontational coping strategies (Holahan and Moos 1987). The former refers to user strategies that try to minimize interaction with the technology and the latter describes strategies that are based on negotiating with technology. We conclude that managing paradoxes in personal technology spaces arises as a major obstacle in people's lives. This presents both a challenge and an opportunity for technology service providers. New innovations like better presence management or service integration are being developed to address some of the problems discussed in this paper, but at the same time, novel features and new gadgets constantly introduce new complexity and ultimately lead to recurring conflicts. Hence, the elimination of technology paradoxes may proof elusive. On the other hand, we suggest that exploring ways to help users better cope with paradoxically behaving technology is a research direction that needs more attention.

ACKNOWLEDGMENTS

This project was funded by a grant awarded to the first author by the Advanced Practices Council of the Society for Information Management.

REFERENCES

Arnold, M. "On the Phenomenology of Technology: The 'Janus-Faces' of Mobile Phones," *Information and Organization* (13), 2003, pp. 231-256.

Auerbach, C. F., and Silverstein, L. B. *Qualitative Data: An Introduction to Coding and Analysis*, New York: New York University Press, 2003.

Balasubramanian, S., Peterson, R. A., and Jarvenpaa, S. L. "Exploring the Implications of M-Commerce for Markets and Marketing," *Journal of the Academy of Marketing Science* (30:4), 2002, pp. 348-361.

Castells, M. *The Rise of the Network Society. The Information Age: Economy, Society and Culture, Volume 1* (2nd ed.), Oxford, UK: Blackwell Publishers, 2000.

Chinn, S. S. "The Technology Paradox," *Industrial Management*, March-April 2001, pp. 25-27.

Easterbrook, G. *The Progress Paradox: How Life Gets Better While People Feel Worse*, New York: Random House, 2003.

Fern, E. F. *Advanced Focus Group Research*, Thousand Oaks, CA: Sage Publications, 2001.

Handy, C. *The Age of Paradox*, Boston: Harvard Business School Press, 1995.

Holahan, C. J., and Moos, R. H. "Personal and Contextual Determinants of Coping Strategies," *Journal of Personality and Social Psychology* (52:5), 1987, pp. 946-955.

Howcroft, D., and Wilson, M. "Paradoxes of Participatory Practices: The Janus Role of the Systems Developer," *Information and Organization* (13), 2003, pp. 1-24.

Hudson, S. E., and Smith, I. "Techniques for Addressing Fundamental Privacy and Disruption Tradeoffs in Awareness Support Systems," in *Proceedings of ACM Conference on Computer Supported Collaborative Work*, New York: ACM Press, 1996, pp. 248-257.

Jarvenpaa, S. L., Lang, K. R., Takeda, Y., and Tuunainen, V. K. "Mobile Commerce at Crossroads," *Communications of the ACM* (46:12), 2003, pp. 41-44.

Krueger, R. A. *Focus Groups: A Practical Guide for Applied Research*, Thousand Oaks, CA: Sage Publications, 1994.

Lyytinen, K., and Yoo, Y. "The Next Wave of Nomadic Computing," *Information Systems Research* (13:4), 2002, pp. 377-388.

Mick, D. G., and Fournier, S. "Paradoxes of Technology: Consumer Cognizance, Emotions, and Coping Strategies," *Journal of Consumer Research* (25), 1998, pp. 123-143.

Orlikowski, W. J. "CASE Tools as Organizational Change: Investigating Incremental and Radical Changes in Systems Development," *MIS Quarterly* (17:3), September 1993, pp. 309-339.

Orlikowski, W. J. "Integrated Information Environment or Matrix of Control? The Contradictory Implications of Information Technology," *Accounting, Management, and Information Technology* (1), 1991, pp. 1, 9-42.

Orlikowski, W. J. "Using Technology and Constituting Structures: A Practice Lens for Studying Technology in Organizations," *Organization Science* (11:4), 2000, pp. 404-428.

Schultze, U., and Orlikowski, W. J. "A Practice Perspective on Technology-Mediated Network Relations: The Use of Internet-Based Self-Serve Technologies," *Information Systems Research* (15:1), 2004, pp. 87-106.

Strauss, A., and Corbin, J. *Basics of Qualitative Research, Techniques and Procedures for Developing Grounded Theory*, Thousand Oaks, CA: Sage Publications, 1998.

ABOUT THE AUTHORS

Sirkka L. Jarvenpaa is the Bayless/Rauscher Pierce Refsner Chair in Business Administration and a cofounder and codirector of the Center for Business, Technology, and Law at the McCombs Business School, University of Texas at Austin. Sirkka can be reached at Sirkka.Jarvenpaa@mccombs.utexas.edu.

Karl R. Lang is an associate professor in Information System at the Zicklin School of Business, City University of New York. Karl can be reached at karl_lang@baruch.cuny.edu.

Virpi Kristiina Tuunainen is a professor of Information Systems Science at the department of business technology, and the director of the Graduate School for Electronic Business and Software Industry,Helsinki School of Economics. Virpi can be reached at virpi.tuunainen@ hkkk.fi.

6 THE ROLE OF UBIQUITOUS COMPUTING IN MAINTAINING WORK-LIFE BALANCE: Perspectives from Women in the Information Technology Workforce

Jeria L. Quesenberry
Eileen M. Trauth
School of Information Sciences and Technology
The Pennsylvania State University
University Park, PA U.S.A.

Abstract   *Transformations in ubiquitous computing and shifts in the domestic nature of home life are placing greater demands on men and women to balance work and life. Although work–life balance has been heavily investigated for many years, the majority of this research gives very little discussion to the role of technology. Thus, the question remains: Can ubiquitous computing address the issues raised by work–life balance? The purpose of this paper is to explore a particular instance of how ubiquitous computing is utilized to maintain work–life balance from the perspectives of women in the information technology workforce.*

Keywords   Ubiquitous computing, IT workforce, gender, under-represented groups, work–life balance, individual differences theory

1 INTRODUCTION

In the transition to an information-based global economy, the lines between work and home are blurring as technology reshapes the workplace and the nature of home life evolves. Ubiquitous computing is facilitating dramatic new alternatives for where, when, and how work is accomplished (Hill et al. 2003; Useem 2000). In addition, the domestic nature of home life is evolving. Since the 1940s, women have entered the labor force in growing numbers at a rate of over 200 percent (Riley and McCloskey

1996). As a result, the labor force consists of more dual-professional couples who have responsibilities for children and elderly dependents, as well as an increase in individuals who have careers, not just jobs (Useem 2000). These transformations are placing greater demands on men and women to balance work and life.

Although work–life balance has been heavily investigated for many years, the majority of this research gives very little discussion to the role of technology. Thus, the question remains: Can ubiquitous computing address the issues raised by work–life balance? The purpose of this paper is to explore a particular instance of how ubiquitous computing is utilized to maintain work–life balance from the perspectives of women in the information technology workforce. The reasons for doing so are twofold. First, it is reasonable to expect that people employed in technical careers are more likely to be surrounded by ubiquitous computing, leading to a higher degree of exposure and expertise with such technologies. Consequently these users serve as an informative case study of the possible projection of these technologies in maintaining work–life balance. Second, although research has found that while men and women both report high levels of work–life imbalance (Duxbury and Higgins 2003; Milkie and Peltola 1999), women commonly do the majority of domestic work (Hochschild and Machung 2003; Perlow 1998). Thus, men and women exhibit different behavior patterns in relation to work–life balance (Mennino and Brayfield 2002). In addition, women in the IT workforce experience higher levels of stress due to work–life imbalance than their male counterparts (Duxberry et al. 1992; Gallivan 2003; Igbaria, et al. 1997). In this paper, we situate the discussion of work–life balance within the context of ubiquitous computing. We then present data from a field study of gender and IT that is directed at understanding the role of ubiquitous computing in maintaining work–life balance. Finally, we present the contribution of this research to theory and practice.

2   BACKGROUND

Work–life balance[1] reflects an individual's orientation across career roles and noncareer life roles as an incompatible inter-role phenomenon (Duxbury and Higgins 2003; Greenhaus et al. 2002). According to Greenhaus and Beutell (1985), the balance of work and life is "a form of inter-role conflict in which the role pressures from the work and family domains are mutually incompatible in some respect" (p. 77). Greenhaus et al. (2002) explain that work–life balance, contains three components: time balance, involvement balance and satisfaction balance. Time balance means devoting an appropriate amount of time to work and life roles. Involvement balance means deriving an equal level of psychological engagement in work and life roles. Satisfaction balance means deriving an equal level of satisfaction from work and life roles.

---

[1]Work–life balance or work-family balance is the management of work–family conflict, work–life conflict, work–life interference, and/or work–life convergence.

2.1 Consequences of Work–Life Imbalance

There is a large body of research on the consequences of work–life imbalance, pointing to negative impacts for individuals. From an individual perspective, work–life imbalance has been found to cause job dissatisfaction (Thomas and Ganster 1995), job stress (Judge et al. 1994), and overall poor well-being (Igbaria et al. 1994). A lack of workplace flexibility is also linked to depression (Googins 1991), difficulty in falling asleep and/or staying asleep, changes in appetite, and tension related aches and pains (Guelzow et al. 1991). A recent study of work–life imbalance in the Canadian workforce showed that the stress level from work–life imbalance almost doubled over the past decade. The resulting reduction of sleep and rejuvenating time contributes to psychological and physical illness (McNaughton 2001). Work–life imbalance also has an effect on home and personal lives. Reeves (2001, in Perrons 2003) explains that work–life imbalance can cause home life to become gloomier and more routine as work–life imbalance creates the need for more rigid and fixed timetables and schedules.

Work–life imbalance can also impair organizational effectiveness, primarily by affecting absenteeism, productivity at work, and high turnover rates (Higgins et al. 1994). The majority of these problems arise as a result of child care and family obligations. Parents who are unable to provide adequate and affordable care for their children may experience time lost from work or a decrease in productivity. In addition, interruptions due to family obligations can infringe on work. Duxbury and Higgins (2003) report that employees with high role overload are three and a half times more likely to have high levels of absenteeism due to physical, mental, or emotional fatigue than counterparts with low levels of role overload. The direct and indirect cost of absenteeism due to role overload is estimated to be between $4.5 billion and $6 billion per year in Canada alone. Another serious impact of work–life imbalance is high turnover rates (Duxbury et al. 1992; Glass and Estes 1997), which are both expensive and disruptive to employers. Duxbury and Higgins report that employees with high role overload are 2.3 times more likely to report high intent to turnover than counterparts with low levels of role overload.

2.2 Promises of Ubiquitous Computing

Weiser (1995) first coined the term ubiquitous computing to explain situations where multiple computers are invisible, indistinguishable, and available to an individual throughout a physical environment, and thus woven into the fabric of everyday life. Not only is ubiquitous computing designed to blend into the user's physical surroundings, but the technology is also engineered to help organize and mediate social interactions wherever these interactions occur (Lyytinen and Yoo 2002). Ubiquitous computing also supports work practices and routine activities (Avital and Germonprez 2003; Chae 2003). Thus, ubiquitous computing enables nothing fundamentally new, but makes tasks faster and easier to do, thereby reducing the strain of mental processing (Lyytinen and Yoo 2002; Weiser 1993).

Researchers are just beginning to investigate the role of ubiquitous computing in work–life balance and their results, to date, have been mixed. Zimmerman (2003) found that ubiquitous technologies such as cell phones, laptops, and text messaging devices make it easier to balance work and life. Several studies report that telecommuting helps parents to work in the home rather than be away for long periods of time (Beasley et al. 2001; Hill et al. 2003; Sullivan and Lewis 2001). Riley and McCloskey (1996) argue that telecommuting reduces costs and commute time, while increasing productivity and flexibility. On the other hand, researchers have concluded that access to ubiquitous computing can increase stress levels. Duxbury and Higgins (2003) found that 70 percent of 33,000 respondents felt that ubiquitous computing increased their stress levels and workloads. Hill et al. (2003) found telecommuting had a negative relationship on work–life balance. These researchers question whether telecommuting is ideal for work–life balance, especially for families with young children. Frissen (2000) further highlights the complexities by reporting that Dutch families do not explicitly perceive technology as a solution to communication and coordination problems, yet they continue to use these technologies. Furthermore, researchers found that ubiquitous computing causes the line of demarcation between work and private life to blur and call for additional investigation in this area (Perrons 2003; Sullivan and Lewis 2001).

The mixed results of these studies, coupled with the complexities in understanding the role of ubiquitous computing in work–life balance, present an interesting opportunity for research. Therefore, the following research question is explored in this paper: What is the role of ubiquitous computing in maintaining work–life balance by women in the IT workforce?

3   METHODOLOGY

Empirical data from an ongoing study of women in the IT workforce was examined for clues to the role of ubiquitous computing in addressing work–life balance. In this study, which has been ongoing since 2000, in-depth interviews are being conducted with female IT professionals. In the course of these interviews, women discuss their work histories, individual and environmental influences on their decision to enter the IT profession, and societal viewpoints about gender that have affected their career progression.

A consistent theme that speaks directly to opportunities for ubiquitous computing is the uneven playing field with respect to domestic responsibilities. Simply put, when both partners have careers, domestic responsibilities are not usually shared equally and it is the women who most often bear more responsibility.[2] Given this situation, coupled with the fact that as IT professionals these women would likely have a heightened understanding of and exposure to new technology, it was expected that this population would represent a meaningful context for examining the strengths and weakness of ubiquitous computing in maintaining work–life balance.

---

[2]While some same-sex couples are included in this research project, the data set is not yet large enough to enable meaningful analysis. Hence, when we refer to "couples" in this paper, we assume them to be heterosexual couples.

Interview transcripts with 136 women working as IT professionals in Australia/New Zealand,[3] Ireland, and the United States were examined for comments about the role of ubiquitous computing in addressing work–life balance. Upon examination of these transcripts, 45 were found to have useable comments.[4] It is these women upon whose voices our analysis is based. Table 1 shows the distribution of respondents by country. The reason for this difference is that the themes of work–life balance and the use of ubiquitous computing to address work–life balance have become more prominent in the interviews as the research project has evolved over time and as ubiquitous computing has evolved. This is evident in the fact that the Australia/New Zealand interviews (which were conducted first) contain the smallest percentage of useful interviews on this topic. Further, women are not specifically asked either about work–life balance or about ubiquitous computing. These themes arise unprompted. While work–life balance issues arise in a majority of the interviews, the use of ubiquitous computing in maintaining work–life balance is mentioned much less frequently.

The women in this study represent a wide range of ages, backgrounds, levels of management responsibility, and degrees of technical specialization. The women range in age from early 20s to late 60s. The ethnic make-up of the women includes Europeans, European-Americans, European-Australians, African-Americans, Asians, Asian-Americans, Indigenous Australians, Hispanic-Americans, and Middle Eastern women. The women have bachelor's degrees, master's degrees, and Ph.D.s. The fields of study include information science, computer science, engineering and information systems, psychology, nursing, communications, mathematics, and liberal arts. Job titles include program/project manager, software architect, quality assurance engineer, IT administrator, system and Web developer, and small IT business owner.

Table 1. Respondent Characteristics

Country	Total # Interviewed	# Interviews Used
Australia/New Zealand	30	6
Ireland	21	9
United States	85	30
Total	**136**	**45**

---

[3]Women working in IT in both Australia and New Zealand were interviewed as part of a single study (Trauth 2002), hence the two countries are listed together in this discussion.

[4]We do not assume that ubiquitous computing influences work–life balance in a persistent and universal manner, or that all women respond to these technologies in the same way. Likewise, we acknowledge that the interviews not included in this analysis could potentially indicate participants' selective considerations to not adopt or use ubiquitous computing. Although, these are interesting aspects of the data, it is outside the scope of this specific paper, as we focus on the ways ubiquitous computing is used to maintain work–life balance.

In this study, we employ Trauth's (2002) individual differences theory of gender and IT, which seeks to explain the observed variation in people's relationship to IT and IT careers by gender. Originally applied to the investigation of the under-representation of women in the IT workforce, the theory is concerned with individual differences among women (rather than differences between men and women) in the ways they experience and respond to characteristics of IT work, the IT workplace, and societal messages about gender and IT. This theory focuses on the individual variations among women that result from a combination of individual characteristics, influencing factors, and environmental factors in order to explain the variation in people's relationships to IT and IT careers by gender. To date, this theory has been used to examine the under-representation of women in the IT workforce through exploration of the socio-cultural environment that shapes a woman's gender identity and her professional development, and her individual responses to these influences (Morgan et al. 2004; Quesenberry et al. 2004; Trauth 1995, 2002; Trauth et al. 2005, 2004).

4   RESULTS

The participants in this study represent a wide range of situations with regard to work–life balance. Some women are the primary source of family income and may have stay-at-home partners. Other women do not have children and view work–life balance in terms of non-child-related factors such as personal responsibilities. To another group of women, work–life balance referred to the strain of elder care of retired parents. Thus, a number of women in our study have chosen nontraditional ways of balancing work and life (i.e., not leaving the workforce to care for domestic responsibilities) and represent a range of work–life balance situations with varying issues and concerns. Several themes about the role of ubiquitous computing in maintaining balance emerged from the interviews and are discussed in the following sections.

4.1 Asynchronous Communication

Of the 45 women included in this study, 19 spoke about asynchronous communication, which allows for more flexibility regarding when and how work is conducted. Many participants felt wireless networks, laptops, mobile phones, electronic calendars, and e-mail allow for flexibility that reduces time barriers and allows for greater control over their schedules. This was a particularly significant theme for Irish women since seven of the nine women in this analysis spoke about asynchronous flexibility and the benefits of communicating with coworkers while out of the office. For example, Cara values ubiquitous computing because it allows her to communicate with her office "from all over the world." Likewise, several women spoke about the benefits of communicating with friends and family while in the office. Karen, an Indian woman who lives in Boston, is able to overcome the time zone differences by using her mobile phone during what are work hours in the United States.

Another positive aspect of asynchronous communication in maintaining work–life balance is the role of telecommuting using ubiquitous computing, including home-to-office network connections, mobile phones, and conferencing capabilities. Ten women felt that telecommuting made it easier to balance their work and home lives, particularly for women in urban areas. Nancy, who lives in North Carolina, enjoys telecommuting from her home: "I get to make my own hours, I do not have a commute, and I do not have to dress up." Denise, who telecommuted to her previous job in Washington, DC, finds it "very good, for raising young children, supporting a husband, and having a family and home." Kimberly telecommuted to her consulting job in Boston during maternity leave and was one of the few women to be promoted to manager while on leave. For Rose, another Bostonian, it is all about control.

I wanted to stay home. I wanted to have more control over my own schedule. ... [And be] able to bring in some income, but at a schedule that was much more convenient to me, in terms of care for my daughter and the amount of time I was actually home.

Despite the positive aspects of asynchronous communication via ubiquitous computing in maintaining work–life balance, a number of negative aspects also emerged from the interviews. One such theme is the 24/7 (twenty-four hours a day; seven days a week) work schedule made possible by ubiquitous computing. Researchers have documented this shift with the expansion of the temporal range and amount of working hours (Perrons 2003). This theme was also supported in our analysis. Eight participants discussed how ubiquitous computing has led to a work environment where they are always accessible, something that negatively impacts work–life balance. While this theme was expressed by American and Irish women of all ages, it was most prevalent among women with children. Candace, an American mother, has experienced a growing expectation that employees work extra hours and be "constantly available by computer or phone." She feels this paradigm is incompatible with home life, and gave responsibility "to advances in technology making it possible for people to be continuously on call." Nuala, a project manager in Ireland, shared her dislike for working on weekends and feels a pressure to check her e-mail messages during time away from the office in order to please her managers.

4.2 Office Relationships and Productivity

The participants also explained the impact of ubiquitous computing on office relationships and work productivity. Six women, generally in their 30s, shared examples of how ubiquitous computing is used to build social networks and to interact with co-workers. For example, Alice uses ubiquitous computing to manage difficulties with co-workers that she does not feel comfortable handling in face-to-face situations. She explained that a student at her university created a website with sexual material which she found highly offensive. Alice used her e-mail and mobile phone to communicate with the student, his professor, and the Dean to resolve the issue without awkward face-to-face conflicts. Helen, a self-proclaimed introvert, does not have time to attend social

functions and feels uncomfortable in such environments. Thus, she uses e-mail to
network with others, without participating in after hour activities:

> *I think a lot of networking is required to further your career in IT, but I am*
> *terrible at it. I do not like to meet new people.* [Helen]

> *But you did mention different times [that you got jobs from networking]?*
> [Interviewer]

> *That was e-mail. It was not personal networking; it just never worked for me.*
> [Helen]

Five women in this study increased their work efficiency through the enhanced
information gathering, multitasking, coordination, and transition to new tasks enabled
by ubiquitous computing, such as wireless networks, laptops, mobile phones, video
conferencing, electronic calendars, and e-mail. Caitlin uses ubiquitous computing to
keep track of her work progress and tasks. Doing so allows her to more easily and
quickly transition projects to coworkers. Many women also spoke about the benefit of
ubiquitous computing to limit the amount of face-to-face communication they have with
coworkers. This reduced face-to-face communication makes it quicker and easier to find
the necessary information to complete work tasks. Faith uses ubiquitous computing to
work more efficiently during the day. In doing so, she remembers key points to discuss
at meetings and ensures that she gets credit for her work.

Five women in this study spoke about the negative influences of ubiquitous
computing on productivity. These influences center around the difficulties associated
with rapid technological innovations and the stress of continuously learning about new
technologies. Emily explained that she can see a difference in ubiquitous computing
adoption by novice and professional users of technology. In her opinion, novice users
are less likely than professional users to quickly learn about new technologies. Jane
feels that women who leave the IT workforce inadvertently "deskill" themselves and
may find difficulty returning to the IT industry with its pervasiveness of ubiquitous
technologies.

4.3 Personal Life Benefits

Six women, five of whom were from North Carolina, also spoke about the role of
ubiquitous computing in maintaining balance in their personal lives. In this sense,
ubiquitous computing is a mechanism for bonding with family and friends through
shared interests. Several women spoke about commonalities they found with their
children from ubiquitous computing. Their common interest was used as a tool to bond
and spend time with family members. June is involved with computers and video games
and uses these technologies to spend time with her children. Several women spoke
about the ways ubiquitous computing makes it easier to help with personal
responsibilities including homework and school projects. Claire uses ubiquitous
computing to mentor young girls in various youth societies to build interest in IT.

I want to encourage things that help girls...to be curious and want to know what is happening underneath [the technology]. What is inside a cell phone? It is really a radio which is why it does not work if there is no antenna within four miles. Knowing a little about the underneath and not [assuming] things are magic and just work.

5 DISCUSSION

We define ubiquitous computing as technologies that are effectively invisible, integrated, and available to individuals throughout their environment (Weiser 1995). However, the participants refer to ubiquitous computing as a tool to support their communication and temporal work arrangements. What was most important to these women was the ability to use technology *anytime* and *anywhere*. Although this definition is narrower in scope, we believe the findings represent wider aspects of ubiquitous computing. First, the women spoke about multiple technologies, not just a single form, thus reiterating a premise of ubiquitous computing as one person utilizing multiple technologies. Second, the women consider these technologies to be unobtrusive and available as they need them. Finally, the women spoke about the technologies as integrated into their environment and daily lives. Hence, the women demonstrate the premise of ubiquitous computing as embedded in the environment where they are able to move around and naturally interact with the technology while breaking away from a desktop paradigm.

We extend the individual difference theory by focusing on the ways that woman, with a range of work–life balance issues, use ubiquitous computing to address their needs. This theory focuses on the differences within rather than between the genders, and enables a deeper understanding of the range of work–life balance considerations for women and their influence on the use of ubiquitous computing. Thus, in answer to our research question, our data demonstrates that ubiquitous computing has a role in work–life balance with regard to asynchronous communication, office relationships, work productivity, and personal life benefits. A detailed explanation requires a nuanced understanding of the range of work–life balance issues and their influence on ubiquitous computing. With regard to asynchronous communication, women in urban areas were more likely to use and value telecommuting. Women who expressed stress from a 24/7 work style typically had children. With regard to office relationships and work productivity, women who were younger in age were more likely to use ubiquitous computing as a social networking tool. Women who were less experienced with technology found the fast-paced change of ubiquitous computing stressful.

The findings presented in this paper highlight several areas for future research. First, additional analysis is needed to identify the role of cultural perspective and societal expectations in the use of ubiquitous computing to balance work and life. The analysis of multiple cultural contexts in this paper suggests differences in societal messages and expectations of women, but very little variance with regard to the use of ubiquitous computing. Likewise, analyzing multiple dimensions will further refine the individual differences theory as it relates to ubiquitous computing use in maintaining work–life balance. Second, additional research is needed to examine how women in industries other than IT view and use ubiquitous computing in maintaining work–life balance. These findings would contribute knowledge to a wider understanding of how women in the IT industry compare to women employed in other areas. Finally, additional research is needed to examine how men inside and outside of the IT industry view and use ubiquitous computing to maintain work–life balance. These findings would contribute knowledge to a wider understanding of the role of ubiquitous computing in maintaining work–life balance.

6 CONCLUSION

The decrease in productivity levels and the increase in absenteeism and turnover resulting from work–life imbalance have serious consequences for the occupational attainment of workers as well as the financial stability of families (Glass and Estes 1997). Addressing work–life balance is essential for organizations as it has been found to impede work productivity and contribute to employee turnover (Duxbury and Higgins 2003). Thus, addressing work–life balance by making an explicit link between employees' needs and business goals can be a catalyst for changing work practices that benefit employees and employers (Bailyn et al. 1997; Honeycutt and Rosen 1997; Perry-Smith and Blum 2000). A crucial step in this process is to think expansively about changing particular work practices and/or the use of ubiquitous computing. The intent of this research is to use a rich data set about women in the IT workforce to identify how they use ubiquitous computing to maintain work–life balance. In doing so, we build on the individual differences theory to demonstrate differences within a gender in their use of ubiquitous computing in addressing a range of interpretations of work–life balance. Continued research is necessary to fully understand how ubiquitous technologies can continue to contribute to positively reshape the workplace and home life.

REFERENCES

Avital, M., and Germonprez, M. "Ubiquitous Computing: Surfing the Trend in Balance Act, " paper presented at the Workshop on Ubiquitous Computing Environment, Cleveland, Ohio, October 24-26, 2003.
Bailyn, L., Fletcher, J. K., and Kolb, D. "Unexpected Connections: Considering Employees' Personal Lives Can Revitalize Your Business," *Sloan Management Review* (38:4), 1997, pp. 11-19.
Beasley, R. E., Lomo-David, E., and Seubert, V. R. "Telework and Gender: Implications for the Management of Information Technology Professionals," *Industrial Management & Data Systems* (101:8/9), 2001, pp. 477-482.
Chae, B. "Ubiquitous Computing for Mundane Knowledge Management: Hopes, Challenges and Questions," paper presented at the Workshop on Ubiquitous Computing Environment, Cleveland Ohio, October 24-26, 2003.
Duxbury, L., and Higgins, C. "Work–life Conflict: Myths Versus Realities, " *FMI Journal* (14:3), 2003, pp. 16-20.
Duxbury, L. E., Higgins, C. A., and Mills, S. "After-Hours Telecommuting and Work-Family Conflict: A Comparative Analysis," *Information Systems Research* (3:2), 1992, pp. 173-190.

Frissen, V. A. J. "ICTs in the Rush Hour of Life," *The Information Society* (16), 2000, pp. 65-75.

Gallivan, M. "Examining Gender Differences in IT Professionals' Perceptions of Job Stress in Response to Technical Change," in *Proceedings of the 2003 ACM SIGMIS Conference on Personnel Research: Freedom in Philadelphia—Leveraging Differences and Diversity i the IT Workforce*, M. Mandviwalla and E. M. Trauth (Eds.), New York: ACM Press, 2003, pp. 10-23.

Glass, J. L., and Estes, S. B. "The Family Responsive Workplace," *Annual Review of Sociology* (23), 1997, pp. 289-333.

Googins, B. K. *Work/Family Conflicts: Private Lives—Public Responses,* New York: Auburn House, 1991.

Greenhaus, J. H., and Beutell, N. J. "Sources of Conflict between Work and Family Roles," *Academy of Management Journal* (10), 1985, pp. 76-88.

Greenhaus, J. H., Collins, K. M., and Shaw, J. D. "The Relation between Work-Family Balance and Quality of Life," *Journal of Vocational Behavior* (63), 2002, pp. 510-531.

Guelzow, M. G., Bird, G. W., and Koball, E. H. "An Exploratory Path Analysis of the Stress Process for Dual-Career Men and Women," *Journal of Marriage Family* (53), 1991, pp. 151-164.

Higgins, C., Duxbury, L., and Lee, C. "Impact of Life-Cycle Stage and Gender on the Ability to Balance Work and Family Responsibilities," *Family Relations* (43:2), 1994, pp. 144-150.

Hill, E. J., Ferris, M., and Martinson, V. "Does it Matter Where You Work? A Comparison of How Three Work Venues (Traditional Office, Virtual Office, and Home Office) Influence Aspects of Work and Personal/Family Life," *Journal of Vocational Behavior* (63), 2003, pp. 220-241.

Hochschild, A. R., and Machung, A. *The Second Shift*, New York: Penguin Books, 2003.

Honeycutt, T. L., and Rosen, B. "Family Friendly Human Resource Policies, Salary Levels, and Salient Identity as Predictors of Organizational Attraction," *Journal of Vocational Behavior* (50:2), 1997, pp. 271-290.

Igbaria, M., Parasuraman, S., and Badawy, M. K. "Work Experiences, Job Involvement, and Quality of Work Life among Information Systems Personnel, " *MIS Quarterly* (18:2), 1994, pp. 175-201.

Igbaria, M., Parasuraman, S., and Greenhaus, J. H. "Status Report on Women and Men in the IT Workplace," *Information Systems Management* (14:3), 1997, pp. 44-53.

Judge, T. A., Boudreau, J. W., and Bretz, R. D. "Job and Life Attitudes of Male Executives," *Journal of Applied Psychology* (79:5), 1994, pp. 767-782.

Lyytinen, K., and Yoo, Y. "Issues and Challenges in Ubiquitous Computing," *Communications of the ACM* (45:12), 2002, pp. 62-65.

McNaughton, A. M. *Family-Friendly Workplaces the Case for Supporting Work–life Balance*, The Calgary Children's Initiative, Calgary, Alberta, Canada, 2001 (available online at http://www.childrensinitiative.ca/media/FFWP.pdf).

Mennino, S. F., and Brayfield, A. "Job-Family Trade-Offs: The Multidimensional Effects of Gender," *Work and Occupations* (29:2), 2002, pp. 226-255.

Milkie, M. A., and Peltola, P. "Playing All the Roles: Gender and the Work-Family Balancing Act," *Journal of Marriage and the Family* (61), 1999, pp. 476-490.

Morgan, A. J., Quesenberry, J. L., and Trauth, E. M. "Exploring the Importance of Social Networks in the IT Workforce: Experiences with the 'Boy's Club,'" in *Proceedings of the 10th Americas Conference on Information Systems*, E. Stohr and C. Bullen (Eds.), New York, 2004, pp. 1313-1320.

Perlow, L. A. "Boundary Control: The Social Ordering of Work and Family Time in a High-Tech Corporation," *Administrative Science Quarterly* (43:2), 1998, pp. 328-357.

Perrons, D. "The New Economy and the Work–life Balance: Conceptual Explorations and a Case Study of New Media," *Gender Work and Organizations* (10:1), 2003, pp. 65-93.

Perry-Smith, J. E., and Blum, T. C. "Work-Family Human Resource Bundles and Perceived Organizational Performance," *Academy of Management Journal* (12), 2000, pp. 1107-1117.

Quesenberry, J. L., Morgan, A. J., and Trauth, E. M. "Understanding the 'Mommy Tracks': A Framework for Analyzing Work-Family Issues in the IT Workforce," in *Proceedings of the Information Resources Management Association Conference*, Hershey PA: Idea Group Publishing, 2004, pp. 135-138.

Reeves, R. *Happy Mondays: Putting the Pleasure Back into Work*, London: Momentum, 2001.

Riley, F., and McCloskey, D. W. "GTE's Experience with Telecommuting: Helping People Balance Work and Family," in *Proceedings of the 1996 ACM SIGMIS Conference on Personnel Research*, New York: ACM Press, 1996, pp. 85-93.

Sullivan, C., and Lewis, S. "Home-Based Telework, Gender and the Synchronization of Work and Family: Perspectives of Teleworkers and Their Co-Residents," *Gender, Work and Organizations* (8:2), 2001, pp. 123-145.

Thomas, L. T., and Ganster, D. C. "Impact of Family Supportive Work Variables on Work-Family Conflict and Strain: A Control Perspective," *Journal of Applied Psychology* (80:1), 1995, pp. 6-15.

Trauth, E. M. "Odd Girl Out: An Individual Differences Perspective on Women in the IT Profession," *Information Technology and People* (15:2), 2002, pp. 98-118.

Trauth, E. M. "Women in Ireland's Information Industry: Voices from Inside," *Eire-Ireland* (30:3), 1995, pp. 133-150.

Trauth, E. M., Quesenberry, J. L., and Morgan, A. J. "Understanding the Under Representation of Women in IT: Toward a Theory of Individual Differences," in *Proceedings of the 2004 ACM SIGMIS Conference on Computer Personnel Research*, M. Tanniru and S. Weisband (Eds.), New York: ACM Press, 2004, pp. 114-119.

Trauth, E. M., Quesenberry, J. L., and Yeo, B. "The Influence of Environmental Context on Women in the IT Workforce," in *Proceedings of the 2005 ACM SIGMIS Conference on Computer Personnel Research*, M. Gallivan, J. E. Moore, and S. Yager (Eds)., New York: ACM Press, 2005, pp. 24-31.

Useem, J. "Welcome to the New Company Town," *Fortune* (8:25), 2000, pp. 62-70.

Weiser, M. "The Computer for the Twenty-First Century," in *Human Computer Interaction: Toward the Year 2000*, R. M. Baecker, J. Grudin, W. A. S. Buxton, and S. Greenberg (Eds.), San Francisco: Morgan Kaufmann Publishers Inc., 1995, pp. 933-940.

Weiser, M. "Hot Topics: Ubiquitous Computing," *IEEE Computer* (26:20), October 1993, pp. 71-72.

Zimmerman, E. "Parent-to-Parent: Using Technology to Stay Connected," *Sales and Marketing Management* (155:7), 2003, p. 58.

ABOUT THE AUTHORS

Jeria L. Quesenberry is currently a doctoral candidate and research assistant at the School of Information Sciences and Technology in the Center for the Information Society at the Pennsylvania State University. Her research interests include the study of social and organizational aspects of information technology, with particular focus on the role of gender and under-represented groups in the IT workforce. From 1999 to 2002, she served as a consultant at Accenture, specializing in the implementation of enterprise resource planning (ERP) packages for human resource and payroll management systems. In 1999, she earned a B.S. in Decision Sciences and Management Information Systems from George Mason University. Jeria can be reached at jquesenberry@ist.psu.edu.

Eileen M. Trauth is a professor of Information Sciences and Technology and Director of the Center for the Information Society at the Pennsylvania State University. Her research is concerned with societal, cultural, and organizational influences on information technology and the information technology professions. Eileen's investigation of socio-cultural influences on the emergence of Ireland's information economy is published in her book, *The Culture of an Information Economy: Influences and Impacts in the Republic of Ireland.* She is currently engaged in a multi-country study of women in the information technology professions in Australia, New Zealand, Ireland, England, and the United States. Eileen has published 8 books and over 100 research papers on her research. She is an associate editor of *Information and Organization* and serves on the editorial boards of several international journals. Eileen received her Ph.D. and Master's degrees in information science from the University of Pittsburgh and her Bachelor's degree in education from the University of Dayton. Eileen can be reached at etrauth@ist.psu.edu.

7 REFLEXIVITY, THE SOCIAL ACTOR, AND M-SERVICE DOMESTICATION: Linking the Human, Technological, and Contextual

Jennifer Blechar
University of Oslo
Oslo, Norway

Lars Knutsen
Jan Damsgaard
Copenhagen Business School
Copenhagen, Denmark

Abstract   *The importance of understanding the factors impacting technology acceptance is well emphasized. However, technology acceptance research is primarily oriented to the individual level in which users or consumers are treated as actors typically making one-way adoption or rejection decisions related to the acceptance of new technology. In this article, we argue that such research stops short of acknowledging the influence of agents' social monitoring of own and other's behavior. By leaning on the process of stratification and the construct of reflexivity, as applied by Giddens (1984), and coupling this with the view that humans are social actors reflexively engaged in the domestication of new technologies, we present the initial progress toward a process model that may guide our understanding of how potential and existing users of new mobile data services learn, draw upon previous and emerging experiences, and thereby bring, or do not bring, new m-services into the performance of everyday practices. Based on the results from our field study, this paper suggests that re-projecting previous experience and reflexivity considerably influences cognition and action in the duration of m-service domestication, thereby bringing complementary understanding to current technology acceptance research.*

Keywords   Domestication, reflexivity, acceptance, adoption, mobile services

1   INTRODUCTION

Adoption and diffusion of innovations theories have for more than half a century been the principal anchors in providing guidance and comprehension of how innovations are generated and evolve as well as how they diffuse and become adopted in populations (Gopalakrishnan and Damanpour 1997; Rogers 2003). Moreover, variance-oriented technology acceptance research has emerged from cognitive-oriented marketing research into technology studies, both in mandatory and voluntaristic technology use domains, to explain and predict attitudes, intention to use, and eventual use of new technologies (Foxall et al. 1998; Venkatesh et al. 2003). Both genres of research have provided a significant and fundamental level of understanding of technology acceptance and use.

However, the compound nature of wireless services (Knutsen and Overby 2004) as well as their multifaceted characteristics, challenge the ability to define specific items or variables related to the particular material or virtual artifact in question. Thus, while technology acceptance research has focused on identifying and determining general impacts of categorical variables (such as ease of use, usefulness, etc.) on technology acceptance and use, the very general nature of these characteristics may render them inappropriate or even work as blinders for exploring the specifics of the artifact and the potentially important alterations emerging during the process of technology acceptance.

Acceptance and use of wireless services can be far messier, more complex, and more ambiguous than nomothetic perspectives of technology acceptance generally convey. Just as scholars of the Austrian School of Economics contend that pure profit opportunities "can not be object to systematic search" because they are unknown until discovered (Kirzner 1997, p. 71), intentions, expectations, and eventual use of wireless services can prove impossible to comprehend and predict until developed, experienced, interpreted, and somewhat incorporated into the everyday lives of users. Thus, before user engagement in the domestication[1] process—the process of adopting and imbedding a product or service into everyday life (Lehtonen 2003; Lie and Sørensen 1996; Ling 2004; Ling and Haddon 2001; Silverstone and Haddon 1996)—the possibilities of understanding potential user cognizance and behavior related to technology acceptance is likely to be nebulous, porous, and amorphous.

Understanding consumer practices related to the acceptance and adoption of new products and services, therefore, needs to be derived in relation to the potential reciprocal impact *integration* with life practices, as well as the emergence of new practices, might have on acceptance, adoption, and diffusion. This is particularly significant for wireless services as the domestication of a distinct artifact in question may depend upon the consumption of *other* material and virtual artifacts and their associated properties. For instance, whereas mobile phones have diffused with unprecedented pace and become the most omnipresent and widely deployed communications

---

[1]Despite etymological connotation to the home sphere and the taming and modification of the wild to domestically fit human needs, domestication has entered technology studies to signify how new technologies enter spheres of everyday social life—in and outside the home—and how meaning is constructed and reconstructed during careers (Haddon 2001, 2004; Lie and Sørensen 1996).

technology in the world (Nokia 2003) and the adoption of voice and text[2] services have unfolded as social epidemics, we see that acceptance and adoption of gateway and mobile Internet services have not reached such tipping points in most of the Western world.

The goal of this article is to outline a framework that can enable enhanced first-(subjective) and second-level (interpretive) understanding (see Lee 1991) of wireless service domestication. We start by reviewing existing acceptance and adoption research. Finding limitations in capturing and explaining changes caused by reflexivity over own and others mobile service actions in the unfolding of domestication, we develop a framework to guide the discussion of our subsequent interpretive inquiry by merging two streams of hitherto disconnected theories: the stratification framework of Giddens (1984) and the domestication approach advocated by Silverstone and Haddon (1996), including recent extensions to this approach (Ling 2004; Ling and Haddon 2001). The results of our research suggest that an analysis of actors' reflexive monitoring of m-service actions can complement technology acceptance research by revealing idiographic accounts of centrally influencing reference technologies impacting the progression of the wireless service domestication process.

2   TECHNOLOGY ACCEPTANCE AND ADOPTION

A large variety of theories and models have been developed, conceptualized, operationalized, and empirically supported with the aim of contingently determining and predicting user actions related to decisions to accept and adopt new technology. Among the most influential are those with roots in the theory of reasoned action (TRA) (Ajzen and Fishbein 1980) such as the theory of planned behavior (TPB) (Ajzen 1985 1991), the technology acceptance model (TAM) (Davis 1989), and the decomposed theory of planned behavior (Taylor and Todd 1995). Resulting from the variety of different constructs proposed, Venkatesh and colleagues (2003) more recently joined root constructs discussed in previous research into the four main latent variables of *performance expectancy, effort expectancy, social influence,* and *facilitating conditions.*

In the mobile arena, several of the constructs and relations found in technology acceptance models have been adopted, adapted, and used to predict user behavior and investigate acceptance (see Khalifa and Cheng 2002; Lu et al. 2003; Pedersen and Ling 2003). However, as has been illustrated by Knutsen (2005), the inflexible nature of such models make them, which is also outside their scope, inapplicable for the purposes of obtaining a deeper understanding of the often multifaceted set of emerging idiosyncrasies transpiring and becoming formed as novel artifacts, or sets of artifacts, permeate the life-worlds of users. Thus, while existing research has been attentive to elements such as current and past experience (i.e., Hubona and Burton-Jones 2003), this work has not explored the evolution of artifacts prior and subsequent to the absolute points of acceptance and adoption; the further socio-technical molding of the artifact.

---

[2]This includes SMS (primarily in GSM areas) as well as mobile e-mail (primarily in Japan and the United States).

Moreover, as these models are directed at the individual level, items such as social influence are treated strictly from the relative social "pressure" the potential accepter may perceive (i.e., Venkatesh et al. 2003). Thus, although technology acceptance scholars acknowledge that human actors exist and act within, often particularly clearly defined, social contexts (usually organizational contexts), less attention seems directed toward the influence that previous as well as emerging experiences with technologies might have on existing knowledge and, thus, users' interpretations and the social aspects therein. In fact, the orientation toward prediction in technology acceptance research *discards* dynamism and thus dialectical changes in (potential) users' knowledgeability concerning technology.

Limitations to diffusion of innovations theory and technology acceptance research have been pointed out (Lyytinen and Damsgaard 2001; Rogers 1995; Van de Ven and Rogers 1988; Wolfe 1994). Interestingly, Venkatesh et al. (p. 470), although maintaining a stringent positivist orientation, encourage researchers to undertake efforts to reach a "richer understanding of technology adoption," which can offer improved guidance to designers of technology. However, this presupposes a technological clarity at the user side that may not exist, or exist only illusorily or nebulously. As Miller (1987, p. 103) contends, "whereas the artefact appears to offer the clarity of realism… which is quite illusory…the object is as likely as the word to evoke variable responses and invite variety of interpretations." Therefore, in order to offer guidance to designers, it is a prerequisite that users have an idea of the designers' technology spirit (DeSanctis and Poole 1994) and the intentions underlying the design of the technology, so that this can be explicated beyond imaginary use and involve more than just an excavated trench of more or less connected juxtapositions. For this, specificity of the properties of the artifact, the product, or the service, beyond general expectations of relative advantage, ease of use, performance expectancies, etc., is needed; specificity is only obtainable as the artifact establishes its meaning through use (Rohracher 2003).

In exploratory technology settings, as for m-services, it may be advantageous to observe Rogers' (1995) encouragement to move research frontiers toward behavioral and social learning aspects of innovation and, more specifically, pay tribute to how overt behavioral changes unfold over time. Although several suggestions have partly accommodated this, for example by calling for closer integration between diffusion of innovations theory, technology acceptance, and domestication (Pedersen and Ling 2003; Pedersen et al. 2002), most research is still at a conceptual rather than empirical level. Despite gains toward more interactive process views, consideration of the malleability caused by actors' cognitive reflection over engagement with m-services or social cues reflecting m-services during the domestication process have, to our awareness, not been under scrutiny. We argue that an alternative approach, which we now turn to present, can bring about such understanding and thereby complement technology acceptance research.

3   REFLEXIVITY AND THE SOCIAL ACTOR: A PROCESS MODEL

Social constructivist approaches have strongly aided in overcoming technological determinism, the idea that technology unidirectionally shapes society, by highlighting social aspects of technology creation, use, and the double hermeneutics of socio-technical impacts. This has occurred from the perspective of influences of user interpretations on the evolution of technology (Pinch and Bijker 1987), and from the constantly fluctuating influence of actors, including living agents and nonorganic objects, within a system (Hughes 1987). In these approaches, users are viewed as constantly negotiating and renegotiating their respective meaning of artifacts, hereunder products and services, shaping and being shaped by them in various ways until *closure* or *stabilization* is considered to finally be reached (Pinch and Bijker 1987: 44). Although the relative structuring capabilities of nonorganic agents and the notion of closure are contestable (is closure ever reached?), the acknowledgement of degrees of circularity and reciprocity between technology and social actors is important because it recognizes that technology has a life beyond the state of acceptance and adoption, and that *as* technology molds interpretations, current interpretive schemes will also mold the interpretation of technology, thus pointing to the social manifestation of emerging technologies.

The above perspective enables the consideration of users as social actors (Lamb and Kling 2003). Despite their focus on actors in organizations, whereas we focus on m-service use in voluntaristic contexts, we concur with Lamb and Kling that in order to understand information systems use beyond laboratory and context insensitive settings, the thin user concept in information systems research needs to embrace a conceptualization of users as social actors. This includes acknowledging that users have social affiliations and can represent larger social-entities through their actions, can influence and be influenced by their environments, engage in interactions that can exert as well as take on influence from and by the social as well as technological, and that identities are expressed as well as shaped through the interactions with technology and other social actors (Lamb and Kling 2003).

If accepting that technology (i.e., m-services) is both a mediator of as well as mediated by practice, emphasis needs to be placed on current socio-technical practices and those emerging in relation to new technology, the contexts in which they occur, and what they socially symbolize. Since practices are enabled and constrained by the actors'[3] knowledgeability—knowledge of actors and their ability to act upon tacit and discursively available knowledge (Giddens 1984)—it is also necessary to understand how knowledgeability of new technology develops. Because knowledgeability is likely to develop with a basis in, and sometimes even challenge, the foundation of what is currently known and instantiated in practice (i.e., current practices with technologies and previous experiences), it seems promising to focus on what Giddens expresses as stratification of action.

In the stratification model, Giddens emphasizes that humans are not only constantly *monitoring their own action*, but also the *actions of others* in the "monitored character of the ongoing flow of social life" (p. 3). In this way, stratification of action involves the embedded processes of *reflexive* monitoring of action occurring within interpretable contexts and human rationalization as well as motivation of action. Thus, the reflexive monitoring of daily life is considered the foundation of the recursive ordering of social

---

[3]Giddens uses the term *agent* rather than *actor*. To avoid terminological confusion, the term actor is used in this paper. Interested readers are directed to Giddens (1984, pp. 20-30).

practices across time and space in which routines preserve the current, while deviation from routines, in the form of unanticipated consequences of action, can cause emergence of new practices. In the presence of *unintended consequences* of own and others' actions, therefore, it is likely that social cues of the action can be picked up and be fed into the reflexive monitoring and thus impact future action decisions. According to Giddens, there is a cyclical relationship from peoples' actions to unintended consequences to *unacknowledged conditions* of these actions, all of which, if recurring over time and space, can reconstruct or promote and inaugurate new social structures which, through actors' reflexive monitoring, can influence future actions.

Interestingly, we have identified that the reflexive nature of human beings and our relations with technology are also central in the work on domestication of technology (Haddon 2001; Lehtonen 2003; Lie and Sørensen 1996; Ling 2004; Ling and Haddon 2001; Silverstone and Haddon 1996). For instance Aune (1996:91-92), sees domestication figuratively as "to handle something alien in such a way that it is adapted to your everyday life, and your everyday life is adapted to this new and hitherto alien artifact" and that this is a "two-way process in which both technology and humans are affected, and in which both technical and social features are changed." Silverstone and Haddon (1996), Aune (1996), and Ling (2004) all illustrate the domestication process to evolve through four or five interrelated phases or steps.[4] These encompass, as illustrated in Figure 1, *imagination, appropriation, objectification, incorporation,* and *conversion.*

Succinctly put, imagination involves the removal of ignorance and/or the awakening of awareness and imagery concerning a new innovation such as a new mobile service or other technology. It is anticipated to develop from an arousal of previously unacknowledged socio-technical opportunities that trigger intuitive and interpretive processes. Although rejection and halt to the progression can occur at any time, imagination can lead to appropriation, the development of knowledge of the innovation to the state where procurement is a substantial possibility or actually occurs. It also symbolizes the step in which an innovation leaves the commercial sphere and enters our sphere of objects (Ling 2004).

Following (ideally) appropriation, objectification denotes the cognizance of how an innovation will fit into our world of objects; essentially, depictions and crystallizations of what identity cues we signal through our consumption and use of the technology (Ling 2004; Silverstone and Haddon 1996). Incorporation can follow, encompassing the process in which the technology (i.e., an m-service) is incorporated with and becomes part of our routines of everyday life. Finally, conversion describes the subprocess in the cycle where instantiations of technology represented through our socio-technical practices "become elements in others' estimation of us" (Ling 2004, p. 30) in various social groups. All of these phases involve the users or consumers making situated and reflexive actions or decisions regarding the new technology in their everyday lives.

By combining the above with the work of Giddens and adapting this to the realm of technology, we construct a process model to illustrate the reflexive nature of how

---

[4]The word *steps* is used illustratively to signify that there ideally, if admitting to a little pro-innovation bias, is a degree of linear progression in the characteristic stages. This progression, however, may not always be as linear as portrayed. Rather it may be messy with several feedback loops and feedback as well as feed-forward step skipping.

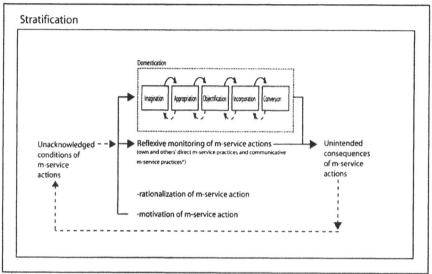

Figure 1. Stratification in the Process of M-Service Domestication.
Adapted and from Giddens (1984) and Silverstone and Haddon (1996)

actors actively engage in acceptance and adoption of new technology *over time* (see Figure 1). In the figure, the stratification process of Giddens is considered to produce as well as take on directions from the domestication process and its progression; stratification is linked reciprocally to the steps in the domestication process.

The process model illustrates how user actions, as instantiations of their interpretations related to the acceptance of new technology, are conceived to evolve and are influenced by previous actions and their possible unintended consequences and unacknowledged conditions. This process model highlights the importance of the reflexivity of peoples' actions and the manner in which users are continuously monitoring both their own and others' practices concerning m-services. While existing theories and models of technology acceptance view users as making primarily one-way action decisions influenced by various constructs, the proposed process model instead illustrates the potential evolving considerations users can place on previous actions and on current routines and their outcomes in their constant renegotiation of the technology within the overall evolving technology domestication process.

This model also emphasizes that the reflexive monitoring of own and others' actions in relation to a technology can both conform with as well as deviate from what is anticipated. Such deviations can lead to *unfaithful appropriations* (DeSanctis and Poole 1994) and, as originally proposed by Fichman and Kemerer (1997, 1999), yield macro-level *assimilation gaps*: differences between cumulative patterns of technology acquisitions versus patterns of deployment. However, rather than focusing on cumulative patterns, the process model attends to the micro and mezzo level negotiations and renegotiations arising (relative to the degree of unfamiliarity) from users reflexive monitoring during the acquaintance with new m-services. Thus, with reflexivity underlying the domestication process, it opens for understanding how cognizance and practice development with respect to m-services (or other technologies) can alter during any typical stage, affecting the progression and directionality of the process, or even bringing the domestication and thus the technology acceptance process to a halt.

4   A FIELD STUDY OF M-SERVICE DOMESTICATION

The study reported in this paper was conducted in Denmark in the spring of 2004 and was undertaken in close collaboration with a mobile operator, device manufacturer, and several content providers. State of the art mobile phones with prepaid SIM cards[5] were distributed to 38 users, providing access to a variety of gateway based m-services (e.g., news, entertainment, e-mail, downloading multimedia content, chat, dating, location-based services, information on contemporary events, etc.). Participants were selected based upon three criteria: (1) they belonged to socio-demographic groups suggested to be among the early adopters of new m-services—students and young professionals (Constantiou et al. 2004), (2) they were members of social or work groups in which social interaction was frequent and monitoring of m-service practices was possible both in the form of physical and virtual co-presence; and (3) they had interest in, but marginal to no mobile data service experience prior to joining the project. The average age of participants was 29 and 43 percent were females.

Data was collected from participants through a variety of qualitative and quantitative methods including surveys, interviews and group interviews. Surveys consisted of both open-ended and fixed response questions and were distributed to participants before, during and after the project period. Open-ended questions in the surveys were based on typical categories previously identified in the technology acceptance literature such as performance expectancy (*In what ways can new mobile data services contribute and be useful in your everyday life?*) and effort expectancy (*How would you describe the efforts you need to make in order to use new mobile data services?*). At the end of the project the participants were asked to describe functions and services that best supported their everyday practices, as well as the most important criteria mobile services should meet to provide value in their everyday life. Importantly, questions were not, at any time, framed in a way so that related technologies were mentioned, and *not* in a way asking the participants to actively report on how they contemplated about past and emerging experience with new m-services. Rather, we targeted our inquiry toward issues concerning performance, efforts, social influence, attitudes, etc. As such, a body of textual data subject for interpretation was gained.

Data analysis for the qualitative data followed Miles and Huberman's (1994) coding procedures. First the respondents' answers to the questions were partitioned based on

---

[5]The prepaid SIM cards provided a budget constraint of 250 DKK per month per user during the project.

descriptive codes guided by a start-list derived from the theoretical model previously presented. Second, to explore patterns, we supplied pattern codes and placed the data into a clustered summary table. Following the clustering, the key findings were extracted and illustrative examples were chosen.

4.1 Results and Discussion

From our analysis we choose to focus on two issues relevant for the theoretical discussion of this paper. This includes what we have registered as a re-projecting of the participants' Internet experience and reflexive monitoring of m-service practices.

4.1.1 Re-projecting Internet Experience

During the study, participants appear to have reflexively drawn upon their experience with the Internet when constructing their expectancies, both related to performance and effort, of new mobile services *as* m-service experience accrued. Although this should not be surprising, it is important with respect to complementing acceptance models as these cannot be utilized for understanding how expectancies are formed when artifacts are introduced. We registered that imagery of m-services before trial rotated around services already available on the regular Internet.

> Many of the services I can envision use of on the mobile are already similar to those I use on the net: e-mail, news, yellow pages, directions, maps, route information and transport information. (Male, 22, before trial)

However, once participants learned the specific efforts and performances of the m-services, this created an assimilation gap as experience emerged which, to a large degree, lead users to become former users or dropouts. Whereas performance and ease were taken for granted before the m-service trial, unexpected or unintended consequences triggered reflexivity over their own and others' experiences and made participants ultimately alter their rationale for engaging in further domestication behavior.

> I thought I would need and use similar services that I use on the net, but I now see that mobile services need to be developed so they serve a mobile setting and take the limitations of mobile phones into account. Annoyed that it still works like a modem on the computer, I turn to the net instead. (Male, 22, after trial)

It is not only when evaluating the usefulness or potential benefits that we see such re-projecting of Internet experience occurs. Through our analysis, we witnessed that participants experience from using the Internet moderated expectancies not only prior to trial but at process stages such as imagination, objectification, and incorporation, and that this re-projecting together with experience gained with new mobile data services fostered correspondence as well as digression from the idealized domestication process. The following quote illustrates not only how expectations changed, but also provide indications that expectancies and motivations were moderated through rationalization over m-service actions:

> Internet was impressing as you did not have any other possibilities. But the mobile is inferior and as an experiential reference it sets the threshold for what to expect. (Male, 21, during trial)

While this statement indicates retrospective reflexivity integrated with the emerging experience, the following illustrates post trial changes in expectancies of new m-service incorporation:

> Using the Internet a few years ago was a hassle too. Nowadays you take it for granted and just use it easy and as part of your everyday. I think much of that goes for the mobile. You really need to get your mind around it in order to get into using it. It takes a while. So, I have more realistic expectations and intentions now after the project. (Female 26, after trial)

4.1.2   Reflexive Monitoring of M-Service Practices

Participants in the field study also exhibited awareness and monitoring of both direct m-service practices, practices in which operation of m-services either have direct or mediating visibility toward others, as well as communicative m-service practices, expressions in which messages contain cues of m-services or use. In accordance with Giddens' (1984) argument that most of our daily behaviors are routine and, therefore, occur almost unconsciously unless something in the daily flow of activities is experienced to bring unanticipated consequences, we see that most comments relating to the domestication of new m-services stem from occurrences that are not in correspondence with previous routines.

> I really had a hard time trying to send an MMS message. And I think I took quite some effort trying to find out about it. However, it was mentioned nowhere that I had to visit a web-page to get registered and obtain the configuration settings. That I found out about after having talked to my colleagues. (Male, 25, during trial)

Thus, although routines are most powerful as they reflect the practices that recur the most and thereby contribute most to the recursive ordering of m-service practices across time and space, it is the little upheavals, such as the one described above, which seem to bring about unanticipated consequences and trigger acknowledgment of newness.

During the project, we also observed several participants belonging to the same cohort starting to use Bluetooth to transmit text and multimedia messages because they experienced that others had started doing so. The typical explanation was, "I started using Bluetooth because some of the others' started." Direct observation of others behavior thus seemed to provide cues into objectifying m-services for the observer.

I admit that the time that I have spent on playing with the "toy" in order to discover the hidden secrets is limited. What I have done is that I have looked over the shoulders of my mates when they have been playing and then tried to see how those services could be useful to me. However, the [name of portal] services are very slow—I have access to the internet everyday at work and if I need information that is where I would find it. (Female, 32, after trial)

Furthermore, reflexivity over influences of others' communicative actions, not only participants, but signals of m-services in the surroundings offered stimuli for engaging in the assessment of motivations and rationalizations of the participant's own m-service agency.

Watching a commercial at the movie theater, I thought the services displayed seemed really smart. But then I started to think: Hey, wait a minute! That's what I have. That's what I don't use. It is mainly because it is too slow and too cumbersome. However, there are some services which can have value, but the value is too small compared to the efforts one must put into utilizing them. (Male, 27, during trial)

5 CONCLUSION AND NEXT STEPS

Through an expanded, integrated framework of domestication and stratification, this paper has presented progress toward a process model introducing user reflexivity in the ongoing evolution of technology consumption. The rationale and theorizing underlying the process model has been illustrated through the results of a field study of new mobile service use. These results suggest that participants actively reflect on previous as well as emerging experiences and observations with related technologies, cues in social surroundings and m-service actions, and that motivations as well as rationalizations indeed occur in a duration, a flow, influencing and revealing the degree of faithful, lasting, and extended appropriation. Hence, initial support has been provided that the monitoring of own and others' actions pertaining to m-services and related technologies, especially the Internet, unfold considerably after access to a technology has been gained. These observations are significant with respect to understanding *dimensions of use* beyond absolute points of acceptance and adoption; dimensions outside the reach of current technology acceptance research.

This paper has also illustrated that imaginative expectancies prior to trial, acceptance, and adoption can be intensely reconstructed, even deconstructed, during post trial, acceptance, or adoption periods. While existing research primarily views acceptance and adoption as absolute outcomes, this paper suggests that there is an array of potentially multifaceted outcomes which can determine not only the relative impact of a certain service or technology in everyday life, but also the relative impact of such outcomes on own and others' further m-service consumption. With the interdependent, varied, and compound smorgasbord of services offered, we contend that reflexivity during the domestication processes can yield unintended and unacknowledged conditions in user cognizance which can later become reflected in different degrees of patronizing m-service actions.

Further research in this area could expand the exploration of the underlying characteristics of the reflexivity at different stages in the domestication process. This can provide insight into what specific properties, attributes, and practices appear to cause progression, digression, or seizure to the process as well as how different properties of m-services may become enacted in physical and virtual co-presence. If carefully attended to, this could reveal narratives and interactions pertaining to m-service properties and their career over time and the meaning and impacts these properties may have in everyday life and in the continuing construction of meaning and practices during the unfolding of domestication. As such, we may avoid equating acceptance and adoption with continued everyday life use.

ACKNOWLEDGMENTS

This research was carried out in the realm of the Mobiconomy project at Copenhagen Business School. The research was in part supported by the Danish Research Agency, grant number #2054-03-0004. The authors made equal contributions to the paper.

REFERENCES

Ajzen, I. "From Intentions to Actions: A Theory of Planned Behavior," in *Action Control: From Cognition to Behavior*, J. Kuhl, and J. Beckman (Eds.), New York: Springer, 1985.

Ajzen, I. "The Theory of Planned Behavior," *Organizational Behavior and Human Decision Processes* (50), 1991, pp. 179-211.

Ajzen, I., and Fishbein, M. *Understanding Attitudes and Predicting Social Behavior*, Englewood Cliffs, NJ: Prentice Hall, 1980.

Aune, M. "The Computer in Everyday Life: Patterns of Domestication of a New Technology," in *Making Technology Our Own. Domesticating Technology into Everyday Life*, M. Lie, and K. H. Sørensen (Eds.), Oslo: Scandinavian University Press, 1996, pp. 91-120.

Constantiou, I. D., Damsgaard, J., and Knutsen, L. A. "Strategic Planning for Mobile Services Adoption and Diffusion: Empirical Evidence from the Danish Market," paper presented at the IFIP TC8 Working Conference on Mobile Information Systems (MOBIS), Oslo, Norway, September 15-17, 2004.

Davis, F. D. "Perceived Usefulness, Perceived Ease of Use, and User Acceptance of Information Technology," *MIS Quarterly* (13:3), 1989, pp. 319-339.

DeSanctis, G., and Poole, M. S. "Capturing the Complexity in Advanced Technology Use: Adaptive Structuration Theory," *Organization Science* (5:2), 1994, pp. 121-147.

Fichman, R. G., and Kemerer, C. F. "The Assimilation of Software Process Innovations: An Organizational Learning Perspective," *Management Science* (43:10), 1997, pp. 1345-1363.

Fichman, R. G., and Kemerer, C. F. "The Illusory Diffusion of Innovation: An Examination of Assimilation Gaps," *Information Systems Research* (10), 1999.

Foxall, G. R., Goldsmith, R. E., and Brown, S. *Consumer Psychology for Marketing* (2nd ed.), Oxford, UK: International Thomson Business Press, 1998.

Giddens, A. *The Constitution of Society*, Cambridge, UK: Polity Press, 1984.

Gopalakrishnan, S., and Damanpour, F. "A Review of Innovation Research in Economics, Sociology and Technology Management," *Omega* (25:1), 1997, pp. 15-28.

Haddon, L. "Domestication and Mobile Telephony," paper presented at the "Machines that Become Us" Conference, Rutgers University, New Brunswick, NJ, April 18-19, 2001.

Haddon, L. *Information and Communication Technologies in Everyday Life*, Oxford, UK: Berg, 2004.

Hubona, G., and Burton-Jones, A. "Modeling the User Acceptance of E-Mail," paper presented at the 36th Hawaii International Conference on Systems Science, Big Island, Hawaii, January 6-9, 2003.

Hughes, T. P. "The Evolution of Large Technological Systems," in *The Social Construction of Technological Systems*, W. E. Bijker, T. P. Hughes, and T. J. Pinch (Eds.), Cambridge, MA: MIT Press, 1987, pp. 51-82.

Khalifa, M., and Cheng, S. K. N. "Adoption of Mobile Commerce: Role of Exposure," paper presented at the 35th Hawaii International Conference on System Sciences, Big Island, Hawaii, January 5-8, 2002.

Kirzner, I. M. "Entrepreneurial Discovery and the Compeititve Market Process: An Austrian Approach," *Journal of Economic Literature* (35:1), 1997, pp. 60-85.

Knutsen, L. A. "M-Services Expectancies and Attitudes: Linkages and Effects of First Impressions," paper presented at the 38th Hawaii International Conference on Systems Science, Big Island, Hawaii, January 3-6, 2005.

Knutsen, L. A., and Overby, M. L. "Strategic Postures and Compound Product-Service Offerings: Supply and Demand-side Implications," paper presented at the International Conference on Mobile Business, New York, July 12-13, 2004.

Lamb, R., and Kling, R. "Reconceptualizing Users as Social Actors in Information Systems Research," *MIS Quarterly* (27:2), 2003, pp. 197-235.

Lee, A. S. "Integrating Positivist and Interpretive Approaches to Organizational Research," *Organization Science* (2:4), 1991, pp. 342-365.

Lehtonen, T. K. "The Domestication of New Technologies as a Set of Trials," *Journal of Consumer Culture* (3:3), 2003, pp. 363-385.

Lie, M., and Sørensen, K. H. *Making Technology Our Own? Domesticating Technology into Everyday Life*, Oslo: Scandinavian University Press, 1996.

Ling, R. *The Mobile Connection: The Cell Phone's Impact on Society* (3rd ed.), San Francisco: Morgan Kaufmann Publishers, 2004.

Ling, R., and Haddon, L. "Mobile Telephony, Mobility and the Coordination of Everyday Life," paper presented at the "Machines that Become Us," Rutgers University, Camden, NJ, 2001.

Lu, J., Lie, C., Yu, C.-S., and Yao, J. "Exploring Factors Associated with Wireless Internet via Mobile Technology Acceptance in Mainland China," *Communications of the International Information Management Association* (3:1), 2003, pp. 101-120.

Lyytinen, K., and Damsgaard, J. "What's Wrong with the Diffusion of Innovation Theory? The Case of a Complex and Networked Technology," paper presented at the IFIP WG 8.6 Working Conference on Diffusing Software Product and Process Innovations, Banff, Canada, April 7-10, 2001.

Miles, M. B., and Huberman, A. M. *Qualitative Data Analysis*, Thousand Oaks, CA: Sage Publications Inc., 1994.

Miller, D. *Material Culture and Mass Consumption*, Oxford, UK: Blackwell, 1987.

Nokia Networks. "A History of Third Generation Mobile," White Paper, July 6, 2003 (available online at http://www.3gnewsroom.com/html/whitepapers/year_2003.shtml).

Pedersen, P. E., and Ling, R. "Modifying Adoption Research for Mobile Internet Service Adoption: Cross-Disciplinary Interactions," paper presented at the 36th Hawaii International Conference on Systems Science, Big Island, Hawaii, January 6-9, 2003.

Pedersen, P. E., Methlie, L. B., and Thorbjørnsen, H. "Understanding Mobile Commerce End-User Adoption: A Triangulation Perspective and Suggestions for an Exploratory Service Evaluation Framework," paper presented at the 35th Annual Hawaii International Conference on System Sciences, Big Island, Hawaii, 2002.

Pinch, T. J., and Bijker, W. E. "The Social Construction of Facts and Artifacts: Or How the Sociology of Science and the Sociology of Technology Might Benefit Each Other," in W

The Social Construction of Technological Systems, E. Bijker, T. P. Hughes, and T. J. Pinch (Eds.), Cambridge, MA: MIT Press, 1987, pp. 17-50.

Rogers, E. M. *Diffusion of Innovations* (4th ed.), New York: The Free Press, 1995.

Rogers, E. M. *Diffusion of Innovations* (5th ed.), New York: The Free Press, 2003.

Rohracher, H. "The Role of Users in the Social Shaping of Environmental Technologies," *Innovation: The European Journal of Social Sciences* (16), 2003, pp. 177-192,

Silverstone, R., and Haddon, L. "Design and the Domestication of Information and Communication Technologies: Technical Change and Everyday Life," in *Communication by Design*, R. Mansell, and R. Silverstone (Eds.), Oxford, UK: Oxford University Press, 1996, pp. 44-74.

Taylor, S., and Todd, P. A. "Understanding Information Technology Usage: A Test of Competing Models," *Information Systems Research* (6:2), 1995, pp. 144-176.

Van de Ven, A. H., and Rogers, E. M. "Innovations and Organizations: Critical Perspectives," *Communication Research* (15), 1988, pp. 15: 632-651.

Venkatesh, V., Morris, M. G., Davis, G. B., and Davis, F. D. "User Acceptance of Information Technology: Toward a Unified View," *MIS Quarterly* (27:3), 2003, pp. 425-479.

Wolfe, R. A. "Organizational Innovation: Review, Critique and Suggested Research Directions," *Journal of Management Studies* (31:3), 1994, pp. 405-432.

ABOUT THE AUTHORS

Jennifer Blechar holds an M.Sc. in Analysis, Design and Management of Information Systems from the London School of Economics and Political Science, UK, and a B.A. in Mathematics from Bryn Mawr College, USA. She is a Ph.D. candidate and research fellow with the Department of Informatics at the University of Oslo, Norway, and has several years experience as a consultant within the telecommunications field. Her research interests involve the design, implementation, and diffusion of high value content services in the mobile industry. Jennifer can be reached at jennifjb@ifi.uio.no.

Lars Knutsen is a Ph.D. scholar at the Department of Informatics at the Copenhagen Business School. He holds a Master of Marketing Management from the Norwegian School of Management and a Master of Science in Strategy from the Aarhus School of Business. His dissertation research analyzes meanings and actions emerging during people's earliest acquaintances with new wireless services and the properties and gratifications these meanings and actions signify. Lars can be reached at lk.inf@cbs.dk.

Jan Damsgaard is professor at the Department of Informatics, Copenhagen Business School, Denmark. He holds a Master's degree in Computer Science and Psychology and a Ph.D. in Computer Science (1996). Jan is the study director of a graduate program in e-business. His research focuses on the diffusion and implementation of networked and standard-based technologies such as intranet, extranet, Internet portals, EDI, and advanced mobile services (GSM/ GPRS/EDGE, UMTS, WiFi, and WiMax). In much of his research, he seeks to explain technology innovation using network economics and technology characteristics. Jan is the research director of the Mobiconomy and DREAMS projects that focus on diffusion and implementation of advanced mobile services. He has presented his work at international conferences (ICIS, ECIS, PACIS, HICSS, IFIP 8.2. and 8.6) and in international journals *(European Journal of Information Systems, Information Systems Journal, Journal of Strategic Information Systems, Information Society, Journal of Global Information Management, Journal of Organizational Computing and Electronic Commerce, Information Technology and People*, and *Journal of the Association for Information Systems*). Jan can be reached at damsgaard@ cbs.dk or at http://www.cbs.dk/staff/damsgaard/.

8 PRIVACY CONSIDERATIONS IN LOCATION-BASED ADVERTISING

Heng Xu
Hock-Hai Teo
Department of Information Systems
National University of Singapore
Singapore

Abstract   *The emergence of mobile communication and positioning technologies has presented advertisers and marketers with a new type of advertising approach: location-based advertising (LBA). Advertisers could deliver contextually appropriate advertising messages through wireless devices on a geographically targeted basis and could reach mobile consumers when they are most likely to make a purchase (Kölmel and Alexakis 2002). However, because LBA could also associate the lifestyle habits, behaviors, and movements with a consumer's personal identity, privacy concern is particularly salient for LBA. Drawing on the privacy literature and the exchange theory, we employ an experimental approach to develop and test an adoption model by including risk-benefit analysis as the major antecedent to behavioral intention. Two environmental variables—industry privacy self-regulation and privacy legislation—are included to further assess the role of industry self-regulator versus government legislator in bearing the responsibility of assuring consumer privacy. Our findings extend individual adoption research into the new L-Commerce context and offer several important implications for various players in the LBA industry: wireless advertising service/content providers, merchants, privacy advocates and government legislators.*

Keywords   Mobile commerce, location-based advertising (LBA), information privacy

1 INTRODUCTION

The emergence of mobile communication and positioning technologies has presented new opportunities and challenges to transform electronic commerce applications for the mobile arena. Spurred by developments in global positioning system (GPS) and sophisticated cellular triangulation techniques, telecommunication operators together with merchants are offering consumers pervasive flexibility to be uniquely reachable and to access networks and services while on the move. These commercial location-sensitive applications and value-added services that utilize geographical positioning information to provide value-added services are termed location-based services (LBS), and are generally marketed under "L-Commerce" (Gidari 2000).

The fast-growing mobile and Internet markets are powering the L-Commerce market evolution. With the advent of sophisticated positioning technologies and the widespread availability of accurate outdoor location information, advertisers and marketers are now presented with a new type of advertising approach: location-based advertising (LBA). With LBA, advertisers could deliver contextually appropriate advertising messages through the wireless devices on a geographically targeted basis and could reach mobile consumers when they are most likely to make a purchase (Kölmel and Alexakis 2002). Wireless devices have become a new medium through which advertisements, promotions, coupons, and other offers that are uniquely customized to an individual's tastes, geographical location, and the time of day are offered. Analysts predict that LBA messages are expected to create 5 to 10 times higher click-through rates compared to the Internet advertising messages (Ververidis and Polyzos 2002).

LBA could take the form of *pull-based* (users request the advertising content based on their locations) or *push-based* (location-sensitive content is automatically sent to users based on their locations) (Kölmel and Alexakis 2002). While LBA has the potential to benefit both merchants and consumers, its acceptance rate among consumers is still relatively low. One of the primary reasons is the consumers' fears of privacy invasion, especially for **push**-based LBA as consumers are wary of being tracked whenever and wherever they are, or being spammed with mobile advertisements (Barwise and Strong 2002). Improper handling of location information would result in the discovery and matching of location data and identity to classify consumers, thereby enhancing the visibility of their behavior, and increasing the scope for potentially personally embarrassing situations (Beinat 2001). Indeed, there is a growing call for "No L-Commerce without L-Privacy" by privacy advocates and consumers (Gidari 2000).

Given that this stance could stymie the development of push-based LBA (Beinat 2001), it is imperative that we develop a complete understanding of the role that privacy, plays in influencing a consumer's evaluation and adoption of push-based LBA. Drawing on the exchange theory, privacy and advertising literature, we aim to predict a consumer's usage intention toward push-based LBA from a privacy lens. Additionally, we seek to understand how merchants and policy makers could also shape the privacy risk perceived by the consumer in the context of adopting push-based LBA. We test our model using one push-based LBA[1] application—mobile coupon (M-Coupon) service—through an experimental approach. This study is novel to the extent that we have yet to find any empirical study that looks at these intertwined issues in the LBA

---

[1]From this point onward, we use the term *LBA* to mean push-based LBA. Our study focuses only on push-based LBA.

context. The marriage of the advertising, privacy, organizational justice, and legal literature streams may provide a deeper understanding of the issues affecting LBA evaluation and adoption, and therefore inform adoption research in the Information Systems discipline. Our findings can potentially be useful to privacy advocates, regulatory bodies and merchants to help shape or justify their decisions concerning L-Commerce.

2   THEORETICAL BACKGROUND AND RESEARCH HYPOTHESES

Figure 1 presents our research model. In this study, we adopt a narrow focus in examining the role of privacy in predicting adoption intention. Based on privacy literature, privacy concern is conceptualized as a *risk-benefit analysis*, which is the basic structure of our model. According to the theory of procedural justice and deterrence theory, we further hypothesize that industry privacy self-regulation and privacy legislation may affect a consumer's privacy risk perception of location information disclosure.[2] Drawing on the advertising literature, we posit that the informativeness and the entertainment value of a LBA message could help shape the perceived benefits of location information disclosure. The following sections develop and elaborate the key constructs and the theoretical rationale for the causal relationships among the constructs in the research model.

2.1 The Role of Privacy Concern in Intention to Use LBA

Information privacy has been generally defined as the ability of the individual to control the terms under which personal information is acquired and used (Westin 1967). Prior research has repeatedly shown information privacy is an utmost concern in diverse organizational and marketing contexts and it is argued that information privacy continues to be eroded as a result of technology innovations (Stone and Stone 1990). One of the key findings within extant privacy studies is that privacy is not absolute and there will be occasions on which privacy can be interpreted in "economic (cost/benefit) terms" (Klopfer and Rubenstein 1977). It was further suggested that individuals should be willing to disclose personal information in exchange for some economic or social benefits subject to an assessment that their personal information will subsequently be used fairly and that they will not suffer negative consequences in the future (Laufer and

---

[2]In this paper, "location information disclosure" refers to all the information disclosed for the purpose of using LBA, including both the dynamic location data and the static personal data such as identity, shopping preferences, mobile phone number, and others. It is the combination of both these groups of data that enhances the visibility of the individual behavior and thus poses a serious threat to individual privacy.

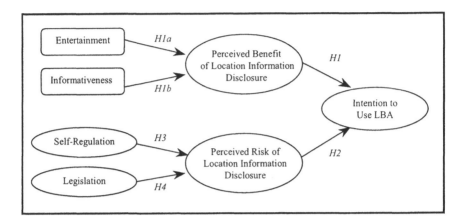

Figure 1. Research Model

Wolfe 1977). Similarly, consumers are likely to behave as if they are performing a privacy calculus in assessing the outcomes they receive as a result of providing personal information to corporations (Culnan 1995).

One theoretical perspective that may help predict a consumer's privacy preference is the exchange theory (Bagozzi 1975; Houston and Gassenheimer 1987). This theory characterizes three classes of meanings of exchange: utilitarian, symbolic or mixed (Bagozzi 1975). A utilitarian exchange is an interaction whereby goods are given in return for money or other goods (Bagozzi 1975, p. 36) and it is considered as the *first exchange* (Culnan and Bies 2003, p.326). The concept of *second exchange* is proposed to explain the privacy calculus phenomenon and refers to the exchange whereby the consumer's personal information is given in return for value such as higher quality service and personalized offers or discounts (Culnan and Bies 2003). Applying the second exchange framework to LBA usage behavior, we can treat the usage of LBA as an exchange where consumers disclose their location information in return for the proper value (e.g., timely personalized discount information based on the consumers' location) provided by the firm. Hence, we predict that mobile consumers should be willing to disclose personal information in exchange for proper value provided by LBA services as long as they perceive that benefits exceed the current or future risks of using LBA. Hence, we hypothesize

H1: *Higher perceived benefits of location information disclosure will lead to greater intent to use LBA.*

H2: *Higher perceived risks of location information disclosure will lead to lower intent to use LBA.*

2.2 Components of Perceived Benefits: Entertainment and Informativeness

Perceived benefits of location information disclosure are gained only when LBA is utilized. According to previous advertising research, consumers mainly value advertising media for the entertainment and informational value (Chen and Wells 1999; Ducoffe 1996; Eighmey 1997; Eighmey and McCord 1998). Entertainment refers to the extent to which the advertising media is fun and entertaining to media users (Eighmey 1997; Eighmey and McCord 1998) and the value of media entertainment lies in its ability to fulfill users' needs for escapism, hedonistic pleasure, aesthetic enjoyment, or emotional release (McQuail 1983). Prior research suggests that providing higher entertainment value is likely to motivate them to use the media more often (Eighmey 1997; Eighmey and McCord 1998). Hence, a corollary to H1 would be

H1a: *Higher level of entertainment will lead to greater intent to use LBA.*

Informativeness is defined as the extent to which the advertising media provides users with resourceful and helpful information (Chen and Wells 1999; Ducoffe 1996). Past studies have suggested that media users consider advertisers' ability to provide audience information as the fundamental reason for accepting the ad itself (Bauer and Greyser 1968). Also, it was indicated that advertising's informational role is its major legitimizing function (Rotzoll et al. 1986). By matching the information on personal preferences provided by consumers with their current location information, LBA is able to provide consumers with personalized and localized up-to-date advertising messages. The increased relevance and timeliness of an advertising message will assist consumers in making a better purchase decision and consequently perceiving LBA to be valuable. Hence, a corollary to H1 would be

H1b: *Higher level of informativeness will lead to greater intent to use LBA.*

2.3 Mitigating Consumer's Privacy Risk Perception: Fair Information Practices

Fair information practices (FIPs), a general term for a set of global principles, has been developed to balance consumer's privacy concerns with a firm's need to use personal information. FIPs regulate the disclosure and subsequent use of personal information by empowering individuals with control over their information as well as giving them an assurance that firms will adhere to a set of principles that most consumers find acceptable (Culnan and Armstrong 1999). Businesses adhering to FIPs can lower the privacy concerns associated with the disclosure of personal information through assuring consumers that the firm will abide by a set of rules (Greenberg 1987) and will not behave opportunistically (Shapiro 1987). However, there is still an ongoing debate on the relative effectiveness of legislation and industry self-regulation in insuring that a firm's implementation of FIPs is available, accurate, and understandable, and that consumers have legitimate choices about how their personal information is subsequently used (e.g., Caudill and Murphy 2000; Culnan and Bies 2003). In response to this debate, we draw on the procedural justice and deterrence theories to provide the theoretical bases for analyzing the relative effectiveness of two different regulatory approaches to the FIPs implementation—industry self-regulation approach and legislation approach—in assuaging consumers' privacy concerns.

2.3.1   *Industry Self-Regulation on FIPs Implementation: Procedural Justice Perspective*

Culnan and Bies (2003) proposed that a justice theoretical perspective provides a useful framework for analyzing consumers' privacy perceptions. Of particular relevance to industry privacy self-regulation is the procedural justice perspective (e.g., Lind and Tyler 1988). Procedural justice refers to the perception by individuals that a particular activity in which they are participants is conducted fairly and how those procedures are enacted (Lind and Tyler 1988). Research has shown that even if outcomes are not favorable to individuals, they are less likely to be dissatisfied with unfavorable outcomes if they believe that the procedures used to bring about those outcomes are fair (Greenberg 1987; Lind and Tyler 1988).

The self-regulation approach to implementing FIPs is one way to enhance consumers' perceptions of procedural justice, because self-regulation provides individuals with control over the disclosure and subsequent use of their personal information via announced privacy policies or privacy seals from trusted third parties (such as TRUSTe, BBBOnline, and Online Privacy Alliance) or other industry association (e.g., Direct Marketing Association). Third party intervention has been employed in self-regulation to provide legitimacy and trustworthiness to companies through seals of approval that are designed to verify adequate privacy compliance. These efforts specifically address FIPs with participating firms agreeing to provide notice, choice, access, security, and enforcement. Previous studies have shown that businesses that conform to the industry self-regulation practices instill greater confidence in consumers to reveal their personal information and thereby lower consumers' privacy risk perceptions (Caudill and Murphy 2000). Hence, we hypothesize

> **H3**: *The presence of industry self-regulation on location information protection should lead to lower perceived risk of using LBA.*

2.3.2   *Legislation on FIPs Implementation: Deterrence Theory Perspective*

Privacy studies suggest that legislation could have a major positive impact on privacy perceptions (Culnan 2000) since the legal system is the most powerful mechanism for the exercise of social control (Spiro and Houghteling 1981). Legal language is powerful because it is oriented toward specific (correlative) rights and duties (Spiro and Houghteling 1981). A general civil right of individual integrity, expressed through various doctrines of tort, property and contract law, protects an individual's freedom of action, ownership and decision from certain kinds of interference by others. Deterrence theory (e.g., Gibbs 1986; Tittle 1980) shows that the legal system requires that offenders be punished in order to maintain the deterrent effectiveness of the system. In essence, illegal behavior can be deterred through the threat of punishment (Tittle 1980).

Deterrence theory has a direct bearing on privacy invasion issues. Recognizing the deterrent effectiveness of a legal system, consumers may perceive a lower level of privacy invasion risks involved in using LBA. Evidence from privacy studies in the Internet usage provides support for the effects of legislation on users' perceptions of privacy protection. The majority, 58 percent, of the American public wants the government to pass laws to protect privacy and 24 percent says that the government should formally recommend privacy standards (Rotenberg 1998). In the LBA context, legislation on location data protection should play an important and direct role in lowering the privacy risk perceptions of using LBA. Hence, we hypothesize

H4: *The presence of legislation on location information protection should lead to lower perceived risk of using LBA.*

2.4 Control Variables Influencing LBA Adoption

Prior research on information privacy and IT adoption suggests a number of additional factors should be included as control variables because of their potential influence on perceived benefit, perceived risk, and intention to use LBA. They are: *prior experience of using mobile applications* (Culnan 1995), *previous privacy experience* (Smith et al. 1996; Stone and Stone 1990), and *innovativeness* (Joseph and Shailesh 1984; Pedersen 2005).

3   RESEARCH METHOD

A laboratory experiment was used to test the proposed model because of its ability to support the testing of causal relationships between manipulated and theoretical constructs with minimal interference from extraneous variables. At present, most of the available mobile applications are delivered to users over different underlying technology platforms such as WAP-based (wireless application protocol) or GPRS-based (general packet radio service) mobile Internet and short messaging service (SMS) (Xu et al. 2003). Since most mobile phones support the SMS functionality, LBA in our study was introduced as the service offered to mobile phone users via SMS based on the cell-identification (cell-ID)[3] technique employed by the network of telecom operators.

---

[3]Cell-ID, or cell of origin (COO), works by identifying the cell of the network in which the handset is operating (Barnes 2003). Such technique is the main technology that is widely deployed in mobile communication networks today. It requires no modification to handsets or

One specific LBA application—the mobile coupon (M-coupon) service—is utilized as the scenario in the experiment. The M-coupon service involves recruiting consumers by service registration and interest subscription: consumers can register their mobile phone numbers and subscribe to a list of merchants who provide M-coupon services, based on their interests and preferred period of time for receiving M-coupons. Profiling information is then used to target the subscribers and their mobile phones will be sent related advertisements when they appear within the vicinity of the merchants.

3.1 The Experiment

The study was designed as a 2 (with/without *self-regulation*) × 2 (with/without *legislation*) factorial experiment design. Participants were randomly assigned to one of the four groups. The gender ratio of each group was kept to 1:1; other individual characteristics and personality factors were controlled by randomization.

A total of 84 undergraduate students in the School of Computing at a large university in Singapore were recruited via an online registration system, and participated in the experiment (42 females, 42 males). They were required to complete an online registration by providing their background information. All of the subjects own mobile phones. As an incentive for participation, each subject received S$15 upon completion.[4] While the use of undergraduate students as potential LBA users might limit the generalizability of the results, we believe that this should not be a major concern because research indicates that younger individuals are among the most avid users of mobile technologies (Pedersen 2005) and, arguably, represent the next generation of mobile consumers.

All subjects began the experiment by answering questions about their personal information as a form of control check. The subjects were then asked to assume the role of a potential LBA user and were presented with the scenario of M-coupon service which was described in the form of a real company Web site to ensure realism (see Appendix F for a detailed description). Next, they were asked to complete a questionnaire regarding their perceptions of benefits and risks, and their intention to use LBA.

Two exogenous variables—*self-regulation* (SREG) and *legislation* (LEGI)—were manipulated to create the environment in which the potential LBA users have to make their choices. *Self-regulation* was manipulated by providing a TRUSTe seal and a privacy policy statement on the service provider's Web site. *Legislation* was manipulated by informing the subjects that L-Commerce transactions are governed by related location privacy protection laws. A summary report containing the gist of the Location Privacy Protection Act was provided to those subjects belonging to the legislation treat-

---

networks since it uses the mobile network base station as the location of the caller (Barnes 2003). However, although locating the caller through this technique is fast (i.e., typically around three seconds), accuracy is relatively low (in the range of 200 meters), depending on cell size (Giaglis et al. 2002). Generally speaking, the accuracy is higher in densely covered areas (for example, urban places) and much lower in rural environments (Zeimpekis et al. 2003).

[4]The reward was framed in Singapore dollars. As of January 2005, one Singapore dollar is about 60 U.S. cents.

ment group. The Location Privacy Protection Act used in the experiment was modified from a proposal by the Senate and House of Representatives of the United States of America.[5] The language used in the Act was localized to suit Singapore's context. During the experiment, no one questioned the authenticity of the Act; however, upon completion of all the experimental treatments, the experiment administrators informed the subjects in the legislation treatments that there was no such legislation in Singapore.

The Web-based system used for this study was programmed to ensure that each subject viewed the treatment conditions before they were allowed to proceed, and that subjects answered all questions before leaving the experiment. These features allowed us to ensure that the subjects had actually read the manipulated conditions completely before they gave their responses to questions asking them about entertainment, informativeness, perceived risk, and intended use.

3.2 Measures

As far as possible, constructs were adapted from existing measurement scales used in prior studies in advertising, consumer behavior, and information privacy to fit the LBA context where necessary. Intent to use and perceived risk were operationalized as reflective constructs, while perceived benefit was operationalized as a formative construct formed from two subconstructs: entertainment and informativeness. The instrument was further validated by assessing the measurement model using confirmatory factor analyses (LISREL 8.51). Appendix C presents the questions measuring each construct in this study.

4   DATA ANALYSIS AND RESULTS

4.1 Manipulation Check

The manipulations on *self-regulation* and *legislation* were checked against true/false questions administered after the experiment. All subjects responded correctly on these questions, suggesting that the subjects have perceived the experiment in the way intended. Additional questions were also posed to assess the level of understanding of the privacy statements and related laws for those subjects belonging to the self-regulation and legislation treatment groups. The subjects' responses to those questions measuring *self-regulation* ($t = 16.88, p < .001$) and *legislation* ($t = 10.26, p < .001$) are all significantly different from the neutral value of four.

---

[5]The details of the proposal are available at http://www.techlawjournal.com/cong107/privacy/location/s1164is.asp.

4.2 Analysis Strategy

Structural equation modeling (SEM) was adopted for data analyses. Following the approach adopted by Teo, Wei and Benbasat (2003), we used both linear structural relations modeling (LISREL) and partial least squares (PLS) for data analysis. LISREL is used to perform confirmatory factor analysis of the measurement items used to capture the dimensions of the subconstructs. Using LISREL for confirmatory factor analyses provides a more rigorous assessment of the fit between the collected data and the theoretical factor structure, and satisfies the minimum requirements of assessing the measurement properties of unidimensionality, convergent validity, and discriminant validity (Bagozzi 1980). PLS is used for hypotheses testing primarily because it follows a component-based strategy and thus does not depend on having multivariate normal distributions, interval scales, or a large sample size (Fornell and Bookstein 1982). PLS is generally more appropriate for testing theories in the early stages of development (Fornell and Bookstein 1982). Given the nature of exploratory study and the use of formative construct (i.e., perceived benefit) in our study, PLS is the preferred technique for testing the structural model. Appendices A and B show the descriptive statistics and the intercorrelations of the study variables respectively.

4.3 Evaluating the Measurement Model

Four multiple-items constructs—entertainment, informativeness, perceived risk, and intent to use—are subjected to confirmatory factor analyses using LISREL 8.51. The validity of the constructs is assessed in terms of unidimensionality, convergent validity, internal consistency and discriminant validity.

Unidimensionality and convergent validity ensure that all the items measure a single underlying construct (Bagozzi and Fornell 1982). Following an iterative procedure of changing one item in each step and the modification indices provided by LISREL (Jöreskog 1993), refinements to this model are made by eliminating two items of the informativeness construct with low loading or high cross loading. The final model comprising 16 items shows some improvement (see Appendices C and D). As is evident, all except two indicator loadings are above the criterion of 0.707 and significant (Hair et al. 1998). The errant indicators, INF2 and INT3, which have no cross-loading problems, are significant, and do not contribute to the problems of convergent validity and internal consistency, are retained. The model fit indices (Appendix D) also provide evidence of the unidimensionality of the items. Except the standardized RMR index, all indices were close to or above the criterion levels.

The internal consistency of each dimension is assessed by computing Cronbach's alpha, composite reliability, and the average variance extracted (Hair et al. 1998). Appendix C presents the results along these dimensions. Cronbach's alpha and the composite reliabilities both exceed Nunnally's (1978) criterion of 0.70 while the average variances extracted for the constructs are all above 50 percent (Hair et al. 1998).

Discriminant validity reflects the extent to which the measures for each construct are distinctly different from each other, and is generally assessed by testing whether the correlations between pairs of constructs are significantly different from unity (Anderson

1987). For each pair of constructs, the correlation between a referent construct and another construct is unconstrained in one model but is set to unity in another model. Constraining the correlation between pairs of constructs to unity suggests that all of the items measure the same construct. Discriminant validity is established if the χ^2 value of the unconstrained model is significantly lower than that of the constrained model. Appendix E shows strong evidence of discriminant validity.

4.4 Evaluating the Structural Model

With adequacy in the measurement models affirmed, PLS is used to assess the structural model. Hypotheses and corollaries testing are performed by examining the sign, the significance of the path coefficients, the weights of the dimensions of the constructs and the explanatory power of the structural model, respectively. A boot-strapping technique is applied to estimate the significance of the path coefficients and the weights of the dimensions of constructs. Since PLS does not generate any overall goodness of fit index, predictive validity is assessed primarily with the examination of the explanatory power and significance of the hypothesized paths. The explanatory power of the structural model is assessed based on the amount of variance in the endogenous construct (intent to use LBA) for which the model could account. All statistical tests are assessed at a 5 percent level of significance using one-tailed t-tests because our hypotheses and corollaries were unidirectional in nature.

Figure 2 depicts the structural model. Our structural model could explain 23.8 percent of the variance for the intention to use LBA. Each hypothesis (*H1* to *H4*) corresponds to a path in the structural model. Perceived benefit (*H1*) and perceived risk of location information disclosure (*H2*) were significant predictors of the intention to use

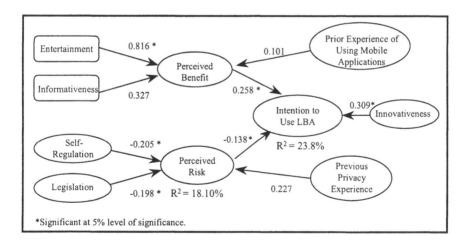

Figure 2. Results of PLS Analyses for Theoretical Model

LBA; and self-regulation (*H3)* and legislation (*H4*) were significant predictors of perceived risk. However, regarding the two corollaries to *H1*, *H1a* was supported but *H1b* was not supported.

5   DISCUSSION AND CONCLUSIONS

This study set out to integrate fragmented theories and research on advertising, privacy, organizational justice, and legal literature streams into a unique adoption model that captures the main inhibiting influences in the new L-Commerce context. Consistent with previous studies (Culnan 1995; Culnan and Bies 2003), the evidence from this study indicates that consumers are rational and are willing to disclose their location information in exchange for some benefits subject to the *second exchange* in LBA context. Our proposed model is able to account for 23.8 percent of the variances in usage intention, which possesses enough explanatory power to make interpretation of path coefficients meaningful. Thus, risk-benefit analysis underpinned by the exchange theory, is shown to be a major antecedent of usage intention in LBA. Furthermore, our findings help provide some initial insights into the controversial issues surrounding the role of industry self-regulation and legislation in assuring consumer privacy. In particular, our results showed that consumers did regard self-regulation and legislation on location information protection as the important factors affecting privacy concern in LBA. Therefore, both procedural justice theory and deterrence theory appear to be suitable theories for identifying the critical factors that have influence on the perceived risk of location information disclosure.

Among the two factors that were hypothesized to form benefit perception, entertainment contributed predominantly to benefit perception. This suggests that consumers could be more likely to use LBA if the advertising messages are perceived to be fun and entertaining. In contrast, informativeness did not contribute significantly to the formation of benefit perception. Two explanations arising from the limitations of this study are plausible. First, our sample population of university students may have placed a higher premium on fun and entertainment when using LBA compared to general mobile users. Second, our laboratory experiment might not be able to fully operationalize the informativeness factor in terms of relevance and timeliness since the subjects were not in a real shopping scenario and they were not actually on the move. Hence, some caution must be exercised when generalizing these findings.

Notwithstanding these limitations, we believe our research contributes to the adoption and information privacy research in the IS field. A number of opportunities exist for further research. Some of these relate directly to overcoming the limitations of this study. First, in our experimental design, we adopted a narrow focus so as to achieve a high degree of control over extraneous variables. There are other negative aspects such as location data quality and service dependability that may affect LBA adoption, which could also be examined in future research. Second, actual adoption behavior was not measured because the objective of this study was to predict the LBA adoption among potential users who do not yet have credible, meaningful information about, or have affective bonds with, the service providers at the initial adoption/usage stage. Future research could move beyond the domain of the initial adoption/usage stage to the domain of continuance/discontinuance of usage whereby consumers already have a longstanding relationship with service providers. Specifically, longitudinal research could be especially useful in investigating how consumers could be motivated to adopt and continue with LBA usage. Third, this study addressed privacy from an institution-based privacy assurance standpoint (i.e., industry self-regulation and government legislation). Nevertheless, it might be expected that consumers' privacy concerns will be lower when they are empowered with the aid of technologies to exert direct control over personal information in the LBA context (Xu and Teo 2004). Future studies could be carried out to examine the effects of device-based privacy enhancing features (Anuket 2003) on alleviating mobile consumers' privacy concerns.

From a practical perspective, this study provides several important implications for the various players in the LBA industry: merchants, wireless advertising service/content providers, privacy advocates, and government legislators. Given that the individual's concern for privacy is not absolute, but rather can be traded off against benefits, there exist ample opportunities for merchants and wireless advertising service/content providers to offer LBA in practice. There seems to be some evidence to indicate that consumers place high expectations on the entertainment value of mobile advertisements. Wireless advertising service/content providers should consider the importance of entertainment value when designing the interface of LBA messages. Our findings further suggest that privacy protection is a fundamental concern that must be addressed in the LBA context. Mobile consumers desire the implementation of FIPs through self-regulation or legislation to protect their privacy during and after the process of using LBA.

The advent of mobile and positioning technologies has brought about multifaceted impacts on mobile consumers. It is thus imperative for adoption researchers, managers, and policy makers to be aware of the issues involved. Although this research has provided some preliminary evidence toward enriching our understanding in some of these aspects, much research remains to be done in shaping the development of this emerging arena. It would be a challenge to continue improving the experiment design, which could be a scenario where consumers are really on the move. Field research along the directions of this study could contribute significantly toward fostering the acceptance of L-Commerce.

REFERENCES

Anderson, J. C. "An Approach for Confirmatory Measurement and Structural Equation Modeling of Organizational Properties," *Management Science* (33:4), 1987, pp. 525-541.

Anuket, B. *User Controlled Privacy Protection in Location-Based Services*, Unpublished Master's Thesis, University of Maine, Orono, ME, 2003.

Bagozzi, R. P. *Causal Models in Marketing*, New York: John Wiley & Sons, 1980.

Bagozzi, R. P. "Marketing as Exchange," *Journal of Marketing* (39), October 1975, pp. 32-39.

Bagozzi, R. P., and Fornell, C. "Theoretical Concepts, Measurement, and Meaning," in *A Second Generation of Multivariate Analysis* (2nd ed.), C. Fornell (Ed.), Westport, CT: Praeger Publishers, 1982.

Barnes, J. S. "Known by the Network: The Emergence of Location-Based Mobile Commerce," in *Advances in Mobile Commerce Technologies*, E-P. Lim, and K. Siau (Eds.), Hershey PA: Idea Group Publishing, 2003, pp. 171-189.

Barwise, P., and Strong, C. "Permission-Based Mobile Advertising," *Journal of Interactive Marketing* (16:1), Winter 2002, pp. 14-24.

Bauer, R., and Greyser, S. *Advertising in America*, Cambridge, MA: Harvard University Press, 1968.

Beinat, E. "Privacy and Location-based: Stating the Policies Clearly," *GeoInformatics*, September 2001 (available online at http://www.geodan.nl/nl/geodan/nieuws/pdf/ GeoInformatics_sept_2001_LBSandPrivacy.pdf)

Caudill, M. E., and Murphy, E. P. "Consumer Online Privacy: Legal and Ethical Issues," *Journal of Public Policy & Marketing* (19:1), 2000, pp. 7-19.

Chen, Q., and Wells, W. "Attitude Toward the Site," *Journal of Advertising Research* (39), 1999 pp. 27-37.

Culnan, M. J. "Consumer Awareness of Name Removal Procedures: Implication for Direct Marketing," *Journal of Interactive Marketing* (9), Spring 1995, pp. 10-19.

Culnan, M. J. "Protecting Privacy Online: Is Self-Regulation Working?," *Journal of Public Policy & Marketing* (19:1), 2000, pp. 20-26.

Culnan, M. J., and Armstrong, P. K. "Information Privacy Concerns, Procedural Fairness and Impersonal Trust: An Empirical Investigation," *Organization Science* (10:1), January-Febraury 1999, pp. 104-115.

Culnan, M. J., and Bies, J. R. "Consumer Privacy: Balancing Economic and Justice Considerations," *Journal of Social Issues* (59:2), 2003, pp. 323-342.

Ducoffe, R. H. "Advertising Value and Advertising on the Web," *Journal of Advertising Research* (36), 1996, pp. 21-35.

Eighmey, J. "Profiling User Responses to Commercial Web Sites," *Journal of Advertising Research* (37:2), 1997, pp. 59-67.

Eighmey, J., and McCord, L. "Adding Value in the Information Age: Uses and Gratifications of Sites on the World Wide Web," *Journal of Business Research* (41:3), 1998, pp. 187-194.

Fornell, C., and Bookstein, F. L. "Two Structual Equation Models: LISREL and PLS Applied to Customer Exit-Voice Theory," *Journal of Maketing Research* (19:11), 1982, pp. 440-452.

Hair, J. F., Anderson, R. E., Tatham, R. L., and Black, W. C. *Multivariate Data Analysis with Readings* (5th ed.), New York: Macmillan, 1998.

Houston, S. F., and Gassenheimer B. J. "Marketing and Exchange," *Journal of Marketing* (51), 1987, pp. 3-18.

Giaglis, M. G., Kourouthanassis, P., and Tsamakos, A. "Towards a Classification Framework for Mobile Location Services," in *Mobile Commerce: Technology, Theory, and Applications*, B. E. Mennecke and T. J. Strader (Eds.), Hershey PA: Idea Group Publishing, 2002, pp. 64-81.

Gibbs, J. P. "Deterrence Theory and Research," in *Law as a Behavioral Instrument*, G. Melton (Ed.), Lincoln, NE: University of Nebraska Press, 1986.

Gidari, A. "No 'L-Commerce^SM' Without 'L-Privacy': Fair Location Information Practices for Mobile Commerce," paper presented at L-Commerce 2000—The Location Services & GPS Technology Summit, Washington, DC, May 2000.

Greenberg, J. "A Taxonomy of Organizational Justice Theories," *Academy of Management Review* (12:1), 1987, pp. 9-22.

Jarvenpaa, S. L., Tractinsky, N., and Vitale, M. "Consumer Trust in an Internet Store," *Information Technology and Management* (1:12), 2000, pp. 45-71.

Jöreskog, K. G. "Testing Structural Equation Models," in *Testing Structural Equations Models*, K. A. Bollen and J. S. Long (Eds.), Newbury Park, CA: Sage Publications, 1993, pp. 294-316.

Joseph, B., and Shailesh, J. V. "Concurrent Validity of a Measure of Innovative Cognitive Style," *Journal of the Academy of Marketing Science* (12), Spring 1984, pp. 159-175.

Klopfer, P. H., and Rubenstein, D. L "The Concept Privacy and its Biological Basis," *Journal of Social Issues* (33), 1977, pp. 52-65.

Kölmel, B., and Alexakis, S. "Location Based Advertising," in paper presented at the First International Conference on Mobile Business, Athens, Greece, July 2002.

Laufer, R. S., and Wolfe, M. "Privacy as a Concept and a Social Issue: A Multidimensional Developmental Theory," *Journal of Social Issues* (33), 1977, pp. 22-41.

Lind, E. A., and Tyler, R. T. *The Social Psychology of Procedural Justice*, New York: Plenum Press, 1988.

Margulis, T. S. "Privacy as a Social Issue and Behavioral Concept," *Journal of Social Issues* (59:2), 2003, pp. 243-261.

McQuail, D. *Mass Communication Theory: An Introduction* (1st ed.), London: Sage Publications, 1983.

Nunnally, J. C. *Psychometric Theory* (2nd ed.), New York: McGraw-Hill, 1978.

Pedersen, E. P. "Adoption of Mobile Internet Services: An Exploratory Study of Mobile Commerce Early Adopters," *Journal of Organizational Computing and Electronic Commerce* (15:2), 2005 (forthcoming).

Rotenberg, M. "Privacy Protection—A US Perspective," *Computer Law & Security Report* (14:1), 1998, pp. 38-40.

Rotzoll, K., Haefner, J., and Sandage, C. *Advertising in Contemporary Society: Perspectives Toward Understanding*, Cincinnati, OH: South-Western Publishing, 1986.

Shapiro, S. P. "The Social Control of Impersonal Trust," *American Journal of Sociology* (93:3), 1987, pp. 623-658.

Smith, H. J., Milberg, J. S., and Burke, J. S. "Information Privacy: Measuring Individuals' Concerns About Organizational Practices," *MIS Quarterly* (20:2), June 1996, pp. 167-196.

Spiro, W. G., and Houghteling, L. J. *The Dynamics of Law* (2nd ed.), New York: Harcourt Brace Jovanovich , 1981, pp. 2-10.

Stone, E. F., and Stone D. L. "Privacy in Organizations: Theoretical Issues, Research Findings, and Protection Mechanisms," *Research in Personnel and Human Resources Management* (8:3), 1990, pp. 349-411.

Teo, H. H., Wei, K. K., and Benbasat, I. "Predicting Intention to Adopt Interorganizational Linkages: An Institutional Perspective," *MIS Quarterly* (27:1), March 2003, pp. 1-31.

Tittle, C. R. *Sanctions and Social Deviance: The Question of Deterrence*, New York: Praeger, 1980.

Ververidis, C., and Polyzos, C. G. "Mobile Marketing Using a Location Based Service," paper presented at the First International Conference on Mobile Business, Athens, Greece, July 2002.

Westin, A. F. *Privacy and Freedom,* New York: Atheneum, 1967.

Xu, H., and Teo, H. H. "Alleviating Consumer's Privacy Concern in Location-Based Services: A Psychological Control Perspective," in *Proceedings of the 25th International Conference on Information Systems*, R. Agarwal, L. Kirsch, and J. I. DeGross (Eds.), Washington, D C, December 2004, pp. 793-806.

Xu, H., Teo, H. H., and Wang, H. "Foundations of SMS Commerce Success: Lessons from SMS Messaging and Co-opetition," in *Proceedings of 36th Hawaii International Conference on System Sciences*, R. Sprague (Ed.), Los Alamitos, CA: IEEE Computing Society Press, January 2003, pp. 90-99.

Zeimpekis, V., Giaglis, M. G., and Lekakos, G. "A Taxonomy of Indoor and Outdoor Positioning Techniques for Mobile Location Services," *ACM SIGecom Exchanges* (3:4), Winter 2003, pp. 19-27.

ABOUT THE AUTHORS

Heng Xu is currently a doctoral candidate in the Department of Information Systems at the National University of Singapore. She received her B.B.A. degree in Information Management and Systems from Shandong University, China, in July 2001. Her research interests include information privacy, technology adoption, and human-computer interaction. Her work has been published in the proceedings of the International Conference on Information Systems, the Hawaii International Conference on System Sciences, and the European Conference on Information Systems, as well as Lecture Notes in Computer Science. She was a recipient of IBM Ph.D. fellowship in 2004. Heng can be reached at xuheng@comp.nus.edu.sg.

Hock-Hai Teo is currently an assistant professor of Information Systems in the Department of Information Systems at the National University of Singapore. He received his Ph.D. (October 1998) in Management of Information Systems from the National University of Singapore. He was a visiting scholar at the Wharton Business School, University of Pennsylvania, from 1999 to 2000. Dr. Teo has published in *MIS Quarterly, Journal of Management Information Systems, International Journal of Human-Computer Studies, Journal of Educational Computing Research, Information and Management, Journal of the American Society for Information Science and Technology, Journal of Database Management,* and *IEEE Transactions on Engineering Management,* and has presented at numerous international conferences, including the International Conference on Information Systems. He had also served on the EDIMAN (Electronic Data Interchange for Manufacturing) Standards Working Committee (1995-96) and had conducted executive seminars for Haw Par Group, Singapore Pools, and Ministry of Foreign Affairs (Singapore-Norway Cooperation Program). Dr. Teo is also currently serving as a Director of Mozat Pte Ltd. Dr. Teo can be reached at teohh@comp.nus.edu.sg.

Appendix A: Descriptive Statistics of Variables

Study Variables	Mean	SD
Theoretical Constructs		
Perceived Benefit—Entertainment **(ENT)**	5.33	0.91
Perceived Benefit—Informativeness **(INF)**	5.09	0.70
Perceived Risk **(RISK)**	4.53	1.56
Intention to Use LBA **(INT)**	4.47	0.87
Control Constructs		
Prior Experience of Using Mobile Applications **(PEXP)**	4.64	1.56
Innovativeness **(INNV)**	5.20	1.01
Previous Privacy Experience **(PPRV)**	1.30	0.65

Appendix B: Intercorrelations among Study Variables

Construct	BEN	RISK	INT	PEXP	INNV	PPRV	SREG	LEGI
BEN	1.000							
RISK	-0.299	1.000						
INT	0.329	-0.177	1.000					
PEXP	0.101	-0.095	0.134	1.000				
INNV	0.097	-0.125	0.317	0.157	1.000			
/PPRV	-0.052	0.248	-0.021	0.069	-0.407	1.000		
SREG	0.223	-0.165	0.158	0.167	-0.146	0.061	1.000	
LEGI	0.011	-0.306	0.145	0.023	-0.050	-0.113	0.167	1.000

Appendix C: Psychometric Properties of the Measurement Model

Measures of Constructs and Sources (measured on seven-point, Likert-type)	SPE	t-value	CA	CR	AVE
Entertainment: (Chen and Wells 1999; Ducoffe 1996) The location-based advertising is…			0.937	0.961	0.810
entertaining (ENT1).	0.72	7.49			
enjoyable (ENT2).	0.88	10.04			
fun to use (ENT3).	0.91	10.63			
cool (ENT4).	0.88	9.99			
exciting (ENT5).	0.93	11.11			
Informativeness: (Chen and Wells 1999; Ducoffe 1996) The location-based advertising…			0.810	0.812	0.519
is a good source of product information (INF1).	0.76	7.60			
supplies relevant product information (INF2).	0.68	6.57			
is a good source of up-to-date product information (INF3).	0.71	6.88			
is a convenient source of product information (INF4).	0.73	7.17			
RISK: (Jarvenpaa et al. 2000; Smith et al. 1996) There would be too much uncertainty associated with providing my personal information (e.g., shopping preferences, mobile phone number, continuous records of my location information, and others) to the service provider (RISK1).	0.87	9.70	0.923	0.925	0.754
There would be a considerable risk if the service provider shares my personal information with other companies without notifying me or getting my authorization (RISK2).	0.93	10.98			
There would be many unexpected problems if the service provider keeps my personal information in a non-accurate manner in its database (RISK3).	0.85	9.35			
There would be high potential for loss if the service provider does not take measures to prevent unauthorized access to my personal information (RISK4).	0.82	8.91			
Intent to Use LBA: (Culnan and Armstrong 1999) How likely would you use such service? (INT1)	0.86	9.28	0.845	0.852	0.660
How likely would you recommend your friends to use such service? (INT2)	0.89	9.74			
Would you actively seek out more information about such service from the service provider's website? (INT3)	0.67	6.61			

(SPE: Standardized Parameter Estimate; CA: Cronbach's Alpha; CR: Composite Reliability; AVE: Average Variance Extracted)

Appendix D: Goodness of Fit Indices for the Measurement Model

Goodness of Fit Indices	Initial Model	Revised Model	Desired Levels
χ^2	191.49	128.35	Smaller
df	129	98	-
χ^2/df	1.484	1.310	< 3.0
GFI	0.79	0.85	> .90
AGFI	0.73	0.77	> .80
Standardized RMR	0.066	0.059	< .05
RMSEA	0.077	0.061	.05 – .08
NFI	0.84	0.90	> .90
CFI	0.94	0.98	> .90
Number of Latent Variables	4	4	–
Total Number of Items	18	16	–

Appendix E: Assessment of Discriminant Validity

Dimensions	Constrained Model χ^2 (df)	Unconstrained Model χ^2 (df)	$\Delta\chi^2$
ENT *with*			
INF	72.06 (27)	42.75 (26)	29.31*
RISK	482.62 (27)	46.50 (26)	436.12*
INT	97.41 (20)	30.06 (19)	67.35*
INF *with*			
RISK	149.78 (20)	27.15 (19)	122.63*
INT	102.82 (14)	10.26 (13)	92.56*
RISK *with*			
INT	145.40 (14)	31.31 (13)	114.09*

*All differences in χ^2 are significant at p < 0.05.

Appendix F: Website Screen for M-Coupon Service
(with *Self-Regulation* Manipulation)

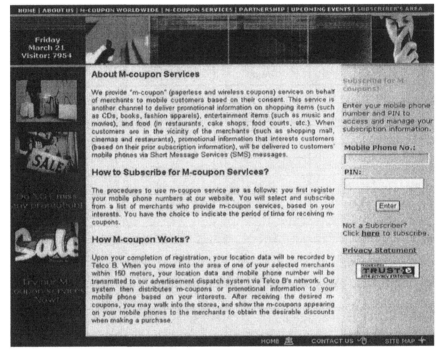

Note: Due to space limitations, we did not provide the screen shot for the M-coupon subscription Web page, the privacy statement page, or other experiment details, which can be requested from the authors.

Part 3

Organizational Impact

9   MOBILITY IN THE ROUND: Use of Wireless Laptop PCs in Clinical Ward Rounds

Henrique M. G. Martins
Matthew R. Jones
Judge Institute of Management
University of Cambridge
Cambridge, UK

Abstract   *It has been suggested that mobile information and communication technologies (MICTs) are better suited than traditional desktop devices to support work practices where participants are either moving around or conduct their work in different spatially dispersed settings. One such practice, which might be expected to benefit from MICT support, is the ward rounds conducted by hospital doctors. After a brief description of this practice, data are presented on the usage of laptop PCs in ward rounds in the Medicine Service of a U.S. hospital with a well-established IT infrastructure. Drawing on questionnaires, interviews, and observational evidence, the paper explores why, 5 years after the laptops were first introduced, a quarter of the clinicians had never used them, and only a quarter took advantage of more than their basic functionality. A number of possible reasons for the failure of doctors to adopt a technology that is seen as offering significant benefits to their work are discussed. In particular, it appeared that the reliability of the technology, differences in senior doctors' ward round practices, and social inertia contributed to the low level of uptake. Other local factors, such as the architecture of the building and departmental practices regarding laptop usage, also affected doctors' use. Implications for research on ubiquitous computing are drawn.*

1   INTRODUCTION

While the precise relationship between ubiquitous and mobile computing is a subject of continuing debate, in the absence of genuinely pervasive computing resources in most work environments, mobile information communication technology (MICT) devices, especially when supported by wireless networks, offer a means of expanding the range of settings in which computation is accessible. This does, of course, provide only partial ubiquity (a contradiction in terms!), and the mobility of the device *per se* is not enough to ensure that computing resources are actually available, as this is likely to be dependent on the correct functioning of a variety of technical and social infra-structures, such as networks, power supplies, and work arrangements, that make device use practicable. Nevertheless, bringing computers to the work practice, rather than the work to computers, constitutes a new opportunity for supporting work that is carried out "on the move," or conducted in a number of spatially dispersed settings.

At least until recently, such settings have received little attention in the literature on ICT implementation, which has tended to focus on situations where desktop computing has been used to support static work practices (Zuboff 1987). The growing mobile computing literature (Esbjörnsson 2002; Esbjörnsson et al. 2002; Esbjörnsson and Östergren 2002), however, typically suggests that MICTs may be better suited to supporting such work practices than static/desktop devices, and hence, that the adoption of MICTs in such settings may be expected to lead to increased efficiency and effectiveness of these work practices.

One specific type of work that is seen as particularly mobile, and therefore likely to benefit from MICT support, is that of hospital doctors (Bardram et al. 2003), espe-cially during their *ward rounds*. Studies of ward rounds (Atkinson 2001; Freeman and Reeder 1957; Martins and Jones forthcoming; Strauss et al. 1997) have identified them as serving a range of functions, such as gathering patient-related information, clinical decision-making, formulation of treatment plans and education. It is suggested (Cox 2002; Davis 2002; Kelly 2001) that MICTs may improve ward rounds by

- making available up-to-date patient data at the point of care, leading to more appropriate treatment
- allowing faster updating of treatment plans, leading to better treatment
- allowing access to reference information, leading to improved clinical decision-making and increased opportunities for learning

Indeed, there have been a number of largely self-reported accounts of the positive effect of such technology on clinical practice (Grasso and Genest 2001; Holleran et al. 2003).

It might, therefore, be expected that if MICTs were made available to doctors, they would use them in their ward rounds. Drawing on an in-depth study of the level and form of usage of MICTs by doctors working in the Medical Service of a large U.S. hospital that has provided wireless access to a comprehensive electronic medical record (EMR) and other resources for more than 5 years, this paper explores possible reasons why such expectations may not be realized. While the findings reported relate to the work practices of hospital doctors, a number of more generic features of support for mobile work practices are identified that may be relevant in other settings.

2   WARD ROUNDS: A BRIEF INTRODUCTION

Ward rounds, also known as *clinical visits* or simply *rounds*, are events when hospital doctors, as a team, typically comprising a senior doctor (Attending Physician), one or two junior doctors (Residents or Interns), and one or two medical students, visit the bedside of each inpatient under their care in turn. Such rounds are necessary because most inpatients are generally bed-bound.

Ward rounds can vary significantly (for example, in terms of their frequency, duration, and the personnel involved) depending on the particular clinical speciality, the clinical setting (wards or intensive care units), and also between countries. The following generic description, based on fieldwork from hospitals in the United States, United Kingdom, Singapore, and Portugal, summarizes some of the key features of ward rounds and helps to place later discussion in context.

The pre-round period, before the senior doctor arrives, can be quite hectic for junior doctors as they try to retrieve and aggregate as much information about patients as possible from the hospital computer systems (typically accessed via desktop computers) and/or paper files held in the doctor's office. To facilitate later recall, the junior doctors may take notes on pieces of paper that they carry in their pockets. The ward round typically starts with the arrival of the senior doctor and proceeds without preliminary discussion of patients. Rather, at each patient bed, a junior doctor (or sometimes a medical student) will be expected to present a summary of the condition and treatment of the patient (drawing, where appropriate, on the notes they may have taken earlier or paper records held at the bedside). Questions and discussion follow the presentation. At some point, the patient is also usually questioned about their condition and physical examinations may be conducted. This information is used by the team for a discussion, of variable duration, about the treatment plan for that patient. During this discussion, further questions may be posed to the patient and further data sought from existing records. Requests for information searches or for tasks to be executed after the ward round may be made at this time. Discussion is often not restricted to the specifics of the particular case, but will include broader medical discussion and teaching, and there can often be an exam-like interrogation of the junior doctors' and medical students' knowledge by the senior clinicians. The ward round normally ends with a plan of action (of varying specificity), which may include ordering of clinical investigations, further analysis of the case, changes to drug regime, or a decision to discharge the patient, all to be executed at a later stage. It is also customary that before the team moves on to the next patient, the senior doctor reminds the junior doctors of topics to study before the next ward round, and either only cordially says goodbye to the patient or does it after a very brief friendly chat.

A variant of the typical ward round, with potential implications for desktop and mobile ICT usage, is the "sitting ward round." In this case, the team often gathers not by the bedside but sitting in a room away from the patients. Each patient is discussed in turn, in more or less the same way, and a plan is often formulated. The team then leaves the room and visits all patients at their beds, in turn. At this stage, however, having already discussed the case, this visit generally serves as a chance for the team to see the patient and exchange some brief words, although sometimes there is some reopening of discussion of the case.

As this shows, ward rounds serve several functions including decision making about short term and long-term patient care, immediate plan formulation for diagnosis and treatment, education (both teaching and evaluative), patient contact and comforting, as well as team-building. In some departments, these tend to be crucial daily, biweekly, or weekly events as they are often the only occasion where the whole medical team caring for a group of patients is actually copresent.

Although, individually, doctors are increasingly reported to be using MICT devices such as handheld/PDAs (Barret et al. 2004; McLeod et al. 2003), predominantly as a source of medical or drug reference information, these are generally not connected to the hospital IT systems. Historically, ward rounds have also not been directly supported by ICTs (even if a complete EMR was available), as the EMR was typically only available via desktop computers. Sitting ward rounds, however, may be supported with desktop technology in some departments.

3   METHODOLOGY

The research reported in this paper forms part of a larger study covering ten sites in eight different hospitals in four countries (Portugal, United Kingdom, United States, and Singapore) carried out between December 2003 and December 2004, where observation, interviews, questionnaires, and data from log files was used to study doctors' and organizations' use of MICTs and technologies to support remote working.

3.1 Case Selection

The particular findings discussed in this paper derive from a study carried out in August 2004 at the Medical Service of the Veterans Affairs Medical Center, Washington, DC. This case was chosen because conditions there appear to be particularly favorable for MICT use: the hospital has a full EMR that, in the Medical Service, has been available for 7 or 8 years via desktop computers and for more than 5 years through wireless laptop PCs. With five similar medical teams using similar devices this case also enables differences in individual and group uptake of MICT to be explored.

3.2 Methods

Research was conducted using three data-gathering methods.

*   Questionnaires about attitudes to, and usage of, desktop and mobile ICT were distributed and collected at regular department meetings, with 33 questionnaires (from a total of 36 collected).
*   Participant observation was conducted on the department wards. Clinicians were accompanied during the course of the day, predominantly before and during their ward rounds, and this was often complemented with informal interviews.
*   A program of semi-structured interviews was carried out with doctors working at the department. Interviews were held in a calm environment and taped with the participants' permission. Transcripts were coded to ensure confidentiality and anonymity.

In all, 16 interviews were carried out, seven with Attendings (senior doctors) who had worked in the department during the last year, eight with junior doctors (Residents and Interns) working on the wards at the time of the study, and one with a medical student. In total, 13 hours of formal interviews and 75 hours of participant observation were conducted.

A grounded theory approach (Glaser and Strauss 1967) was used to identify emergent themes from the interviews and observation data as well as from open-ended answers in the questionnaire.

4 CASE DESCRIPTION

4.1 The Department and its Wireless Laptops

The VA Medical Center is a multi-speciality tertiary care facility. At any given time there may be around 60 doctors working in the Medical Service, distributed between a 12-bed intensive care unit, wards (with 87 beds), or outpatient clinics. The MICT devices made available for ward rounds were (at the time of study) standard laptop PCs with WiFi wireless connection. These were attached to a food trolley (as illustrated in Figure 1) and could not be removed. The AC adapter was also attached with a conventional power cable that could be extended to only a nearby wall socket. No mouse or extra battery were attached.

This apparatus was only movable as a whole, but the height of the tray could be adjusted and there was some free space on the tray to the sides of the Laptop. Although the particular model of laptop used had changed over time, this set-up had been constant. While recognizing that the

Figure 1. Sketch of the Resident from Team Beta Using the Wireless Laptop

food trolleys were not ideal, the Head of Department, explained that they had been used because funding for laptops did not include a budget for carts to hold them.

The laptops provide full access to Windows software, two hospital systems (a full EMR which includes the availability of all imaging studies and a drug administration system mostly used by the nurses), and the Internet. The hospital has its own intranet resources (links to departments guidelines and protocols, library holdings, and online resources), and broadband access to the Internet through a network filter for some sites considered less appropriate. The department policy toward computer usage (desktop and laptop) was liberal.

We've never told them not to [use Internet Explorer]....It's not that we had any constraints...you could do other things that you're not supposed to do either on them, and that has gotten people into trouble here (Head of Department).

Of the 33 staff studied, 24 were Attendings and 9 were Residents or Interns, with almost equal numbers of men and women. Less than half of the doctors owned a handheld/PDA. All doctors used a desktop every day for clinical work, 60 percent of them more than 10 times a day. Attending clinicians reported a higher frequency of use than Residents. The Internet was used for clinical work related with the department by all respondents at least once a week.

4.2 Wireless Laptop Usage in the Department

While two-thirds of the doctors had been using the wireless laptops for more than a year, almost a quarter (equally distributed between Attendings and Residents/Interns) claimed that they never used them and the remainder (mostly Residents/Interns) reported shorter periods of use.

About one-fifth of the doctors were high frequency users, using the laptops more than five times a day for clinical work, 35 percent were medium frequency users, while another fifth used them less than once a week (one-quarter were nonusers). All doctors used the laptops to check patient data, but only two for medical calculations and one to send clinical-related e-mails. No doctor reported using the laptops for checking hospital guidelines. The users thus comprised three groups: multi-task users, who browsed the Internet for medical information, checked medical and drug reference information, as well as consulting the EMR; standard users, who used the laptops only to access the EMR; and nonusers.

Age, gender, seniority, and usage of technologies other than MICTs showed no significant difference between the user group and the nonuser group. The multi-task user group reflected the seniority and gender make-up of the department, but included predominantly high- and medium-frequency users, most of whom owned a handheld/PDA (compared to almost none of the other groups).

One distinctive aspect of the Medical Service was the high turnover of staff. Residents, Interns, and medical students joined the department on a 4-week rotation from nearby universities and hospitals (each with different EMR systems and ward layouts), while the Attendings typically covered the wards for 4 weeks per year. All the rotations occurred asynchronously, meaning that knowledge of EMR use had to be continuously replaced. Using the laptops during ward rounds was, thus, one of the few occasions when all team members were together as a group, and provided an important opportunity for Attendings to teach others about the operation and capabilities of the hospital's systems.

Another distinctive aspect of the Service was that most of its patients were located in wards on two consecutive floors of the hospital building. Each ward had a central area (with several desktop computers) from which six corridors of patient rooms lead off. Each floor had two or three doctors' rooms (with five desktop PCs). The floors were connected by service stairs, but the elevator was located away from the center of the wards. Normally teams had patients on both floors and doctors identified this layout as affecting their usage of laptops.

Each of the teams has a laptop, chained, nailed, spiked, or something to a portable table, which makes it quite cumbersome, by the way, because we tend to go up and down between the third and fourth floor and you have to carry the table with you or go use the elevators which are painfully slow (Resident, Team Alpha).

4.3 Views of Nonusers

One team of doctors in particular (Team Alpha) never used the laptop PCs during the observation period; instead the Resident wrote out file-cards with relevant data for each patient and updated this with new data and action plans during the ward round. The Interns also kept their own, paper-based notes. The Resident, who was a charismatic individual, seemed to be more influential than the Attending in this team. He often spoke on behalf of the team and seemed to have been responsible for the team's non-usage of the laptops.

Well I guess on rounds it's the Resident's call. We never even had that as an option (Intern, Team Alpha).

This was not because he was unaware of the potential benefits of MICT use on ward rounds, however.

It's quite unusual for all the labs that are of interest to be complete by the time we round. I suppose it would be nice to have that available, but we simply discuss our plan based upon what we have, we have some notion of what lab values are likely to change if there are going to be values that change, and so we usually can make most planning decisions ahead of time by giving criteria for what lab we expect (Resident, Team Alpha).

The Intern in the team did not use the wireless laptops at other times either. His reasons for this reflect issues raised by a number of other doctors on the ward.

If I'm pushing the laptop around, I can't use the stairs, I can't carry it with me, it's hooked up to that desk, and then you know if I'm running around back and forth between the nurses station and the patient rooms and going here and there, I find that when I'm walking around the wards I'm running all over the place so I don't want to have to be responsible...for the laptop, if it gets damaged or stolen or anything. So it's not really a benefit. And [there are] so many computers available anywhere I am, I'm no more than 5 or 10 seconds away from sitting down at a desktop and getting the information I need (Intern, Team Alpha).

The Resident based his decision not to use the wireless laptops on his earlier experience working on a team where the devices were used daily.

Last year....Rounds tended to be more administratively frenetic when we had the laptop with us. There was more a temptation to do orders immediately, there was more waiting for lab results to come back and interrupting a chain of thought regarding the patient (Resident, Team Alpha).

Another concern was that laptops could affect education by reducing junior doctors' information processing capabilities and distracting their attention during the actual rounds.

I didn't want [the laptop] with us because I wanted folks on rounds to focus on the pieces of information that struck them as they were collecting it....The likelihood was [also] that there would be nothing more than one or two data points on a couple patients that we miss and that would be required for a decision at that point (Resident, Team Alpha).

The Resident felt very confident that ward rounds without the laptop were as good as those with it in almost every situation, although he identified one exception where the team was responsible for a large number of patients, including a significant number of patients from other teams.

During the observation period there were two Attendings covering the team, although laptops were not used with either. The second Attending had been working with the team for less than a week and, although she had previously used wireless laptops for ward rounds in her last job, perceived their use as valuable, she did not insist on their use in Team Alpha. This may have been because she was unfamiliar with the devices in the particular hospital.

I haven't actually seen them [but]I think [using laptops will] be a nice idea. We had them at Hopkins and we ended up using them a lot. They were fairly new...and I thought it was helpful on rounds to have information (Attending, Team Alpha).

4.4 Views of Users

The most active users at the time of the study were Team Beta, who had two laptops in their room, one of which served as a backup in case the first laptop failed. Even this team, however, did not always use laptops, as a medical student explained,

[With] the first Attending... we'd have more sit down rounds in our team room discussing things. So at that point we would be putting...the orders directly onto our desktops and then when we would round, we wouldn't really take the computer with us. The second Attending...would prefer us to have the computer with us but at that time we were having a lot of glitches with the com-

puters. The last Attending we've had, again she seems to be more sit down, get things kind of under our grasp, and then go from there. Although we still take the laptop with us. But again taking the laptop with us helps just getting orders done quicker and as something comes up you can order it at that time, or looking again at radiology is useful (Medical Student, Team Beta).

Another of the team members explained the team's usage of the laptops as being due to a combination of junior and senior clinician styles.

If you have a team that...really likes to get things tucked away early in the day and doesn't like to wait for things that you could have at your fingertips like lab results and sort of come back as you round on the patients, then I think that the laptops would be utilized more. And that was our case. ....It was driven by the Resident and the Attending, sort of the tone and the pace, and it's my impression that other teams didn't have the same sort of drive (Intern, Team Beta).

Team Beta's enthusiasm for laptop use did not appear to be dimmed by the unreliability of the technology (a problem specifically highlighted in almost half the comments on the questionnaires). While the team showed frustration when their ward rounds were frequently disrupted by the laptop crashing or losing power, they generally tried to solve the problem while continuing their discussion. For example, the Attending would continue asking questions about the patient while rebooting the laptop or searching for a wall plug. Occasionally they would even have to conduct

Figure 2. Sketch of Two Members of Team Beta Carrying the Laptop and Trolley Upstairs

rounds without a laptop because both were not working. Again, however, the Attending responded to this by chasing the IT department for prompt maintenance.

I mean usually we go a couple of days and then something goes wrong. But that's been a constant. And everyday I'm going to a computer person going, they're not working again (Attending, Team Beta).

Team Beta were based predominantly on the upper floor, but would visit patients on the lower floor daily. Except for occasions when there were only a few patients to be visited, two of the male Interns or medical students would take hold of the trolley with the laptop and carry it downstairs. The elevator was never used, despite the problems with carrying the device (on its trolley) upstairs (see Figure 2).

During the observation period, two Attendings covered the team. Both were enthusiastic about technology in general and the laptops in particular. As one of them put it,

And I guess depending on the attending some people just want to hear about the things...I am a data person. So I like the availability of data (Attending, Team Beta).

Because the hospital's systems also allowed remote access, both sometimes worked from home.

The main reason cited by members of Team Beta for use of the devices was that they increased team efficiency by allowing ready access to patient information and the input of at least some of the most urgent orders while rounding.

Because all of the orders are on the computer, it just makes things run smoother if during rounds you come up and say, I need this order done, rather than waiting 'til the end of rounds to do it, you know you can do it right there....The round's a lot more complete I think, also, much more efficient (Medical Student, Team Beta).

These benefits, however, were seen to depend on the team's capacity to work collaboratively. For example, orders would be entered, or the Resident would retrieve information with the laptop, while a patient was being presented by the Interns or medical students. Most team members were also in agreement about the advantages of being able to check the most up-to-date laboratory information.

When we come in and see the patients early in the morning, often times results are not there but by the time we round, almost certainly they are and that makes everything a lot easier because we can adjust issues (Intern, Team Beta).

Another common theme was the usefulness of the laptops as a support for additional information requests or to look at patterns of data from the patient's whole medical record.

The seven other Attendings working in the department mostly used the laptops for ward rounds because they liked to have easy access to data and immediate action like order entry. One Attending, in particular, saw this as giving him greater control.

I want up-to-date information, I want to see the information myself rather than relying on somebody else's recitation of it.....And then of course I do want to be able to review all the medications and not only rely on what somebody tells me the patient's on. Because they sometimes are mistaken.....[and] I want to be able to implement whatever plan we're concerned about immediately. I do not want to delay, I want to enter it into the system as we talk (Attending, Team Gamma).

Another Attending, in contrast, explained that she favoured laptop use because it encouraged a particular style of work and she saw it as better for education.

It's largely to keep the tradition of walk ward rounds going despite the fact that we had technology that would otherwise tie us into that room....without the laptop we would sit in the team room and talk about 12 or 15 patients, all in sequence, and then we'd go around and see everybody....The teaching was much stronger when we talked about patients as we went to see each one of them...and we weren't doing walk rounds before we had mobile laptops (Attending, Team Delta).

The same concern for education was voiced by an attending who was supportive of students retrieving data from online sources during rounds.

It's quite typical that while we're talking about this patient a student is looking up something on Up-to-Date. That happens frequently on rounds. They'll say, oh, Up-to-Date says, you know (Attending, Team Gamma).

5 CASE ANALYSIS: ACCOUNTING FOR THE ADOPTION OF MICT IN WARD ROUNDS

Contrary to claims in some of the literature (McLeod et al. 2003), age, gender, seniority, and usage of desktop technology do not seem to be related to laptop usage. Similarly, previous experience of MICT use for ward rounds did not always lead to greater uptake. Moreover, despite all teams being of a similar size, having access to a full EMR (both on desktops and on the laptop PCs, with the same application view) and ample desktop computing, about a quarter of the doctors claimed never to have used the laptops and three out of five teams were not using them at the time of study. It would seem, therefore, that some traditional explanations for the uptake of MICTs in ward rounds did not apply, at least in this setting.

In terms of reasons for non-usage of the laptops, unreliability of the technology was widely identified, although it is unclear whether this reflected significant technical problems (that might be overcome by future technological advances) or difficulties in establishing routines that would make the existing technology more reliable in practice (such as ensuring that batteries were always recharged). It was noticeable, however, that teams who used the laptops regularly seemed to deal with problems in a constructive way, rather than dismissing the technology as unworkable.

The other major reason for non-usage was not necessarily that teams perceived no benefit from using the laptops, but that influential members preferred other ward round practices (such as sitting ward rounds or walking ward rounds supported by paper notes).

Interestingly, the architecture of the building appeared to influence laptop usage, as all teams based on the upper floor were users, while those on the lower floor were, at best, irregular users. This may be due to other factors and interview data showed it was not always the rule, but it seemed that the particular way the laptops were set up made carrying them upstairs especially cumbersome. The department practice of teams being assigned specific machines meant they kept them in their (often locked) offices;

this, in turn, often prevented teams visiting a different floor from using the laptops available there.

The study was not able to find any measurable data on the effects of using wireless laptops on ward rounds, nor did users have access to such evidence. Rather, individuals held particular beliefs about the benefits (or otherwise) of laptop use. Thus both users and nonusers agreed that laptops could provide better data access and the possibility of immediate and supervised order entry. Three types of data that could be accessed were identified: standard data that an Intern/medical student might forget to present, or present incorrectly; timely data, for instance, the latest lab results; and data that would not normally be expected to be required (or necessarily available), such as a full medical history or recent research findings relevant to a particular case. Access to the latter two types, at the bedside, was seen to be a distinctive contribution of MICT use.

Users and nonusers differed, however, in whether they believed that such data were beneficial for medical education, patient care, or the efficiency of their work. This may relate to different views on the use of data in ward rounds. Thus nonusers tended to believe that the laptops made too much data available on ward rounds and encouraged doctors to rely on them rather than developing their own judgement beforehand. This was seen as making decision-making more variable and plan-formulation more con-tingent by emphasizing immediacy and creating more interruptions and distractions. As a result, in these doctors' opinion, data analysis and synthesis before the round was reduced, and decisions became less consistent and considered, to the detriment of junior doctors' education. For the multi-task users, on the other hand, the data-intensive environment created by the laptops enabled better team discussion and decision-making, leading to more concrete and immediately implemented care plans, and more effective education.

From the nonusers' perspective, clinical decision-making involved the considered evaluation of available data and the preformulation of an appropriate treatment plan that could be revised in the light of collegial debate or significantly discrepant evidence of the patient's condition. Hence students needed to be trained in presenting and defending their assessment of the available data. Enthusiastic laptop users, however, saw decision-making as a more collective process involving real-time data analysis leading to the immediate implementation of appropriate treatment. Hence students needed to learn to access and integrate data quickly from many sources and to take prompt action.

Some other, less important, reasons for use included caseload, especially in peak periods or when one team was temporarily looking after another's patients (because this made it difficult to recall every patient) and the extent to which individual patients' results might be updated during the course of ward round. The latter would, of course, depend on the duration of the ward round which could vary from one Attending to another.

The personal style of senior doctors appeared to influence usage significantly by determining the type of ward round (walking or sitting) and their willingness to instigate a change of practice, especially in a situation of high team membership turnover. The senior doctors' attitudes to technology, however, seemed to relate more to how the laptops were used than with if they were used or not. These findings are summarized in Table 1.

Table 1. Influences on Laptop Use for Ward Rounds

No association with use or non-use	• Age • Gender • Seniority • Use of desktop technology/Internet • Previous experience • Team size • Availability of desktop computing • Availability of full EMR on the laptops
Some association with non-usage	• Unreliability of technology • Building layout • Device characteristics • Senior doctors' satisfaction with existing ward round practices • Senior doctors' preference for decision-making with data available before the round • Senior doctors' belief that junior doctors need to be able to present and defend their decisions • Senior doctors' concern about distraction of junior doctors during ward round • Sitting ward round
Some association with usage	• Senior doctors' belief in the benefits of laptop use • Senior doctors' willingness to instigate new practices • High case load • Senior doctors' perception of benefits of rich data availability for education and decision-making • Senior doctors' perception of need for timely data and action • Senior doctors' belief in collective, real-time decision-making
Association with both usage and non-usage	• Walking ward round

6   DISCUSSION

In contrast to findings of other studies, it appeared that characteristics such as age, gender, and seniority did not seem to influence MICT device use. This may be because all users were highly skilled professionals working in an IT-intensive setting and where senior doctors, especially, had many years experience of EMR use.

This case also suggests that, contrary to suggestions in the literature, the benefits of MICT use in ward rounds were not self-evident and a significant proportion of doctors did not use the laptops at all. While the immaturity (and hence unreliability) of the technology was widely cited as a reason for non-use, this can, at best, only partly explain such behavior as a number of doctors used the laptops regularly despite this.

Five points, in particular, may be relevant to understanding this situation. First, it seems that all ward rounds are not equal: they are not the uniform, highly mobile practice suggested by some advocates of MICT use. Sitting ward rounds, for example, would seem well supported by desktop computers. Second, doctors appeared to have different perceptions of the function of ward rounds (for example decision-making with available data and testing of junior doctors' presentations or collective decision-making moments with all possible data) and whether this could be supported by MICT. Third, doctors' attitudes varied toward technology, but also regarding the importance of rich and timely data in clinical decision-making, the effectiveness of existing practices, and their willingness to change practices. Fourth, the costs and benefits of MICT use were necessarily based on individual perceptions as measurable evidence was lacking. So, while some reasons for non-use, such as device reliability or the inconvenience of carrying the laptop upstairs, may not have been as serious as they were said to be, without strong evidence of benefits, even small costs may be enough to discourage use. As the enthusiastic laptop users also showed, individuals could often do something about the situation, such as pressuring for better hardware maintenance. Fifth, strong social influences, such as the power relationships between grades of doctors, existing work routines, team dynamics, and department practices such as on device sharing, shaped laptop usage and were also influenced by it.

Local circumstances seemed to play an additional role. High staff turnover, for example, meant that training needs were high and continuous but also that using laptops on ward rounds provided an important opportunity for sharing of experience on EMR use. Similarly, the hospital architecture, combined with specific device characteristics, caused problems for even the most enthusiastic users. Thus the particular pattern of MICT adoption would seem likely to vary even among apparently similar settings.

The influence of hospital architecture also illustrates how, even though the laptops themselves may have been highly mobile, by attaching them to trolleys to enable them to be used by a doctor who would normally be standing during a ward round, their effective mobility was reduced (indeed this restriction was, in part, a deliberate strategy by the hospital to reduce the risk of the laptops being stolen). Even without the trolley, the ubiquitous use of the laptops was constrained by their battery life. *Mobility of the device* itself is, therefore, not necessarily the same as its *mobility in practice*.

Finally, the findings emphasise the active role of users in the adoption of MICT devices. This operates in a variety of ways, from their perceptions of the costs and benefits of wider availability of information to their willingness to change routines to accommodate device usage. This would seem particularly the case in the current state of MICT use, where individual users' access to mobile, computer-based resources is often dependent on whether they bring the devices to the work setting themselves. Moreover, if the purpose of MICT use is seen to be the provision of ubiquitous information resources, rather than devices per se, then users may feel that their needs are adequately met by static devices, providing these are sufficiently numerous and available, without needing to have the device at the exact point of use. Ubiquity may, therefore, be seen not as an objective characteristic of a technological resource, but as dependent also on users' perceptions.

7   CONCLUSION

While the findings reported here relate to only one site and one type of MICT use, evidence from other sites in our study suggests that they raise common issues that may extend beyond the particular medical setting studied. Recognising, for example, the variability of apparently standard work practices, the importance of individual perceptions (and the social processes influencing them), the role of established organizational routines, and the way in which these are shaped by, and shape, work practices would seem relevant in other contexts.

Thus, while it may, as the call for papers for this conference proposes, increasingly be "possible to create ubiquitous information[-rich] environments [that provide] new possibilities and opportunities for organizations to improve their productivity and effectiveness," the evidence presented suggests that these possibilities do not arise automatically or instantly. Moreover, perhaps especially in the context of current attempts to provide such environments through mobile devices, the realization of these possibilities appears to be subject to significant social influences. Even if some technical, architectural, and policy barriers to MICT use may be overcome in time, therefore, without clear evidence of unequivocal benefits, adoption will rely on users' beliefs about the value of ubiquitous information. It would appear, moreover, that such beliefs cannot be assumed to be universally positive. Whether this reflects the persistence of social influences that may be expected to diminish as the opportunities provided by MICTs achieve greater recognition, or represents an enduring alternative understanding of particular work practices, however, remains to be seen.

ACKNOWLEDGMENTS

Funding for this research was received from Fundação para a Ciência e Tecnologia, Lisbon, and St. Edmunds College, Cambridge. The support of Dr. David Nashel and all his staff at the VA Medical Center is gratefully acknowledged. This study received IRB approval (Protocol 00882).

REFERENCES

Atkinson, P. *The Clinical Experience*, London: Gower, 1981.

Bardram, J., Kjær, T. A. K., and Nielsen, C. "Supporting Local Mobility in Healthcare by Application Roaming among Heterogeneous Devices," in *Proceedings of the Fifth International Conference on Human Computer Interaction with Mobile Devices and Services (Mobile HCI'03)*, Berlin: Springer Verlag, 2003 (available online at http://www.daimi.au.dk/~bardram/docs/mobile_HCI.pdf).

Barret, J. R., Strayer, S. M., and Schubart, J. R. "Assessing Medical Residents' Usage and Perceived Needs for Personal Digital Assistants," *International Journal of Medical Informatics* (73:1), 2004, pp. 25-34..

Cox, J. "Wireless Woos Doctors: Networked Mobile Devices Help Improve Patient Care and Diagnosis," *Network World Fusion,* December 9, 2002 (available online at http://www.nwfusion.com/research/2002/1209sector.html).

Davis, G. B. "Anytime/Anyplace Computing and the Future of Knowledge Work," *Communications of the ACM* (45:12), 2002, pp. 67-73.

Esbjörnsson, M. "Mobile Reporting: Supporting Road Inspectors," in *Proceedings of Interact'01–IFIP TC 13 International Conference on Human-Computer Interaction*, Amsterdam: IOS Press, 200, pp. 747-748 (available online at http://www.tii.se/mobility/publications.htm).

Esbjörnsson, M., Juhlin, O., and Östergren, M. "Making Motor Bikers Come Together—Fast Moving Users and Mobile Ad Hoc Networks," in *Proceedings of 25th Information Systems Research Seminar in Scandinavia*, Bautahøj, Denmark, 2002.

Esbjörnsson, M., and Östergren, M. "Hocman: Supporting Mobile Group Collaboration," in *Extended Abstracts of the Conference on Human Factors in Computing Systems*, New York: ACM Press, 2002, pp. 838-839 (available online at http://www.tii.se/mobility/Files/Hocmanpaper.pdf).

Freeman, H. E., and Reeder, L. G. "Medical Sociology: A Review of the Literature," *American Sociological Review* (22:1), 1957, pp. 73-81.

Glaser, B. G., and Strauss, A. L. *The Discovery of Grounded Theory: Strategies for Qualitative Research*, New York: Aldine, 1967.

Grasso, B. C., and Genest, R. "Use of a Personal Digital Assistant in Reducing Medication Error Rates," *Psychiatric Services* (52:7), 2001, pp. 883-884, 886.

Holleran, K., Pappas, J., Lou, H., Rubalcaba, P., Lee, R., Clay, S., Cutone, J., Flammini, S., Kuperman, G., and Middleton, B. "Mobile Technology in a Clinical Setting," in *Proceedings of the AMIA Annual Fall Symposium*, 2003, p. 863.

Kelly, J. "Going Wireless," *Hospital Health Networks* (74:11), 2001, pp. 65-66, 68.

Martins, H. M. G., and Jones, M. R. "What's So Different about Mobile Information Communication Technologies (MICT) for Clinical Work Practices: A Review of Selected Pilot Studies," *Health Informatics Journal* (forthcoming).

McLeod, T. G., Ebbert, J. O., and Lymp, J. F. "Survey Assessment of Personal Digital Assistant Use among Trainees and Attending Physicians," *Journal of American Medical Association* (10:6), 2003, pp. 605-607.

Strauss, A. L., Shizuko, F., Suczek, B., and Wiener, C. *Social Organization of Medical Work*, New Brunswick, NJ: Transaction Publisher, 1997.

Zuboff, S. *In the Age of the Smart Machine*, New York: Basic Books, 1987.

ABOUT THE AUTHORS

Henrqiue M. G. Martins is a medical doctor and holds a Master's in Management Studies. He is finishing a Ph.D. at the University of Cambridge, working within the Information Management area on the topic "The Use of Mobile Information and Communication Technologies in Clinical Settings." His interests are the interface between the areas of medicine and management, namely mobile clinical information systems, as well as management education to medical students and junior doctors. He has presented work in several conferences and has some forthcoming publications in these areas. Henrique can be reached at hmgm2@cam.ac.uk.

Matthew R. Jones is a University Lecturer in Information Management in the Department of Engineering and the Judge Institute of Management at the University of Cambridge. His research interests concern the relationship between information systems and social and organizational change. He has published widely in this area, including several studies in the healthcare domain. Matthew can be reached at mrj10@cam.ac.uk.

10 BELIEFS ABOUT COMPUTING: Contrary Evidence from a Study of Mobile Computing Use among Criminal Justice Personnel

Andrea Tapia
Steve Sawyer
School of Information Sciences and Technology
Pennsylvania State University
University Park, PA U.S.A.

Abstract   *In this paper, we explore how technological determinism can act as a belief system. To do so, we draw on a multi-organization field trial of uses of mobile computing by criminal justice personnel. Our findings make clear that mobile computing does not yet meet operational needs. In high contrast, we find that the belief these mobile computing technologies will solve the preponderance of organizational, informational, and communication problems that beset contemporary criminal justice efforts is unchanged by the shortcomings of the current environment. While the devices, applications, and telecommunications network never worked as intended or expected, their introduction was met with acceptance, enthusiasm, and the deterministic belief that they would make work better. We go beyond the common explanation of learning from a field trial and explore the contradictions inherent to the findings through the lens of technological determinism. In doing this, we highlight several implications that deterministic beliefs have regarding organizational value of field trials and research conceptions regarding the introduction of new computing technologies.*

1   INTRODUCTION

Through this paper we make two contributions. We provide empirical evidence on workers' experiences with increased levels of connectivity while mobile. This serves as a means of gaining insight into what mobile computing might mean in organizational settings. Second, we examine the implications of technological determinism relative to introducing new computing by drawing on our empirical evidence.

These two contributions arise from a multi-organizational field trial of mobile workers in criminal justice organizations. We found that the mobile devices and wireless access never were successfully incorporated into the already complex network of information and communication technologies (ICT) used and often worn by each participating officer. This, however, did not diminish the belief that such mobile technologies will solve the preponderance of organizational, informational., and communication problems that plague criminal justice in the United States (e.g., Rudman et al. 2003).

In studying mobile access to computing resources in criminal justice, we note that at present most criminal justice personnel are unable to access valuable resources when mobile. Instead, they have learned to rely on the limited resources they bring with them and that dispatchers and dispatch centers can provide for most of their information needs. With the increased bandwidth available via third-generation (3G) wireless networks, however, it becomes theoretically possible to deliver data to criminal justice personnel wherever they are. This change with respect to access by users has potentially profound implications for organizational strategies in this space and can serve as a lens into the value and opportunities for ubiquitous access to information in other industries and other organizational sectors.

This paper continues in four parts. First, we provide a short overview of the institutional (criminal justice) and computing elements that together serve as the focus of this field trial. Second, we review the conceptual basis for our research, outline our research design, and explain our data collection methods and analysis. Third, we present our findings. In the fourth section, we build on concepts of technological determinism and cognitive dissonance to explore how the evidence from the trial contradicts the beliefs about the ICT held by the participants.

2   CRIMINAL JUSTICE, COMPUTING AND MOBILITY

There are at least three reasons why criminal justice is an appropriate domain for studying mobile work. First, the work of criminal justice officers is (and has been) highly mobile, knowledge intensive, and pervasive. Second, recently there is great interest in using ICT to better support these workers' information needs. Third, criminal justice has long been a focus of academic study and that provides us with an extensive reference literature (see Klockars and Mastrofski 1991; Manning 1977, 2003; Nunn 2001).

Current research findings provide contrary views regarding adoption and use of ICT in criminal justice (Allen and Wilson 2004; Brown 2001; Lin et al. 2004; Nabbubg 29931 Pica and Kakihara 2003). Some departments have well-structured programs to bring computing together with their work practices. These departments either select off-the-shelf systems or have vendors develop systems suitable to fulfill specified needs or roles. This stretches into wireless technologies as well (NASCIO 2003; Taylor et al.

1998). Evidence exists that the adoption of new ICT and uses of mobile technologies (beyond the nearly omnipresent radio communications suite in most cars and with most police officers in the United States) is accelerating in the United States (Nunn 2001). Partly this is in response to the country's increased attention to homeland security (Rudman et al. 2003); although efforts to improve policing through advanced computing predate this current attention (Northrup et al. 1995).

For the purposes of the trial on which we report, the 3G network is one of three elements of a technical infrastructure that underlies an integrated criminal justice information system. Beyond the mobile data network access, the technical infrastructure includes access to and use of Pennsylvania's justice network (JNET)[1] via mobile devices that the users have with them. This focal application was JNET, a secure Web-based portal connecting authorized users to a set of 23 federated criminal justice and law enforcement databases via a query-based interface. The JNET architecture is characterized by three elements. First, it acts as a portal to the criminal-justice-related databases of the Commonwealth of Pennsylvania (and the U.S. Federal government). Second, JNET is a secure system. Users are carefully vetted before they get access, their use is tied to specific roles, and these roles grant them varying levels of access to the range of data available. Third, JNET provides electronic messaging, e-mail and reporting functions. JNET has been operational since early 2000 and it supports thousands of queries each month (and use has grown by nearly 10 percent per month since inception).[2]

The third part of the technical infrastructure is the device being used to provide mobile access to JNET (and to the Internet more broadly). We studied both laptop and personal digital assistant (PDA) technology. These must have a special 3G modem card. Most police cruisers have an integrated laptop PC, making this seemingly a trivial effort (put in the wireless modem card, load on the security software, and use a browser). However, there were a number of operational and legal issues that made this a nontrivial effort. For example, many of the laptops are not equipped with space to load the modem card. Battery draw on police cruisers is substantial, and this further limits laptop use (and the 3G modem cards draw substantial power to run the antenna and maintain connectivity). Moreover, some cruiser's laptops have other software whose security and operational or licensing requirements preclud additional applications from being added.

For officers not in a cruiser, the mobile device must be carried on their person. Again, this is not a trivial effort considering that almost every square inch of the average police person's body is covered by some piece of gear. Moreover, the combination of current equipment (including communications, weapons, body armor, etc.) weighs nearly 25 pounds. This means that adding a mobile device is a significant decision.

---

[1]For more information about JNET, see www.pajnet.state.pa.us.

[2]JNET 2004 usage statistics, available online at http://www.pajnet.state.pa.us/pajnet/ site/default.asp. JNET is one of the earliest and most visible examples of a small and growing group of integrated criminal justice information systems that are a focus of homeland security efforts in the United States. Others include the Capital Area Wireless Integrated Network (CAPWIN, see www.capwin.org), the automated regional justice administration system (ARJIS, see www.arjis.org) and a fast-growing number of municipal efforts such as systems in Montgomery County, Maryland, and Los Angeles County, California.

3   FIELD TRIAL DESIGN, DATA COLLECTION, AND ANALYSIS

The research reported on here is guided by the belief that field trials of mobility provide insights into how work will be organized, governed, and supported by ubiquitous and information technology-intensive infrastructures (e.g., Green 2002; Lyytinen and Yoo 2002a).[3] Heeding Orlikowski and Iacono's (2001) call to better theorize the IT artifact, we conceptualize mobile access to JNET as a socio-technical ensemble. This view helps to highlight interdependencies among people (workers and managers) who use the ICT, the organizational rules and roles that guide both people's actions and the ICT's uses, and the situated nature of these relationships (that occur in specific times and places, in specific events).

A second source of guidance in designing the field trial comes from Jessup and Robey (2002), who suggest that studies of mobile computing in the workplace environment focus on individual, team and organizational levels of analysis. Lyytinen and Yoo (2002b) suggest an organizational perspective and within that focus on network externalities and coordination or control uses as drivers of these changes. Sawyer, et. al. (2003) suggest an institutional perspective and focus on identifying value and negotiating governance (control) as central issues.

The design of our field trial focused on collecting data at and across three levels of analysis. At the *technical* level, we focused on the 3G network's coverage, access, connectivity, and security, uses of applications (particularly JNET), and device operations. At the *individual* level, we focused on the adoption and uses of the devices and JNET relative to officers' work processes and relevant tasks changed. At the *organizational* level,[4] we focused on structural and governance changes relative to the tasks and business processes such as the role of dispatch, operational control, and inter-organizational interactions and, in doing so, leverage the extensive knowledge of policing and partially control for institutional factors.

The field trial was designed as a structured intervention: mobile workers were provided with a mobile device and secure access to the public 3G network. For pragmatic reasons, this was done in two phases. The first phase lasted 3 months, included 5 participants and focused on laptop usage. The second phase began directly after the completion of the first phase, involved 13 participants, lasted 3 months, and focused on personal digital assistant (PDA) usage. Participants in both trials were police

---

[3]Lyytinen and Yoo (2002b) note the terms mobile, ubiquitous, and pervasive are too often used interchangeably with respect to computing. They argue that mobility refers to devices that are mobile, but not embedded. Pervasive devices are embedded, but not always mobile. Ubiquitous devices are both mobile and embedded. A ubiquitous device is commonplace, portable, and nearly invisible. A pervasive device is one that is commonplace, but not very portable. In the case of the field trial we report on here, officers currently have mobile devices (such as radios and in-cruiser computers) and the interest was in increasing their embeddedness. To do this, we focused on leveraging the pervasive value of JNET by making it accessible from mobile computers.

[4]The organizational level of analysis is drawn from the criminal justice institutional field.

and other criminal justice officers from three organizations (one county-level and two local-level) located within one U.S. county.

We used seven forms of data collection. First, we did interviews of all users at the beginning and end of each trial period. Second, we led focus groups of users following the trials. These were voluntary, and only two participants did not participate (for schedule reasons). Third, all users completed a 1-week time diary of work behavior during the field trial. Fourth, members of the research team did ride-alongs. Fifth, we gathered documents during all interviews, observations, and visits (and did extensive Web and library research to support the field work). Sixth, we engaged in informal weekly interactions (via phone, e-mail, and in person). Finally, we gathered data about laptop uses, wireless data transmission, and JNET usage via unobtrusive means (such browser logs, server logs, and telecom activity logs). Data from the first six sources were either transcribed into digital format or collected at the source in digital format. Data from the usage logs came in digital format.

4 FINDINGS

In the first part of this section, we summarize six findings drawn from the data on the field trial (see Table 1).

Table 1. Findings from the Field Trial of 3G Mobile Access to JNET

Level	Finding
Technical	1. Current ICT infrastructure is unable to support production needs at this time
Technical	2. Users used their mobile devices other than expected
Individual	3. Value of mobile access to criminal justice work is certainty of access
Individual	4. Officers need access for smaller percentage of their work time than expected
Organizational	5. Mobile access does not replace the need for central coordination or dispatch.
Cross-level	6. There is minimal support for a complex and often chaotic ICT infrastructure

4.1 Current ICT Infrastructure Is Unable to Support Production Needs at this Time

The officer in this trial had to grapple with the constraints of secure access, limited coverage, and unstable access to the 3G wireless network. For example, the "always on" possibility that 3G networks provide (due to their use of packet-based, Internet protocol, spread-spectrum transmission) was never realized because of the mandated constraints of JNET application security. The (required) two-factor login was both difficult to follow and time-consuming to initiate. The virtual private network (VPN) would shut down if the bandwidth fell below a certain point (and this meant users had to re-authenticate). Moreover, JNET requires periodic validation of users and will shut down if this is not done. Trial participants were highly conscious of security of information and they valued the steps taken by JNET to keep information secure during the field trial even though it added several steps to the logon process.

A common problem with this trial was the lack of 3G coverage within the rural areas that the trial covered. Coverage maps provided by the vendor indicated more than 70 percent of the area was covered. In practice, coverage was far less than expected. Furthermore, the life of the PDA battery was not sufficient to maintain connection to the 3G network over long periods and this led trial participants to stop using their PDAs for mobile access.

4.2 Users Used Their Mobile Devices Other than Expected

While officers did not use the wireless network to the degree expected, they made great use of their mobile devices. Officers began to use the PDAs for scheduling, contacts, note-taking, and a host of other tasks. As Manning (2003) notes, criminal justice officers are willing to take on new tools and eager to adapt them to their needs. But criminal justice officers are not willing to compromise their (or anyone else's) safety if the device or application does not work. Further, they are unwilling to tinker with applications that are used infrequently. We note that JNET applications, which are very useful for deskbound workers, are neither fast enough nor focused on the needs of mobile workers, making it difficult for them to use by themselves in active incidents. The officers did not stop using JNET; they just stopped accessing JNET via mobile devices.

4.3 Value of Mobile Access to Criminal Justice Work Is Certainty of Access

The measure of value is not volume or frequency of use for these officers. Their measure is certainty of access when needed. In the same way that a gun is important to have (even if 97 percent of all officers never fire their side-arm as part of their job), access to JNET (and more specifically photos) is highly valued (officers must be certain that it will work when they "draw it from their holster"). The value is driven in great part by the reliability of their mobile connectivity (otherwise it is just as likely that the officer will return to their fixed office to access this data). These officers' work worlds revolve around geographies of local communities, and they live balancing routine with emergency. A quiet drive around their beat can be shattered by a horrific traffic accident or domestic disturbance, and this puts their life at risk. In these moments of crisis, the officer cannot doubt that the weapon will function as expected. In that same moment, even if the mobile technology has not been used for weeks, the offier must be certain that device will work on cue and as expected. We learned that connection reliability and incident management is more important to these officers than are data download speed.

4.4 Officers Need Access for a Smaller Percentage of Their Work Time than Expected

Trial participants are not always engaged in tasks that require mobile access to JNET. The value of mobile access seems to be tied to particular aspects of their work. Mobile access and JNET use seems important to only certain tasks and events in the work of our participants. For example, in the 8-hour shifts we observed through ride-alongs, officers typically were engaged in information seeking tasks for less then 15 percent of the total shift time. Self-reported time diaries corroborate that information-seeking activities are a small but very critical aspect of the police officer's work.

4.5 Mobile Access Does Not Replace the Need for Central Coordination or Dispatch

Wireless communication devices may have a role in facilitating communications between criminal justice personnel, but in this case they do not reduce the number of people involved in the process of completing any task, change the role that any person currently plays, nor reduce the number of steps in any process. The real implication for wireless technology is using the current people and processes—but allowing information to flow more quickly from repositories to people, and from person to person, at very important critical moments. Mobile JNET is not cost saving—but it is likely to be life saving.

4.6 There Is Minimal Support for a Complex and Often Chaotic ICT Infrastructure

Criminal justice organizations have limited ICT support and diverse ICT infrastructures. The officers in our trial relied chiefly on themselves and on each other to learn to use and troubleshoot the devices. This seems to be the way they have learned and supported all of their ICT. Each of the three units participating in the trial had different IT infrastructures and often these were supported through a of variety contracts with different third party vendors.

5   IMPLICATIONS AND ISSUES WITH
THE MYTHOLOGY OF UBIQUITY

In the last week of the field trial, no officers attempted to log on from a mobile device to the 3G network or to access JNET from a mobile device. In our post-trial focus groups and debriefing, officers reported that they were pleased to have participated. Many spoke highly of their experiences with the trial sponsors and research staff, praised the idea, the potential, and the value of JNET. This exuberance seemed an odd contrast to the record of use. Moreover, three of the officers rarely, if ever, used their mobile access (once or perhaps twice a shift). Three others used it for several hours a shift at their most engaged point. But even the most aggressive users had come to closure on the field trial before the trial had come to an end.

How can we reconcile their behaviors to these espoused beliefs? Trial participants welcomed the mobile devices and advanced ICT in general, but they did not use the devices or service to any great extent. Trial participants are hopeful about the roles that mobile devices and wireless access can play in making their work life safer and also better enable them to perform their duties, but they are critical of the operation of these devices and the services. The officers in our trial took a long-term perspective: they were willing to wait until something is proven to work before taking it on as part of their daily routine. Despite the connection, battery, and logon problems, the officers continued to see the potential for these mobile devices as creating greater efficiency, better communication, and added safety.

In this final section, of the paper we reflect on the meanings and implications of these findings. In Table 2 we illustrate that in several areas the officers held to a set of beliefs concerning this new ICT despite evidence contrary to what they expected. For example, officers believed that the mobile access to JNET via 3G wireless networks would offer increased efficiency, would make their jobs easier, would reduce the workload of the dispatch personnel, and would increase criminal justice effectiveness in general. However, the mobile devices never functioned as promised and there was never any evidence they would. Even at the end the trial period, officers held fast to the belief that the ICT would solve problems. This claim was even more ironic and more powerful because each of the participating officers was able to relate tales of failed computing interventions from previous experiences. Several officers discussed failed report-writing software, poor in-vehicle devices, limited technical support, and other failures in policing.

Through this trial, we expected that the integration of mobile computing would be relatively seamless. Officers were using laptops in their cars and cruisers. However, we found that the officers made use of a very small range of laptop functionality and onboard applications (relying primarily on voice interactions with central dispatch instead).

We anticipated that the mobile devices and 3G network would function with little support needed by us. We found that the operational environment was much more demanding, the officers were much harder on the equipment, and the coverage far less than we expected. So, our expectation that there would be little or no need for organizational and technical support was woefully optimistic. In phase two of the trial, we added technical support (essentially 1.5 hours per person per week) and it was not

Table 2. Myths of Ubiquity

	Myth	*Evidence*
Integration of new devices	Seamless	Poor
Function of devices	Perfectly	Poorly
Function of third generation wireless network	Well	Poorly
Need for organizational and technical support	Little need	Highly needed
Role of dispatch	Dispatch less central	No change
Criminal justice	Catch more "bad guys" and close more cases (efficient and effective)	No change
Instances used	High/often/regularly	Rarely

enough. We learned that there is little ongoing organizational-level technical support for the small police departments in our field trial. This meant that for us to get our applications and devices operational, we often had to first resolve the existing backlog of technical issues (with e-mail, applications, access, and hardware breakdowns). This, in turn, was a complicated effort because it required us to negotiate across a host of outsourced IT units and internal IT people working (with or) for a range of state, county, and local governments.

We expected that the use of mobile 3G access to JNET would alter the ways in which officers interacted with dispatch (less reliance) and more interaction with other units and personnel (because it was easier to share information). We saw no change across the 7 months of our study. Dispatch remained the undisputed center of inter-organizational interaction and there were no discernable changes in the number or structure of officer-to-officer interactions.

One aspect of the study was to focus on the officer's efficiency (measured in terms of incidents and cases that were closed). We expected that greater access to information would improve efficiency. However, this was not supported. Further, we expected that use of the mobile access to JNET would become regular, common, and often. As we noted above, use was sporadic, tied to tasks that account for about 15 percent of the officer's field work, and inhibited by a host of recurring operational shortcomings.

5.1 Technical Determinism and Mythic Conceptualizations

One explanation for these contradictory findings is technological determinism. It seems that the ICT ensemble represented here by 3G wireless-enabled mobile devices accessing JNET is viewed by organizational members through the lens of technological determinism.[5] Organizational members believed that mobile access to JNET would improve their work, their organizations, and their lives. Participants viewed the results with the acceptance that current problems are a result of a temporary setback (in the case of negative findings), enthusiasm (in the case of positive findings), and the deterministic belief (seemingly independent of the findings) that they would eliminate the problems uncovered here in future trials and deployments.

This deterministic perspective stands in contrast to the evidence drawn from the trial. This contrast leads us to consider the concept of technological determinism as a belief (and not solely a theory). Technological determinism is a philosophical stance about both technology and the human condition. Technological determinists (Adorno and Horkheimer 1944; Ellul 1964; Ferkiss 1974; Heidegger 1977; Marcuse 1941) argue that technology itself is capable of restructuring the social world in its own image. These determinists tend to have polarized responses to technology in that they find technology's effect as either socially liberating or socially oppressive. Technological change is viewed as both a necessary and a sufficient condition determining all other social change. (McGinn 1991, p. 74). In organizational terms, the social system of an organization is compelled to mold itself to the technology. In other words, changes in the technical system of an organization translate directly into changes in organizational structure or functioning (Adler 1987; Khandwalla 1974; Thompson 1967; Woodward 1965).

Winner (1986), in his famous work "Do Artifacts Have Politics?," rejected the technological determinist's framework and claimed that technologies should be judged not only for their utilitarian effects on organizational efficiency, but perhaps more importantly for the symbolic ways in which they embody power and authority. Thomas argued in his work, *What Machines Can't Do*, that social and technical systems are jointly responsible for organizational structuring and change and that the relationships among technology and organization are mediated by the exercise of power (1994, p. 5).

This development in the social study of technology opened the doors to the study of technology in a cultural light. Several authors have begun to discuss the emotional framing of technology by modern Western society (Alexander 1992; Davis 1998; Grosso 1995; Postman 1992; Rozak 1994; Tenner 1996). They propose that through the interplay between technology and culture, technology is interpreted and framed as either the savior or the destroyer of humanity.

Alexander (1992, p. 40) goes further, arguing that as an object is made sacred by being sealed off from the profane world, gaining access to its power becomes a problem in itself. Priests emerge as intermediaries between the divinity (computer) and the laity. A technological expert class is created. In contemporary information systems literature, Kaarst-Brown and Robey (1999) build on this mysticism and the creation of a technological expert class. They draw on the metaphor of magic using dragons and wizards to produce cultural insights for IT management. In this paper, we focus on myth as an imaginative story using powerful symbols and colorful images to help people

---

[5]For this study, this view is essentially positive, although this does not need to be the case. For example, Kling (1980) identifies that both utopian and dystopian views of technology are powerful lenses that provide, at best, a partial understanding of the roles of computing in organizations.

understand concepts either too complicated or too difficult to express in words. Myths may have originated in truth or may continue to hold a kernel of truth as they are told, but what most clearly defines them are their exaggeration, fanciful elaboration, and interpretation of that kernel. We suggest that modern myths are passed from person to person through the telling of stories through a variety of media. These stories serve to build aspects of our wider American culture, as well as smaller, organizational cultures, and may prompt individuals to behave in new, culturally specific ways.

Seen this way, technological determinism is mythic. This elevation of a relatively simple theory to become a myth is both subtle and profound. In mythic terms, the value of ICTs is framed as a (if not the) means forward, out of the crises and complexities of contemporary policing. Manning (2003) grapples with this, noting on one hand the pragmatic pro-orientation toward ICT: "Each information technology at first competes for space, time and legitimacy with other known means and is judged in policing by somewhat changing pragmatic, often nontechnical values" (p. 133). In contrast, though: "There is little evidence that thirty years of funding technological innovations has produced much change in police practice or effectiveness" (p. 134).

At the trial's end, then, do we interpret the limited success as a basis for the next trial's grand improvements, or do we confront the starkness that increasingly ubiquitous computing (at least in criminal justice) is not likely to bring significant value? If the former is true, then our first six findings are where the value lies. If the latter is true, what evidence is required to change one's beliefs from focusing on the first? What happens if the next trial also fails?

5.2 Cognitive Dissonance in Reconciling Evidence and Belief

How can we reconcile the evidence with the belief? Festinger et al. (1956) argue that when an individual holds a strong conviction and is faced with unequivocal and undeniable evidence, their belief was wrong: "The individual will frequently emerge, not only unshaken, but even more convinced of the truth of his beliefs than ever before. Indeed, he may even show a new fervor about convincing and converting other people to his view" (p. 3). For Festinger et al., the moment of realization that a deeply held conviction was wrong creates a sense of cognitive dissonance in the mind of the believer.

All of the officers in this study experienced this form of cognitive dissonance in that their beliefs of the potential of mobile access to JNET to change their lives were challenged. It seems, though, that they emerged unscathed, holding fast to their previously strong beliefs of technological determinism.[6] Their dissonance was mediated by the fact that in the case of all myths, there usually is a kernel of truth. Most officers

---

[6]It may be that readers of this paper struggle with this also. Is this paper reporting on a "failed" field trial or is it reporting on a failed premise? It is easier to respond to the former concern: the six findings provide substantial guidance on what to do next, and that is clearly not a sign of a failure.

knew of an instance, had heard a rumor, or had read an article that declared the success of an implementation of a technology into policing that had met with unprecedented workplace change, efficiency and success. This one instance was strong enough that it provided a base on which these officers could anchor their beliefs concerning the power and potential of technology. Despite the failure of several trials and several devices in their own organization, they believed that somewhere out there, something was working well for someone.

These officers dealt with their cognitive dissonance by making claims that the timing was not quite right, that if the wireless providers were given a bit more time to improve their rural networks, the coverage would be improved and the devices would transform into the desired object. They also claimed that perhaps the laptop or PDA was not "the one" device that would transform their jobs, that device was coming.

5.3 The Blinding Power of Technological Determinism

Thinking about mobility leads us to more closely examine the deterministic theme running through these organizations concerning ICT. There are at least three pragmatic consequences that arise from (the seemingly unsupportable) confidence in the future values of ICT. First, that organizational decision-makers, users, and technology evaluators will likely continue to seek ICTs that will provide them the simple path forward. Second, these same people will have trouble making sense of evidence drawn from failed attempts to implement and use ICTs (since the direct effects model is unlikely to be empirically supported). The inability to understand this data is driven by the unsound basis of direct effects thinking, not by the measurements taken or instruments used to gather evidence (e.g., Sawyer et al. 2003). A third consequence is that the cognitive dissonance arising from the seemingly unsupportable confidence in technological determinism suggests that these officers are willing, if not eager, to take on additional trials. This further suggests that proactive systems design approaches are likely to lead to useful applications and, in doing so, the interactions are likely to reinforce the belief that mobile, ubiquitous computing is possible. This seemingly self-replenishing reservoir of good will towards working toward a better technological infrastructure provides technology developers, scholars, and organizational leaders the opportunities to continue experimenting (and studying) new devices, access methods, and services. It is not clear to us what experiences with a trial might drain this reservoir.

Brooks (1987) noted, in the context of automating software development, that there is no silver bullet. No one seems to think there is a silver bullet for uses of ICT in criminal justice. It may be that they think the better response is to fire more bullets. If technological determinism is a belief—and not just a theory—then our analysis suggests that efforts such as the work being done in criminal justice to engage pervasive and ubiquitous computing may provide an empirical opportunity to understand the consequences.

REFERENCES

Adler, P. (Ed.). *Technology and the Future of Work*, New York: Oxford University Press, 1992.

Adorno, T., and Horkheimer, M. "The Culture Industry: Enlightenment as Mass Deception," in *Dialectic of Enlightenment*, 1944.

Alexander, J. "The Promise of a Cultural Sociology: Technological Discourse and the Sacred and Profane Information Machine," in *Theory of Culture*, R. M. Smelser (Ed.), Berkeley, CA: University of California Press, 1992, pp. 293-323.

Allen, D., and Wilson, T. "Action, Interaction and the Role of Ambiguity in the Introduction of Mobile Information Systems in a UK Police Force," in *Proceedings of the IFIP TC8 Working Conference on Mobile Information Systems*, September 15-17, 2004, pp. 15-36.

Brooks, F. "No Silver Bullet: Essence and Accidents of Software Engineering," *Computer* (4:1), 1987, pp. 10-19.

Brown, M. "The Benefits and Costs of Information Technology Innovations: An Empirical Assessment of a Local Government Agency," *Public Performance & Management Review* (24:4), 2001, pp. 351-366.

Davis, E. *Techgnosis*, New York: Random House, 1998.

Ellul, J. *The Technological Society*, New York: Alfred A. Knopf, 1965.

Ferkiss, V. *Technological Man: The Myth and the Reality*, New York: George Brazilier, 1969.

Festinger, L., Riecken, H., and Schachter, S. *When Prophecy Fails*, Minneapolis, MN: University of Minnesota Press, 1956.

Green, N. "On the Move: Technology, Mobility, and the Mediation of Social Time and Space," *The Information Society* (18:4), 2002, pp. 135-152.

Grosso, M. *The Millennium Myth*, Wheaton, IL: Theosophical Publishing Press, 1995.

Heidegger, M. *The Question Concerning Technology*, New York: Harper and Row, 1977.

Jessup, L., and Robey, D. "The Relevance of Social Issues in Ubiquitous Computing Environments," *Communications of the ACM* (45:12), 2002, pp. 88-91.

Kaarst-Brown, M. L., and Robey. D "More on Myth, Magic and Metaphor: Cultural Insights into the Management of Information Technology in Organizations," *Information, Technology and People* (12:2), 1999.

Khandwalla, P. N. "Mass Output Orientation of Operations Technology and Organizational Structure," *Administrative Science Quarterly* (19), 1974, pp. 144-156.

Kling, R. "Social Analysis of Computing: Theoretical Perspectives in Recent Empirical Research," *ACM Computing Surveys* (12:1), 1980, pp. 61-110.

Lin, C., Hu, P. J-H., and Chen, H. "Technology Implementation Management in Law Enforcement," *Social Science Computer Review* (22:1), 2004, pp. 24.

Lyytinen, K., and Yoo, Y. "Issues and Challenges in Ubiquitous Computing: Introduction," *Communications of the ACM* (45:1), 2002a, pp. 62-65.

Lyytinen, K., and Yoo, Y. "The Next Wave of Nomadic Computing," *Information Systems Research* (13:4), 2002b, pp. 377-388.

Manning, P. *Police Work: The Social Organization of Policing*, Prospect Heights, IL: Waveland Publishing, 1977.

Manning, P. *Policing Contingencies*, Chicago: University of Chicago Press, 2003.

Marcuse, H. "Social Science Implications of Modern Technology," *Studies in Philosophy and Social Sciences* (9:3), 1941, p. 425

McGinn, R. *Science, Technology and Society*, Englewood Cliffs, NJ: Prentice Hall, 1941.

NASCIO. "Concept for Operations for Integrated Justice Information Sharing Version 1.0," National Association of State Chief Information Officers, July 2003 (available online at https://www.nascio.org/publications/index.cfm).

Northrup, A., Kraemer, K., and King, J. "Police Use and Computers," *Journal of Criminal Justice* (23:3), 1995, pp. 259-275.

Nunn, S. "Police Information Technology: Assessing the Effects of Computerization on Urban Police Functions," *Public Administration Review* (61:2), 2001, pp. 221-234.

Orlikowski, W., and Iacono, S. "Desperately Seeking the 'IT' in IT Research—A Call to Theorizing the IT Artifact," *Information Systems Research* (12:2), 2001, pp. 121-124.

Pica, D., and Kakihara, M. "The Duality of Mobility: Designing Fluid Organizations through Stable Interaction," in *Proceedings of the 11ᵗʰ European Conference on Information Systems*, C. Ciborra, R. Mercurio, M. DeMarco, and O. Hanseth, Naples, Italy, June 19-21, June 2003, pp. 259-275.

Postman, N. *Technopoly*, New York: Vintage Books, 1992.

Rozak, T. *The Cult of Information*, Berkley, CA: University of California Press, 1994.

Rudman, W., Clarke, R., and Metzel, J. "Emergency Responders: Drastically Underfunded, Dangerously Unprepared," Report of an Independent Task Force Sponsored by the Council on Foreign Relations, July 29, 2003 (available online at http://www.cfr.org/pdf/ Responders_TF.pdf).

Sawyer, S., Allen, J., and Lee, H. "Broadband and Mobile Opportunities: A Sociotechnical Perspective," *Journal of Information Technology* (18:2), 2003, pp. 31-50.

Taylor, M., Epper, R., and Tolman, T. *Wireless Communications and Interoperability among State and Local Law Enforcement Agencies*, Report 168945, National Criminal Justice Institute, Washington, DC, 1998.

Thompson, J. *Organizations in Action*, New York: McGraw-Hill, 1967.

Thomas, R. J. *What Machines Can't Do*, Los Angeles: University of California Press, 1994.

Winner, L. "Do Artifacts Have Politics?," *The Whale and the Reactor: A Search for Limits in an Age of High Technology*, Chicago: University of Chicago Press, 1986, pp. 19-39.

Woodward, J. *Industrial Organizations: Theory and Practice*, London: Oxford University Press, 1965.

ABOUT THE AUTHORS

Steve Sawyer is a founding member and associate professor at the Pennsylvania State University's School of Information Sciences and Technology. Steve holds affiliate appointments in Management and Organizations; Labor Studies and Industrial Relations; and the Science, Technology and Society. He does social and organizational informatics research with a particular focus on people working together using information and communication technologies. Steve can be reached at sawyer@ist.psu.edu.

Andrea Hoplight Tapia is an assistant professor of Information Sciences and Technology at the Pennsylvania State University. Prior to her arrival at Penn State, Andrea completed a National Science Foundation funded post-doctoral fellowship at the University of Arizona entitled "Universities in the Information Age." Her Ph.D. is in the area of Sociology and focuses on the study of technology, culture, and workplace organizations. Her most recent work examines the nature of computer-centered, high-tech industry. She is particularly interested in the how the workplace and employer-employee relations change when in a high-tech environment. At the core of her research is her interest in the social values attributed to technology and the power structures that arise within organizations due to the manipulation and use of those techno-values, in other words, techno-social capital. Andrea can be reached by e-mail at atapia@ist.psu.edu.

11 ASSESSING THE MOBILE–STATIONARY DIVIDE IN UBIQUITOUS TRANSPORT SYSTEMS

Magnus Andersson
Rikard Lindgren
Ola Henfridsson
Telematics Group
Viktoria Institute
Göteborg, Sweden

Abstract   *Many transport organizations seek to develop seamlessly integrated computing environments. A central problem in attempts to realize such **ubiquitous transport systems** is the divide that exists between stationary transport management systems and mobile applications such as embedded vehicle sensor networks and in-vehicle services for message handling. Originating from different innovation regimes, these technologies are heterogeneous in that they rely on different technological platforms and knowledge bases, as well as the institutionalized settings from which they have emerged. This paper assesses how the mobile–stationary divide plays out in practical efforts to develop ubiquitous transport systems in road haulage firms. This assessment is conducted through a multiple-case study that identifies socio-technical challenges associated with this divide. Building on this assessment, the paper contributes a set of implications for enterprise-wide ubiquitous computing environments where coordination of diverse sets of mobile units is central to organizational performance. On a general level, these implications are important for any organization attempting to integrate mobile and stationary information systems.*

1   INTRODUCTION

Facilitated by improved mobile and wireless communication services and continuing miniaturization of computing devices, the emergence of ubiquitous computing has enabled distributed computing capabilities with which highly mobile organizations can address core information processing problems and opportunities (Lyytinen and Yoo 2002; March et al. 2000). In particular, the promises of ubiquitous computing technologies are attractive to organizations in which coordination of diverse sets of mobile units is central to organizational performance.

As an example of such organizations, the typical road haulage firm coordinates a workforce mainly consisting of drivers who are geographically distributed and constantly moving, providing timely pickup and delivery of goods. Plagued by low margins and intensive competition, road haulage firms have implemented a wide variety of distributed IT support tools to conduct their day-to-day business (Lindgren and Henfridsson 2003). Such IT support includes services that offer dispatchers overviews of their mobile resources by positioning individual trucks, drivers route calculation services to minimize time and fuel expenditures of assignments, and managers vehicle performance recording services are maintained for accurately following the mobile workflow (see Akinci et al. 2003; Giannopoulos 2004; Roy 2001).

While such technology investments promise to redefine the ways business can be organized and conducted, evident in these investments is also the desire to integrate people and the systems they use. In Andersson and Lindgren (under review) the term ubiquitous transport systems (UTS) is used to discuss seamlessly integrated computing environments applicable to the transport industry. Attempting to understand infrastructure capabilities of such distributed and heterogeneous computing environments (see March et al. 2000), they present typical service requirements in the Swedish road haulage sector. In the quest of a "total solution" to the service requirements of road haulage firms, however, a central problem is the mobile–stationary divide. The mobile–stationary divide refers to the set of socio-technical problems associated with the integration of stationary office systems (transport order and cargo planning systems) and mobile applications (embedded vehicle sensor networks and in-vehicle telecommunication services for order management and message handling).

Overcoming the mobile–stationary divide is vital for transport organizations seeking to interconnect various technological, social, and organizational elements into an assemblage that enables physical and social mobility of computing and communication services (see Lyytinen and Yoo 2002). Realizing the vision of UTS involves dwelling with the multitude of applications emerging in the road haulage business. Indeed, as noted in the literature, a significant challenge is to create, integrate, and maintain heterogeneous computing resources as effective components of well-functioning architectures (Lyytinen and Yoo 2002; Sambamurthy and Zmud 2000). An important first step is thus to explore organizational efforts to develop integrated computational solutions (involving heterogeneous, geographically distributed computing resources) spanning far beyond the stationary parts of transport organizations.

In this paper, we present a multiple-case study that assesses the mobile–stationary divide in practical efforts to implement UTS in road haulage firms. The study is part of an ongoing action research project (see Baskerville and Wood-Harper 1996) involving academics at the Viktoria Institute, road haulage industry representatives, a number of road haulage firms, and system vendors. Contributing to the early stage of the ubiquitous computing research tradition in the field of information systems, this paper reports an assessment of organizational attempts to bridge the mobile–stationary divide.

Discussing socio-technical challenges associated with such attempts, the paper contributes a set of implications for enterprise-wide ubiquitous computing environments where coordination of diverse sets of mobile units is central to organizational performance.

2 THE MOBILE–STATIONARY DIVIDE IN UBIQUITOUS TRANSPORT SYSTEMS

A ubiquitous computing environment can be described as "a heterogeneous assemblage of interconnected technological and organizational elements, which enables the physical and social mobility of computing and communication services between organizational actors both within and across organizational borders" (Lyytinen and Yoo 2002, p. 378). One central issue in developing and using ubiquitous computing environments in organizations is to handle its inherent heterogeneity. Manifested in new requirements on the construction of ubiquitous enterprise architectures (Lyytinen and Yoo 2002), the heterogeneity of such architectures typically follows from the challenges surrounding attempts to interconnect technologies belonging to different innovation regimes. Indeed, innovation regimes, such as technological platforms and knowledge bases, as well as institutionalized settings in which technological innovations emerge (Godoe 2000), are vital in understanding and handling heterogeneity.

In utilizing technologies originating from different innovation regimes, organizations face organizational, social, and technological challenges. At the organizational level, there are challenges related to the managerial rationale for designing and evolving their IT activities in response to the imperatives of changing business and technological environments that need to be tackled (Sambamurthy and Zmud 2000). Indeed, the organizing logic must be adapted to the heterogeneous assemblage of interconnected social and technical elements of ubiquitous computing environments. Moreover, in weaving together technologies originating from different innovation regimes, ubiquitous computing environments promise to involve redefinitions of social action as well as new social behavior (Jessup and Robey 2002). In particular, the seamlessness sought over multiple contexts not only triggers such social changes but it also occasions new socio-technical design challenges (Henfridsson and Lindgren 2005). Finally, there exist a number of technical challenges associated with heterogeneous and distributed computing environments (Lyytinen and Yoo 2002; March et al. 2000). For example, realizing interoperability between different innovation regimes typically requires software components that can work as gateways between different standard sets (Hanseth 2001).

In the transport industry, two broad categories of innovation regimes can be distinguished (see Andersson and Lindgren, in review). The first regime relates to the mobile side of transport organizations, that is, the set of technologies and corresponding knowledge bases surrounding the vehicles and their drivers in daily work practice. These technologies include both vehicular systems (e.g., embedded vehicle sensor systems) and driver-centric computing systems (e.g., in-vehicle services for order management and message handling). The second regime relates to the stationary side of transport organizations, that is, the set of office systems and corresponding knowledge bases associated with controlling and coordinating transport assignments and mobile resources. These technologies include systems for transport order management and cargo planning, resource coordination, and route calculation.

Belonging to different innovation regimes, the alignment of mobile and stationary technologies in transport organizations is difficult to achieve. While such integration is central to realizing the vision of UTS (as seamlessly integrated computing environments applicable to the transport industry), the divide existing between these innovation regimes also appears in their deployment in user organizations. In line with Andersson and Lindgren, we here refer to this divide as the mobile–stationary divide, highlighting the set of organizational, social, and technical problems related to integration of stationary office information systems and mobile applications. Viewing this literature review as a backdrop and context for the research problem, we here present a multiple-case study of the ways in which the mobile–stationary divide plays out in practical attempts to realize the vision of UTS. Whereas this divide and its associated challenges can be traced in the literature, there exist few, if any, studies that seek to explore these and their mutual interdependencies in greater depth.

3   RESEARCH METHOD

3.1 Research Design and Sites

The research presented here is part of an ongoing action research project (see Baskerville and Wood-Harper 1996) called "Value-Creating IT Support for Road Haulage Firms" in which researchers from the Viktoria Institute, system vendors, and road haulage representatives collaborate. Our previous work reports socio-technical problems related to the capability of the underlying technical infrastructures to support services required in road haulage firms (Andersson and Lindgren, in review). This paper assesses the nature of the mobile–stationary divide through a multiple-case study (Yin 1994), covering organizations that try to address issues pertaining to this divide. We used our prior study as input for case selection (applicability to the research themes), purpose (elaboration of early results), and analysis (themes used to structure analysis of new data).

In our research design, we were specifically interested in cases where attempts to integrate mobile and stationary systems were evident. Finding such cases in the Swedish transport context has proven to be a challenging task, due to the low market penetration of technology specifically designed for road haulage. In order to acquire a sample of such cases, we approached six major system vendors actively involved in the action research project for recommendations of user organizations of interest. Guided by our action research agenda, the proposed cases were then evaluated using the service requirements previously reported on and a set of criteria. From this process, six cases were selected to be included in the study (see Table 1).

Table 1. Case Overview

| Organization | Size | Ownership | Systems | | Transports |
			Mobile	Stationary	
A	325	Independent	CoDriver	SAdata	Bulk, foods, oil, goods
B	300	Member owned	Barkfors	TDXlog	Goods
C	100	Independent	Dynafleet	Transport 2000	Foods, goods
D	40	Independent	FAS	In-house system	Foods, goods
E	300	Member owned	Hogia Innovation	Hogia Mobilast	Waste, foods
F	11	Independent	Transics	TUF 2000	Chemicals

3.2 Data Collection and Analysis

This study includes six data sources. These are interviews with system users, documents produced by users in daily practice, notes from user observations, system vendor documentation, notes from vendor interviews, and observation notes from vendor demonstrations. To cover experiences of technology use, where applicable, we interviewed individuals involved in three different levels of work (dispatchers, drivers, and managers) in each of the six organizations, focusing on socio-technical impacts. Questions concerned the user's experience of interaction with the technology and social effects on work practice. The resulting 15 semi-structured interviews, lasting between 1 and 2 hours, were recorded and later transcribed. While these interviews provide the bulk of the empirical data, supplementary data was also gathered. Where needed to resolve ambiguity emerging in these interviews, short observations of systems in use were made. For example, a driver using an in-vehicle order management system would be observed and field notes taken. Further information includes documents from vendors and user organizations describing systems and intended use.

As previously mentioned, early results from the same project were used to direct our attention on emerging themes and issues. While not explicitly following the grounded theory approach (Strauss and Corbin 1990), the overall process exhibits similarities in that the initial research was conducted in an open-ended manner, while this subsequent stage is more directly concerned with emerging themes from the initial stage.

The analysis was performed iteratively and concepts were discovered, defined, and refined. Statements formed candidate concepts, verified or modified by similar occurrences elsewhere in the data. When all empirical data had been analyzed in this fashion, a second iteration was performed, this time to test the relations between the candidates and further refine them. From this process, a set of concepts emerged. This set was compared to the prior three categories to test the viability both of the prior categories themselves and of the newly formed set of concepts. Finally, the categories and the concepts were used to elicit a number of socio-technical challenges associated with practical efforts to overcome the mobile–stationary divide.

4   FINDINGS

On the basis of our multiple-case study, this section outlines key categories and concepts related to the mobile–stationary divide. In addition, it presents socio-technical challenges surrounding attempts to realize UTS in the six investigated road haulage firms. Table 2 summarizes these findings and associates each concept with the case organizations in which they were evident.

Table 2.   Mobile–Stationary Divide: Categories, Concepts, and Socio-Technical Challenges

Categories	Concepts	Socio-Technical Challenges
Mobile resource evaluation	• Driver control (A, C) • Resource consuming control (A, D, E) • Ambiguous context interpretation (D)	• Digital traces in mobile resource management
Transport data management	• Workflow transparency (E, D, C, B) • Manual manipulation elimination (C, B, F) • Process control (B, E) • Task reallocation (A) • Transparency enabled empowerment (B)	• Organizational work-flow configuration in distributed environments
Dispatcher-driver communication	• One way communication (A, C) • Communication confidence (C, D) • Delivery apprehension (D, F) • Sensemaking difficulties (C)	• Time independence in *ad hoc* communication

4.1 Mobile Resource Evaluation

Mobile resource evaluation concerns the ability of the stationary part of the organization to accurately follow the mobile workflow using system support. Concepts found in the analysis are driver control, resource consuming control, and ambiguous context interpretation.

Driver control refers to the ability of the stationary personnel to assess the compliance of the mobile workforce with organizational policies such as speed limits, drive time legislation, and other vehicle-related metrics. Controlling the mobile workforce from a central location was largely viewed as difficult. Some case organizations (A and C) aimed to measure and control technical and human components through embedded vehicle systems. An illustrative example is systems that constantly remind drivers to use efficient driving styles. As illustrated by a dispatcher from case organization A, experiences pertaining to use of such technology were positive.

> *Before we got this system, you didn't really know about these things. Well, you knew that a certain driver drove too fast, but did it really have that much effect on fuel consumption? Now you get a really good view of the costs of driving too fast, and when you get that, it is easier to tackle the problem.*

Resource consuming control concerns the balance between invested resources and outcomes of follow-up activities. While embedded vehicle systems generated huge sets of data describing performance down to individual driver and vehicle levels, however, many managers found that the time invested in assessing newly available metrics mitigated the potential benefits. Although satisfied with the increased level of detail provided, a dispatcher from case organization A commented,

> *I work more now, since I've got access to more information. With this system I get information on each driver or truck. The time I invest, that's probably the main difference. On the other hand, the analyses are better, more reliable. Earlier, I had nothing to work with, so yes, I work more with this now.*

However, there were also concerns that decisions would be taken on false grounds. For example, concentrating on fuel consumption as a variable could prove incorrect as many other factors have to be considered such as the conditions in which a particular driver operates and the load factor and cargo weight of the assignments carried out. Such a detailed analysis was not available in the systems studied. As asserted by the manager of case organization D, it was not deemed feasible to perform it manually due to the complexity and time involved.

> *Well, we have made some remarks, but we have not taken it very far actually. There are lots of things beyond their [the drivers] control that influence their driving. For example, we have a number of trucks involved in high security assignments where you can't stop. They have to follow the convoy and they can't deviate. There are also other things that are more important. If you choose a smaller non-toll road you might save money while the fuel consump-*

tion goes up. So it's not that easy. If you want that kind of analysis, it takes a lot more time and that's something that I don't have.

While the positive consequences illustrate opportunities to follow the workflow of multiple mobile resources, the challenges involved in resource management of mobile resources are evident. The digital trace of mobile work created in systems was at worst found incomplete and/or inconsistent with the context in which the mobile resources operate and at best resource consuming in terms of analysis and use.

4.2 Transport Data Management

Transport data management refers to the ability of the systems to rationalize the process of continually documenting and analyzing transport assignments. Analyzing the empirical data, we found five interrelated concepts: workflow transparency, manual manipulation elimination, process control, task reallocation, and transparency-enabled empowerment.

Workflow transparency concerns effects of horizontal information sharing. Generally, an individual dispatcher is responsible for managing and reporting on the workflow of a certain group of vehicles. By granting dispatchers access to each others' system views, the introduction of transport management support created a workflow transparency. A dispatcher from case organization B explained,

If I get a booking and enter it into the system, I don't have to be there personally if that customer calls and wants to know something. All information is there. It becomes an asset for everyone. I think that is good.

The reoccurring task of responding to customer information needs become less dependent on individual dispatcher availability as individual knowledge was in a sense transferred to the traffic controller collective.

Manual manipulation elimination refers to the ability of the systems to seamlessly integrate the process of transport data management. With separate stationary transport data systems and mobile order systems, information transfer was conducted manually. As noted by several respondents, this manual information input was regarded a problem with important implications. Primarily, manual handling of information transfer was time consuming. Also, the risk of information corruption increased with the number of manual replications and/or modifications performed. As recognized by the manager of case organization C, stationary users of integrated systems saw these problems with manual input eliminated in that the need for manual information transfer was minimized.

If you had an assignment in the transport management system, you had to enter it once more into Dynafleet before you could send it to the driver. Now it's sent immediately. It saves a lot of time.

Process control concerns the ability of the systems to trace transactions performed. Before the introduction of mobile order systems, paper documents pertaining to goods delivered or picked up were handled by drivers. This fragmented manual process made follow-up an arduous process. Resulting from integrated mobile and stationary systems, case organizations B and E experienced positive effects of an unbroken chain of computerized information exchange. This made possible automated repositories, easily scanned in search for anomalies. Respondents at the managerial level with access to such records experienced greater possibilities to follow up transactions in less time than before, as noted by the manager of case organization E.

Now I can use the system to follow a vehicle thoroughly. I can go back months. Before [the introduction of the system] I had no idea. It's a lot easier to get statistics. I can accomplish in 10 minutes what used to take 2 hours.

Many drivers asserted that mobile order systems changed their work designation. As a driver from case organization A commented, they now had to perform work previously related to the stationary workforce.

It all started when we got mobile phones, which was all right. Then we got an order system and had to manage all order documentation ourselves. And now this! [Referring to the in-vehicle order management system.] Some feel that we get more and more of the paper work. On the other hand, we don't have to wait for them [the dispatchers] to sort the order receipts out before leaving. Now, when you have loaded, you do it yourself on the mobile terminal when you want to.

While this indicates that such a task reallocation was unwelcome and regarded as an additional burden, it also rendered drivers the opportunity to manage their workflow themselves.

Transparency-enabled empowerment concerns the potential of technology to alter the power balance through making information globally available. In umbrella organizations consisting of independent road haulers, increased information access was viewed as potentially disruptive by the stationary part of the organization. As they previously were the sole owners of searchable and detailed information pertaining to revenue on assignment level, they now feared that drivers would question the authority of the dispatchers, demanding access to the most profitable assignments while shunning those less lucrative. The manager of case organization B was acutely aware of such potential effects.

They get a lot more information now, so hopefully it has become easier for the haulers to follow up so they get paid for their assignments. They might also get an idea of what assignments are better to take than others. All are not equally profitable. This is for good and for worse, because if you discover that some assignments yield little in return, you won't take those assignments.

Since the stationary organization has other priorities than optimizing the revenue of individual member road haulers, this was seen as potentially disruptive to the current way of managing mobile resources.

In sum, the positive and negative consequences related to seamless transport data management support showed a clear organizational impact. Indeed, the introduction of technology highlights a challenge of work flow management in distributed environments. The integration of mobile and stationary computing resources entails a previously unavailable transparency as well as a redistribution of tasks and responsibilities among actor groups who see new threats and opportunities arise.

4.3 Dispatcher-Driver Communication

Dispatcher–driver communication concerns the ability of the systems to rationalize the communication between stationary and mobile actors. Such system support includes messaging services for reducing redundant verbal communication between dispatchers and drivers. Our empirical analysis generated four interrelated concepts: one-way communication, communication confidence, delivery apprehension, and sensemaking difficulties.

While messaging services imply two-way communication between drivers and dispatchers, actual usage indicated a different mode of interaction. Dispatchers posted textual messages to drivers, thereby gaining the benefit of a one-way communication channel. Drivers were by comparison passive recipients, probably at least partly attributed to mobile device manipulation difficulties. Still, as noted by the dispatcher of case organization A, this time independent communication was regarded as beneficial and time saving in dispatcher–driver communication.

> *If I call someone [a driver] and the phone is busy, I just send a message "call me" and in a short while I'll get a call. It could be something concerning vehicle maintenance or that the driver needs to contact someone or something similar. I find that very good. And what's really good is that even if the driver is not at work, you can send a message in the evening, and then the following morning when he logs on he'll get it.*

Furthermore, the introduction of messaging systems linking mobile and office workers offered the possibility to track communication history. This brought a greater sense of communication confidence in that both drivers and dispatchers experienced that conversations were subject to fewer interpretational disputes and less frustration later. A driver from case organization A explained,

> *This gives us drivers a sort of protection. Because if we have sent a message, they [the dispatchers] have got the time it was sent and everything on the computer. It is stored there, so there can't be any unnecessary arguments.*

Despite these positive and intended consequences, we also discovered a type of delivery apprehension relating to the reliability of current mobile–stationary communication technologies. As illustrated by the manager of case organization C, senders were not confident that messages actually reached the recipients in time.

The way drivers and dispatchers interact is different now. Sometimes, when there is a lot of communication going on, the drivers have felt that they were not getting answers fast enough. They then wonder if their messages have been read at all. This can be especially frustrating when waiting for a return load.

Indeed, technical problems related to the underlying information transfer protocols (most notably GSM/SMS) rendered a new and unwelcome uncertainty. In some cases, this caused senders to confirm the reception of textual messages by phone, thereby eliminating the time saving benefits sought, if not making communication even more resource demanding. A dispatcher of case organization D commented,

It sometimes happens that they [the drivers] get important messages much later than they should have. If you take for granted that they arrived in due time, things go wrong and you have to correct them later. So the only way to know is to call them.

Sensemaking difficulties relate to the inability of the systems to comprehensibly embody communication practices between mobile and stationary actors. While the case organizations introduced communication systems to minimize communication ambiguity, sensemaking limitations to structured and formalized communication were evident. Taking for granted *ad hoc* information that does not fit the format of systems messaging or relying solely on textual messaging was regarded a dangerous approach, as the recipient's interpretation could not be confirmed as is the case with synchronous verbal conversation. The manager of case organization C exemplified,

They would send a message, "Load eight pallets there and five there." But with this system you can't add, "You must put those pallets in front because..." The misunderstandings can be very costly, if you don't communicate properly. It [the system] must never replace talking.

Summarizing the positive and negative consequences of mobile–stationary communication technologies, we identified a clear effect on the communication patterns between dispatchers and drivers. While several respondents appreciated the time independence in *ad hoc* communication created by technology, users also experienced a diminished control of the communication process. The cooperative effort involved in constructing the meaning of conversation became subject to limitations imposed by the communication systems. Such sensemaking efforts are challenging in attempts to reduce temporal dependence in communication between stationary and mobile actors in road haulage firms.

5   DISCUSSION

Following the ongoing diffusion of mobile and wireless communication services in our everyday life, ubiquitous computing environments have emerged as a vital area of research in information systems. As indicated in recent research, its implications span multiple levels of analysis and call for new research approaches (Lyytinen and Yoo 2002). Indeed, the heterogeneous and distributed nature of these computing environments requires both technology-intense (March et al. 2000) and socially informed (Jessup and Robey 2002) research. In fact, most ubiquitous computing research issues can be productively approached with research efforts that tackle the intertwining of social and technical elements playing out in attempts to design, implement, and use seamless services (Lyytinen and Yoo 2002).

In view of the socio-technical challenges of ubiquitous computing, this paper sets out to explore the mobile–stationary divide in UTS. This divide plays out as the set of socio-technical problems surrounding the integration of stationary office systems and mobile applications required for ubiquitous transport services. A central problem associated with such integration is the heterogeneity inherent in this type of attempt. Belonging to different innovation regimes (Godoe 2000), attempts to interconnect technologies with heterogeneous platforms, knowledge bases, and institutionalized settings are difficult. We have identified three socio-technical challenges associated with the mobile–stationary divide: digital traces in mobile resource management, organizational workflow configuration in distributed environments, and time independence in *ad hoc* communication. These challenges have implications for enterprise-wide ubiquitous computing environments where coordination of diverse sets of mobile units is central to organizational performance.

At the organizational level, attempts by road haulage firms to realize seamlessly integrated computing support caused new workflow configurations that changed organizational structure. The information transparency created by such integrated solutions rendered changes in the relation between the mobile and stationary workforces. As an example, mobile workers found themselves in a position where they performed tasks previously attributed to the stationary personnel. Moreover, in a situation where independent drivers were confronted with detailed information on the financial viability of individual assignments, stationary personnel saw their authority to coordinate and control the way in which transport assignments were allocated undermined. This example suggests that organizations have to adapt their organizing logic to the structural changes imposed by interconnected organizational and technical elements of heterogeneous and distributed computing environments (see Lyytinen and Yoo 2002; Sambamurthy and Zmud 2000).

At the social level, the desire of road haulage firms to rationalize mobile–stationary communication by employing new technology occasioned both positive and negative effects on communication patterns. The independence of time in *ad hoc* communication was widely recognized as beneficial. While establishing this independence, however, the cooperative effort involved in constructing the meaning of conversation became subject to limitations imposed by the communication systems. Users viewed the diminished opportunities for individual interpretation as helpful, but simultaneously noticed new issues of uncertainty related to their common understanding of mobile work. Indeed, such sensemaking difficulties had direct consequences for mobile work practice as well as social interaction. Left unattended, these adverse effects of efforts to achieve time independent communication are likely to impede the development of skills and organizational commitment on behalf of the mobile workers (see Jessup and Robey 2002).

At the technology level, there are several unresolved issues regarding development of ubiquitous computing architectures with the capacity to meet the service requirements of transport organizations. In filtering and combining information from both mobile and stationary sources lies the potential of increased understanding of the organization (see Jessup and Robey 2002). However, our case organizations were largely unsuccessful in their attempts to utilize the digital trace of mobile work created in systems as it was found incomplete and/or inconsistent with the context in which the mobile resources operate. According to our respondents, a contributing factor here was that the knowledge bases of mobile and stationary system vendors, including their understanding of mobile and stationary work practice, differed. This suggests that the development of architectures with the capability to facilitate mobile resource evaluation will be complex due to the diverse technological regimes involved (see Godoe 2000). In the context of the transport business, the heterogeneous assemblage of embedded vehicle systems and stationary systems requires a common platform of protocols and data standards to ensure interoperability of systems and to enable the integration of distributed technologies (see Lyytinen and Yoo 2002; March et al. 2000).

6 CONCLUSION

A central problem in attempts to develop seamlessly integrated computing environments for transport organizations is the existing divide between mobile and stationary systems. This paper has reported an assessment of how the mobile–stationary divide plays out in organizational efforts to realize such computing environments. On the basis of this assessment, we have also discussed implications for development of enterprise-wide ubiquitous architectures including distributed technical, social, and organizational elements. Indeed, these implications are important for any organization attempting to integrate mobile and stationary information systems.

An important task for researchers and practitioners is to assist transport organizations in their efforts to overcome the mobile–stationary divide. However, realizing the vision of UTS requires a thorough understanding of the nature of the multitude of both mobile and stationary technologies in the transport business. We have observed intricate organizational effects created by such technology. Further work is needed to uncover the underlying reasons for the adverse effects described. This includes shedding light on the relationship between key actors involved in development of the required computing components of UTS. As our findings indicate, seamlessly integrated ubiquitous computing environments are going to be the result of the combined efforts of a diverse set of innovation regimes.

REFERENCES

Akinci, B., Hendrickson, C., and Karaesmen, I. "Exploiting Motor Vehicle Information and Communications Technology for Transportation Engineering," *Journal of Transportation Engineering* (129:5), 2003, pp. 469-474.

Andersson, M., and Lindgren, R. "Ubiquitous Transport Systems: Towards Seamlessly Integrated Computing Environments for Road Haulage Firms," in review.

Baskerville, R. L., and Wood-Harper, A. T. "A Critical Perspective on Action Research as a Method for Information Systems Research," *Journal of Information Technology* (11), 1996, pp. 235-246.

Giannopoulos, G. A. "The Application of Information and Communication Technologies in Transport," *European Journal of Operational Research* (152:2), 2004, pp. 302-320.

Godoe, H. "Innovation Regimes, R&D and Radical Innovations in Telecommunications," *Research Policy* (29), 2000, pp. 1033-1046.

Hanseth, O. "Gateways—Just as Important as Standards. How the Internet Won the 'Religious War' about Standards in Scandinavia," *Knowledge, Technology and Policy* (14:3), 2001, pp 71-89.

Henfridsson, O., and Lindgren, R. "Multi-Contextuality in Ubiquitous Computing: Investigating the Car Case through Action Research," *Information and Organization* (15:3), Special Issue on Ubiquitous Computing Environments, 1995 (forthcoming).

Jessup, L. M., and Robey, D. "The Relevance of Social Issues in Ubiquitous Computing Environments," *Communications of the ACM* (45:12), 2002, pp. 88-91.

Lindgren, R., and Henfridsson, O. "Local Road Hauling in a Global Context: An Action Research Study-in-Progress of Fleet Management Systems," in *Proceedings of Americas Conference on Information Systems*, J. Ross and D. Galletta (Eds.), Tampa, FL, 2003, pp. 1975-1980.

Lyytinen, K., and Yoo, Y. "Research Commentary: The Next Wave of Nomadic Computing," *Information Systems Research* (13:4), 2002, pp. 377-388.

March, S., Hevner, A., and Ram, S. "Research Commentary: An Agenda for Information Technology Research in Heterogeneous and Distributed Environments," *Information Systems Research* (11:4), 2000, pp. 327-341.

Roy, J. "Recent Trends in Logistics and the Need for Real-Time Decision Tools in the Trucking Industry," in *Proceedings of the 34th Hawaii International Conference on System Sciences*, R. Sprague (Ed.), Los Alamitos, CA: IEEE Computer Society Press, 2001.

Sambamurthy, V., and Zmud, R. W. "Research Commentary: The Organizing Logic for an Enterprise's IT Activities in the Digital Era—A Prognosis of Practice and a Call for Research," *Information Systems Research* (11:2), 2000, pp. 105-114.

Strauss, A., and Corbin, J. *Basics of Qualitative Research: Grounded Theory Procedures and Techniques,* Newbury Park, CA: Sage Publications, 1990.

Yin, R. K. *Case Study Research: Design and Methods* (2nd ed.), Thousand Oaks, CA: Sage Publications, 1994.

ABOUT THE AUTHORS

Magnus Andersson is a member of the Telematics Group at the Viktoria Institute, Göteborg, Sweden. He is also Ph.D. Student at the Department of Informatics, Göteborg University. Magnus can be reached at magnus.andersson@viktoria.se.

Rikard Lindgren is currently managing an action research project on ubiquitous transport systems at the Viktoria Institute, Göteborg, Sweden. He is also an assistant professor in Informatics at the School of Economics and Commercial Law, Göteborg University, and at the School of Information Science, Computer and Electrical Engineering, Halmstad University. Dr. Lindgren holds a Ph.D. degree in Informatics from Göteborg University, Sweden. Dr. Lindgren has published his research in *MIS Quarterly, Information and Organization, European Journal of Information Systems, Scandinavian Journal of Information Systems,* and other journals in the information systems discipline. He can be reached at rikard.lindgren@viktoria.se.

Ola Henfridsson manages the Telematics Group at the Viktoria Institute, Göteborg, Sweden. He is also an assistant professor in Informatics at the School of Information Science, Computer and Electrical Engineering, Halmstad University. Dr. Henfridsson holds a Ph.D. degree in Informatics from Umeå University, Sweden, and is a member of the editorial board of *Scandinavian Journal of Information Systems*. Dr. Henfridsson has published his research in journals such as *Information Technology and People*, *Information and Organization*, and *MIS Quarterly*. He can be reached at ola.henfridsson@viktoria.se.

12 THE IMPACT OF UBIQUITOUS COMPUTING TECHNOLOGIES ON BUSINESS PROCESS CHANGE AND MANAGEMENT: The Case of Singapore's National Library Board

Anand Ramchand
Paul Raj Devadoss
Shan L. Pan
Department of Information Systems
National University of Singapore
Singapore

Abstract   *Ubiquitous computing technologies are reaching a stage of technical maturity that is enabling their application in everyday business environments. As organizations increasingly adopt these technologies, such as radio frequency identification (RFID), a deeper understanding of their impacts on business process management and design will reveal innovative opportunities for organizations to leverage upon in achieving their objectives. The case of RFID adoption at the National Library Board (NLB) reveals how the technology has enabled deskilling, modularity, and motility in business processes. As a result, NLB has enjoyed higher levels of efficiency, developed novel and differentiated services, and achieved greater customer satisfaction.*

1 INTRODUCTION

The concept of *ubiquitous computing* (Weiser 1991) is the result of advanced developments in computing and communication technologies, coupled with their widespread adoption by individuals and organizations. The rapid diffusion of such technologies has profoundly altered the way computing has been utilized and exploited to make personal and work lives more effective and efficient. Computing and technological capabilities are no longer viewed from the depreciatory perspective of machines that simply perform tasks using a repository of custom software in isolated environments that users enter and leave. Instead, an increasingly popular and desired notion of computing is that of enabling integrated information- and application-enhanced physical spaces, with the perceptual capability to allow users to interact naturally with their information (Saha and Mukherjee 2003). This is achieved through the use of increasingly mobile and pervasive communication and computing devices. This notion forms the basic premise of ubiquitous (or "anytime, anyplace") computing: "an assemblage of interconnected technological elements that enable the mobility of computing and communication services" (Yoo and Lyytinen 2003, p. 2).

Ubiquitous computing technologies are reaching a stage of technical maturity that enables their application in everyday business and social environments (Fleisch 2001; Stanford 2002). Recent literature suggests ubiquitous computing technologies present considerable potential to significantly change how work is performed at organizational, team and individual levels in numerous ways (e.g., Davis 2002; Jessup and Robey 2002; Lyytinen and Yoo 2002; Lyytinen et al. 2004). The design of organizational business processes and the exploitation of information technologies constitute a recursive relationship, in which IT is a key enabler in transforming, as well as supporting, business processes (Davenport and Short 1990; Venkatraman 1994). With increasing intelligence and mobility, seamless integration into physical environments, and declining costs, the adoption and application of ubiquitous computing technologies by organizations are enabling substantially new and distinctive service options and business processes, and, consequently, creating a variety of impacts on organizations (Strassner and Schoch 2002).

The intent of this paper is two-fold. First, based on an exploratory study of the adoption of *radio frequency identification* (RFID) in Singapore's National Library Board's (NLB) as part of strategy-driven process changes, we provide empirically based insights into the strategic use of ubiquitous computing technologies in enabling innovative business processes, with particular regard to their impact on process owners and process design. Second, we highlight the enablers of such impacts and their implications on organizations. In the discourse of these issues, we discuss areas where future research may provide a deeper understanding of the effects of ubiquitous technologies in organizations.

2   LITERATURE REVIEW

Business processes, "logically related tasks performed to achieve a defined business outcome" (Davenport and Short 1990), typically consist of structure, inputs, outputs, internal or external customers, and owners (Al-Mashari and Zairi 2000; Davenport and Short 1990). Processes reflect how work is performed and can be strategically changed or redesigned to provide organizations with significant improvements. The role of IT has been shown to be fundamental and multifaceted in this endeavor (Attaran 2004), enabling and facilitating organizations in implementing radically improved processes, rather than merely automating current ones (Al-Mashari and Zairi 2000; Hammer 1990). Process change efforts, however, consist of a continuum of approaches and may not only be radical in nature, but may also be evolutionary and incremental (Stoddard and

Jarvenpaa 1995). Such strategy-driven process change efforts are characterized by the transformation of organizational subsystems, such as people, IT, or coordination mechanisms, and aim to improve process outcomes (Kettinger et al. 1997).

RFIDs, an automatic identification technology, represent an enabler of emerging ubiquitous computing technologies and applications (Want et al. 1999), and have had strong impacts on business processes. In RFID systems, *tags* (small chips with antennas and information storage capabilities) are attached to and used to identify physical entities through radio waves using an RFID reader. RFIDs are significantly better than earlier auto-identification technologies as they do not require human intervention in the identification process, do not need line of sight between the reader and entities, can identify many entities simultaneously, and have larger data storage capacity (Stanford 2003; Strassner and Schoch 2002).

Due to the automated nature of data input into enterprise systems, RFIDs eliminate media breaks (the need for human intervention in transferring data from one medium to another), thus simplifying and accelerating business processes, reducing input and processing errors, and allowing organizations to achieve higher levels of data integration (Fleisch 2001). As a result, RFID systems bridge existing and cumbersome gaps between the transference of physical data into digital domains. RFIDs also provide opportunities to achieve significant process freedoms by removing more human intervention from business processes than previous technologies, as well as enabling greater information visibility throughout organizational supply chains (Angeles 2005). RFID systems have frequently been employed in supply chain and logistics tracking business processes to permit the automatic capture of product location and information, supplementing data input into organizational systems and allowing organizations to streamline their processes and minimize errors.

Effective process design should not be merely techno-centric; it requires a balanced socio-technical perspective (Markus and Robey 1995; Sarker and Lee 2002). Process change initiatives not only change the IT capabilities and infrastructure of the organization, but also the roles and responsibilities of organizational members and the structure of the organization itself. Process redesign efforts driven by traditional IT typically result in a need for greater ownership and direct responsibility over the operation of processes by process owners, as outmoded hierarchies are replaced with flattened, leaner structures and decentralized decision making (Cunningham and Finnegan 2004). Process owners are made completely responsible for and maintain complete authority over their processes, from their initial design to implementation and performance evaluation, as well as planning training efforts for front-line employees. Process owners also play a vital role in guiding the evolution and adaptation of the new processes, ensuring the outmoded methods do not resurface, managing process employees, and incrementally improving the process over time (Hammer and Stanton 1999). However, the ownership over cross-functional processes introduces significant operational burdens on senior managers, making the realization of true strategic effectiveness from newly implemented processes and their management difficult (Lee and Dale 1998).

As the adoption of nontraditional, ubiquitous computing technologies in organizations increases, a deeper and more detailed understanding of the consequences and opportunities afforded by such technologies on newly designed business processes and their management is necessary to bring about effective implementation and suitable practices for organizations.

3   RESEARCH METHOD

An exploratory case study was conducted at the National Library Board (NLB) of Singapore, investigating the adoption of RFID technologies and the subsequent implementation of a first-of-its-kind system. Data was collected in September 2003 from a total of 43 semi-structured interviews with staff from various divisions of NLB. As the investigation studied the adoption and implementation period from 1996 to 2003, interviewees were drawn from a wide variety of business functions and managerial levels, as well as with varying seniority of service (ranging from 6 months to 32 years). The open-ended interviews allowed the researchers to gather data on a wide variety of issues and perspectives from interviewees. Interviews were recorded and subsequently transcribed verbatim and supplemented with field observations.

Further data for the study was drawn from interviews with NLB's RFID-technology partner, ST Logitrack, in order to gather insights into the technical details of the technology adoption, as well as useful secondary opinions on the use of RFIDs in NLB. Data was also gathered through various documents such as press releases, internal reports, internal magazine write-ups, other research reports, and popular press articles. Such data supplemented information gathered on scope of projects, objectives, achievements and issues handled during the various stages of adoption at NLB. Further data was also gathered through personal observations at NLB's libraries and office premises during visits to 13 different libraries, NLB's headquarters, and its supply center.

4   CASE DESCRIPTION

Based on a vision drawn up in consultation with an extensive cross section of the society to expand the learning capacity of the nation, the Singapore government formed the National Library Board in 1995 to transform Singapore's library services in the information age. In its current form, NLB provides services for 70 libraries in Singapore including 39 national public libraries, of which 3 are large regional libraries, 18 community libraries, and 18 children's libraries.

NLB set about the task of increasing its annual book loans of about 10 million in 1994. It began with an extensive business process reengineering exercise in 1996 targeting the consolidation and optimization of business processes that were concurrent, identifying the need for radical solutions due to mismatches between existing capabilities and targets set by NLB's vision. This exercise also presented the organization with a complete idea on all processes and involved key process owners in the development of performance targets. As the CEO of NLB noted,

We knew we had to start right now because we had such high targets set for us through Library 2000 for the following years. If we didn't start now [1996], we'd never reach there!

Several technology solutions were considered potentially useful, including the implementation of self service stations for library services and the introduction of more services that delight the customers. In the words of the CEO,

We started to look at three things that people didn't like in our libraries... long queues, time to provide new items and serving open-ended enquiries.

Existing barcode systems were difficult to use for library patrons since they required aligning the book physically with the reader in order to be read by the machine. The manager of the Innovation and Services Department (ISD) reported,

You might wonder what's so hard in aligning the book, but considering the number of people who require assistance, the average time for a loan shoots up rendering it relatively inefficient.

Also, book returns were handled manually despite book return chutes, located at library entrances, through which users could drop off books anytime of the day. However, this system didn't work well since it left users waiting for the staff to update the system before they could borrow again.

Scouting for a better technology to handle the books, NLB identified RFID as a potential technology. In Singapore, Singapore Technologies Logistics and Singapore Technologies Electronics had explored RFID applications for logistics operations. Along with NLB, the three partners developed a prototype demonstrated in November 1997. As a project manager recalled,

When the book with RFID chip was dropped down a reader-embedded container, the reader successfully recognized the drop! There began the long journey toward its application in libraries,

4.1 Deploying RFIDs

A passive RFID chip embedded in the spine of the book (currently, with the availability of smaller chips, it is pasted on the last page of the book) identifies a book to scanners in close proximity. All library items are tagged with an RFID chip, containing information identifying the book, the library branch, and rack numbers where the book is shelved. In a book loan or return process, the data would be used together with the library user's identity to manage the library user's loan information. The data is initially stored in a local server, which operates with a backup and is then synchronized with the centralized data servers.

In the months following the demonstration, ST Electronics developed a prototype for a new library that NLB was renovating at Bukit Batok Community Library. The manager of ISD noted,

In those 9 months from early 1998 to November 1998 to when the Bukit Batok Community Library was opened after renovation, we worked on designing the system, developing the software, the interfaces...the whole package. I can say that we were the first fully functional library with over 100,000 items on loan using RFID.

A manager from NLB summed up the library user reaction to the new technology.

There's a sense of amazement. I can put the book in any direction...it still works. We approached this library as a prototype, it worked great, the public loved it and that is why it is still there!

Self service book loan counters were designed with a simple interface with options for all four official languages (English, Chinese, Malay, and Tamil). Users log into the system by placing their identity cards into the machine and place each book they wish to check out on the reader. The screen confirms by displaying the books checked out and the account status. A book return chutes were equipped with a scanner to log returned books instantly. At the book drop, the user drops the book through a chute, where RFID scanners update the systems on users' book loans instantaneously. The book drop service is located at the entrance of a library, in order to make the service available 24 hours a day. Books can now be returned at any of NLB's libraries through book drop counters, anytime of the day. A manager at NLB stated,

The technology can support many books being dropped in at a time, but we'd rather that the users drop one at a time since that will help our users be aware of the books they drop in...this is a human constraint.

The technology had to be reined in, to make it easier for the users and save NLB the task of handling too many lost items from users. A library officer also noted this about users:

Sometimes [they] drop in their own books though it can only accept one book at a time....Or they even drop other library books like school library books or school text books! We then take care of such books through "lost and found" during sorting and shelving.

Since the loan information was instantly updated to their library user's record, it encouraged more loans by library users. As a manager commented,

With the old system, they sometimes ask why their account is not credited when they've already returned a book...and our staff would have to retrieve it from the overnight pile of books and speed up this users return.

A librarian summed it up as follows while commenting on the processes in sorting:

With the RFID systems in place, the sorting process is a breeze because this computer [attached to the scanner] even shows the shelf number for the book.

The efficiency of loaning books and returning them at book drops at any library improved user experience at libraries, helping in the growth of book loans at NLB. The organization was learning from the deployment of the system, observing it in operation and working on improving at the next implementation within a year. The whole implementation was again piloted at the next library in 1999. Two more libraries were piloted before the systems were functioning to the satisfaction of NLB. NLB then invited global tenders for implementing the system across all its libraries in 2000. Singapore Technologies Logitrack, a joint venture by ST Electronics and ST Logistics, was awarded the tender and has since rolled out the RFID systems in all NLB libraries in Singapore. The entire process was completed in April of 2002. The success of the technology during pilot testing prompted other libraries to start requesting its implementation. As the project manager reported,

> *When the other libraries saw what we could do with RFID, they too wanted it. RFID was helping them achieve targets which would otherwise consume tremendous resources.*

With increasing adoption of IT, awareness of its potential was recognized and accepted by users. The CIO added,

> *Now we had the pleasant problem of managing this demand....We achieved our targets without retrenching any staff. Our retraining was focused on service quality, rather than technology since it was easy enough to use. To the library users, we have given a better service quality. In face to the library users, there is no need to even talk to our staff, but if they need to, our staffs have more time to do so!*

4.2 Impacts of IT at NLB

The immediate objective of the organization in adopting RFID was accomplished by removing queues, delivering better service quality, and giving employees more time to do value added tasks. Further, innovation of new services was possible at libraries. According to the CEO,

> *The introduction of this technology... eliminated the queues; it eliminated the staff from the mundane work of having to stand there to attend to the customers. Now the customers can just go to the machine and check it out and our staff can do some other value-added work. Librarians are not there just to shelve books or stamp books; they are there to help you find information, which is higher value-added work.*

With the introduction of IT, training was necessary in using such technologies. Also, with the savings in time spent at counters, staff were retrained to do greater value-added tasks. The CIO noted,

> *IT helped relieve mundane work. Staff are then trained to do more productive work in the back room or trained to become professional librarians where they help to organize information, help to select books, catalogue books, and they get to read what's the latest in the publishing industry. That adds to their intellect. So that's how staff would accept: "Yes, IT helps me in that."*

To the staff, the new systems literally liberated them from the loan counters. They now had more time to devote to improving services. A librarian noted that,

> *With the new systems, we now have more time to walk around the library answering queries from users instead of being tied to a desk. Our job satisfaction is driven by our ability to quickly answer user queries satisfactorily.*

To manage book returns, NLB has an operations room behind the book return chutes where books are sorted. Returned books are sorted by shelf numbers or prepared for pickup by the postal service for delivery to other branches. A computer displays the shelf code encoded in the RFID chip in order to simplify the sorting process. A library officer demonstrating the process noted,

> *This system makes it easy to sort out the books and recognize their shelves.*

Books are then carted off for shelving. The staff requested a color coded label on the spine indicating the collections to which a particular book belongs. This coding is uniform across all NLB libraries, and helps staff visually pick out incorrectly shelved books. Explaining the request by the librarians, the project manager noted,

> *The library staff gave us feedback that it was difficult to pick out a wrongly shelved book among all these books. So we accepted their feedback and put a label on the spine of the book.*

Growing loans meant an increasing number of returns, thus placing a heavy burden on the shelving staff. An older staff involved in the shelving process commented,

> *This is a tedious process, returning books to the shelves all day! Especially during school vacations, the volume increases a lot. I wish this could be automated. It's a hard thing to do all day...but it can't be automated, putting books to open shelves. It can only be done with closed shelves.*

NLB employs part-time employees who help the staff with shelving. This strategy helps NLB carve the tedious work process into smaller, manageable schedules sourced to the part-time staff. In addition, several community programs bring in volunteers to help shelve books. Such programs also benefit NLB by helping them reach out to the community and engage them in a daily work process.

One of the junior staff, who has gone from *"stamping books all day,"* commented,

> *If I can answer a user's query well, then I am most satisfied with my job...we now have plenty of resources to do just that.*

The management recognized the fact that some staff were unwilling to take the step into the future that the introduction of RFID systems heralded, namely greater use of IT in daily work routines. The management took into consideration the other events that were happening in the organization to understand the mixed feeling toward the introduction of the RFID systems. The management reacted appropriately, which the CEO summarized as follows:

> *We had so many things changing...the front office with the RFID systems...our back office with our HR FIS systems, and there was an overlap for about three years. It was a huge strain on the organization and naturally people were stressed. This is when we had to show patience, trust, and give time.*

The top management engaged the staff in a dialogue and conveyed the message that these technologies were meant to help increase productivity. Commenting on the organization after the formation of NLB, the CIO noted,

> *When a new management introduces something...staffs worry if their job is safe. So we introduced tea talks, when the CEO was in direct touch with staff, explaining the objectives and allaying their fears.*

To help staff cope with the changed environment in the organization, NLB provided training sessions, opportunities for skill development, and redeployment of some staff into other jobs.

With increasing adoption of RFID technologies at more branches, book loans were growing annually at NLB in addition to annual library user visits to the branches. The increased productivity was managed with retrained staff from other functions that had become redundant due to the introduction of IT. As the RFID technologies were adopted at each new library with incremental services being automated, less staff were needed to man the library. NLB countered this by increasing the responsibilities of lower rank staff to the extent that the first fully self-service DIY (do it yourself) styled library was launched with just one Systems Library Officer and one concierge who manage approximately 2,000 loans a day. Using a call center, NLB now provides support for user queries at libraries through its interactive Cybrarian kiosk. Users can see directions and demos of services while consulting a library call center staff.

NLB is now equipped to quickly deploy a loaning service even at remote community events using a virtual private network, thus taking the library to the people. One library manager commented,

> *It is now much more efficient...we used to write down the call numbers and then key them in later, which was error prone and slow.*

The RFID-tagging of its collections has also drastically reduced the time spent in stocktaking of collections. None of the libraries now close for stocktaking, and the entire exercise at a library is completed overnight, except for the anomalies in reports which are followed up later. NLB constantly strives to identify potential business problems and find a solution that addresses a set of related processes. The CEO summed up the approach as

> *An optimized, automated solution to an immediate problem is our objective.*

5 FINDINGS AND IMPLICATIONS

The adoption of RFIDs by NLB demonstrates the efficacy of ubiquitous computing technologies in providing organizations with radical and novel approaches to solving traditional business problems using nontraditional and modern technologies. Permeating this usage are interesting insights and new perspectives into the impact of these technologies on transforming the management and design of business processes, namely, by enabling deskilling, modularity, and motility in business processes.

5.1 Process Deskilling

Prior to the RFID-tagging, customers experienced prolonged waiting times for services, caused both by physical and information delays. For instance, when returning an item, customers had to queue up at counters for service (physical delay), and subsequently wait for their loan records to be updated (information delay). Similarly, NLB had to update records manually (information delay) and proceed to shelve returned items for future loans (physical delay).

The initial implementation of book return chutes succeeded in dissociating the information and physical delays of the processes from the customer's perspective. While the system meant customers need not incur any waiting time to manually return loaned items, the updating of customer records was still manually performed, failing to remove haunting delays in service from NLB's back-office perspective.

With the adoption of RFIDs, NLB was able to further *deskill* the processes of loaning and returning—simplifying them significantly enough to be performed through the use of RFID technology. When loaned items were automatically scanned at the book return chute, NLB membership records were instantaneously updated, eliminating all information delays in the process. This new capability was enabled by the embedded and communicative nature of the RFID tags in each book, which allowed the physical books to *informate* (Zuboff 1988) NLB systems without the need for human intercession, eliminating the media breaks inherent in the regular process. The calm nature of such ubiquitous technologies (Weiser 1991) makes it possible to minimize human interaction and control over the technology while it performs its tasks invisibly, making only its outcome noticeable (Want 2004).

The deskilling of the process had implications on the existing staff of the library. The removal of human intervention from the process led to the deskilling (Burris 1998) of many staff. Where librarians previously were needed to engage with customers, facilitate the acceptance of loan items, and update systems, these processes were now, through the use of embedded RFIDs, technology-enabled. NLB's employment of volunteers and part-time staff to carry out manual reshelving tasks meant that full-time librarians could be *upskilled* (Burris 1998) to solely perform other back-office and service-oriented tasks. As a result, NLB enjoyed significant savings in terms of human resource costs and time incurred to provide higher quality levels of service.

5.2 Process Modularity

In addition to deskilling, the RFID system enabled the modularization of processes (Sanchez 1997) by moving input and output information dependencies to the interface of the customers with the technology. In modular process architectures, components of processes are standardized and can be reused for the creation of different functionalities and levels of performance (Sanchez 1997).

Prior to the RFID-tagging, reducing waiting times for services offered to customers involved the spawning of multiple, concurrent instances of those processes, and incurred the necessary resources for their deployment. For instance, in order to lower waiting times, NLB would deploy more staff at manual service counters. Such instances of service processes not only entailed increasing utilization of resources, but also increased the managerial monitoring and control efforts of process owners, who mediated and oversaw the activities of process employees.

With the RFID-enabled processes, not only were employees deskilled from the process, but process owners could focus on evaluating and improving the process from an abstraction created through the use of the technology (Zuboff 1988). The uniformity of the technology-enabled process allowed it to be replicated, based on this abstraction, numerous times and in various locations within and across libraries with little or no additional management or control activities by process owners. The inherent responsibilities of process owners were, therefore, assuaged and subsequently refocused, as they could focus on the activities of process evaluation and improvement, rather than process control and training, while being able to deploy and reuse the process effectively and efficiently to meet organizational objectives. As a result, the organizational capability to fully realize the efficiency gains from the new process are increased (Sanchez 1997).

The ubiquitous technology enabled such modularity by simplifying the process to a reduced, technology-enabled form, without the loss of information requirements, while embedding coordination between process functions (Sanchez 1997). Subsequent to deskilling the process, its initiation and dependencies were refocused onto the interface with the customer, rather than the intervention of NLB employees throughout its execution. Such process modularity further enabled the creation of new and novel services with greater ease. Being able to instantiate their RFID-enabled processes with little effort was vital in facilitating the creation of the self-serviced DIY library, manned by only two NLB staff. Furthermore, the capability to manage the process from an abstraction frees process owners to not only focus their efforts on process improvement, but also to combine efforts across core processes to deterministically seek gains from convergence, commonality, and overlaps, allowing organizations to truly enjoy the benefits of a process-oriented view of the organization.

5.3 Process Motility

The ability to adapt and duplicate processes easily in new, *ad hoc* and spontaneous situations at NLB is a result of the technology-enabled deskilling and process modularity achieved through the use of the RFID system. *Process motility* here refers to the flexibility to reuse modular processes innovatively to provide new services and functionalities in diverse contexts and locations. This view of processes looks beyond reconfiguring unbundled and independent process modules into new processes, and instead suggests that by enabling a supportive and coordinated IT architecture, ubiquitous technologies facilitate the relocation and reapplication of processes outside the firm's traditional location and context without a loss in process quality and functionality.

NLB sought advantages from the technology-enabled simplification of its processes, as well as their easy reproducibility and unmanned operations, to frequently provide services at *ad hoc* locations for short periods of time and during special events held at remote locations. Processes were motile as they could be quickly and easily implemented at locations previously inaccessible due to the cumbersome technical and human requirements of capturing data effectively and with minimal errors while at these locations. With the use of the RFID technology, however, tag readers could easily be set up so that self-service loan return counters could easily be deployed, thus permitting customers to access library services at locations previously unavailable.

The adoption of the ubiquitous technologies to enable process motility eliminated the spatial dependence of NLB's services. Traditional approaches, such as using book chutes at the libraries themselves, only managed to provide customers with the ability to access library returns services at any time, removing temporal restrictions on such services. The capability of process motility enabled by the RFID systems, however, facilitated the creation of novel services to bridge the spatial restrictions of service provision as well, allowing NLB to flexibly break through the notion that its services were only available at fixed locations, bringing its services closer to customers.

6   CONCLUSION

The newly implemented processes at NLB enabled by RFID technologies demonstrate how ubiquitous computing enables the deskilling, modularity, and motility of processes, signifying greater flexibility from organizational processes and their easier management. As a result of their adoption and usage, organizations stand to gain tremendous business value from the use of ubiquitous technologies such as RFIDs, including automation and information operations savings in terms of human resources, throughput, and operational flexibility, as well as transformational advantages such as the ability to create differentiated and innovative services across spatial and time dimensions previously inaccessible to the use of traditional technologies in processes. Furthermore, the process owner activities of controlling, monitoring, and managing processes and training staff are subsequently lightened, potentially enabling process owners to exert more effort on achieving holistic and strategic cross-process advantages for the organization to truly enjoy the benefits of newly designed, technology-enabled processes.

Further research is needed, however, to gain a deeper understanding of the impacts of such ubiquitous technologies on organizational processes. In particular, investigations into how organizations should rethink their approach and technology considerations in process change initiatives to fully exploit the advantages enabled and driven by ubiquitous technologies needs to be carried out. While customer-focused process redesign is a primary guideline, the development and deployment of new services and process efficiency gains enabled by the technologies can be underestimated. Organizations need to be imaginative and creative not only in their process change efforts, but also in their consideration of future capabilities enabled by ubiquitous computing technologies.

REFERENCES

Al-Mashari, M., and Zairi, M. "Revisiting BPR: A Holistic Review of Practice and Development," *Business Process Management Journal* (16:1), 2000, pp. 10-42.

Angeles, R. "RFID Technologies: Supply-Chain Applications and Implementation Issues," *Information Systems Management*, Winter 2005, pp. 51-65.

Attaran, M. "Exploring the Relationship Between Information Technology and Business Process Reengineering," *Information and Management* (41), 2004, pp. 585-596.

Burris, B. "Computerization in the Workplace," *Annual Review of Sociology* (24), 1998, pp. 141-157.

Cunningham, J., and Finnegan, P. "Process Improvement (PI) Programs and Information Systems: A Cross-Case Analysis of Impact," *Journal of Information Technology* (19), 2004, pp. 59-70.

Davenport, T., and Short, J. "The New Industrial Engineering: Information Technology and Business Process Redesign," *Sloan Management Review* (31:4), 1990, pp. 11-27.

Davis, G. B. "Anytime/Anyplace Computing and the Future of Knowledge Work," *Communications of the ACM* (45:12), 2002, pp. 67-73.

Fleisch, E. "Business Perspectives on Ubiquitous Computing," M-Lab Working Paper No. 4, University of St. Gallen, 2001.

Hammer, M. "Re-engineering Work: Don't Automate, Obliterate," *Harvard Business Review* (68:4), July/August 1990, pp. 104-112.

Hammer, M., and Stanton, S. "How Process Enterprises Really Work," *Harvard Business Review* (77), November/December 1999, pp. 108-118.

Jessup, L., and Robey, D. "The Relevance of Social Issues in Ubiquitous Computing Environments," *Communications of the ACM* (45:2), 2002, pp. 88-91.

Kettinger, W., Teng, J., and Guha, S. "Business Process Change: A Study of Methodologies, Techniques, and Tools," *MIS Quarterly* (21:1), 1997, pp. 55-80.

Lee, R. G., and Dale, B. G. "Business Process Management: A Review and Evaluation," *Business Process Management Journal* (4:3), 1998, pp. pp. 214-225.

Lyytinen, K., and Yoo, Y. "Research Commentary: The Next Wave of Nomadic Computing," *Information Systems Research* (13:4), 2002, pp. 377-388.

Lyytinen, K., Yoo, Y., Varshey, U., Ackerman, M. S., Davis, G., Avital, M., Robey, D., Sawyer, S., and Sorenson, C. "Surfing the Next Wave: Design and Implementation Challenges of Ubiquitous Computing Environments," *Communications of the AIS* (13), 2004, pp. 697-716.

Markus, M. L., and Robey, D. "Business Process Reengineering and the Role of Information Systems Professionals," in *Business Process Change: Reengineering Concepts, Methods and Technologies* V. Grover and W. J. Kettinger (Eds.), Harrisburg, PA: Idea Group Publishing, 1995, pp. 591-611.

Saha, D., and Mukherjee, A. "Pervasive Computing: A Paradigm for the 21st Century," *IEEE Computer*, March 2003, pp. 25-31.

Sanchez, R. "Preparing for an Uncertain Future: Managing Organizations for Strategic Flexibility," *International Studies of Management and Organization* (27:2), 1997, pp. 71-94.

Sarker, S., and Lee, A. S. "Using a Positivist Case Research Methodology to Test Three Competing Theories-in-Use of Business Process Redesign," *Journal of the Association for Information Systems* (2:7), 2002, pp. 1-72.

Stanford, V. "Pervasive Computing Goes the Last Hundred Feet with RFID Systems," *IEEE Pervasive Computing*, April-June 2003, pp. 9-14.

Stanford, V. "Pervasive Computing Goes to Work: Interfacing to the Enterprise," *IEEE Pervasive Computing*, July-September 2002, pp. 6-12.

Stoddard, D., and Jarvenpaa, S. "Business Process Reengineering: Tactics for Managing Radical Change," *Journal of Management Information Systems* (12:1), 1995, pp. 81-108.

Strassner, M., and Schoch, T. "Today's Impact of Ubiquitous Computing on Business Processes," in *Proceedings of the First International Conference on Pervasive Computing (Pervasive 2002), Short Paper Proceedings*, Zurich, August 26-28, 2002, pp. 62-74.

Venkatraman, N. "IT-Enabled Business Transformation: From Automation to Business Scope Redefinition," *Sloan Management Review* (35:2), Winter 1994, pp. 73-87.

Want, R. "RFID: A Key to Automating Everything," *Scientific American*, January 2004, pp. 56-65.

Want, R., Fishkin, K., Gujar, A., and Harrison, B. "Bridging Physical and Virtual Worlds with Electronic Tags," in *Proceedings of the ACM Conference on Human Factors in Computing Systems*, Pittsburgh, May 15-20, 1999, pp. 370-377.

Weiser, M. "The Computer for the 21st Century," *Scientific American*, September 1991, pp. 94-104; reprint: *IEEE Pervasive Computing*, January-March 2002, pp. 19-25.

Yoo, Y., and Lyytinen, K. "Measuring the Consequences of Ubiquitous Computing in Networked Organizations," *Sprouts: Working Papers on Information Environments, Systems and Organizations* (3), Summer, 2003 (available online at http://weatherhead.cwru.edu/sprouts/2003/030309.pdf).

Zuboff, S. *In The Age of the Smart Machine: The Future of Work and Power*, New York: Basic Books, 1988.

ABOUT THE AUTHORS

Anand Ramchand is a doctoral student with the Department of Information Systems, School of Computing, National University of Singapore. His research interests include ubiquitous and pervasive computing environments and the management of organizational knowledge. He can be reached by e-mail at ANAND@comp.nus.edu.sg.

Paul Raj Devadoss is a doctoral candidate with the Department of Information Systems, School of Computing, National University of Singapore. His research interests include e-governments, enterprise systems, IT use, and metastructurational activities in organizations. He can be reached by e-mail at PAULD@comp.nus.edu.sg.

Shan Ling Pan is the coordinator of Knowledge Management Laboratory in the Department of Information Systems of School of Computing at the National University of Singapore (NUS). Dr. Pan's research work has been published in *IEEE Transactions on Engineering Management, Journal of the American Society for Information Systems and Technology, IEEE Transactions on Systems, Man, and Cybernetics, IEEE Transactions on Information Technology in Biomedicine, Journal of the Academy of Marketing Studies, Communications of ACM, Information and Organization, Journal of Strategic Information Systems, Journal of Organizational Computing and Electronic Commerce, European Journal of Operational Research, European Journal of Information Systems*, and *Decision Support Systems*. He can be reached by e-mail at PANSL@comp.nus.edu.sg.

13 UBIQUITOUS COMPUTING AND THE DOUBLE IMMUTABILITY OF REMOTE DIAGNOSTICS TECHNOLOGY: An Exploration into Six Cases of Remote Diagnostics Technology Use

Katrin Jonsson
Jonny Holmström
Department of Informatics
Umeå University
Umeå, Sweden

Abstract   *The aim of this paper is to display the use a specific type of ubiquitous computing technology—remote diagnostics technology—in organizations and, in particular, the way in which the technology is enacted in remote and local maintenance groups. By taking a case study approach, we look into the use of remote diagnostics technology in the maintenance industry. Drawing from actor-network theory, and in particular the notion of double immutability, we argue that we need to establish a stable relationship that uses remote diagnostics technology for monitoring machine performance from a remote place while also keeping a level of local responsiveness toward machine performance. The stability of the remote diagnostics technology is seemingly effective in that critical data can be collected, diffused, and manipulated. The stability of the network of relations surrounding the technology is, however, yet to emerge. The borders between the central group and the local maintenance workers must be considered and we need to acknowledge that it takes effort to sustain stable networks of relations. We need to establish a new relationship that uses ubiquitous computing technology for monitoring processes and activities from the remote group while also keeping a level of local responsiveness toward machine performance. Taken together, the remote and the local group, along with the remote diagnostics technology, constitute a maintenance work collective.*

1   INTRODUCTION

Information technology has revolutionized contemporary business life as it has changed the ground rules of strategic management, marketing, logistics, and organizational design, to name but a few disciplines. As the most recent, and arguably most challenging, "wave of technology," ubiquitous computing technology is designed to blend into the surrounding and to serve specified purposes as knowledge work (Davis 2003), learning (Chae 2003), communication and collaboration (Grudin 2003) or businesses (Giles and Purao 2003; Medovich 2003). This wave of computerization is characterized by mobility and embeddedness (Avital and Germonprez 2003; Lyytinen and Yoo 2002) making it possible to collect large amounts of data from physical environments, users, and products. Ubiquitous computing is also characterized by a separation of data from the technology through which it was collected (Avital and Germonprez 2003) and the possibility to transfer it to remote places.

In this paper, we focus on a particular type of ubiquitous computing that is commonly referred to as remote diagnostics technology. Sensors and network access are installed into physical products, mostly machines, making it possible to collect and access their performance parameters remotely. The performance of products such as shipboard cranes and hydraulic engines can thereby be monitored in some detail to ensure continuous product performance and enable timely maintenance. Traditionally, monitoring is done periodically by local technicians visiting the product, but with remote diagnostics technology, central service centers can monitor products remotely. These remote groups can offer problem solving services as well as new value adding services, something that has been optimistically forecast for in the vehicle industry (Kuschel and Ljungberg 2004). To date, efforts in developing and using remote diagnostics technology have primarily been concerned with making maintenance work on the products more timely and effective.

The remote group enabled by remote technology is dependent on data collected by the system. The transformation of the machine's physical condition into a digital representation is crucial if remote diagnostics technology is to be adapted and used well. The remote group must rely on data displayed by the system, showing the details of the product's condition. Traditional local groups, on the other hand, are skilled in using their senses and manual collection of data as sources in maintenance planning. Remote diagnostics technology seems to challenge the way traditional local groups perform maintenance planning by enabling remote groups specialized in collecting and analyzing data.

The aim of this paper is to display the use of remote diagnostics technology in organizations, in particular the way in which the technology is enacted in central and local maintenance groups. There is a gap between those two groups that needs to be bridged in order to establish a maintenance collective that works well. Remote diagnostics technologies create a remote closeness between physically dispersed objects and actors, while at the same time creating a local physical distance when actors and objects move their interaction into the digital environment. Drawing from actor-network theory, and in particular the notion of double immutability, we argue that we need to establish a stable relationship that uses remote diagnostics technology for monitoring machine performance from a remote place while also keeping a level of local responsiveness toward machine performance. Taken together, the remote and the local group, along with the remote diagnostics technology, constitute a maintenance work collective.

2   LITERATURE REVIEW

2.1 Ubiquitous Computing

The development of information technology with increased computing power, smaller devices, and improved network capabilities has radically affected how and where computing technology can be used. The computer has moved from dedicated operating rooms, via the desktop into our homes, and has now reached traditional objects in our environment. Terms like traditional business computing, mobile computing, pervasive computing, and ubiquitous computing are used to describe this progress of technology and its usage (Lyytinen and Yoo 2002). The relation between those stages is outlined in Figure 1.

A low level of both embeddedness and mobility characterizes traditional business computing since the size of the computer makes it visible as well as stationary in the office environment. With decreased component size, the computer becomes mobile, making it possible to carry it with us. Input to the computer is still manual, so the amount of data is finite. When the level of embeddedness increases, the computer is provided with the capability to collect data automatically from the environment in which it is embedded. Pervasive computing is such an area where sensors, identifiers, and virtual models of the physical environment are used to provide the computer with information about the environment. The level of mobility is what differentiates pervasive computing from ubiquitous computing, the fourth type of computing mobility (Lyytinen and Yoo 2002).

Remote diagnostics technology is embedded into physical products, making them literally invisible. Sensors are installed to collect data from the product; the data are then transferred via network connections for further analysis. The level of mobility, that is the other characteristic of ubiquitous computing, could be interpreted in different ways. One way is to ask if the product is mobile or not. The answer to that question varies between the different cases in this study. Some products are mobile and have wireless network connections, but some products are stationary and transfer data via a permanent telecommunications network. Mobility could, however, be viewed from a user perspective and not from an infrastructure perspective. Remote diagnostics technology is designed and developed to enable seamless monitoring of the product's condition. Alarms are automatically sent to the responsible technician via e-mail or SMS. The technology thus enables mobile monitoring of the product, independent of whether or not the local technician is in the building. We interpret mobility in the perspective of the use the technology enables and not solely in the perspective of the infrastructure: that is, whether a wireless connection is required or not. Remote diagnostics technology is thus interpreted as a ubiquitous technology, both embedded and mobile.

The development of objects that are provided with tags and sensors allows interaction and automatic data collection. Passive and active tags, microprocessors, sensors, and transmitters have enabled a continuous collection and processing of data that is cheaper and less time consuming compared to manual interaction (Alt and Zimmermann 2001). Figure 2 illustrates how the physical world and the information world merge through the development and use of ubiquitous computing.

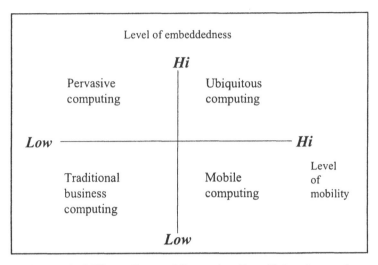

Figure 1. Different Types of Computing (from K. Lyytinen and
Y. Yoo, "Issues and Challenges in Ubiquitous Computing," *Communications
of the ACM* (45:12), 2002, pp. 63-65. Used with permission).

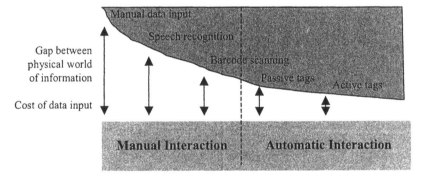

Figure 2. The Merge of the Physical World and the Information World
through Ubiquitous Computing (from E. Fleisch, "Von der Vernetzung
von Unternehmen zur Vernetzung von Dingen," in *Roadmap to
E-Business*, EM. Schögel, T. Tomczak, and Ch. Belz (Eds.),
Verlag Thexis, 2002, pp. 124-136. Used with permission.)

With traditional manual data input, the gap between the two worlds is high since the information processing is time consuming and noncontinuous, something that is changed with automatic data collection. Automatic interaction reflects the embedded perspective of ubiquitous computing as presented by Lyytinen and Yoo (2002) and the world of information enables mobility, which was the other characteristic they presented. The bits can flow in the digital network, making it possible for people to be mobile and be in different places and still have information access. In the case of remote diagnostics technology, the local group has developed skills based on the physical world, while the remote group is specialized in analyzing data in the digital world.

2.2 Actor-Network Theory and Double Immutability

With one group based on data analysis and another group skilled in physical assessments, a gap emerges. Drawing from actor network theory, and in particular the notion of double immutability, we argue that we need to establish a stable relationship that uses remote diagnostics technology for monitoring machine performance from a remote place while also keeping a level of local responsiveness toward machine performance.

The digital representation of a machine's condition is created through a transformation from the physical to the digital. A transformation process raises questions of what is gained and what is lost (Latour 2000). In Latour's studies of the transformation between the local and the universal, he showed how locality and particularity are lost in the transformation into the universal, while compatibility, standardization, and universality are gained. The transformation between the local and the universal described by Latour (2000) can be compared with the transformation between the physical and the digital with remote diagnostics technology. Both transformation processes raise questions of what is gained and what is lost and they both deal with the local and the remote. The digital world could be compared with the universal, and the physical world could be compared with the local. In order to succeed with the transformation between the local and the universal the object must have the properties of being mobile but also presentable, readable and combinable with one another, labeled by Latour (1987) as *immutable mobility*. The immutable mobile can move in time and space more or less unchanged. The immutable mobile (Law 1987; Mol and Law 1994; Singleton and Michael 1993) could, for example, be writings, maps, graphs, figures, and formulas.

Data in the digital world could be described as immutable mobile in the sense that it can be transferred all over the world and still be the same. Networks make it perfectly mobile by making it possible to transfer data thousands of kilometers in milliseconds. It is also possible to combine binary data. We can receive files from different sources, open them in the same computer, cut and paste them into the same file, and then send it further. The immutable mobile makes it possible for actors on the periphery to become familiar with events that are remote by giving them access to stable information; they can act at a distance (Latour 1987).

An immutable mobile provides a way of structuring vision and, moreover, enabling whatever is presented to be rapidly manipulated and controlled and it can be understood as the product of a series of transformations where inscriptions and translation processes are played out. Put into a technical context, inscription refers to the way technical artefacts embody patterns of use. As programs of actions are inscribed into technology, it becomes an actor that imposes its inscribed program of action on its users (Hanseth and Monteiro 1998). Inscriptions may vary in strength. Strong inscriptions leave little room for interpretative flexibility, whereas weak inscriptions leave some room for interpretation (Monteiro 2000). Translation refers to the process in which actors re-interpret and appropriate each other's interest to their own. Translation also refers to the process in which the meaning of the technology is negotiated with other elements in the environment. This process of translation embeds technology into the context of use, producing stability and social order (Callon 1986; Mähring et al. 2004).

Immutable mobiles are, in effect, examples of strong inscriptions. They are immutable in that they move in time and space more or less unchanged. But we need to pay close attention to the double nature of immutability.

> Thus the first take-home lesson from ANT and post-ANT studies is that objects often display—may be understood as being constituted in—a double immutability. On the one hand they probably have a more or less stable shape in physical space—though the definition of that stable physical shape is likely to depend on relational and interactive work of one kind or another (and it may also be that "abstract objects" don't occupy Euclidean space). On the other, they certainly have, display, or are constituted by, a more or less stable structure in a network of relations (Law and Singleton 2003, p. 6).

This notion of double immutability leads us to focus not only on remote diagnostics technology per se, but also on the network of relations in which it is embedded and the processes of translation of which it is part. In exploring this, following Law and Singleton (2003), we should pay close attention to what they refer to as the "double immutability": the stability of entities both in their physical shape and in their network of relations.

3 TRAVELING BETWEEN THE REMOTE AND THE LOCAL IN THE CONTEXT OF MAINTENANCE WORK

3.1 Method

This article is based on qualitative case studies of companies developing or using remote diagnostics technology within the maintenance industry. Six different organizations with different relations to this kind of systems have been part of the study. The organizations are MacGregor Cranes, Monitoring Control Centre (MCC), Alpha, Beta, Gamma, and PowerDrive (fictitious names on the last four). MacGregor is a manufacturer of cranes and has developed a remote diagnostics system. MCC is a service provider that offers different services based on remote diagnostics. Alpha and Beta are organizations that use remote monitoring/diagnostics in their plants. Gamma and PowerDrive are both manufacturers that have developed their own systems and offer services based on these. All companies thus have experience of either developing or using this kind of system, which give us a more overarching view of the area of remote diagnostics and the gains and losses with this kind of system from a local and remote perspective. In total, three organizations are manufacturers developing remote diagnostics technology. One organization is a pure service provider that bases their services on collected data. Two organizations are customers who have systems installed in their plants. In total, 31 people have been interviewed, ranging from engineers, technicians, after-sales personnel, remote diagnostics developers, maintenance managers, and sellers. All interviews have been recorded and transcribed. The interviews have ranged from 45 minutes to 3 hours and have been focused on how this kind of system is used and what experiences the person has from working with the technology.

Our interviews tapped into the experiences of working with remote diagnostics technology, with a particular emphasis on maintenance work. One of the aims with remote diagnostics is to enhance the maintenance process by enabling predictive or condition-based maintenance. The technology is used for monitoring and the maintenance decisions are based on both scheduled and actual condition of the product (Campbell 1995). In the following section, we will describe the use of remote diagnostics technology from a local and a remote perspective.

3.2 Remote Diagnostics Technology: A Remote Perspective

When a digital model of a physical world is created (the world of information), it becomes possible to do calculations on collected data. When the world of information is growing, the computing model contains more and more data about the product's condition and analyses are done in order to detect abnormal conditions and trends. In the maintenance industry, there seems to be a trend toward collecting more and more data to get an even more all-embracing model of the physical object. The director of maintenance at Alpha expresses it as,

We do measure parameters that we don't get any benefit of. But if you haven't measured them, the data is lost.

When this world of information is growing, it creates new conditions for how the condition-based maintenance could be performed. Remote monitoring of products makes it possible to collect data, analyze it, and do predictions at a distance from the physical product. Since the data gathering is automatic and the data could be transferred via a network, the physical dependency disappears. MCC, for example, has one office in the northern part of Sweden but envisions becoming a global service provider without opening any new offices. MacGregor is another company highlighting decreased physical dependency in promotion of their remote diagnostic service. In their brochures, their service is promoted as,

We provide seamless service solutions.....we monitor the condition and performance of your cargo handling equipment, wherever the ship is in the world.

The world of information can be created without an engineer physically visiting every product. The development of automated data collection with a decreased gap between the physical and the digital world allows for a new kind of condition-based monitoring. The engineers no longer have to visit the products; instead, more of their daily work is done in the office and consists of analyzing collected data. This data lets the engineer detect abnormal variations and, hopefully, prevents breakdowns. To companies offering services based on collection and analysis of data, the technology allows for a seamless service solution since the technology is always present in the plant.

Automated data collection also creates a stable and regular flow of data, whereas manual collection could result in corrupt data due to irregularities in time and use of instruments. A developer of remote diagnostics systems at Gamma view it as,

Manual measuring is not acceptable. People are not good at repeatable accuracy. You don't pressure [the instrument] in the same way each time, you don't hold it in the same way and you are not able to place the measuring circuit in the same position each time. What people are good on are analyses.

With computerized measuring, the regularity and measuring technique is always the same. Computerized automated data collection will thus enhance the creation of a stable and regular data collection. The Gamma developer indicated that this would make the data automatically collected more reliable. The stability of data would thus be enhanced.

The technical development has also allowed for other actors to offer services based on remote monitoring of products. A manufacturer can collect data from a product located in another part of the world, analyze it, and take actions based on the information. PowerDrive has developed a remote service offer where they collect data from products all around the world and then transfer it back to their main office where analysis takes place. Collection of data from many dispersed objects in one place enhances the possibility of comparing data and the people doing the analyses get experience from many different machines and settings. MCC and MacGregor have developed similar services. MacGregor promotes their service as, *"Wherever you are—we are there."* This should, of course, be interpreted in a virtual sense. MacGregor is not present physically but their remote diagnostics system, through which they can follow the use and condition of the crane in its actual environment, is always present. MacGregor is thus present in the crane's environment in a virtual manner via the technology.

To the manufacturer, the use of remote diagnostics technology is an interesting area since it creates new business opportunities in the after-sale market while at the same time giving them important feedback about the products in use. With remote monitoring of products the manufacturer gets a picture of how they work in actual settings and if common problems within product runs exist. PowerDrive, for example, has been using their system to test products before they are launched to the market. To PowerDrive, the system has been valuable in product development since it gives them an overall picture about certain product categories.

3.3 Remote Diagnostics Technology: A Local Perspective

Although the products are constantly monitored with remote diagnostics technology, only a specified number of parameters can be collected. Thus, the picture the distant technician gets is not total. As the director at MCC expresses it,

When you physically walk around in the plant, you get a lot of other signals; you see, hear, and feel.

The diagnoses that can be performed with the system are limited to the number of parameters that are monitored. A physical walk-around by an experienced engineer who can see, hear, and feel when something is abnormal can detect things that the remote diagnostics technology cannot. As a hydraulic engineer at Beta expresses it,

You have to learn to know the machines individually. You don't do that remotely.

This highlights a clear limitation with the remote diagnostics technology compared to an experienced engineer walking around in the plant. Although the system can detect conditions by detailed analysis that the engineer cannot, many of the respondents point out the importance of keeping in mind that there is a world out there and the collected data on its own is not enough. The limitations of the technology are expressed by the hydraulic engineer at Beta as,

With more monitoring, you can work more and more online and less people will be out among the machines. You won't get the same feeling of the machines. The only things you see are, for example, temperature, pressure, and flow. You don't know how it sounds.

The system and, therefore, also the remote technicians are limited to the data collected by the sensors. The limited depiction of the reality is a technological constraint that always has to be kept in mind and considered. Another constraint related to this kind of system is highlighted in an event at Alpha. An engineer at the company described how they installed a diagnostics system at one of the oil pumps that monitored the oil level. This system was supposed to be a complement to the operators' traditional regular walk rounds in the plant. When the oil level sank, an engineer located in another building called the operator and instructed him to fill it with more oil. After a while the operator got used to the phone calls and stopped walking around in the plant. The system, however, only measured the oil level and did not give the engineer in the office an overall depiction of the machine and its environment. One day the machine almost broke down due to other problems that the system did not detect, but the operator would have seen it if he had walked by. To him, the phone calls had become a work practice indicating problems and, therefore, he viewed the walk rounds as unnecessary.

The example highlights the constraint of remote diagnostics technology described earlier; the depiction of the reality is limited and all problems cannot be detected. But the example also gives us insight into another potential constraint with the remote technology: the technology can create a remote closeness where engineers in another room, house, organization, or even part of the world can get close to the equipment. However, at the same time, this may create a local physical distance in the plant, as happened in the case above. The operator stopped walking by the machine physically since he relied on the digital information environment and the procedure of getting an alarm when something had to be done. The operator experienced that the use of the technology created new working procedures on which he comfortably relied. The example highlights the benefit of a remote closeness but, more important, it shows a potential loss when a local physical distance is created. The operator in this case stopped doing the walk rounds and, although the operator was in the same building as the machine, the technological environment made him view the traditional physical closeness as unnecessary; thus a local physical distance was created. As has been pointed out, the technology has its own benefits and the physical walks rounds by the local group have other benefits.

3.4 The Relation Between the Local and the Remote Perspective

Both the local and the remote group seem to have their own benefits and con-straints. All of the organizations involved in this study report perceived benefits related to the use of remote diagnostics technology in terms of an increased remote awareness of their processes. There are advantages for maintenance work in terms of a better understanding of how machines and procedures function. The advantages to the local group are, however, also raised. Physical presence gives information impossible to transform into the digital world.

The introduction of remote diagnostics technology makes it important to handle the relationship between the two groups, especially since there seems to be a perceived shift in responsibility in the eyes of the local group. As the director at MCC expresses it,

> *It's very important that the border between the two groups is clear. The local groups must be well fuctioning...they must have basic control of the machines. This doesn't work today. The borders are very unclear. When the company buys services from the remote group, the local group seems to view the remote group as responsible for everything, at the same time as the remote group views the local group as responsible for basic monitoring and walk rounds. This happens when the borders are not clear; the responsibility has to be clearly expressed.*

The increased "remote closeness" came as a result of the use of remote diagnostics technology, but we could also see a certain increase in the "local physical distance," which has to do with local groups assessing walk rounds as unnecessary and shifting responsibility. This seems to be a challenge to be bridged.

4   DISCUSSION

The findings illustrate how remote diagnostics technology is a ubiquitous and increasingly critical part of the fabric of the modern organization, supporting its operations. In particular, remote diagnostics technology influences which organizational actions, and their consequences, become more visible. Arguably more than anything else, ubiquitous computing is characterized by a separation of data from the technology through which it was collected (Avital and Germonprez 2003) and the collected data represents a digital model of the physical world. Introducing an actor-network perspective on these cases highlights the role that remote diagnostics technology plays in shaping organizational realities through the norms and values embedded within it. We focus on double immutability in this process, and, taken together, this gives us insight into the relationship between the central and the local maintenance groups in the maintenance of products embedded with remote diagnostics technology.

4.1 The Local and the Remote

The remote diagnostics technology has in these cases shown a degree of immutability in its character. Respondents at all companies view the technology as effective in that critical data can be easily collected, diffused, and analyzed. The data is perceived as stable in the sense that it can be transferred via the digital network to remote service groups without being corrupted. The involved companies see a great potential in the possibility of combining data from dispersed products, making it possible to compare them and hopefully drawing valuable conclusions. The three characters of the immutable mobile—mobility, stability, and combinability—thus seem to be characteristics suited for remote diagnostics technologies. The other side of double immutability concerns the stability of the network of relations. In our cases, it seems as if this stability is a challenge yet to be bridged.

The digital world of information enabled by remote diagnostics technology can be seen as an abstracted view of the machines in the physical world; it is a snapshot including some specified parameters. On an aggregate level, these parameters are to capture the performance of the machine in which the remote diagnostics technology is embedded. Focusing on the transformation between the local and the remote can help to explain the remote diagnostics process. As is told by some of the respondents, a physical visit to the machines give maintenance workers information through all of the senses. This is lost when the machine is diagnosed remotely via a specified number of parameters. The sensors only detect what they are designed to detect; the local maintenance worker can get additional information other than the parameters he his checking. One should, however, bear in mind that the sensors can register data that maintenance workers cannot, but nevertheless a sense of locality is lost when specified data is collected and transferred away via the digital network to a remote place.

While qualities related to locality are lost, factors like compatibility and relative universality are gained with remote diagnostics technology. The transformation of the machine's condition into digital numbers makes it possible for a central service center to compare different machines with their ideal condition and with each other, independent of their physical location. It also becomes easier to do calculations in order to predict what is about to happen with the machine in order to perform timely maintenance. The technology thus enables a *remote closeness* in the sense that the central service center can constantly diagnose the product, independent of the physical distance. They can, in a virtual sense, always be present in order to help the customers maintain their products. At the same time as the remote closeness is gained, there is a potential loss. As illustrated by the cases in this study, the remote closeness can create a *local distance* when the monitoring of the machine is digitalized. The remote group cannot collect the same data as the local technician, nor can the technician collect the same detailed data as the remote group do via the technology. When diagnostics are based solely on technology and the responsibility is shifted to the remote group a local physical distance emerges. The network of relations between those two groups must be clear and stable so each groups' benefits are used, otherwise the local distance may destroy the benefits of the central service group when remote diagnostics technology is to be used.

4.2 Creating a Maintenance Collective

Remote technology is used for leveraging the "digital information world"—the representation of machine performance of importance for maintenance work. This enable more effective control from the side of the central service group. In the companies studied, both the local maintenance group and the remote service group examined in this study were aware of both their own and the other party's roles and responsibilities. The remote group knew that they were not able to diagnose the product to 100 percent. The local group perceived their own work in the same way; they knew they were not able to predict the condition of the machines with the same precision as the remote diagnostics technology.

Although both parties were aware of the limitations in their own work, the network of relations between them has not been addressed in such a way that seems to be necessary in order to establish a maintenance collective that works well. Instead the local groups perceived a shifted responsibility from themselves to the central groups, which can have damaging effects on maintenance work. Neglected maintenance from the local group could result in an overall unsuccessful maintenance strategy since these two groups do not replace each other. Instead, they should be viewed as complementary and, woven together, they could constitute a strong maintenance collective.

Through such a collective, stability in the network of relations can be achieved. This other face of immutability thus seems to be something that the involved parties have to take into consideration during the design work. Instead of focusing only on the technology per se and the remote group's work, both faces of the immutability have to be considered. Thereby, a maintenance collective can emerge where all parties—the technology, the remote group, and the local group—contribute to the double immutability.

5 CONCLUSIONS

The purpose of this paper has been to display the use of remote diagnostics technology in organizations, in particular the way in which the technology is enacted in central and local maintenance groups. To address the various circumstances that surround the use of remote diagnostics technology, the notion of double immutability was introduced and discussed. This provided a language to talk about the efforts needed to establish a maintenance collective that works well and that can face the challenges involved in the maintenance of machines in which remote diagnostics technology has been embedded.

The results revealed that information technology was used for leveraging the information world—the representation of machine performance of importance for maintenance work. In our cases, we have seen how the remote diagnostics technology creates a *remote closeness* between objects and actors physically dispersed but at the same time it creates a *local physical distance* when actors and objects physically close to each other move their interaction into the ubiquitous computing environment. The possibilities to transfer data have opened up the possibilities to *get knowledge about objects that are distant* and *combine data from these physically dispersed objects*, which enhances the creation of an overall depiction. Ubiquitous computing could thus enhance the creation of a *global depiction of remote phenomenon*.

Following Law and Singleton (2003) and their idea of the double immutability— that the stability of entities is found both in their physical shape and in a network of relations—we find that stability is sustained in two partially related ways. The stability of the remote diagnostics technology is seemingly effective in that critical data can be collected, diffused, and manipulated. But the stability of the network of relations surrounding the technology is yet to emerge. In our application of the notion of double immutability, we identified the challenge of better integrating central and local maintenance group in the maintenance of products embedded with remote diagnostics technology. The borders between the remote group and the local maintenance workers must be considered and we need to acknowledge that it takes effort to sustain stable networks of relations. We need to establish a new relationship that uses ubiquitous computing technology for monitoring processes and activities from the central group while also keeping a level of local responsiveness toward machine performance. Taken together, the remote and the local group, along with the remote diagnostics technology, could constitute a maintenance work collective.

REFERENCES

Alt, R., and Zimmermann, H.-D. "Introduction to Special Section—Business Models," *Electronic Market* (11:1), 2001, pp. 3-9.

Avital, M., and Germonprez, M. "Ubiquitous Computing: Surfing the Trend in a Balanced Act," paper presented at the Workshop on Ubiquitous Computing Environment, Cleveland, OH, October 23-26, 2003.

Callon, M. "Some Elements of a Sociology of Translation: Domestication of the Scallops and Fishermen of St Brieuc Bay," in *Power, Action and Belief: A Sociology of Knowledge?*, J. Law (Ed.), London: Routledge and Kegan Paul, 1986, pp. 196-233.

Campbell, J. D. *Uptime: Strategies for Excellence in Maintenance Management*, Portland, OR: Productivity Press, 1995.

Chae, B. "Ubiquitous Computing for Mundane Knowledge Management: Hopes, Challenges and Questions," paper presented at the Workshop on Ubiquitous Computing Environment, Cleveland, OH, October 24-26, 2003.

Davis, G. B. "Affordances of Ubiquitous Computing and Productivity in Knowledge Work," paper presented at the Workshop on Ubiquitous Computing Environments, Cleveland, OH, October 24-26, 2003.

Fleisch, E. "Von der Vernetzung von Unternehmen zur Vernetzung von Dingen," in *Roadmap to E-Business*, M. Schönegel, T. Tomczak, and Ch. Belz (Eds.), St. Gallen, Switzerland: Verlag Thexis, 2002, pp. 124-136.

Giles, C. L., and Purao, S. "The Role of Search in Ubiquitous Computing," paper presented at the Workshop on Ubiquitous Computing, Cleveland, OH, October 23-26, 2003.

Grudin, J. "Implications of Technology Use throughout Organizations," paper presented at the Workshop on Ubiquitous Computing, Cleveland, OH, October 23-26, 2003.

Hanseth, O., and Monteiro, E. "Changing Irreversible Networks: Institutionalization and Infrastructure," in *Proceedings of 6th European Conference on Information Systems*, W. R. J. Baets (Ed.), Euro-Arab Management School, Granada, Spain, 1998, pp. 1123-1139.

Kuschel, J., and Ljungberg, F. "Decentralized Remote Diagnostics: A Study of Diagnostics in the Marine Industry," in *People and Computers XVIII: Design for* Life, S. Fincher, P. Markopoulos, D. Moore, and R. Ruddell (Eds.), London: Springer, 2004,pp. 211-226.

Latour, B. *Pandora's Hope: Essays on the Reality of Science Studies*, Cambridge, MA: Harvard University Press, 2000.

Latour, B. *Science in Action,* Cambridge, MA: Harvard University Press, 1987.

Law, J. "On the Methods of Long-Distance Control: Vessels, Navigation and the Portuguese Route to India," in *Power, Action and Belief: A New Sociology of Knowledge*, J. Law (Ed.), London: Routledge and Kegan Paul, 1987, pp, 234-263.

Law, J., and Singleton, V. *Object Lessons*, Lancaster, UK: The Centre for Science Studies, Lancaster University, 1987.

Lyytinen, K., and Yoo, Y. "Issues and Challenges in Ubiquitous Computing," *Communications of the ACM* (45:12), 2003, pp. 63-65.

Mähring, M., Holmström, J., Keil, M., and Montealegre, R. "Trojan Actor-Networks and Swift Translation: Bringing Actor-Network Theory to IT Project Escalation Studies," *Information Technology and People* (17:2), 2004, pp. 210-238.

Medovich, M. "Pervasive Computing and Pervasive Economies in the 21st Century," paper presented at the Workshop on Ubiquitous Computing Environment, Cleveland, OH, October 23-26, 2003.

Mol, A., and Law, J. "Regions, Networks and Fluids: Anaemia and Social Topology," *Social Studies of Science* (24:4), 1994, pp. 641-671.

Monteiro, E. "Actor-Network Theory," in *From Control to Drift: The Dynamics of Corporate Information Infrastructure*, C. U. Ciborra, K. Braa, A. Cordella, B. Dahlbom, A. Failla, O. Hanseth, V. Hespo, J. Ljungberg, E. Monteiro, and K. A. Simon (Eds.), Oxford: Oxford University Press, 2000, pp. 71-83.

Singleton, V., and Michael, M. "Actor-Networks and Ambivalence: General Practitioners in the UK Cervical Screening Programme," *Social Studies of Science* (23:2), 1993, pp. 227-264.

ABOUT THE AUTHORS

Katrin Jonsson is a Ph.D. student and instructor at the department of Informatics, Umeå University, Sweden. Her research is situated within ubiquitous information environments and investigates its implications in organizations. Her thesis project focuses on remote diagnostics technology use in the industry and she is collaborating with a number of manufacturing and process-industry companies. Katrin can be reached at katrin.jonsson@informatik.umu.se.

Jonny Holmström is an assistant professor in Informatics at the University of Umeå, Sweden and a research manager the Centre of Digital Business. His current research includes empirical examinations of innovation networks with particular emphasis on the technologies that support them. He has published his research in Information and Organization, Information Technology and People, Journal of Global Information Technology Management, Scandinavian Journal of Information Systems, and at major international conferences. Jonny can be reached at jonny.holmstrom@informatik.umu.se

14 WIRELESS GRIDS: Assessing a New Technology from a User Perspective

Lee W. McKnight
Raed M. Sharif
Syracuse University
Syracuse, NY U.S.A.

Lidwien van de Wijngaert
Utrecht University
Utrecht, The Netherlands

Abstract   *The objective of this paper is to assess the value of wireless grids from the perspective of users. In a ubiquitous information environment, wireless grids allow the ad hoc sharing of resources (e.g., microphones, screens, processing power) of edge devices (e.g., mobile phone, laptop, PDA). Wireless grids are one of the emerging wireless communication concepts that have been developed in university and industry research laboratories. So far, literature about wireless grids has tackled some of the technical and policy issues about the technology. This paper provides the first empirical study about wireless grid technology from the user perspective.*

Using Rogers' diffusion of innovations model, this paper focuses on the future diffusion of this technology. Using the results of two focus group meetings, we suggest that the introduction of the technology and its future diffusion will be a complex process. The future acceptance and use of this technology requires not only social and mental changes to move from one stage to another in the diffusion process, but also changes in the coordination and pricing mechanisms, and even changes in the technology itself.

1 INTRODUCTION

"Wireless communications is a rapidly evolving and promising sector of the communications arena, and even in a challenging time for the telecommunications industry, represents a significant development opportunity for companies and organizations in creating a global market" (McKnight et al. 2002, p. 11). The products and services of this sector, mainly wireless devices, are increasing in numbers, and their power is growing (Gaynor et al. 2003). People are increasingly using wireless devices in their professional and personal lives. Different research and development efforts are taking place in industry and universities to further develop these devices and find new potentials for their use. One of the new emerging concepts of wireless communications is wireless grids. As the concept of wireless grids is new, we will first provide a description of what the technology encompasses. After that, we will present the goals of our research and the results in the rest of this paper.

1.1 Wireless Grids

According to McKnight et al. (2004), "Wireless Grids is a new type of resource sharing network that connects sensors, mobile phones, and other edge devices with each other and with the wired grid. Ad hoc distributed resource sharing allows these devices to offer new resources and locations of use for grid computing" (p. 24).

The ultimate vision of the grid is that of an adaptive network offering secure, inexpensive, and coordinated real-time access to dynamic, heterogeneous resources, potentially traversing geographic, political and cultural boundaries but still able to maintain the desirable characteristics of a simple distributed system, such as stability, transparency, scalability and flexibility (McKnight et al. 2002, p. 2).

To give more insight about the nature of this technology and its use, we present a number of wireless grids applications that were developed by the wireless grids research team at Syracuse University. These application can be used both in an organizational as well as an end user context.

1.1.1 Distributed Audio Recording

Most small devices have the ability to record simple audio. Cell phones, PDAs, and most laptops have a simple microphone built in. The problem with these simple audio recording devices is that they produce simple audio. They don't produce stereo sound, and they might not pick up subtle sounds in the background, like a person talking on the other side of a room.

What distributed audio recording application does is build a small wireless network of these devices and then share the recorded audio between them. By combining the audio from these different devices, it is possible to make a stereo recording. Another possibility is to combine several streams in a lecture or office meeting and get a good recording of questions without having to pass around a microphone or have people aim their conversation toward a tape recorder.

Figure 1 provides a graphical outline of the service architecture for the distributed audio recording and other wireless grid applications.

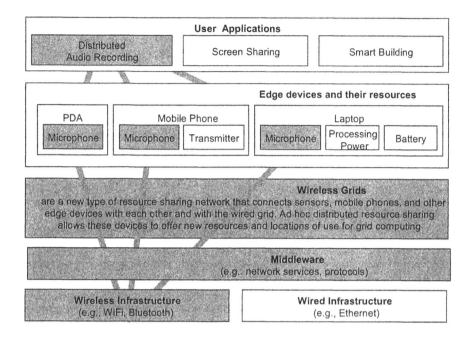

Figure 1. Wireless Grid Architecture

There are two resources being shared with the distributed audio recording application: a recorder resource and a mixer resource. The recorder is simply a resource that will capture a live audio stream using a microphone of some kind. The mixer resource can take advantage of multiple recorder resources and mix them together to create a unified audio stream.

1.1.2 Wireless Ad Hoc Screen Sharing

Another example of a wireless grid application can be found at a typical business meeting where more than one person will be presenting something, using slides. Often, each person has their own laptop which contains the presentation, and people take turns connecting their machines to a projector. The projector tends to become a bottleneck because each person who wants to present using the projector needs to (1) hook up their laptop to the projector and (2) find and change the settings needed to use the projector. While this may not seem like a big ordeal, it gets to be more of a problem when there are more people making presentations (for example, at academic conferences). The wireless ad hoc screen sharing application gets rid of having to make a physical connection to a projector by essentially sharing the projector with one or more different laptops over a wireless network.

In order to share a projector, two different pieces of software are needed. The first software, the display manager, resides on a single machine that is hooked up to the projector. This software is in charge of deciding who is the current "owner" of the projector. The second piece of software, the display client, runs on the laptop of anyone who wants to use the projector. The two pieces of software talk to each other over a wireless network and share the graphics shown on a given screen (McKnight et al. 2004).

1.1.3   Smart Buildings and Location Aware PDAs

A third example of a wireless grid application is that of a PDA connecting to the wireless network inside a building. Not only does it connect to the wireless network, but also it becomes a location-aware device within the building. It shows a map of the building, with an indicator of where you are on that map. Using the building intranet site on the PDA, it is possible to retrieve directions and announce arrival, for example, by using voice over IP (VoIP) technology to turn your PDA into a local communicator.

1.2 Research Goal

During the past decade, the concept of wireless grid technology has emerged in different industrial and academic labs (e.g., Intel Research at Berkeley and the TeleCom City project of Syracuse University, MIT, Tufts, and Boston University). Most of this research has focused on the technical challenges and developments of wireless grids. Although theoretical work has been done in the areas of economic and future market challenges of wireless grids; no empirical studies were directed to the potential individual users themselves to hear about their perceptions, beliefs, attitudes, and concerns about this technology. Gaynor et al. (2003) and McKnight et al. (2002) suggest that further research is needed in the area of the economic and market challenges of wireless grid technology.

This empirical study is the first of its kind in the area of wireless grid technology where empirical evidence about the future use of this technology by individual users was collected. Using the basic elements of Rogers' (1995) model for the diffusion of innovations, our aim is to assess the value of wireless grids outside the laboratory from a user perspective and its potential diffusion model.

We will proceed by describing our theoretical framework, which strongly draws on the work of Rogers. In section 3, we will describe how two focus group meetings were set up and analyzed. Section 4 describes the results from these focus groups and, in section 5, we will discuss the conclusion and limitations of the research and opportunities for further research.

2   DIFFUSION OF INNOVATIONS

Several theories help to explain the adoption and use of new technologies: diffusion of innovations (Rogers 1995), domestication (Silverstone and Haddon 1996), sense making (Dervin 1986), and (unified) technology adoption model (Davis 1989; Venkatesh et al. 2003) are just a few examples of the many possible theoretical frameworks. Although we are aware of the fact that each of these theories, models, and frameworks can provide important insights with regard to the adoption and use of wireless grids, we chose to start this paper, the first that investigates wireless grids from a user rather than a technical perspective, with Rogers' classic work on the diffusion of innovations.

Rogers' work on the diffusion of innovations provides us with a starting point to understand how wireless grids might diffuse through time and space. Rogers defines the diffusion of innovations as "is the process by which an innovation is communicated through certain channels among the members of a social system" (p. 5). Looking from the perspective of individual-level adoption decisions, Rogers identifies five characteristics of the innovation that can either facilitate or impede the adoption of an innovation.

- *Relative advantage* is the degree to which the innovation is perceived as being better than the idea it supersedes. The degree of relative advantage is, for example, expressed in economic profitability or social status.
- *Compatibility* is the degree to which an innovation is perceived as consistent with the existing (socio-cultural) values, past experiences with previously introduced ideas, and the need for innovations by potential adopters.
- *Complexity* is the degree to which an innovation is difficult to understand and use.
- *Triability* is the degree to which an innovation can be experimented with on a limited basis.
- *Observability* is the degree to which the benefits of the proposed innovation are visible.

Besides these characteristics of the innovation, Rogers mentions numerous other factors that explain the rapid diffusion of an innovation. These factors not only relate to the individual's decision to adopt or reject an innovation, but place it in a broader context. Rogers, for example, mentions the type of innovation decisions and the way in which communication channels and change agents function.

In this paper, we will also address another important factor in the diffusion process: diffusion networks. The S-shaped curve is used to describe the process of more and more people joining in the innovation. In the beginning of the process, diffusion is slow and the number of new users is small. Oliver et al. (1985) argue that people who adopt an innovation in this phase choose to make a big contribution to the collective action while the majority do little or nothing. Once a "critical mass" is reached, Markus (1987) states that enough individuals have adopted an innovation so that the innovation's further rate of adoption becomes self-sustaining. In the last phase of the S-shaped adoption curve, the number of new users again diminishes. Here the market is reaching saturation: the moment in which the maximum number of adopters is reached. This does not necessarily need to be 100 percent of the population, but rather 100 percent of the potential adopters. In addition, the traditional S-shaped curve changes when the innovation is an interactive service (like telephone, fax, e-mail, and wireless grids). Economides (1991) states that network externalities occur when "the buyer of the last unit of a good has a higher benefit than the buyer of the first unit because the sale of the earlier units has created some benefit in a related dimension." In other words, network externalities are a quality of certain goods and services such that they become more valuable to a user as the number of users increases. This makes reaching a critical mass even more difficult than for products that do not have network externalities.

3   RESEARCH METHOD

Our research is aimed at obtaining insight into the starting position of the technology. As mentioned above, the main goal of this study is to predict the future diffusion model of wireless grid technology through listening to the thoughts and concerns of potential individual users about this new technology. Therefore, we have performed two focus group meetings. Volunteers for the focus groups were recruited through e-mail and personal invitations. The invitations were sent to three categories: faculty members, staff members, and graduate students (Ph.D. and Master's levels). Twenty volunteers were divided into two separate focus group meetings. Because it is a new technology and given the lack of awareness about this technology and its potential use, it was decided to start the meetings with a 20 minute introductory presentation about the technology with another 20 minutes to answer the participants' questions. During the 1-hour discussion, the participants were asked the same questions, which focused on the potential individual user's perceptions, attitudes, concerns, and future intentions regarding wireless grid technology.

The video recordings of the focus groups were transcribed and entered into the content analysis software Kwalitan (Peters 2004). This software allows systematic ordering of open, qualitative, unstructured data. The data from focus group meetings were analyzed using content analysis and a coding scheme developed by the researchers. The coding scheme was based on the theoretical framework presented earlier in this paper.

4   RESULTS

In this section, we will provide an overview of the discussion that took place during the focus group meetings. We will examine how wireless grids as an innovation hold up to the factors that were enumerated by Rogers.

4.1 Relative Advantage

From a very theoretical and abstract point of view, the participants' could see many values and benefits in using this technology. Their first and immediate reaction and reflections on the technology consisted of a strong agreement that using this technology is valuable especially in terms of time and effort saving and in providing them with new resources and capabilities. The participants went even further and provided different scenarios where sharing resources through the wireless grid technology might help in making their lives easier and more efficient.

It's very promising technology. The resources are extensive; there are lots of things to share and the case of cell phone is one of them. Many times you have the cell phone but don't have the signals and it is a common problem these days. If I am next to someone with a signal, which is a common situation too, given that we have different cell phones companies with different coverage capacities, and my cell phone will immediately pick the signal from this person, this is all what I need, at the end of the day I want to use the cell phone to have my work done.

Yes, I think it is absolutely useful. For example, I am still carrying my laptop wherever I go to do my work, which is still very heavy. If we reduce the size to the PDA and I can do everything on the PDA including my homework, for example, through sharing others' resources, this will definitely help me and make my life easier.

Wow, this seems to be very cool technology and will allow me to be more mobile with my smart devices.

However, from a practical point of view, especially after discussing the use of this technology in real-life scenarios and after being asked if they would share their resources in real-life cases under different circumstances, the participants started to realize and identify some concerns might be associated with the use of this technology. The focus of these concerns was mainly on security, privacy, and trust issues. In the context of wireless grid technology, the participants' security concerns were mostly related to loss of information, information and/or device damage, and other security consequences.

For me, the security will be a very big concern; it is just related to the human tendency. For example, if I have this small device and people are going to request the processing power of my device, I am going to worry about viruses and other security and privacy issues, so to reduce this complexity, I would probably say no.

If people ask me to share some of my resources, I might say no. Yes, no because this is my device and I don't want to run into technical problems later because I let people use it.

I definitely think that security would be an issue. I guess I should be able to choose whom I can give or share information with. That would make me feel so much safer.

4.2 Compatibility

Using IT is almost synonymous with fast change. In general people are used to the fact that new technologies build on existing ones (e.g., a mobile phone with an Internet connection, a laptop with a wireless connection, a PDA that can send e-mail). A mobile phone that can use the signal of another phone or a laptop that can share a screen with another laptop seems like a logical next step. In that sense, the use of wireless grids seems like an innovation that is very compatible with other existing technologies.

However, the trust and privacy issues that were mentioned by the participants strongly relate to the concept of compatibility. Sharing a personal item like a laptop or mobile phone is something that would require at least a mental and social change of how we perceive devices and their resources as our own.

How people will be able to protect their personal and private information and what will make sure that this personal information will not be accessed and/or stolen were among the participants' questions and concerns when using wireless grid technology and sharing their resources with others. Some of the reactions to this issue were extreme and tended toward total rejection, which was also reflected by one participant's body language and signs of fear of losing something.

> Of course I will never let anybody share my resources and to give them the chance to access my private and personal stuff. Oh my God! It's my privacy.

Others, however, expressed moderate but conditional reactions and responses and they seemed to be willing to compromise some of their security and privacy in case the technology would provide some solutions.

> Yes, I fully agree that sharing resources with others will be very valuable, but I think the privacy and ownership issues will be of very special concern not only for me, but for most of the people I guess.

> I am OK in this community and this environment of sharing resources, but I would need somewhere in my computing world where I could block some of my stuff away so not everything is accessible in every way. I think that there has to be identified levels of accessibility.

Participants put a high level of trust as an important condition to share resources with others; they also suggested that different levels of trust could be found in this kind of relationships. The participants identified two levels of trust. Trust at a personal level (e.g., family and friends) and trust at a professional level (e.g., work colleagues).

4.3 Complexity

Of special concern for the participants about sharing resources with others and the consequences of this process is the pricing and coordination mechanism that will coordinate, regulate, and manage the way people use and deal with this technology.

> The question is not whether it is valuable or not, the question is what is the best business model that can make it work?

I don't want to personally negotiate with people the sharing of resources, I just want to know what is available and to have it, there must be a system that manages this process, If I need to get into negotiations, then it is not worth my time.

Another thing that would also be of concern is the price factor. How much I will charge? For what service? And how to get the money? These are questions need to be answered.

So, as long as the sharing is limited within a small and known community or work group context, complexity will be relatively low as the people that want to share are trusted friends or colleagues. But when the use of wireless grids grows and enters the public space, complexity increases considerably. Once outside a small community of friends or colleagues, it will be quite complex to find a model in which people are willing to share their resources and still understand the system. People may be willing to share, if there is something in it for them as well. A business model in which people can exchange credits or real money may be too much to ask, at least at the early stages of the diffusion process. So people will need to find a balance between security (allowing strangers to use their device), the degree of disruptiveness and the risk of losing valuable assets, and the possible benefits of sharing.

4.4 Triability

When asked about possible solutions for the problems and concerns they raised, and as an indicator of the willingness of people to balance the potential cost (financial and nonfinancial) and benefits (financial and nonfinancial) of the technology, the participants suggested starting to use wireless grid technology in communities. These communities with, to a large extent, known and trusted members (e.g., project teams, faculty members, doctors) can serve as a role model or a demonstration site of the technology for other future individual users. Within this community, where sharing resources will be free of charge, the participants believe the security and trust issues will not be a big concern.

I would want to be sure that I am sharing with only the people that I know and trust, for example my coworkers, and then once I am comfortable with it and comfortable with what is out there and what is happening, I probably would go to the next level and I would share with the public. There would be A-level users, and B-level users, etc.

After some period of time, where they will have the opportunity to test this technology with known and trusted people, the participants said that they can move to another level outside their community where other coordination, pricing, and payment mechanisms need to be identified.

4.5 Observability

In order to see what observability means for wireless grids, we need to look at the technology from a broader perspective. Over the past few years, we have seen how mobile phones (and other small devices like PDAs and notebooks) have turned into fashion items (Fortunati 2001). New technologies are not only purchased for their functionality, but also as a social statement. Although many people will not actually use all these features, people like having the opportunity to use them, if only to show off to other people. Innovators and early adopters are especially sensitive to this opportunity (Rogers 1995). Wireless grids could be an addition to the list of capabilities of laptops, mobile phones, and PDAs. When adopting (and not actually using) the technology is a sufficient reason for purchasing it, one could argue that observability of the technology is very high. Peer-to-peer communication with regard to the advantages of wireless grids could then become an important factor in the fast diffusion of the technology. Finally, once people have the technology installed in a device, it is easy to play around and experiment with it in different situations, increasing the level of observability.

4.6 Network Effects

Finally, we want to focus on network externalities and the diffusion effect as an important factor in the fast diffusion of wireless grids. The use of wireless grid technology requires some other devices that also have this technology installed. This situation is unlike the use of a mobile phone which can be used to contact another mobile phone as well as a fixed phone. Because the installed base of fixed phones is very high, purchase of a mobile phone has immediate value. Early adopters of wireless grids are confronted with a lack of other users with whom to share their devices. This interdependence on the system level has a negative effect of the diffusion of wireless grids. The lack of a critical mass of users is a threat to the diffusion of wireless grids. This stresses the importance of the wireless grid as a social statement (no network externalities) and the use of Wireless Grids within small communities (critical mass is easily reached). That also reaffirms the importance of having good marketing strategies for the wireless grids, especially free trials and subsidized communities.

5   CONCLUSION AND DISCUSSION

5.1 Limitations and Further Research

This paper is based on the results of two focus groups of highly educated people who were familiar with the field of information technology. Although the level of subjectivity of the qualitative and interpretive approach we used is relatively high, and although it might be difficult to generalize the findings, this was one of the few relevant approaches, especially in the case of the first paper on this topic, to collect some insight into the future of this technology from the perspective of the user.

We intend to follow further development of wireless grids. Currently, we are conducting a policy capturing study. The goal of this study is to obtain insight into the conditions under which people are willing to share their resources and to be confronted with some of their security, privacy, and trust concerns. By presenting respondents with different real-life scenarios, we can see in which cases people are or are not willing to share. Factors that are being studied, for example, are the degree of trust in the situation, the degree to which the request is related to an emergency or a regular situation, who benefits from sharing (only the person who wants to share or both), and the gender of the asker. Besides these situational characteristics, we also take user characteristics (such as gender, IT experience, and altruism) into account.

Furthermore, we will study a group of high school students who will be experimenting with wireless grids during a summer course in 2005. These students will be equipped with PDAs that are enabled for wireless grids. By closely watching how the process of mutual shaping develops, we will be able to draw conclusions not only on the diffusion of wireless grids, but also on the diffusion of future related new technologies.

5.2 Conclusion

Rogers' concept of relative advantage was clearly described by participants in the focus groups in terms of benefits of the technology. Other issues, such as trust, privacy, and security relate to Rogers' concepts of compatibility and triability. The respondents search for a viable business model also relates to Rogers' concept of complexity. Observability and network externalities, although important theoretical measures in the diffusion of wireless grids, were not explicitly mentioned by people in the focus groups.

From the findings we should conclude that the introduction of wireless grids is not a simple process. Drawing on theories that stress the introduction of new technology as a dynamic process, the authors suggest that people need to learn how to share their resources in a process of mutual adaptation (Williams and Edge 1996). Therefore, we argue that the introduction of wireless grids should follow a step-wise process. In this process, critical mass is not reached once, but several times, in different situations, and with different technologies (Bouwman et al. 1992). Figure 2 illustrates how we see this process.

We can also conclude that the technology has three immediate potential groups of users. The first group is the group of people who are already up to date with the latest wireless communication technologies (e.g., Wi-Fi and Bluetooth). Such a group of people might include, but not be limited to, engineers, managers, faculty members, students, and IT professionals. We believe that this group will be one of the easiest groups to target. The second group is teenagers, who are inclined to obtain new technologies in order to underline their social status. Based on the past examples of cell phones, digital cameras, and PDAs, we expect this group to behave similarly with regard to wireless grid technology and to show high interest in adding this technology to their other fashion technologies. A third opportunity is to introduce the technology within specific communities (e.g., hospitals, police, fire fighters).

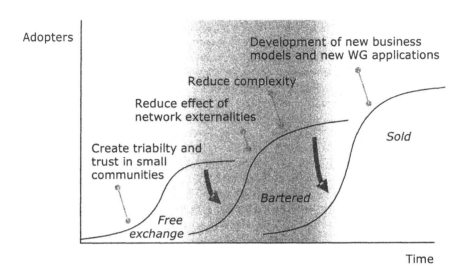

Figure 2. Mutual Shaping of Technology and Diffusion

On the diffusion road of wireless grids, there are many pitfalls that might prevent wireless grids from becoming successful. Lack of trust and network externalities are factors that need to be addressed with care. In this process, the technology will change and adapt itself to the new situation.

REFERENCES

Bouwman, H., Christoffersen, M., and Ohlin, T. "Introduction. Videotex: Is There a Life After Death?," in *Relaunching Videotex*, H. Bouwman and M. Christoffersen (Eds.), Dordrecht: Kluwer Academic Publishers, 1992, pp. 7-15.

Davis, F. D. "Perceived Usefulness, Perceived Ease of Use, and User Acceptance of Information Technology," *MIS Quarterly* (13:3), 1989, pp. 319-341.

Dervin, B. , and Nilan, M. "Information Needs and Uses," *Annual Review of Information Science and Technology* (21), 1986, pp. 3-33.

Economides, N. "Compatibility and the Creation of Shared Networks," Chapter 3 in *Electronic Services Networks: A Business and Public Policy Challenge*, M. E. Guerin-Calvert and S. S. Wildman (Eds.), New York: Praeger, 1991.

Fortunati, L. "The Mobile Phone: An Identity on the Move," *Personal and Ubiquitous Computing* (5:2), 2001, pp. 85-98.

Gaynor, M., McKnight, L., Hwang, J., and Freedman, J. "Wireless Grid Networks and Virtual Markets," in *Proceedings of the International Conference on Computer, Communication and Control Technologies (CCCT '03)/ 9th International Conference on Information Systems Analysis and Synthesis (ISAS '03)*, Orlando, FL, July 31-August 2, 2003 (CD-ROM).

Markus, M. L. "Toward a Critical Mass Theory of Interactive Media: Universal Access, Interdependence, and Diffusion," *Communication Research* (14:5), 1987, pp. 491-511.

McKnight L, Anius, D, and Uzuner, O. "Virtual Markets in Wireless Grids: Peering Policy Obstacles," paper presented at the TPRC 30th Annual Research Conference on Communication, Information and Internet Policy, Alexandria, VA, September 2002 (available online at http://tprc.org/papers/2002/88/virtualmarkets.pdf).

McKnight, L. W., Howison, J., and Bradner, S. "Wireless Grids: Distributed Resource Sharing by Mobile, Nomadic, and Fixed Devices," *IEEE Internet Computing* (8:4), July-August 2004, pp. 24-31 (available online at http://csdl.computer.org/comp/mags/ic/2004/04/w4024.pdf).

Peters, V. *Kwalitan: A Supportive Program for Qualitative Analyses, Version 5.0*, Nijmegen, The Netherlands: Katholieke Universiteit Nijmegen, 2004.

Oliver, P., Marwell, G., and Teixera, R. "A Theory of the Critical Mass, I: Interdependence, Group Heterogeneity, and the Production of Collective Action," *American Journal of Sociology* (91), 1985, pp. 522-556.

Rogers, E. M. *Diffusion of Innovations*, New York: Free Press, 1995.

Silverstone, R., and Haddon, L. "Design and the Domestication of Information and Communication Technologies: Technical Change and Everyday Life," in *Communication by Design: The Politics of Information and Communication Technologies*, R. Mansell and R. Silverstone (Eds.), Oxford, UK: Oxford University Press, 1996, pp. 44-74.

Venkatesh, V., Morris, M. G., Davis, G. B., and Davis, F. D. "User Acceptance of Information Technology: Toward a Unified View," *MIS Quarterly* (27:3), 2003, pp. 425-479.

Williams, R., and Edge, D. "The Social Shaping of technology," *Research Policy* (25:6), 1996, pp. 865-899.

ABOUT THE AUTHORS

Lee W. McKnight is an associate professor in the School of Information Studies, Syracuse University. He is a research affiliate of the Program on Internet and Telecoms Convergence at MIT, which he founded in 1996. He is also a Research Associate Professor of Computer Science at Tufts University, and President of Marengo Research, a consultancy. Lee's research interests span policy, economic, business, and technical aspects of the emerging global information economy. His research focuses on wireless grids, nomadicity and mobility, networked multimedia, innovation systems, national and international technology policy, the convergence of the Internet and telecommunications industries, and Internet telephony policy. Lee can be reached at lmcknigh@syr.edu.

Raed M. Sharif is a Ph.D. student in the Information Science and Technology Program, School of Information Studies, Syracuse University. In addition to his background in Economics and Political Science and 5 years of experience in IT management, Raed has an MBA (2002) from Birzeit University, Palestine. His research interests include innovation and development, ICT for development, knowledge and technology transfer, and national and international technology ICT policy and strategy formulation. Raed can be reached at rmalshar@mailbox.syr.edu.

Lidwien van de Wijngaert is an assistant professor at the Institute for Information and Computing Sciences at Utrecht University in The Netherlands. Currently she is a visiting professor at Syracuse University. Her research focuses on the adoption and use of new technologies such as broadband Internet and wireless grids. Her research always focuses on the perspective of the user. She has published in international journals such as *New Media and Society* and she is a member and reviewer for the International Communication Association. Recently, she coauthored a textbook on ICT in organizations. Lidwien can be reached at L.vandeWijngaert@cs.uu.nl.

15 FLUID ORGANIZING OF WORK IN THE UBIQUITOUS INFORMATION ENVIRONMENT

Masao Kakihara
Kwansei Gakuin University
Hyogo, Japan

Abstract   *The strong trend of miniaturization and personalization of computing devices that continues in our everyday lives has become inseparably linked to the various services and functions these technological artifacts offer. Mobile workers can do their jobs, not just in formal office space, but in locations as varied as hotels and train stations. These workers are actively utilizing various ICTs in their highly mobile work practices. This paper explores an emerging pattern of work practice in the ubiquitous information environment, namely, **fluid organizing of work**. In rapidly changing businesses such as media, entertainment, and ICT-related areas, an increasing number of workers perform their jobs independently and bring their distinct skills and expertise to organizations on an ad hoc basis. Since business activities are increasingly knowledge-intensive, the importance of effective utilization of external professional workers is increasingly important as well. Such a pattern of organizing work practice has blurred the formal boundaries of organizations. This paper addresses structural changes of those work practices, particularly in the context of **mobile professional work**, and the technological impacts on those changes. The paper concludes by proposing that in order to appreciate the emerging pattern of work practice in today's ubiquitous information environment, we should take seriously the fluid perspective of work and organization.*

Keywords   Mobile work, professional, work practice, ICT

1   INTRODUCTION

In the last two decades, we have seen the rapid diffusion of information and communication technologies (ICTs) into all levels of our social lives. The strong trend of miniaturization and personalization of computing devices that continues in our everyday lives has become inseparably linked to the various services and functions these technological artifacts offer. The mobile phone, for example, was first developed and utilized as a consumer product rather than a business service. A number of innovative firms are adopting ICTs for restructuring their business processes and organizational forms. Wireless communication services and applications support mobile workers doing their jobs at various places, not just formal office spaces, but locations such as hotels and train stations as well. The Internet-based technological environment available today, offering ubiquitous accessibility to a broad range of information, serves as a critical foundation for mobile work practices.

This paper tries to explore an emerging pattern of work practice in the ubiquitous information environment, namely, *fluid organizing of work*. In order to cope with today's turbulent business environment, firms are flexibly mobilizing human resources outside formal organizational boundaries. Outsourcing has become an important strategic option for efficient and effective management, particularly in rapidly changing businesses such as media, entertainment, and ICT-related areas. An increasing number of workers perform their jobs independently and bring their distinct skills and expertise to organizations on an *ad hoc* basis. Since business activities are increasingly knowledge intensive, the importance of effective utilization of external professional workers is increasing as well. Such a pattern of organizing work practice has blurred the formal boundaries of organizations. This paper addresses structural changes of work practices, particularly in the context of *mobile professional work*, and the technological impacts on those changes.

2   MOBILE PROFESSIONAL WORK

As Schön (1983) argues, professionals have become "essential to the very functioning of our society" (p. 3). Among the oldest professionals would be the clergy and teachers, although they might not have been called or even recognized as professionals at the time. Architects also have a long history of contributing to society as professionals with their expertise of designing and constructing buildings. However, in contemporary society, we recognize more diversity in professionals, including accountants, designers and artists, writers, doctors and nurses, engineers, lawyers, pharmacists, psychologists, counselors, social workers, scientists, librarians, professors, urban planners, and so on.

The existing research has tended to study professionals only within organizations, private or public. As a result, professionals working independently have been largely neglected in contemporary research on professional work. Obviously, most of the "modern" professionals are employed within organizations. As Whalley and Barley (1997) argue, the need for the professionals' expertise was "created" in response to changes of inner conditions of the firms. However, in the light of today's turbulent business environments, addressing only professionals inside the organizational structure clearly does not suffice. In fact, during the last two decades, we have seen a rapid growth of workers who are independent of a formal organization and, in many cases, do their jobs on a freelance or contract basis, establishing ongoing relationships with several different client firms (Segal and Sullivan 1995, 1997). Most of them are knowledge-based rather than material-based professionals such as consultants, designers, writers, journalists and planners of various kinds (Meager 1992). Their livelihood depends on selling their own distinct skills, knowledge, and/or tangible and intangible products to firms.

The emergence and rapid growth of such post-modern professionals, freed from conventional employment relationships, is becoming a critical factor in contemporary business environments, especially in knowledge-intensive sectors. Yet surprisingly little research has been done on such post-modern professionals and their work practices, which are not bounded by formal organizational structures, rules, and constraints but play critical strategic roles in organizational contexts.

Among the notable exceptions is Malone and Laubacher's (1998) work. Seeing the success of the Linux open source community, the emergence of virtual companies, the rise of outsourcing and telecommuting, and the proliferation of freelance and temporary workers, they argue

> The fundamental unit of such an economy is not the corporation but the individual. Tasks aren't assigned and controlled through a stable chain of management but rather are carried out autonomously by independent contractors. These electronically connected freelancers—e-lancers—join together into fluid and temporary networks to produce and sell goods and services (p. 146).

This kind of independent professional workers, *e-lancers* in their words, can be seen at the forefront of the contemporary business environment. Although independent professionals outside organizations already existed in various forms (such as lawyer and accountants) since the middle of the 20th century, their numbers have remained quite small when compared with workers (both white- and blue-collar) employed by firms. This is mainly because, as traditional economic theories of organization suggest, firms have benefited from internalizing a wide range of labor forces into the formal organizational structure and placing them in the same, fixed locations such as offices and factories to effectively manage them in a centralized manner. In other words, firms deemed it costly and risky to utilize people who are outside of the organizational boundaries and largely distributed in a wide area due to limited communication and coordination technologies available in the industrial age such as trains, cars, telegraph, fixed telephone, and mainframe computers. In consequence, firms have remained large.

However, in today's ubiquitous information environment supported by powerful and reasonably affordable computing devices and services, firms have become capable of coordinating their business processes and utilizing outside workers, particularly those who have distinct skills and expertise. They no longer have to hold a large number of permanent workers inside the organizations for the sake of centralized coordination of business processes (Malone et al. 1987). Many of the highly skilled people in firms are actually spinning out and finding their workplaces outside firms, since being free and independent can provide them with greater benefits such as gaining more reward for their work and managing their career and lives more flexibly. Some of these people are getting together and forming loosely bound partnership-based organizations such as consulting firms and design studios, but each of them still retains much more autonomy and freedom than professionals inside firms. Therefore, considering these shifts occurring around post-modern, mobile professionals and their impact upon contemporary business activities, we must give careful consideration to how such professionals work with organizations and how particular ICTs are utilized in their everyday work practices.

3   A FIELD STUDY

In order to acquire a realistic picture of actual work practices of mobile professionals, an empirical field study was conducted from April to July 2002 in Tokyo, Japan. The field study adopted the inductive qualitative research approach employing open-ended interviews based on an interview guide and *ad hoc* participant observations. In addition to the recorded interviews based the interview guide, highly contextualized data about work practices was collected immediately before, during, and after each interview session.

Tokyo was chosen as the site for this study for two primary reasons. First, the distinctive institutional background of Tokyo is particularly interesting with a work environment distinctly different from that of Western countries. The Japanese corporate system has typically been associated with three institutionalized traditions: lifetime employment, promotion by seniority, and the enterprise union system (Aoki and Dore 1996). A widely persistent, steep vertical structuring still exists, as well as administrative and corporate bureaucracy (Nakane 1983). Within such a distinctive world, almost all Japanese professionals have been employed by the government or large corporations, which led to the highly elitist internal structure of organizations. This institutional distinctiveness of the Japanese work environment could benefit us in understanding actual opportunities, problems, obstacles, and hopes that emerging professional workers are currently facing with more clarity and contrast than looking at work environments in Western contexts.

Second, Japan's unique and advanced technological environment is also critical for the choice of fieldwork location. It is widely recognized that Japan has enjoyed advanced technological innovations that resulted largely from Japanese industries' strength in research and development and manufacturing of technical devices, systems, and large infrastructures. Japan is in the middle of dramatic technological innovation and diffusion of mobile technology (Rheingold 2002). Such a unique technological environment potentially influences Japanese mobile professionals' work practices. The specific socio-technical environment in Tokyo, therefore, makes it a highly suitable setting for studying the emerging realities of mobile technology use.

The informants were selected based on the following definition of the mobile professional:

The mobile professional is a worker:
(1)   who owns distinct and competitive work skills and/or knowledge;
(2)   who works independently, largely freed from formal organizational constraints and rigid employment relationships; and

(3) whose work activities are highly mobile in terms of operation, location, and interaction with the support of ICT, particularly mobile technology.

Table 1 lists the informants interviewed in this field study.

The occupation of the mobile professionals interviewed ranged widely. The largest (11) group of occupation consisted of *independent consultants*. There could be several reasons for this group being the largest. Independent consultants represent distinct skills and knowledge, they are independent in their work practices and can flexibly organize their work.

The second largest group (9) was *entrepreneurs*. Although entrepreneurs are not likely to be seen as mobile professionals, their working lives display significant characteristics common to other kinds of mobile professionals. They have a clear vision of their business and highly distinct skills and knowledge combined with a high enthusiasm aimed at making their vision materialize. In terms of high competitiveness in skills and knowledge, independent consultants and entrepreneurs present common-alities; whereas independent consultants utilize their skills and knowledge for their clients, entrepreneurs do so for their own. Entrepreneurs, too, can manage their work activities flexibly. While they usually own their office, their work activities span a wide range of areas for meetings and negotiation with various business partners. Considering these unique characteristics, entrepreneurs should also be regarded as an important group of mobile professionals. *Designers* (six) and *journalists* (four) are also distinct informant groups in this field study.

4   FOCUS CASES

Three *focus cases* of mobile professionals that proved to be particularly exemplary among all the informants are presented here. First is the case of *an independent town planning consultant*, which shows the high degree of mobility in terms of work sites. Second is the case of *a freelance computer graphics (CG) designer*, where various Internet-based tools and applications play critical roles in his highly independent but collaborative work style. Third is the case of *an e-business entrepreneur*, which demon-strates various consequences of the use of mobile technology in mobile professional work. Obviously, in each case, only a small portion of the entire transcript is presented here. Some descriptions drawn from *ad hoc* observation in the cases are also used to complement the interview data.

4.1 Case A: Independent Town Planning Consultant

Jun,[1] 38, started his independent consulting business in 2000. His main consulting field is town planning for small- and medium-sized municipalities. He works alone with

---

[1]All names have been changed to protect privacy.

Table 1. List of Informants

No.	Job	Gender	Age	No.	Job	Gender	Age
1	Independent consultant	M	50s	32	Corporate manager (employed)	F	40s
2	Corporate manager (employed)	M	50s	33	Consultant (employed)	F	20s
3	Entrepreneur	M	30s	34	Architect	M	40s
4	Independent consultant	M	30s	35	Independent consultant	M	30s
5	Independent consultant	M	50s	36	Sales coordinator (employed)	M	30s
6	Corporate researcher (employed)	M	30s	37	Consultant (employed)	M	30s
7	Corporate researcher (employed)	M	30s	38	Marketing planner (employed)	M	30s
8	Consultant (employed)	F	30s	39	Entrepreneur	F	50s
9	Marketing planner (employed)	M	30s	40	Independent consultant	M	50s
10	Marketing planner (employed)	F	30s	41	Designer (freelance)	M	50s
11	Consultant (employed)	M	30s	42	Journalist	M	30s
12	Entrepreneur	M	30s	43	Journalist	M	30s
13	Entrepreneur	M	50s	44	Sales coordinator (employed)	M	20s
14	Corporate researcher (employed)	M	30s	45	Independent consultant	M	50s
15	Designer (freelance)	M	30s	46	Marketing planner (employed)	M	30s
16	Journalist (employed)	M	20s	47	Independent consultant	M	30s
17	Marketing planner (employed)	M	30s	48	Entrepreneur	M	30s
18	Designer (freelance)	M	30s	49	Sales coordinator (employed)	M	30s
19	Corporate manager (employed)	M	40s	50	Independent consultant	M	50s
20	Entrepreneur	M	20s	51	Independent consultant	M	30s
21	Entrepreneur	F	20s	52	Independent consultant	M	50s
22	Designer (freelance)	M	20s	53	Designer (freelance)	M	50s
23	Independent consultant	M	20s	54	Consultant (employed)	M	40s
24	Entrepreneur	M	30s	55	Consultant (employed)	M	40s
25	Entrepreneur	M	20s	56	Marketing planner (employed)	M	30s
26	Corporate manager (employed)	M	30s	57	Marketing planner (employed)	M	30s
27	Designer (employed)	F	30s	58	Corporate researcher (employed)	M	20s
28	Journalist (employed)	F	20s	59	Corporate researcher (employed)	M	20s
29	Freelance producer	F	30s	60	Sales coordinator (employed)	M	20s
30	Consultant (employed)	M	30s	61	Academic researcher	M	30s
31	Corporate researcher (employed)	M	30s	62	Academic researcher	M	30s

no employees but collaborates with many people including other consultants and developers. The majority of his current clients are small- and medium-sized municipalities, mainly in rural areas hundreds miles away from big cities such as Tokyo and Osaka.

He finds the high degree of mobility in his work activities the most conspicuous advantage as a professional worker. Town planning projects typically require the project members to see the actual site in which a certain plan is to be implemented. He also argues that visiting the site and seeing it with his own eyes is crucial for the town planning business, since observation of the site offers invaluable data and insights for the project. Acquiring a Subnote PC and a mobile phone changed his way of working dramatically. With his mobile phone, he was able to easily contact and be contacted by his clients and coworkers virtually (not completely) anytime, anywhere. The Subnote PC connected with the mobile phone provided him with almost the same PC environment during business trips and site observation.

His work practices clearly show two basic patterns of geographic movement. First is the long-distance travel. He follows a working style where he can spend a considerable amount of time at the actual sites where his clients' problem issues reside. Most of his clients are local governments in areas far away from Tokyo. Therefore, it is inevitable that he frequently travels hundreds of miles for a visit and explores the sites physically. Second is the intensive local travel. He moves around the Tokyo area intensively to meet his clients and other members of the projects, since meeting those people fact-to-face is extremely important for his business. In such local travel, he usually uses underground trains and taxis, or he walks. Just like moving around Tokyo, he also travels intensively in and across the local areas when visiting the clients' sites.

4.2 Case B: Freelance Computer Graphics Designer

Yoshi, 35, is working as a freelance CG designer in Tokyo. He uses a room in his home in central Tokyo as his workspace where he does almost all of his design work. After graduating from a university with a degree in graphic design, he got a job in one of the biggest design firms in Japan. Having worked as a graphic designer for 8 years in the firm, he became freelancer 5 years ago. He is an expert of on three-dimensional CG (3D-CG) design, but most of his work revenue comes from projects relating to Web site design and coding. He gains most of his revenue from Web site design work for music production companies.

Due to the nature of CG design, he spends a considerable amount of time in front of the computers in this room. In this regard, he is mostly a static home-worker. However, he engages in intense interaction with people outside by actively using the Internet technologies. Particularly interesting is that his corporeal movement is largely static, sitting in a room for a long period of time, but the range of his interaction with other people through the Internet spans the globe and the patterns are significantly intense and diverse.

Even though the intense interaction with various people through the Internet greatly helps Yoshi gain access to the latest information about hardware and software, he is still faced with a considerable lack of physical human interaction. In this regard, he has a special place. In 1997, Yoshi received the highly respected CG design award founded by a large entertainment company, one of the most reputable and widely known CG design awards in Japan. This company has established a special design studio in one of their office buildings in central Tokyo exclusively for the winners and finalists of the award. For Yoshi, the special design studio seems to function as a *Ba* (Nonaka and Konno 1998), a place where people can share a distinct context of working and exchange a variety of tangible and intangible goods. Such a place can provide people with broad opportunities for "real" human interaction, which facilitate exchange of valid information concerning new clients and jobs. Furthermore, the studio is also a place for collaboration. Since each of the designers coming to the studio has a distinct background and expertise of design, they can easily find each other as complementary in their design work.

4.3 Case C: E-Business Entrepreneur

Hiro, 35, is CEO of a small software company. After being involved in the Internet service provider (ISP) business for a few years, he founded the company in 1998. The company primarily develops entertainment software and digital content such as network-based games on the Internet, a music-composing tool for PCs, and, more recently, various tools and network content for Internet-enabled mobile phone services such as the NTT DoCoMo i-mode platform

In contrast to the two previous cases, Hiro is subject to much more intense and dynamic interaction with other people. Whereas Jun and Yoshi primarily work alone and only interact with a limited number of clients and members of projects at one time, Hiro has 20 members of staff in his company. Moreover, he is involved in constantly changing business situations where he has to interact with a diverse range of current and prospective stakeholders. In order to cope with this, he utilizes the combination of e-mail and mobile phone technologies as the primary means of managing his interaction: He forwards all incoming e-mail to his Internet-enabled mobile phone. In fact, during the interview, his mobile phone notified him about received e-mail several times, and he checked them immediately. This emphasized the fact that he was engaged in a constant flow of multiple interaction threads. For him, it proved impossible at one particular time to focus on a single interaction at hand and to exclude others. He needed to juggle multiple interaction threads by effectively using technology.

5 FLUID ORGANIZING OF WORK

As clearly shown in the three focus cases above, mobile professional work is in rapidly changing work settings and in a constant flux of interaction with various stakeholders. In the ubiquitous information environment where people can interact with others by using such emerging technologies as e-mail, Web services, mobile phones, and PDAs, relational disposition of human interaction is becoming ambiguous and transitory. In particular, the dynamic and heterogeneous work practices of mobile professionals inherently involve the capacity of boundary formation at various levels of organization.

These findings offer us a new perspective on work practice as a *fluid* (Mol and Law 1994; Urry 2000). A fluid is "a world of mixtures" and "variation without boundaries and transformation without discontinuity" (Mol and Law 1994, p. 600). A fluid world ensured by multiple mobilization of interaction can be characterized as "the remarkably uneven and fragmented flows of people, information, objects, money, images and risks across regions in strikingly faster and unpredictable shapes" (Urry 2000, p. 38). This is clearly the world of the contemporary mobile professional work. As the fieldwork results show, mobile professionals get their jobs done not only in formal offices but at various sites such as home, clients' offices, hotels, moving vehicles, and so on; anywhere can be their office. With the powerful support of ICTs, their work practices permeate across various regions of work (projects, teams, organizations, etc.) and networks (private and public, formal and informal, etc.). The fluid nature of work practice cannot be fully captured from static perspectives, since it always transforms the work context. Mobile professionals' work practices are always in transition, extensively moving around, participating in several different projects, and interacting with diverse stakeholders.

Contemporary businesses, especially in media, entertainment, and ICT-related areas, increasingly utilize nontraditional labor forces such as contract-based workers, people from staffing service companies, various kinds of freelancers, and contract-based technicians (Barker and Christensen 1998; Cappelli 1999). Furthermore, companies are actively adopting newly developed, flexible organizational practices such as task forces, project-based teams, and virtual teams, which typically include various "outside" professional members such as consultants, designers, and planners (Snow et al. 1999; Townsend et al. 1998). Given these emerging company practices, it seems that an organization as a distinct unit of operation and hence of analysis is far from self-evident or well-defined, since the unity of today's organization in turbulent business environments, particularly knowledge-intensive industries, is predicated less and less on stable organizational structure, constant and well-defined business processes, or long-lasting membership of the staff.

Mobile professionals are one of the most radical groups of workers whose work activities deconstruct the traditional sense of unity of organizations. Mobile professionals are keen to liberate themselves from organizational structures, processes, and conventions that are likely to hamper their knowledge-intensive, autonomous ways of working. In the case of the independent consultant discussed above, for example, Jun should be seen as an outsider from a traditional point of view, as he does not have a formal employment relationship with any organization. However, from the project members' point of view, he should be seen as an insider in the sense that due to his distinct skills and knowledge, his work practices are tightly linked to the client's business processes and hence competitiveness. Acting as knowledge brokers, mobile professionals constantly straddle boundaries at various levels and form new boundaries of a group of practitioners, or a community of practice (Wenger 1998), through their fluid work practices over time.

Given such fluid organizing of work, the traditional image of organization might require reconsideration. When considering the fact that mobile professionals' work practices typically cut through and reformulate boundaries at various levels over time, the distinction between organization and environment and between inside and outside becomes vague. Many have already proposed the network-based view of organization (e.g., Castells 1996; Jarvenpaa and Ives 1994; Powell 1989; Rockart and Short 1991; Snow et al. 1992; Van Alstyne 1997). Largely supported by the development and diffusion of ICTs in general and the Internet in particular, today's organizations have become capable of coordinating business operations and processes by directly reaching to and connecting with a variety of players in the market such as foreign business partners, suppliers of raw materials and parts, famous designers in the world, and their own customers. Castells (1996) describes this transformation by stating that "networks constitute the new social morphology of our societies, and the diffusion of networking logic substantially modifies the operation and outcomes in processes of production, experience, power, and culture" (p. 469). Powell (1989) argues that the networked forms of organization can be an alternative to the transactions of markets and the hierarchical governance structures of firms in some industrial sectors. However, despite the implications of those theories for our understanding of contemporary organizations, it appears that their theorization is still largely static, specifically because of the network metaphor. The network metaphor is typically described by the assemblage of inter-connected nodes, hubs, and spokes. While this metaphorical approach is particularly useful for explaining complex relationships between the organization and its diverse stakeholders, it seems to be implicitly but firmly predicated on static, snapshot depictions of the ongoing operations and processes that dynamically constitute and reconstitute emergent relationships among the stakeholders.

Imai and Kaneko (1988) point out the fundamental difference between the tradi-tional image of networks and the one in actual organizational contexts (see Figure 1). Through their investigation of Japanese manufacturing and other industries, they insist that the network organization in actual organizational settings is

> constructed not through individuals' activities as discrete functional elements in the organization but through each individual's personal and spontaneous activities that create self-organizing relationships amongst the members, redefine boundaries between "self" and "others," and then produce dynamic and diverse contexts in which real innovations emerge (p. 149; translated by the author).

This view greatly resonates with the fluid metaphor by Mol and Law (1994). As opposed to computer networks, the configuration of social networks is always in a dynamic transformation. Relationships and boundaries in social networks in work settings can never be fixed but are iteratively produced and reproduced through the stakeholders' work practices, which in turn create work contexts in which they interact with each other. This view does not deny the existence of relationships and boundaries in organizational settings; however, it requires us to pay specific attention to the emergent aspects of ongoing formation of the relationships and boundaries in actual work contexts.

Some scholars have discussed such a fluid perspective of work and organization. Morgan's (1997) comprehensive review of various images of organization provides a useful overview. Along with many other images of organization such as machines, organisms, brains, cultures, political systems, psychic prisons, and instruments of domination, he offers a distinct image of organization as flux and transformation. By

The traditional image of networks 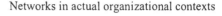 Networks in actual organizational contexts

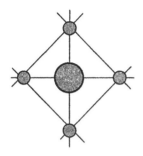 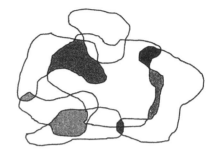

Figure 1. Comparison between the Traditional and Actual
Views on Networks (Adapted from Imai and Kaneko 1988)

applying autopoiesis theory (Maturana and Varela 1980, 1992), Morgan explains that organizations can be seen as constant flow and change that can hardly be captured from a static, external observer's view. From this fluid perspective, the distinction between organization and environment is just a product of external observation, insisting that relations with any environment are internally determined and boundaries are continuously produced and reproduced through continuous enactment of self-referencing acts.

Ciborra's (1996) discussion of "the platform organization" is related more closely to fluid organizing of work discussed in this paper. He explains that the platform organization is

[A] virtual organizing scheme, collectively shared and reproduced in action by a pool of human resources, where structure and potential for strategic action tend to coincidence in highly circumstantial ways, depending upon the transitory contingencies of the market, the technology and the competitors' moves (p. 115).

More succinctly, the platform organization, he argues, can be characterized by "fragmentation, fuzziness and displacement" (p. 116). Through his detailed case study of Olivetti, a leading European computer company at the time of his study, the organization sometimes markedly exhibited organizational features far from the traditional images of specific organizational structure, authority lines, and communication flows. It is full of chaotic events, contingencies, and surprises, which in turn produce new organizational configuration. While Mintzberg (1983) proposes a similar form of organization, *adhocracy*, characterized as organic, flexible, nonhierarchical and highly informal, Ciborra's platform organization places much more emphasis upon transformation and improvisation in and around the organization. Although Ciborra's focus is mainly on internal events of the company, his study clearly indicates that an organization can be perceived as a fluid.

As clearly seen above, a fluid pattern of organizing work practices has been discussed *sporadically* in the history of study on the relation between organization and ICT. It can be argued that in the light of today's emerging ubiquitous information environment, it is more and more important to address a fluid pattern of organizing work practices in relation to ICTs in general and mobile and wireless technologies in particular. As we have seen in the field study of mobile professionals in Japan, mobile professional work would be one of the most conspicuous cases that vividly present various consequences of fluid organizing of work. Mobile professionals reconstruct organizational settings and boundaries through their fluid work practices largely supported by their active utilization of ICTs. Such fluid work practices could not be fully appreciated through the traditional organizational perspectives predicated on static understanding of work and organization.

6   CONCLUDING REMARKS

This paper discusses the emerging pattern of work in today's ubiquitous information environment through an empirical field study of mobile professionals. The fieldwork results show that the work practices of mobile professionals should be best appreciated through a fluid perspective capturing the dynamic and heterogeneous nature of work practices. Mobile professionals' fluid organizing of work is heavily based on and supported by their active utilization of ICTs for interaction and collaboration. Furthermore, the fieldwork results put into question the traditional understanding of organization predicated on the *a priori* assumption of organizational boundaries.

It should be noted, however, that such a fluid perspective of work and organization cannot be applied to all of the realities of today's organizational phenomena. For instance, mobile professionals currently account for a fraction of the entire workforce even in urban areas of developed countries. Furthermore, industries that actively utilize mobile professionals as a competitive and flexible workforce are still quite limited, mainly to knowledge-intensive and/or ICT-related industries. Therefore, the fluid nature of work practice might appear in few occasions and in organizations in a small number of industries.

Nevertheless, it would be fair to say that a fluid perspective of work and organization will be more and more important in the age of the ubiquitous information environment. It is widely acknowledged that knowledge has become a critical resource for competitiveness in a wide range of industries. As many argue, dealing with knowledge in organizational contexts is always an issue spreading across boundaries between teams and between organizations, and the configuration of such boundaries are constantly transformed over time through face-to-face and mediated interaction among diverse stakeholders (Ciborra and Andreu 2001; Knights et al. 1993). In such dynamic intra-, inter-, and transorganizational contexts, it is important to address actual work practices of people in and around organizations not from a rigid and static perspective but from a fluid perspective that can shed light upon the ever-changing nature of organizational knowledge. Individuals, teams, organizations, institutions—all are being faced with the upheaval of existing work settings, structures, and conditions, shifting from relatively stable and static states to dynamic and constant transformation. In order to address these fluid social realities in the ubiquitous information environment, our perspective also has to be dynamic and flexible. The perspective of fluid organizing of work can be one such distinct analytical lenses.

REFERENCES

Aoki, M., and Dore, R. *The Japanese Firm: The Sources of Competitive Strength,* Oxford, UK: Oxford University Press, 1996.

Barker, K., and Christensen, K. "Controversy and Challenges Raised by Contingent Work Arrangement," in *Contingent Work: American Employment in Transition,* K. Barker and K. Christensen (Eds.), Ithaca, NY: ILR Press, 1998, pp. 1-20.

Cappelli, P. *The New Deal at Work: Managing the Market-driven Workforce,* Boston: Harvard Business School Press, 1999.

Castells, M. *The Rise of the Network Society,* Malden, MA: Blackwell, 1996.

Ciborra, C. U. "The Platform Organization: Recombining Strategies, Structures, and Surprises," *Organization Science* (7:2), 1996, pp. 103-118.

Ciborra, C. U., and Andreu, R. "Sharing Knowledge Across Boundaries," *Journal of Information Technology* (16:2), 1996, pp. 73-81.

Imai, K., and Kaneko, I. *Nettowaku Soshikiron (The Theory of Network Organizations)* (in Japanese), Tokyo: Iwanami, 1988.

Jarvenpaa, S. L., and Ives, B. "The Global Network Organization of the Future: Information Management Opportunities and Challenges," *Journal of Management Information Systems* (10:4), 1994, pp. 25-57.

Knights, D., Murray, F., and Willmott, H. "Networking as Knowledge Work: A Study of Strategic Interorganizational Development in the Financial Services Industry," *Journal of Management Studies* (30:6), 1993, pp. 975-995.

Malone, T. W., and Laubacher, R. J. "The Dawn of the E-Lance Economy," *Harvard Business Review* (76:5), September-October 1998, pp. 145-153.

Malone, T. W., Yates, J., and Benjamin, R. I. "Electronic Markets and Electronic Hierarchies," *Communications of the ACM* (30:6), 1987, pp. 484-497.

Maturana, H. R., and Varela, F. J. *Autopoiesis and Cognition: The Realization of the Living,* Dordrecht: Reidel, 1980.

Maturana, H. R., and Varela, F. J. *The Tree of Knowledge: The Biological Roots of Human Understanding* (Revised Edition), Boston: Shambhala, 1992.

Meager, N. "The Characteristics of the Self-employed: Some Anglo-German Comparisons," in *The New Entrepreneurs,* P. Leighton and A. Felstead (Eds.), London: Kogan Page, 1992, pp. 69-99.

Mintzberg, H. *Structure in Fives: Designing Effective Organizations,* Englewood Cliffs, NJ: Prentice-Hall, 1983.

Mol, A., and Law, J. "Regions, Networks and Fluids: Anaemia and Social Topology," *Social Studies of Science* (24), 1994, pp. 641-671.

Morgan, G. *Images of Organization.* (2nd Edition), Thousand Oaks, CA: Sage Publications, 1997.

Nakane, C. *Japanese Society,* Middlesex, UK: Penguin, 1983.

Nonaka, I., and Konno, N. "The Concept of 'Ba': Building a Foundation for Knowledge Creation," *California Management Review* (40:3), 1998, pp. 40-54.

Powell, W. W. "Neither Market Nor Hierarchy: Network Forms of Organization," in *Research in Organizational Behavior Vol. 12.,* B. M. Staw and L. L. Cummings (Eds.), Greenwich, CT: JAI Press, 1989, pp. 295-336.

Rheingold, H. *Smart Mobs: The Next Social Revolution*, Cambridge, MA: Perseus Publishing, 2002.

Rockart, J., and Short, J. "The Networked Organization and the Management of Inter-dependence," in *The Corporations of the 1990s: IT and Organizational Transformation*, M. S. Scott-Morton (Ed.), Oxford, UK: Oxford University Press, 1991, pp. 189-216.

Schön, D. A. *The Reflective Practitioner: How Professionals Think in Action*, New York: Basic Books, 1983.

Segal, L. M., and Sullivan, D. G. "The Growth of Temporary Services Work," *Journal of Economics Perspectives* (11:2), 1997, pp. 117-136.

Segal, L. M., and Sullivan, D. G. "The Temporary Labor Force," *Economics Perspectives* (12:2), 1995, pp. 2-19.

Snow, C. C., Lipnack, J., and Stamps, J. "The Virtual Organization: Promises and Payoffs, Large and Small," in *Trends in Organizational Behavior: Vol. 6. The Virtual Organization*, C. L. Cooper and D. M. Rousseau (Eds.), Chichester, UK: John Wiley & Sons, 1999, pp. 15-30.

Snow, C. C., Miles, R. E., and Coleman, H. J. "Managing 21st Century Network Organizations," *Organizational Dynamics* (20:3), 1992, pp. 5-20.

Townsend, A. M., DeMarie, S. M., and Hendrickson, A. R. "Virtual Teams: Technology and the Workplace of the Future," *The Academy of Management Executive* (12:3), 1998, pp. 17-29.

Urry, J. "Mobile Sociology," *British Journal of Sociology* (51:1), 2000, pp. 185-203.

Van Alstyne, M. V. "The State of Network Organization: A Survey in Three Frameworks," *Journal of Organizational Computing* (7:3), 1997, pp. 83-151.

Wenger, E. *Communities of Practice: Learning, Meaning, and Identity*, Cambridge, UK: Cambridge University Press, 1998.

Whalley, P., and Barley, S. R. "Technical Work in the Division of Labor: Stalking the Wily Anomaly," in *Between Craft and Science: Technical Work in U.S. Settings*, S. R. Barley and J. E. Orr (Eds.), Ithaca, NY: Cornell University Press, 1997, pp. 23-52.

ABOUT THE AUTHOR

Masao Kakihara is an assistant professor at the School of Business Administration, Kwansei Gakuin University, Japan. He holds a B.Econ. From Kwansei Gakuin University and both an M.Sc. and a Ph.D. in Information Systems from the London School of Economics and Political Science. Prior to his postgraduate studies, he worked for four years as a corporate strategy consultant in Tokyo. His research concerns ICT-enabled work practices and mobile professional workers and those organizational consequences. His current research project looks at how various professional workers in the music industry collaborate with each other in their music production practices. Masao can be reached at kakihara@kwansei.ac.jp.

16 THE RECONSTRUCTION OF PORTABLE COMPUTERS: On the Flexibility of Mobile Computing in Mobile Activities

Gamel O. Wiredu
Interaction Design Centre
Department of Computer Science and Information Systems
University of Limerick
Limerick Ireland

Abstract   *The remote distribution of contemporary activities has direct implications for the mobility of humans and associated actions. Remote distribution inherently entails parameters such as the mobility of individuals, artifacts, tasks, and information; and potential conflicts between objective and personal motives of individuals. The interactions of these parameters bear directly on the range of mobile computing services derivable from the use of these artefacts. Based on an activity-theoretical perspective, this paper presents a discussion of the dynamics of mobile computing services through an analysis of the process of reconstruction of personal digital assistants (PDAs) in a mobility-saturated work-integrated learning project. Upon this analysis, the flexibility of mobile computing as a direct function of the reconstruction process is discussed and a conceptual framework for the analysis of flexible mobile computing in mobile activities proposed.*

Keywords   Reconstruction, motives, flexibility, mobile computing

1   INTRODUCTION

Portable information and communication technologies (ICTs) have invaded us, and human activities are increasingly being mobilized and distributed. Yet the present level of mobility and distribution is so seldom problematized, so often taken for granted within IS research (Sørensen 1999). Mobility presents a significant challenge for IS research which, in the past, has largely concerned itself with desktop ICTs such as mainframe and desktop computers.

More significantly, the remote distribution of contemporary activities has direct implications for the mobility of humans and associated computing actions. Remote distribution inherently entails parameters such as the mobility of individuals, artifacts, tasks, and information; and potential conflicts between objective and personal motives. For instance, how professionals compute in mobile or distributed environments with portable ICTs, as well as the dynamics of how they reconstruct these artifacts as they derive mobile computing services, has seen little investigation and clarification in the literature. This paper takes up the challenge to tease out the dynamics of mobile computing services through an analysis of the process of reconstruction of personal digital assistants (PDAs) in a mobility-saturated work-integrated learning project. It is aimed at theorizing the flexibility of mobile computing based on an understanding of the reconstruction of portable computers.

The next section is a brief discussion of the theoretical foundations of this task, followed by a description of the empirical study and its relevant findings. Analysis of the findings follows and concludes with the proposition of a conceptual model of flexible computing.

2   THEORETICAL FOUNDATIONS

2.1 Motives and the Theory of Activity

The theory of activity[1] is a "philosophical and cross-disciplinary framework for studying different forms of human practices as development processes, with both individual and social levels interlinked at the same time" (Kuuttin 1995, p. 25). Activity theory originates in Vygotsky's (1978) idea of the mediated stimulus-sign-response relationship which is transformed into a subject-tool-object relationship by Engeström (1987): the subject's *responses* to external object *stimuli* are mediated by psychological tools and *signs*.

In any conscious human activity at the individual level, there is a *subject* who pursues an *object* with a motive to transform the subject and object into an *outcome*, a product. It is these transformations that motivate the existence of the activity. At the social level, where the individual performs an activity in collaboration with other people, an activity is more complex because of its collective nature. In his theory of expansive learning, Engeström drew on Marx's (1867) and Zinchenko's (1983) knowledge of the economics of human labor to remodel the subject-tool-object structure to reflect the

---

[1]Although the historical roots of activity theory are traced to various sources by various contemporary authors, it is mostly claimed that its foundation was laid in the cultural-historical psychological works of Lev Vygotsky during the 1920s and early 1930s. However, the understanding of activity in the works of psychologists such as Vygotsky, Leont'ev, Engeström, and Ilyenkov is inspired by Karl Marx.

collective nature of an activity. The resultant activity system incorporates the community-based elements of human activity: subject, tools, object, rules, community, division of labor, and outcome.

In this system, the relationship between the subject and the object are mediated by tools in addition to interactions with community members and the rules governing the division of labor among community members. Engeström's conceptualizations suggest that all the elements of the structure are interconnected and they shape each other based on a transition from human adaptation to consumption. An activity is directed by a motive, and the motive is to transform an object: an activity "answers a definite need of the subject, is directed toward an object of this need, is extinguished as a result of its satisfaction, and is produced again, perhaps in other, altogether changed conditions" (Leont'ev 1978, p. 62). The motivation is aroused when the person has identified an object which he or she perceives will satisfy his or her need. The motive is a result of stimulation in the consciousness of the subject by biologically and sociologically satisfying external objects; it gives an activity a determined direction. The motive, according to Leont'ev, may be "either real or ideal, either present in perception or exclusively in the imagination or in thought" (p. 62). The general macro structure of an activity incorporates both internal and external activities of the subject; it is constituted by a series of conscious and goal-oriented *actions* which are also constituted by subconscious *operations.*

A series of actions together constitute an activity, and they are conducted through a planning–orientation–execution phase. This implies that actions are performed consciously and are directed at the achievement of immediate or intermediate goals. Generally, goal-oriented actions result in objective products which satisfy the motives by which an activity was stimulated.

Compared with actions that are consciously performed, operations are subconsciously performed. An operation is determined by the goal which is given in certain conditions requiring a certain mode of action, and operations can degenerate into actions when the subject encounters adverse conditions in an activity. The back-and-forth movements and transformation of actions and operations have direct implications for the analysis of the flexibility of computing actions.

2.2 Mobility Modalities and Technology Affordances

The uses of mediating physical and psychological tools may constitute activities, or may constitute actions and operations of an activity depending on the pertaining conditions. In other words, the analysis of mediation by physical instruments has to open up to the fact that the instrument can assume any of the activity levels depending on several other environmental conditions that impact directly or indirectly on the activity. The identification and analysis of the dynamic properties of physical tools are particularly important when one considers the complexity of modern portable ICTs. To understand this problem, we draw upon Kristofferson and Ljungberg's (2000) argument that the utility of portable ICTs is dependent on three factors: modality, environment, and application. The immediate nature of the physical and social surroundings defines the environment; applications represent the design properties of ICTs such as hardware, software and data; and modality stands for the fundamental patterns of human movement. Thus, the ease and/or clumsiness of their uses are, primarily, factors of conditions representing the *modalities* of human mobility and their *affordances* (based on the user's perception of their physical, interface, and system design properties).

Modality, in the sense of Kristoffersen and Ljungberg, is the description of the fundamental patterns of motion of humans as they move around: traveling, visiting, and wandering. Traveling is the process of movement from one point to another in which the distance between those two points is such that a vehicle is required to convey the person in the process. Visiting demands some form of traveling but its essential component is the prolonged time a person spends at one location to perform some function before moving to another location. A wanderer is a person whose movements exhibit "extensive local mobility in a building or local area" (p. 142). He or she does some limited traveling and visiting in a localized environment. These fundamental patterns represent a modest and simple functional characterization of the complexly variegated nature of human mobility; however, they are useful in the sense of their intrinsic linkage with portable ICTs and the conditions of their use.

According to Gibson (1979), the affordances of an object of the environment, natural or artificial, are the perceptible properties it "offers the animal, what it provides or furnishes, either for good or ill" (p. 127). Affordances point to both the environment and the observer, and are realized in the interaction between organisms and environmental objects.

> An affordance cuts across the dichotomy of subjective-objective and helps us to understand its inadequacy. It is equally a fact of the environment and a fact of behavior. It is both physical and psychical, yet neither. An affordance points both ways, to the environment and to the observer (Gibson 1979, p. 129).

ICTs may have affordances for information capture, processing, and transmission, and their ease of use is very much dependent on perceived ease of use in action. Therefore, "making affordances perceptible is one approach to designing easily-used systems" (Gaver 1991, p. 2). It follows from this that ICT affordances are derived from their physical, interface, and system design properties, from previous information based on socio-cultural experience, and are founded on the motives of the activities they mediate.

Socio-cultural experience is premised on the objective and social sense of external objects as demonstrated in Ilyenkov's (1977) analysis of the concept of the *ideal*. The ideal is a sign or symbol historically and culturally built collectively by society for society which mediates human activities. The ideal

> confronts the individual as the thought of preceding generations realized ("reified," "objectified," "alienated") in sensuously perceptible "matter"—in language and visually perceptible images, in books and statues, in wood and bronze, in the form of places of worship and instruments of labor, in the

designs of machines and state buildings, in the patterns of scientific and moral systems, and so on. All these objects are in their *existence*, in their "present being" substantial, "material," but in their *essence*, in their origin they are "ideal," because they embody the collective thinking of people, the "universal spirit" of mankind" (Ilyenkov 1977; emphasis added).

Thus, there is a distinction between crude material matter of natural origin and idealized material of socio-cultural origin built through the collective sense-making of people.

These parameters—motives driving an activity, technology affordances, and modalities of human mobility—have some bearing on the degrees of reconstruction of ICTs by users, and reflect the enabling and limiting capacities of ICTs.

2.3 Technology Reconstruction

Reconstruction of technology is based on a user's teleological "assignment—or imposition—of function" to the artifact (Searle 1995, p. 14) and it is the accumulation or individual reconstructions that evolve into a socially shared understanding seen as a social construction (Berger and Luckmann 1967; Searle 1995). The enabling and limiting capacities of ICTs can be situated within arguments founded on technological determinism and social constructivism which provide contrasting insights about the nature of technology in human activities. Technological determinists (e.g., Winner 1997, 1993, 2001) argue in favor of the imposing nature of technology, that technology invites human action and not the other way round. Thus, one can perform many actions with a car, but one cannot fly the car like an airplane. The social constructivists (e.g., Bijker 2001; Bijker et al. 1987; MacKenzie and Wajcman 1985; Orlikowski 1992, 2000; Woolgar 1991), on the other hand, argue for the supple nature of technology systems based on the social context of use.

While the technological determinists seem to base their arguments mostly on the design properties of technology, the social constructivists seem to base their arguments on the activity- or context-based interpretation of the design properties of technology. But technology possesses both determining or limiting and socially constructed or enabling properties. Technology is both imposing and flexible, both a determinant of actions and socially constructed.

It is reasonable to say that actions are constrained by the physical properties of technology, and moreover the "situated use of technology is confined to a set of predefined options and reflects the instantiation of a context-free logic embedded in the artifact" (Kallinikos 2002, p. 291). However, it is also reasonable to say, at the same time, that an overemphasis of technological determinism can be misleading because technology is interpretively flexible. Bijker (2001), for example, argues that "this *interpretive flexibility...*shows that neither an artifact's identity nor its technical 'success' or 'failure,' are intrinsic properties of the artifact but subject to social variables" (p. 26). This implies that particular affordances of an artifact and the modalities in which it is used can induce a flexible interpretation and reconstruction of the its properties.

3   MOBILE COMPUTING IN MOBILE WORK-INTEGRATED LEARNING: AN EMPIRICAL STUDY

3.1 Information Management Through Mobile Computing

A 12-month empirical study of mobile computing in a work-integrated learning (WIL) project in the National Health Service of the United Kingdom commencing in April 2003 was undertaken to understand the complexities of portable technology use in mobile activities.

This was a pilot project in which 12 health professionals were being trained for a new professional role in surgical care. The new role was being created to fill an impending man-hour or skills shortage gap which would be caused when the weekly hours of junior doctors were cut from an average of 72 to 56 by the European Union Working Time Directive.

The project was characterized by remote distribution and mobility—of the 12 trainees/learners, of the learning activity, of the PDAs, and of information. It entailed both local mobility within each learner's hospital and remote mobility to and from the training coordination center in London. In the parlance of Kristoffersen and Ljungberg (2000), these forms of mobility are respectively conceptualized as wandering and visiting. PDAs were officially adopted and deployed to provide computational support for this activity. Particularly, the highly critical issues of monitoring and remote control of the learners' activities in their individual hospitals and the development of learning portfolios were the targets of the computing support.

Remote monitoring and control of clinical actions, and the development of portfolios of evidence of those actions undertaken, were requirements whose fulfillment was aimed at satisfying two parties. First, the sponsors of the project, the European Union, had to be supplied with reports and statistics of proceedings of the training project. These reports would convey the details of the activities that were actually undertaken by the learners in their hospitals with the aim of underlining the credibility of the whole training exercise and hence of the new professional role. Second, the wider community of existing medical professionals had to be satisfied that this new professional role was credible. Since professions in the medical field have existed for centuries, the success of this new profession depended on the acceptance and trust given by existing medical professionals. Thus, the portfolios were meant to provide evidence of the depth and breadth of learning activities undertaken by the learners in the event anyone doubted their relevance.

Each learner was provided with a Compaq iPAQ H3970 model PDA which was running a Pocket PC 2002 operating system. Each was also given a foldable keyboard to facilitate their input of written reflections-on-action (Schön 1983). This PDA model has an inbuilt appointment calendar, address book, and limited or "pocket" versions of Microsoft® Word®, Excel®, and Outlook®. These were deployed to be used by the learners as tools for capturing information on the spot, for reading information, for recording clinical and learning activities, for writing reflections right after every learning activity, for sharing information, and for transfer of relevant data to the monitoring center in London. The PDAs were supposed to be used to process notes and other information while roaming from one ward to another and in other locations of the hospitals as training demanded. Crucial to the learning process was to record what was done when it was done, not at the end, and the PDAs were deployed to fulfil immediate and easy capture and processing of information.

An activity logging database with recorded details of patient encounters on the wards was to be developed by each trainee. Clinical activities were to be selected from a predefined "pick list" through tapping a stylus directly on the PDA screen. Additional data included details such as the initials of any supervisor and whether a performed activity was an elective or an emergency. The patient's age and gender were recorded but, in accordance with data protection legislation, their names were not.

There was also a learning reflective journal, which consisted of a set of templates with headings such as "thoughts and feelings?" and "what worked and what didn't?" These were intentionally open-ended questions that would allow the learners to frame the answers as they wished. Answers to these questions were to be typed as reflections-on-actions at the end of each learning day using the foldable keyboard.

It was envisaged that the PDAs would provide learning support to the learners through the accumulation of relevant learning resources—medical literature, drug calculators, and formulary[2]—which could be available to the learners anywhere during their learning maneuvers. Although access to learning resources was implemented 6 months into the project, it eventually became the key factor that sustained any hope which the learners had in the PDA. Compared with the scenario in which learners have to make visits to libraries to gain access to learning resources, or the one in which the learner is burdened with the task of carrying paper versions of those resources, the PDA would alleviate such problems by saving the time to visit a library and the effort to carry many books while roaming. It was envisioned that when a PDA is inscribed with theoretical medical information and used in practical learning environments, the user/learner could intermittently refer to this information to shape meaning-making from the practical clinical actions.

3.2 Failure and Success Perceptions

As far as the training project was concerned, the PDA and all the custom applications that were designed to provide mobile computing support for the learners were deemed as a failure after the implementation period. The artifact could not be used in the clinical setting because of both design and environment condition problems. The systemic design of the PDA itself was a major limitation (low level processors, slower to manipulate, smaller memory, and limited input mechanisms are typical examples). This in turn affected the custom applications that were designed into the PDAs. In the end, the highly mobile nature of clinical duties around the hospital wards ensured that contemporaneous mobile computing was not feasible or possible.

---

[2]British National Formulary was the particular formulary in this instance.

For example, the performance of a typical clinical action such as taking a surgical patient's history could not happen contemporaneously with logging of actions into the PDA. Nor could the learner, in the event when he or she was in the company of the surgical team examining patients in the wards, be audacious enough to pull out the PDA to read, take notes, or log in actions. Apart from the issue of audacity, experiential learning—which relies on direct practice and observation—would not take place in such an instance. From the perspective of interaction, the outcome of Sørensen and Pica's (2005) study of police work in the UK corroborates the fact that portable ICT use on-the-move occurs in "rhythms" between "physical and virtual contexts of work." In other words, more physical work undermines virtual working with a portable artifact and vice versa. It was, therefore, not surprising when the project manager officially called for the abandonment of the PDA as a tool of information management in the project.

Alongside the failure perception, the learners reported that the PDA was an excellent personal organizer which many of them could not "live without." These reports were received during and after the project. It was clear that the custom applications—such as calendar, task scheduler, and address book—had proven to be extremely useful as far as personal organization alongside learning activities was concerned. In the final analysis, the learners were ambivalent toward the PDAs.

4   FLEXIBILITY OF MOBILE COMPUTING

In respect of this brief case description, the intriguing question is, *what are the dynamic conditions which engendered the success-and-failure perception of mobile computing services?* First and foremost, it has to be noted that whether a portable ICT is perceived to offer any mobile computing service at all depends on a combination of three factors: the *affordances* of the artifact, the *modalities* of human mobility, and the *motives* of the activities they mediate and which engender their use (Wiredu 2005). The degree of influence of these factors is dynamic. For example, affordances are dependent on factors such as design properties, experience, and previous socio-cultural information; modalities of mobility appear in various forms from extremely remote to local; and changing conditions and needs of people induce them to switch motives. Although the case clearly shows that the design properties of the PDAs offered few affordances, and that mobile computing was inflexible and a failure in the project, it is noteworthy that the learners' final evaluation and perception of the PDA as a wonderful tool was indicative of its ability to satisfy their other personal motives. In order to unveil the dynamics underlying the success-and-failure perception of the artifact, it is interesting to analyze the reconstruction of the artifact, based on its *interpretive flexibility* (Bijker 2001) within the trajectory of its use, and within the confines of the artifact's deterministic design properties.

4.1 Ideality and Reconstruction of the PDA

The trajectory of use of the PDA was situated within the learners' mutating perception of the PDA as a *tool* or *object* depending on the activity and motive on the one hand, and flexible use on the other hand. As a tool, which was what it was envisioned to be from the outset, it would figuratively represent a transparent screen through which the subject could see the learning object and transform it. As an object, it would represent an opaque device standing between the subject and object: its use would represent another activity existing alongside the learning activity. Evidence from the project suggested that, in terms of the central activity, the device represented an object, an opaque piece of equipment, which interfered with the learners' clinical routines and contravened its initial tool-functionality. The source of this problem is to be found precisely in the idealization of the PDA; that is, the design of PDAs and the marketing gimmicks that promote their diffusion, which influenced their adoption and deployment in the project.

Over the years, the gap between expected and actual use of ICTs have founded many accounts of information systems failure. Expectations of technology success, usually conceived before expensive technology integration projects, are largely informed by the pseudo accomplishments of such technologies. Such information results from the conception of the ideal PDA, of either designers' and hence marketers' touted ease of use or accounts from successful use in entirely different contexts. In the work-integrated learning case, the integration of the PDAs was a result of their perceived ease of use to support activity logging and reflections writing in distance and distributed learning. Since this ideal is a reflection of the designers' construction of these artifacts, and thus their motives, the *social variables* (Bijker et al. 1987) within the use conditions engendered processes of reconstruction of the PDA and re-conceptualization of its ideal.

The ideal or *essence* (Ilyenkov 1977) of PDAs at the outset of the project was a simple extrapolation of the ideal functionalities of desktop computers: their automating, informating, and transforming capabilities (Zuboff 1988). Stated differently, the PDA is itself a portable prototype of a desktop computer inputted with miniature versions of desktop computer applications. Even in certain respects, the portability of the PDA gives it an added advantage over desktop computers. One such respect is its mobility, and hence its ostensible facilitation of mobile computing. Here was an extremely volatile and ambitious training project, implementation of which would undoubtedly be characterized by crucial challenges. It would be work-integrated, activity-based, con-ducted in distant and distributed locations, function under the direct control of surgical staff and hence out of immediate control of the project team, highly locally mobile, confrontational, unstable, and slippery. Since it was a distance and distributed learning exercise, it was imperative for the project team to institute measures to control—to scaffold, monitor, and coordinate—the learners' distant activities. Upon this, the adoption and deployment of the PDAs, based on their ideal, was deemed an efficient controlling and stabilizing measure.

An intriguing aspect of the evidence from the PDA use over the period was its simultaneous rejection and acceptance by the learners. Its nonutility in the clinical setting, software problems, and data losses caused its eventual formal abandonment in the project. As far as the learning activity was concerned, the ideal PDA proved to be illusive in its utility. However, the uses of its generic or standard applications at the personal level proved to be a fantastic experience, a tool that many of the learners could not "live without." Thus, while the perception of the PDA as a learning support tool in the project was a failure, the same device was deemed a success as far as its standard or

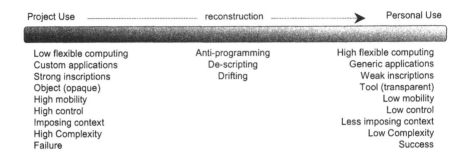

Project Use	----------------- reconstruction -----------------➤	Personal Use
Low flexible computing	Anti-programming	High flexible computing
Custom applications	De-scripting	Generic applications
Strong inscriptions	Drifting	Weak inscriptions
Object (opaque)		Tool (transparent)
High mobility		Low mobility
High control		Low control
Imposing context		Less imposing context
High Complexity		Low Complexity
Failure		Success

Figure 1. Reconstruction of the PDA

factory-built applications were concerned. Even at the end of the project, by which time the PDA had long been abandoned, the learners found the PDAs useful, but this usefulness lived alongside prior disappointment, signifying ambivalence. It is within this ambivalence, based on the social variables in the context of use, that reconstruction of the PDA is attributable.

To begin with, the fact that the success of a PDA manifests in its usage as an action or operation rather than activity, leading to its perception as a tool rather than an object, has to be emphasized. In other words, the flexibility of mobile computing determines its successful use. To be sure, evidence and accounts of ICT failures coupled with the efforts of IS developers attest to the fact that technology users instinctively desire and strive continuously toward a state of flexible computing. Over the course of the work-integrated learning project, this striving for flexibility on the part of the learners was obvious; circumstances of low flexible computing, symbolizing failure, were continuously being substituted for higher flexible computing. Given that the project-use of the PDA was deemed a failure and personal-use a success, the process of reconstruction from uselessness to usefulness was situated within the continuum between these two sets of uses (see Figure 1).

Specifically, reconstruction was rooted in and embodied by the strength of inscriptions (Akrich 1992) of the original designers and of the project manager. The framework of learning actions and reflections, which underpinned the design of the three different applications, was grounded on pedagogical principles to surrogate the project manager's monitoring and instructions from the training center in London. Given the strong focus of the project on surgical care skills acquisition toward the assumption of junior doctors' functions, and the aim to satisfy accreditation and acceptability requirements, the pedagogical principle underlying the clinical actions and reflections framework was instructive and objectivist-oriented. Hence, the applications that emanated were characterized by strong inscriptions of the project manager's desired patterns of expected use by the learners. These attributes of instructive learning—such as monitoring, scaffolding, and facilitation—were all inscribed into the PDAs based on implicit and explicit assumptions about the technology's capacities, its ideal capacities, for providing mobile computing services. The automation of these attributes, the strong inscriptions, because they were imposing on the users, and because they added to existing structures represented by the design properties of the PDAs and the learning conditions, exemplified high complexity and an overload of structures (Sørensen et al. 2002). In short, the PDA could not be idealized as it was desired. In reality, "anti-programming" (Latour 1991), "de-scripting" (Akrich 1992), and "drifting" (Ciborra 2000) were inevitable.

Instead of activity logging after the completion of every action, the learners, on realizing the clinical impracticality of such actions, used paper-based logging sheets and later transferred these into the PDA when they returned home. Instead of writing reflections-on-action at the end of every day's learning, most of them wrote them weekly; worse still, they wrote on paper before typing into their PDAs. Worst of all, many of them even found it more convenient to perform these computing actions on their desktop computers and subsequently synchronize them into the PDA. It was clear that the learners were following an anti-program. These counter-actions were performed to alleviate the imposition and intrusion associated with the custom application; that is, they were de-scripting the inscribed remote-controlling measures of the project manager—not rebelliously, but in their instinctive orientation toward flexible computing.

The failure of the technology under the custom applications and its success under the standard applications suggest that the learning conditions were more accountable for anti-programming and de-scripting than the design properties. These conditions contained the social variables upon which, Bijker (2001) conceptualizes the interpretive flexibility of technology. In truth, the learners' interpretation of the applications built into the PDA, leading to a mix of success-and-failure perceptions, was premised on whether the learning actions allowed flexible computing or otherwise. In low flexible computing, the PDA was an object. As an object, if it ever satisfied a need, the learners' motive to transform it was implicit in its reconstruction into a tool; its tool perception reflects highly flexible computing which, in the learners' case, could only be accomplished in less mobile and less imposing conditions—at home or after work, for instance. Reconstruction was witnessed in a drift from uselessness in objective circumstances toward successful personal use. Wartofsky (1973) argued similarly:

> On this reconstruction, we may speak of a class of artefacts which can come to constitute a relatiely autonomous "world," in which the rules, conventions and outcomes no longer appear directly practical, or which, indeed, seem to constitute an arena of non-practical, or "free" play or game activity....So called "disinterested" perception, or aesthetic perception, or sheer contemplation then becomes a possibility; but not in the sense that it has no use. Rather, in the sense that the original role of the representation has been, so to speak, suspended or bracketed (p. 208).

It is exactly the phenomena of *suspension* and *bracketing* which characterized the reconstruction of the PDA.

Of course the PDA ended up as a tool, but a tool for other personal activities and motives of the learners contrary to the originally purported tool function of the learning activity. To wit, at the collective level of the 12 learners, it was clear that the PDA had been socially constructed—personalized and reconstructed at the individual level—into a useful and successful tool.

It is therefore argued that the set of conditions of an activity, which determine the flexibility of mobile computing, must be the focal point of determining whether an artifact offers any mobile computing service. On the balance of the flexibility of mobile computing in the project, the PDA offered optimum computing services during its use in less frustrating conditions (Ortega y Gasset 1941), that is, when it was being used to fulfil personal motives.

5   HUMAN MOBILITY AND FLEXIBLE COMPUTING: A CONCEPTUAL MODEL

The preceding arguments shape up into relationships between the various factors which have dominated the analysis: human mobility, motives, conditions, ICT afford-ances, and flexibility of mobile computing. These relationships are condensed into a conceptual model which suggests a path for analyzing mobile computing in human activities and for ascertaining the flexibility of mobile computing. In view of the murky nature of the concept of *mobility*, it is necessary to develop this conceptual model to ground the analysis of the impact of portable ICTs as mediators in human activities. Thus, the whole concept of mobility, in terms of portable ICTs and mobile computing, is properly dissected to depict its constituent levels and their interrelationships between these levels (see Figure 2).

The spatial, temporal, and contextual dimensions of mobility are fundamental and inseparable: all other forms, types, or modalities of mobility can be properly understood along the lines of a combination of their space, time, and context dimensions. This inseparability is depicted by the oval that embodies the mobility levels in Figure 2.

It is well known that human mobility is most fundamental due to the purposeful movement of humans caused by their biological and environmental needs. An aspect of this idea can be found in Wiberg's (2001) argument that human mobility is inspired

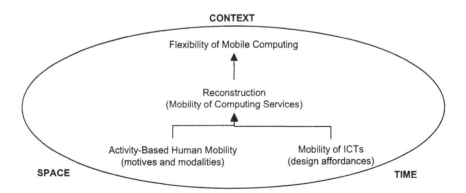

Figure 2. Conceptual Framework for the determination of Flexible Computing from Mobility of Humans Activities and ICTs

by the social need to interact. While human mobility is basic, an understanding of the mobility of ICTs cannot be achieved when human and object mobility are separated. In other words, since portable ICTs are incapable of self-mobility, understanding their impact relies on understanding the modalities of human mobility that engender the mobility of ICTs: the mobility of ICTs, in the context of purposeful human activities, is always dependent on human mobility. Even though self-moving robotic machines seem to be exceptions, we have to remember that humans design the machines that enable them to exhibit self-mobility. The inseparability of human and object mobility is a result of the ontogenetic and phylogenetic development efforts of individuals and society which stimulate human activities (see Leont'ev 1978, 1981; Marx 1867; Vygotsky 1962, 1978). Objects are either the targets or mediators of human activities, thus they are always intrinsic aspects of activities which embody human movements. Human and object mobility, therefore, serve as a substrate upon which other forms of mobility develop or depend.

Mobile computing services comprise the next level of mobility and are direct resultants of the mobility of ICTs and the conditions within those activities they mediate. Note that whether a portable ICT is perceived to provide any mobile computing service at all depends on a combination of three deciding factors: the *affordances* of the artifact based on its physical, systemic, and interfacial design properties; the *motives* that engender their uses; and the *modalities* of human mobility. These three factors can be derived from a task-technology fit (Goodhue and Thompson 1995) analysis of activity-based human mobility and technology-in-use at the base level of the model.

It may be misleading to argue simplistically that portable ICTs automatically provide mobile computing services. Mobile humans carry portable ICTs to draw on their computing services potentiality for satisfying particular motives in their activities; if the affordances of the ICT, the motives of those activities, and the modalities of human mobility exhibited make it impossible to draw on the information services, then the ICT virtually becomes a white elephant and this engenders the reconstruction process. Since mobile human activities are performed within changing dimensions and modalities of mobility, the degree of accessibility of mobile computing services within mobile artifacts for supporting mobile activities vary considerably (see Weilenmann 2001; Wiberg and Ljungberg 2001). Accessibility resonates well in reconstruction because it is one of reconstruction's key attributes.

Based on the state and quality of mobile computing services that can be obtained from portable ICTs, the flexibility of mobile computing can be deciphered. In the work-integrated learning case, accessibility to computing services shaped the reconstruction and personalization of the PDA, leading to our determination of the flexibility of mobile computing. Furthermore, it is the determination of this flexibility which informs on the transformative impact of a particular ICT in an activity. Portable ICTs mediate activities and transform them into technology-mediated activities. A typical example is the technology transformation of learning into technology-mediated learning (e.g., Alavi and Leidner 2001) and mobile learning which is increasingly attracting attention in current technology-mediated learning research. Work is also increasingly being mobilized in various forms leading to current popular themes such as occupational mobility and mobile professionals (Kakihara and Sørensen 2002), nomadic working (Dahlbom 2000), tele-activities (Castells 2001), and e-lancers (Malone and Laubacher 1998). However, mobile computing services are not automatic enhancers of mobile activities (see Weilenmann 2001, Wiberg 2001). In fact they can be corrupters of those activities, just as the "technologizing" of the word, espoused by Ong (1982) and Fichtner (1985), could possibly lead to rote and unproductive learning.

6 CONCLUSION

To conclude, for the purposes of analysing the utility of portable ICTs in purposeful human activities, the mobility levels presented in the model, are valuable. The model places the analysis of mobile information services and reconstruction in a pivotal position, brings the complexities and complications associated with the uses of portable ICTs in human activities into focus, and displaces the tendency to oversimplify its problematic nature. The model proposes a shift in perspective from focusing on the factory-based design properties of portable ICTs for making judgements about their utility toward a focus on the mobile computing services they offer in human activities. Hence, it is in the analysis of the reconstruction of the artifact—the causes by affordances, motives and modalities of mobility, as well as the enhancing or debilitating effects on those activities—that will unearth a clearer understanding of the flexibility of mobile computing. This is the most effective way of informing the design of portable ICTs for mobilising human activities.

REFERENCES

Akrich, M. "The De-scription of Technical Objects," in *Shaping Technology/Building Society* W. E. Bijker E. and J. Law (Eds.), Cambridge, MA: MIT Press, 1992.
Alavi, M., and Leidner, D. E. "Research Commentary: Technology-Mediated Learning—A Call for Greater Depth and Breadth of Research," *Information Systems Research* (12:1), 2001, pp. 1-10.
Berger, P. L., and Luckmann, T. *The Social Construction of Reality: A Treatise in the Sociology of Knowledge,* Harmondsworth, UK: Penguin, 1967.
Bijker, W. E. "Understanding Technology Culture through a Constructivist View of Science, Technology and Society," in *Visions of STS: Counterpoints in Science, Technology and Society Studies,* S. H. Cutliffe and C. Mitcham (Eds.), Albany, NY: State University of New York Press, 2001.
Bijker, W., Hughes, T., and Pinch, T. *The Social Construction of Technology Systems,* Cambridge, MA: MIT Press, 1987.
Castells, M. *The Internet Galaxy: Reflections on the Internet, Business and Society*, NewYork: Oxford University Press, 2001.
Ciborra, C. U. (Ed.). *From Control to Drift: The Dynamics of Corporate Information Infrastructures,* Oxford, UK: Oxford University Press, 2001.
Dahlbom, B. "Networking: From Infrastructures to Networking," in *Planet Internet* K. Braa, C. Sorensen, and B. Dahlbom (Eds.), Lund, Sweden: Studentliteratur, 2000.
Engeström, Y. *Learning by Expanding: An Activity-Theoretical Approach to Developmental Research,* Helsinki: Orienta-Konsultit, 1987.
Fichtner, B. "Learning and Learning Activity," in *Education for Cognitive Development*, E. Bol, J. P. P. Haenen, and M. Wolters (Eds.), The Hague: SVO/SOO, 1985.

Gaver, W. "Technology Affordances," in *Proceedings of the Computer Human Interaction (CHI 1991)*, New York: ACM Press, 1991, pp. 79-84.

Gibson, J. J. *The Ecological Approach to Visual Perception*, Boston: Houghton Mifflin, 1979.

Goodhue, D. L., and Thompson, R. L. "Task-Technology Fit and Individual Performance," *MIS Quarterly* (19:2), 1995, pp. 341-356.

Ilyenkov, E. V. "The Concept of the Ideal," in *Problems of Dialectical Materialism*, E. V. Ilyenkov (Ed.), Moscow: Progress Publishers, 1977 (available online at http://www.marxists.org/archive/ilyenkov/works/ideal/ideal.htm).

Kakihara, M., and Sørensen, C. "Post-Modern Professionals' Work and Mobile Technology," in *Proceedings of the New Ways of Working in IS Conference: 25th Information Systems Research Seminar in Scandinavia (IRIS25)*, Denmark: Copenhagen Business School, 2002.

Kallinikos, J. "Reopening the Black Box of Technology Artifacts and Human Agency," in *Proceedings of the 23rd International Conference on Information Systems*, L. Applegate, R. D. Galliers, and J. I. DeGross, Barcelona, Spain, 2002, pp. 287-294.

Kristoffersen, S., and Ljungberg, F. "Mobility: From Stationary to Mobile Work," in *Planet Internet*, K. Braa, C. Sorensen, and B. Dahlbom (Eds.), Lund, Sweden: Studentliteratur, 2000.

Kuuttin, K. "Activity Theory as a Potential Framework for Human-Computer Interaction Research," in *Context and Consciousness: Activity Theory and Human-Computer Interaction*, B. A. Nardi (Ed.), Cambridge, MA: MIT Press, 1995.

Latour, B. "Technology is Society Made Durable," in *A Sociology of Monsters: Essays on Power, Technology and Domination*, J. Law (Ed.), London: Routledge, 1991, pp. 103-131.

Leont'ev, A. N. *Activity, Consciousness and Personality*, Englewood Cliffs, NJ: Prentice-Hall, 1978.

Leont'ev, A. N. *Problems of the Development of the Mind*, Moscow: Progress Publishers, 1981.

MacKenzie, D., and Wajcman, J. (Eds.). *The Social Shaping of Technology: How the Refrigerator Got its Hum*, Milton Keynes, UK: City University Press, 1985.

Malone, T. W., and Laubacher, R. J. "The Dawn of the E-Lance Economy," *Harvard Business Review*, September-October 1998, pp. 145-153.

Marx, K. *Capital, Volume 1: The Process of Production Capital*, Moscow: Progress Publishers, 1867 (available online at http://www.marxists.org/archive/marx/works/1867-c1/index.htm).

Ong, W. J. *Orality and Literacy: The Technologizing of the Word*, London: Routledge, 1982.

Orlikowski, W. J. "The Duality of Technology: Rethinking the Concept of Technology in Organizations," *Organization Science* (3:3), 1992, pp. pp. 398-427.

Orlikowski, W. J. "Using Technology and Constituting Structures: A Practice Lens for Studying Technology in Organizations," *Organization Science* (11:4), 2000, pp. 404-428.

Ortega y Gasset, J. "Man the Technician," in *Towards a Philosophy of History*, J. Ortega y Gasset (Ed.), New York: W. W. Norton, 1941.

Schön, D. A. *The Reflective Practitioner: How Professionals Think in Action*, New York: Basic Books, 1983.

Searle, J. *The Construction of Social Reality*, New York: Free Press, 1995.

Sørensen, C., Mathiassen, L., and Kakihara, M. "Mobile Services: Functional Diversity and Overload," Working Paper #118, Department of Information Systems, London School of Economics and Political Science, 2002.

Sørensen, C., and Pica, D. "Tales from the Police. Mobile Technologies and Contexts of Work," *Information and Organization* (15:3), 2005 (forthcoming).

Sørensen, T. "Rush-Hour Blues of the Whistle of Freedom," STS Working Paper, Center for teknologi of samfunn, Norges teknisk-naturvitenskapelige universitet, Trondheim, Norway, 1999.

Vygotsky, L. S. *Mind in Society: The Development of Higher Psychological Processes*, Cambridge, MA: Harvard University Press, 1978.

Vygotsky, L. S. *Thought and Language,* Cambridge, MA: MIT Press, 1962.

Wartofsky, M. "Perception, Representation, and the Forms of Action: Towards an Historical Epistemology," Chapter 11 in *Models: Representation and the Scientific Understanding,* M. Wartofsky (Ed.), Dordrecht: Reidel, 1973, pp. 188-209.

Weilenmann, A. "Negotiating Use: Making Sense of Mobile Technology," *Personal and Ubiquitous Computing* (5:2), 2001, pp. 137-145.

Wiberg, M. "Knowledge Management in Mobile CSCW: Evaluation Results of a Mobile Physical/Virtual Meeting Support System," in *Proceedings of the 34th Hawaii International Conference on System Science,* Los Alamitos, CA: IEEE Computer Society Press, 2001.

Wiberg, M., and Ljungberg, F. "Exploring the Vision of 'Anytime, Anywhere,' in the Context of Mobile Work," in *Knowledge Management and Virtual Organizations,* Y. Malhotra (Ed.), Hershey, PA: Idea Group Publishing, 2001, pp. 157-169.

Winner, L. *Autonomous Technology. Technics-Out-of-Control as a Theme in Political Thought,* Cambridge, MA: MIT Press, 1977.

Winner, L. "Upon Opening the Black Box and Finding it Empty: Social Constructivism and The Philosophy of Technology," *Science, Technology and Social Values* (18), 1993, pp. 362-378.

Winner, L. "Where Technological Determinism Went," in *Visions of STS: Counterpoints in Science, Technology and Society Studies,* S. H. Cutliffe and C. Mitcham (Eds.), Albany, NJ: State University of New York Press, 2001.

Wiredu, G. O. *Mobile Computing in Work-Integrated Learning: Problems of Remotely Distributed Activities and Technology Use,* Unpublished Ph.D. Thesis, Department of Information Systems, London School of Economics, University of London, 2005.

Woolgar, S. "The Turn to Technology in Social Studies of Science," *Science, Technology and Human Values* (16:1), 1991, pp. 20-50.

Zinchenko, P. I. "The Problem of Involuntary Memory," *Soviet Psychology* (12:2), 1983, pp. 55-111.

Zuboff, S. *In the Age of the Smart Machine: The Future of Work and Power,* New York: Basic Books, 1988.

ABOUT THE AUTHOR

Gamel O. Wiredu is a research fellow at the Interaction Design Centre of the Department of Computer Science and Information Systems at the University of Limerick, Ireland. He holds M.Sc. and Ph.D. degrees in Information Systems from the London School of Economics. His doctoral research centered on mobile computing in remotely distributed activities in which he investigated the motivational, control, and political dimensions of remote distribution, and their impact on the mobile computing actions. His current research concerns are the social and cultural aspects of globally distributed software engineering in which he is investigating the coordination and control challenges that are presented by the socio-cultural accidents associated with particular software engineering locations in the distribution. Gamel can be reached via e-mail at Gamel.Wiredu@ul.ie.

Part 4

Development Issues

17 MOBILE SYSTEMS DEVELOPMENT: A Literature Review

Jens Henrik Hosbond
Peter Axel Nielsen
Department of Computer Science
Aalborg University
Aalborg, Denmark

Abstract   *This article reviews 105 representative contributions to the literature on mobile systems development. The contributions are categorized according to a simple conceptual framework. The framework comprises four perspectives: the **requirements** perspective, the **technology** perspective, the **application** perspective, and the **business** perspective. Our literature review shows that mobile systems development is overlooked in the current debate. From the review, we extend the traditional view on systems development to encompass mobile systems and, based on the identified perspectives, we propose core characteristics for mobile systems. We also extend the traditional focus found in systems development on processes in a development project to encompass the whole of the development company as well as interorganizational linkage between development companies. Finally, we point at research directions emerging from the review that are relevant to the field of mobile systems development.*

Keywords   Mobile systems development, software development, literature review, mobile requirements, mobile technology, mobile applications, mobile business

1   INTRODUCTION

Information systems development has been researched for decades both from the viewpoint of software engineering and the viewpoint of the information system in use in organizations. In this article, we address the branch of systems development dealing with developing mobile applications. The present advances in mobile technologies necessitate a rethinking of systems development for this particular domain (Krogstie et al. 2004). Traditional software engineering has much to offer mobile systems development, but the limitations caused by the uniqueness of mobile applications are not clear. The organizational approaches to information systems development or approaches directed at developing Web applications for the consumer market may also have much to offer mobile systems development, but again, these limitations are not clear.

In this paper, we review the literature on mobile systems development (i.e., the research literature that purport to address mobile systems development and mobile applications, irrespective of whether these applications are for the consumer market or for organizational purposes). We do this to sort out what characterizes mobile systems development and the contributions that have already been made in this domain.

The next section outlines our research approach. In section 3, we present the perspectives we have found and how the literature fits into these perspectives. In the discussion in section 4, we elaborate on the structure of the research knowledge on mobile systems development and, in particular, we discuss what is unique about mobile systems development compared to traditional systems development. In section 5, we conclude the article.

2   RESEARCH APPROACH

Along the lines suggested by Webster and Watson (2002), we have pursued a structured approach to selecting articles and we have used a concept matrix to arrive at a conceptual structuring of the domain of mobile systems development.

2.1 Article Selection

We have systematically searched journal articles through the Danish Article Database Service, a portal to all major journals either published by or indexed by Wiley, Siam, Emerald, Blackwell, ACM, IEEE, Kluwer, Elsevier, Proquest, JSTOR, ArticleFirst, EBSCO, FirstSearch, or Ingenta (to name a few). We have also systematically searched conference proceedings indexed by ACM, IEEE, and AIS. We have further searched through conference proceedings on mobile systems, m-commerce, and systems development that we otherwise came across. We have focused on contributions with title, abstract, or keywords hinting that they would be relevant for this literature review and only contributions thus relevant have been reviewed in detail. We have limited our search to contributions dated 2000 or later. In effect, contributions were included in the literature review if they satisfy two criteria:

- They mention mobile systems one way or the other in the title, abstract, or keywords.
- They are relevant for the task of development.

2.2 Conceptual Structuring

The structure of the literature review in the following section was developed through a concept matrix. The conceptual structure emerges from the review. The categorization of contributions is not based on an *a priori* conceptualization. The first-level categories are the primary concern of each contribution as we assess it (e.g., a contribution on how to prototype a wireless LAN is categorized as having a primary concern for requirements). The other first-level categories that emerge from the literature are technology, application, and business. The review reveals in this way four first-level categories, thus providing four primary *perspectives* on mobile systems development.

At the second level, we focus on the concepts addressed in each contribution as we assess it, for example, a contribution (Pedersen and Ling 2003) within the business perspective is categorized at the second level as providing an adoption and diffusion study. The review reveals 8 second-level concepts thus providing 8 areas. The areas are modeling techniques; design studies; wireless communication; architecture; security; application; adoption and diffusion studies; and business models and strategic alliances.

3 PERSPECTIVES

The relevance of the different discourses within the existing research on mobility has been considered by applying a systems development lens. We end up with 105 articles revealing four perspectives (first-level categories) in total covering 8 different areas (second-level concepts) of the literature on mobile systems development. The reviewed contributions and their distribution on perspectives and areas are shown in Table 1; the numbers in brackets are the number of contributions in this area.

We suggest that the four perspectives all have a role to play or influence the practice of mobile systems development. It should be noted that in the following presentation only a representative subset of the articles are used.

3.1 The Requirement Perspective

The *requirement* perspective is here applied as a category comprising two areas within mobile systems development: (1) the literature on modeling techniques for designing architecturally sound mobile systems and (2) the large number of studies focusing on design and human-computer interaction (HCI). In mobile systems development, both research directions play an important role in getting the requirements right for mobile systems.

Table 1. The Distribution of Papers in Each of the Perspectives and Areas

PERSPECTIVES	AREAS	REFERENCES
Requirements	Modeling techniques [4]	Drosos et al. 2004; Sauer 2004; Smith 2000, 2004
	Design studies [26]	Ahlström et al. 2002; Andersson et al. 2004; Andreasson et al. 2002; Brunnberg 2004; Condost et al. 2002; Dahlbom and Ljungberg 1998; Esbjörnsson 2001; Forsberg 2002; Gallis et al. 2001; Gustavsson et al. 2001; Hardless et al. 2001; Kjeldskov and Graham 2003; Kjeldskov et al. 2004; Lindroth 2002; Lindroth et al. 2001; Lundin and Magnusson 2002; Lundin and Nuldén 2004; Messeter et al. 2004; Nilsson 2001; Olsson 2004; Pareto and Snis 2004; Pica 2002; Östergren 2004; Smith-Berndtsson and Åström 2001; Weilenman 2001; Xu and Teo 2004
Technology	Wireless communications [18]	Carneiro et al. 2004; Chen et al. 1998; Gao et al. 2004; Hang et al. 1997; Hsieh and Sivakumar 2004; Hu and Zhang 2004; Huang and Zhuang 2004; Iraqi et al. 2000; Jiang and Zhuang 2004; Kim et al. 2003; Lindgren et al. 2003; Lu et al. 2004; Mahadevan and Sivalingam 2001; Mohapatra et al. 2003; Niebert et al. 2004; Wei and Gitlin 2004; Wu and Chuang 2001
	Architecture [17]	Braun et al. 2004; Bruno et al. 2001; Cannataro and Pascuzzi 2001; Dahlberg et al. 2001; Davies et al. 2002; Fife and Gruenwald 2003; Jing et al. 1999; Karimi and Krishnamurthy 2001; March et al. 2000; Metafas et al. 1996; Pierre 2001; Pitoura and Bhargava 1994; Sanneblad 2001; Schoeman and Cloete 2003; Shih and Shim 2002; Straub and Heinemann 2004; Thorstensten et al. 2004

PERSPECTIVES	AREAS	REFERENCES
	Security [18]	Bahl et al. 2002; Bierman and Cloete 2002; Capra 2004; Dogac and Tumer 2002; Gupta and Montenegro 1998; Køien 2004; Langeheinrich 2001; Mishra et al. 2004; Park et al. 1998; Phillips et al. 2002; Ravi et al. 2004; Schwiderski-Grosche and Knospe 2002; Sklavos et al. 2005; Tang et al. 2003; Tang and Veijalainen 2001; Wang and Pang 2003; Weippl and Essmayr 2003; Yang et al. 2004
Application	Application [6]	Christensen et al. 2002; Lipic and Osmanovic 2001; Olla and Atkinson 2004; Raatikainen et al. 2002; Senn 2000; Varshney and Vetter 2002; Yen and Chou 2000
Business	Adoption and diffusion studies [7]	Aarnio et al. 2002; Fogelgren-Pedersen 2002; Ling 2000; Ioanna et al. 2004; Naruse 2003; Pedersen and Ling 2003
	Business models and strategic alliances [9]	Alphonse 2004; Barnes 2002; Haaker et al. 2004; Olla and Patel 2002; Pedersen and Methlie 2004; Sabat 2002; Siau et al. 2001; Tsalgatidou and Pitoura 200; Van de Kar et al. 2003

3.1.1 Modeling Techniques

Because of the advances in wireless technologies, the level of complexity for the underlying system architecture rises. Furthermore, as complexity rises, time-to-market is as important as ever. This calls for a powerful modeling and design methodology ensuring robust and rapid development.

The increased complexity leads to at least four desirable capabilities within modeling and development of mobile systems: controllable abstraction, reusability, analysis of capabilities, and a high level of abstraction (Metafas et al. 1996). Considering these desired capabilities we may say that this "implies the need for an object-based approach" (Metafas et al. 1996, p. 123). These modeling and architectural considerations seem to have been agreed upon in the later contributions within this field. Smith (2004) proposes an extension of the specification language Object-Z (Smith 2000) to enable scalable and intuitive implementation of mobile applications. The Object-Z specification language is an object-oriented approach. Smith (2004, p. 193) argues that the properties of "inheritance and polymorphism allow us to exploit commonalities in mobile systems by defining more complex models in terms of simpler ones." Similar attempts at applying object-oriented approaches to modeling of mobile systems have been proposed. Drosos et al. (2004) apply an extension of the unified modeling language (UML), namely UML-R (unified modeling language for real-time). The obvious benefit of UML is the already predominant use of UML in practice, implying that the applicability of UML must be conceived as high among designers. To test the applicability of UML-R, Drosos et al. evaluate a development project applying the UML-R design language. The evaluation showed a reduction in development time and the methodology also proved to be highly beneficial as a tool for abstraction when several development teams collaborated in codesign of the resulting mobile system.

3.1.2   Design Studies

We treat design studies and mobile HCI under the common area of *design studies*. The huge interest in research on design and use of mobile systems dates back to the late 1990s. Dahlbom and Ljungberg (1998) proposed *mobile informatics* as a new research direction within IS. The core of mobile informatics is the exploration into how mobile work may be supported by wireless technologies and how users apply these. The contributions within design studies have been many.

Another, related school of thought is the research discourse of mobile HCI. One of the research areas within mobile HCI shares strong relations with mobile informatics, even though the term *usability test* is used more frequently in mobile HCI. In mobile HCI, there is an interest in evaluating the research approach by which evaluations of usability are carried out. Kjeldskov and Graham (2003) provide a review of the applied mobile HCI research methods. The review indicates that the laboratory testing approach dominates the mobile HCI domain even though the real-world context obviously cannot be compensated for in such settings. Consequently, they advocate for an increased interest in more context-rich research approaches (e.g., field studies or case studies). However, a recent study (Kjeldskov et al. 2004) shows that a usability test in a laboratory may be just as effective.

3.2 The Technology Perspective

The continuous advances of wireless technologies imply a complex and uncertain area for development companies. Developing mobile systems, therefore, necessitates in-depth analysis and consideration of what technology to use as the foundation for coming mobile systems. The *technology* perspective covers broadly the technical contributions adding to an increased body of knowledge on how to understand, exploit, and deal with the new technological capabilities from a technical viewpoint, and the issues and challenges emerging from these wireless innovations. Pierre (2001) contributes to the field by providing an overview of the predominant concepts and nontrivial areas (e.g., cellular systems, network infrastructure, application architecture, and security). Our literature review has revealed contributions in the three areas: wireless communications, application architecture, and security.

3.2.1   Wireless Communications

In this context, wireless communications covers research on or strongly related to cellular systems and network infrastructure. The increasing number of new or improved wireless network technologies is immense. The primary challenge is no longer just to go wireless, but seems to be "the ability to provide seamless and adaptive quality of service in such [a] heterogeneous environment" (Gao et al. 2004, p. 24). Currently, this field seems to attract particular interest both in practice and in research. Examples of some the latest contributions are a discussion of the challenges of mobile *ad hoc* networks (MANETs) and future directions and challenges (Mohapatra et al. 2003), a presentation of challenges and solutions in an attempt to solve the interoperability problems in the UMTS network (Kim et al. 2003; Niebert et al. 2004), a proposed a framework for integration of cellular wide wireless area networks (WWAN) and wireless local area networks (WLAN) (Wei and Gitlin 2004), and attacks on the challenges associated with turning the 4G platform into an open architecture including different wireless networks (Carneiro et al. 2004; Jiang and Zhuang 2004; Lu et al. 2004).

3.2.2   Architecture

The architecture is an essential area for development organizations. If we are developing location-based services, which imply an enormous load of requests on the underlying database management system, what architectural implications does this have? The architectural challenges have received a great deal of attention (see Davies et al. 2002; Jing et al. 1999; Pitoura and Bhargava 1994; Sanneblad 2001; Schoeman and Cloete 2003; Shih and Shim 2002). Two examples of studies in which a specific system architecture has been discussed and elaborated are Schoeman and Cloete (2003) and Shih and Shim (2002). Schoeman and Cloete discuss the architectural requirements for a mobile agent system. They contribute by developing a framework adding to an increased understanding of the architectural requirements and issues related to designing and implementing a mobile agent system. The other example represents system architectures within mobile commerce. One of the complex issues for architectures in mobile commerce is that of ensuring correct management of monetary transactions (Dogac and Tumer 2002; Shih and Shim 2002). Shih and Shim propose a scalable framework based on the Java Intelligent Network Infrastructure (JINI) capable of handling complex business transactions from a varied set of services.

3.2.3   Security

Another important area within mobile systems is security. Security in mobile systems exists at many levels; for example, security in wireless networks, security in embedded systems (Ravi et al. 2004), security in mobile agent systems (Bierman and Cloete 2002), security in mobile commerce systems (Schwiderski-Grosche and Knospe 2002), and security in the shape of engineering trust (Capra 2004) ensuring user integrity in mobile information sharing environment (Phillips et al. 2002). The contributions provided by this debate are of outmost relevance and importance to mobile systems development.

3.3 The Application Perspective

The *application* perspective covers articles with the aim of classifying and categorizing existing mobile applications and markets/sectors in which these may be of particular interest. The main contribution of this research is an increased insight into and understanding of the various classes and types of applications that exist as potential future business objects (Lipic and Osmanovic 2001; Olla and Atkinson 2004; Senn 2000). Varshney and Vetter (2002), for instance, propose a framework for classification of different types of mobile applications and end up with 10 different classes, including mobile financial applications, mobile advertising, and mobile office. Raatikainen et al. (2002) take a different path and discuss the requirements for future middleware (i.e., a set of generic services above the operating system) in order to support mobile applications. Yen and Chou (2000) take the discussion a step further and address the question of business application, managerial issues, and future developments.

3.4 The Business Perspective

The *business* perspective comprises the following two areas of research: (1) adoption and diffusion studies and (2) business models and strategic alliances. Both of these areas may play a significant role when companies consider the business potential of a mobile system. What is the potential with respect to adoption and diffusion of the product on the market? Is it necessary to initiate strategic alliances in order to ensure a solid product and minimize the costs of failure and how are such strategic alliances handled? These are just some of the questions that are relevant in the business-oriented considerations that to some extent steer and influence the development activity.

3.4.1 Adoption and Diffusion Studies

Adoption and diffusion studies, in general, constitute a broad research area. In recent years, there has been an interest in applying models from this research discourse on the area of m-commerce (see Aarnio et al. 2002; Fogelgren-Pedersen 2002; Han 2002; Ling 2000; Naruse 2003). The studies are broadly categorized as either diffusion studies, adoption studies, or domestication studies (Pedersen and Ling 2003). In diffusion studies, the focal point is how adoption of, for example, mobile systems takes place at the macro level (Pedersen and Ling 2003). That is, how segments or groups of end-users adopt technology. Adoption studies represent a more individualized focus and are interested in the adoption at the micro level, for instance, individual user adoption (Pedersen and Ling 2003). In the last category, domestication studies, the focus is on the use of technology and its socio-technical consequences. The focus on socio-technical issues associated with technology use is not limited to either defined end-user groups or individual users (Pedersen and Ling 2003). Domestication studies are, therefore, not limited to either a macro or micro level focus. In this way, domestication studies of end-users' habits and use patterns share concerns with design studies (section 3.1).

3.4.2 Business Models and Strategic Alliances

In an environment characterized by much uncertainty, such as the mobile industry, there has been a trend toward strategic alliances also refereed to as value chains (Barnes 2002; Haaker et al. 2004; Kar et al. 2003; More and McGrath 1999; Pedersen and

Methlie 2004; Sabat 2002;Tsalgatidou and Pitoura 2001). The emergence and organization of such interorganizational networks requires that "multiple actors have to balance different design requirements, strategic requirements, and business logics to create a win-win situation, in which each actor has an incentive to cooperate" (Haaker et al. 2004, p. 1). Actors in these networks may be technology platform vendors, network and infrastructure vendors, application developers, or content providers (Sabat 2002; Tsalgatidou and Pitoura 2001).

In a case study of the business model applied in the design and launch of i-mode's ringtunes service, Kar et al. (2003) propose four elements that together represent the business model for the ringtunes service concept. The four elements are (1) service formula, (2) network formation and coordination, (3) enabling technology, and (4) revenue model. The literature within mobile commerce seems to agree largely on these dimensions as constituting elements of a business model (see Haaker et al. 2004; Pedersen and Methlie 2004). According to Kar et al., the service formula is concerned with defining the service strategy for adding value to the end-customer (e.g., what and how content is to be offered). The network formation and coordination—or the governance dimension (Pedersen and Methlie 2004)—defines the rules of engagement in the interorganizational alliance. Finally, Kar et al. emphasize the importance of getting the technological issues solved and reaching, for all parties, an acceptable revenue model.

4. DISCUSSION

The literature review reveals the current state of the mobility debate and also its contribution to mobile systems development. The distribution of the reviewed articles on the different perspectives is depicted in Figure 1.

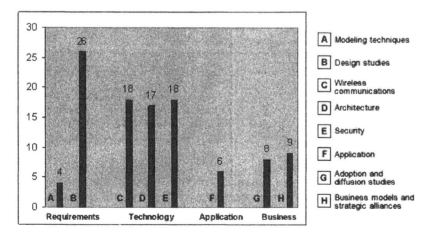

Figure 1. Histogram of the Different Perspectives
and the Distribution of Articles

Interpreting the distribution of contributions brings forth several issues. Clearly, the distribution shows an overweight of technology-related contributions. The three areas within the technology perspective represent 50 percent (53 papers out of 105) of the articles in this review. Arguably, we may say that the mobility debate so far has been largely technology-driven. The strong focus on technology is an obvious indicator of continuous development and innovation within this field, which reflects somewhat immature technologies, but also emphasizes a strong demand for more robust and flexible mobile technologies.

The requirements perspective shows an uneven distribution between the two areas (modeling techniques and design studies; see Table 1). Modeling techniques are covered in only four articles whereas design studies are covered in 26 articles. Both areas are important in a mobile systems development context when trying to understand the requirements. However, the current state of the research literature reveals that much needs to be done in the area of modeling techniques in order to develop a sufficient body of knowledge of how to actually model these systems. The role of modeling techniques should not be underemphasized as these contributions are necessary as a first step toward conceptualizing mobile systems from a development perspective. In a discussion of the characteristics of mobile systems, Krogstie et al. (2004) propose model-based techniques as a way forward to understand the particularities of these systems. In general, the implications of mobility have been extensively studied, taking many different perspectives. The varying types of contributions may all have a role to play in mobile systems development, but the limitations are unclear. As a first step, we propose an extension of the scope of traditional systems development that may contribute to a framing of mobile systems development.

The literature review shows that the scope of mobile systems development is an extension of the scope of traditional systems development.

From the literature on mobile systems development, it is easy to get the impression that all that has been learned and written about traditional systems development is neglected as it is hardly mentioned in the literature we have reviewed. It is, however, necessary to look at the recent research on mobile systems development as an extension of the existing body of knowledge on systems development (see Figure 2).

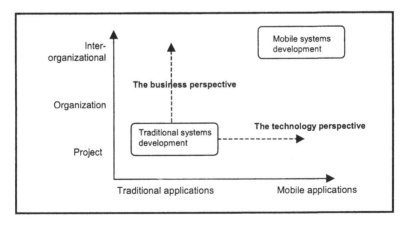

Figure 2. The Extended Scope of Mobile Systems Development

Traditional systems development tends to focus on methodologies and techniques that are focusing on stationary information systems in organizations, enterprise resource planning systems, and, lately, Web information systems. The particulars of the mobile technologies as outlined in the technology perspective (section 3.2) extend the scope (horizontally in Figure 2) because of the focus on mobile wireless communications, application architectures, and security. The technology perspective has immediate implications for the requirements perspective (section 3.1) as that is directed at modeling techniques and design studies. It is striking that very little research has been directed at establishing requirements that do not merely reflect the mobile technologies, but also the organizational and social context of mobility. The technology perspective has also immediate implications for the application perspective (section 3.3) with its outline of the different types of mobile applications and their uniqueness.

Traditional systems development tends to focus primarily on the task of development at the level of the project and very little on the task of development at the level of the company or at the level of inter-organizational development. The tremendous focus within mobile systems development on the business perspective extends the scope toward higher organizational levels (vertically in Figure 2).

Business models and strategic alliances have been of some concern in traditional systems development. The increasing complexity of the task of developing mobile systems and its character in terms of both task uncertainty and business risks makes it less likely that these complexities can be handled at the level of the development project. Mobile systems development thus often involves several development projects in several development companies. Collaboration between some of these is then organized in strategic alliances (Haaker et al. 2004). Hence, the concern for strategic alliances becomes crucial in mobile systems development. Strategic alliances are not new to systems development, but seem to be more common among mobile development companies, although so far there is little research documenting this.

The increased technical complexity in mobile systems and the increased complexity of business models may well lead companies to enter into strategic alliances. Strategic alliances, on the other hand, do not reduce the complexities per se. The partakers in the alliance exercise specialization of development capabilities and competencies as well as specialization of system components or provided services. Effectively, that can increase the process complexities, as the complexity of the added collaboration also needs to be handled.

We propose that strategic alliances stand out as a unique characteristic of mobile systems development and thus deserve further attention in the pursuit of framing and understanding the implications of this concept.

5   CONCLUSION

In this paper, we have reviewed 106 papers and their contributions to mobile systems development. The review shows that the field is still at an early stage.

We found that little research addresses mobile systems development directly. The reviewed literature is relevant to mobile systems development, but not central. Traditional systems development may have much to offer, but is largely directed at the project level. The technological challenges in mobile systems development are significant, but research in these areas is not well connected to the development tasks. Strategic alliances and interorganizational development surface as one of the characteristics of mobile systems development, but remain a significant challenge for future research.

Effectively, we propose to view mobile systems development as an extension of traditional systems to encompass these new challenges.

Further research is needed in order to understand the implications of the technological challenges and challenges stemming from business models and strategic alliances on mobile systems development.

REFERENCES

Aarnio, A., Enkenberg, A., Heikkilä, J., and Hirvola, S. "Adoption and Use of Mobile Services: Empirical Evidence from a Finnish Survey," in *Proceedings of the 35th Hawaii International Conference on System Sciences*, Los Alamitos, CA: IEEE Computer Society Press, 2002, pp. 1097-1106.

Ahlström, P., Berg, M., and Winberg, A. "Stationary Mobility: Designing for Train Travellers." in *Proceedings of the 25th Conference on Information Systems Research in Scandinavia*, K. Bødker, M. K. Pedersen, J. Nørbjerg, J. Simonsen, and M. T. Vendelø (Eds.), Bautahöj, Denmark, August 10-13, 2002.

Alphonse, J. "Re-creating the Norwegian Model for Selling Mobile Content in Malaysia," in *Proceedings of the 27th Conference on Information Systems Research in Scandinavia*, P. Flensburg and C. Ihlström (Eds.), Falkenberg, Sweden, August 14-17, 2004.

Andersson, M., Wridell, Y., and Lindgren, Y. "A Qualitative Interview Study Investigating the Role of Transport Information Systems in Road Haulage Firms," in *Proceedings of the 27th Conference on Information Systems Research in Scandinavia*, P. Flensburg and C. Ihlström (Eds.), Falkenberg, Sweden, August 14-17, 2004.

Andreasson, N., Axelsson, J., and Kuschel, J. "Sharing of Mobile Tools: An Ethnographic Workplace Study in a Car Repair Shop," in *Proceedings of the 25th Conference on Information Systems Research in Scandinavia*, K. Bødker, M. K. Pedersen, J. Nørbjerg, J. Simonsen, and M. T. Vendelø (Eds.), Bautahöj, Denmark, August 10-13, 2002.

Bahl, P., Russel, W., Wang, Y., Balachandran, A., Voelkner, G., and Miu, A. "PAWNs: Satisfying the Need for Ubiquitous Secure Connectivity and Location Services," *IEEE Wireless Communications* (9:1), 2002, pp. 40-48.

Barnes, S. J. "The Mobile Commerce Value Chain: Analysis and Future Developments," *International Journal of Information Management* (22:2), 2002, pp. 91-108.

Bierman, E., and Cloete, E. "Classification of Malicious Host Threats in Mobile Agent Computing," in *Proceedings of the Annual Conference of the South African Institute of Computer Scientists and Information Technologies*, Port Elizabeth, South Africa, September 16-18, 2002, pp. 141-148.

Braun, P., Müller, I., Geisenhainer, S., Schau, V., and Rossak, W. "A Service-Oriented Software Architecture for Mobile Agent Toolkits," in *Proceedings of the 11th IEEE International Conference and Workshop on the Engineering of Computer-Based Systems*, Brno, Czech Republic, May 24-27, 2004, pp. 550-556.

Brunnberg, L. "The Road Rager— Making Use of Traffic Encounters in a Mobile Multiplayer Game," in *Proceedings of the 27th Conference on Information Systems Research in Scandinavia*, P. Flensburg and C. Ihlström (Eds.), Falkenberg, Sweden, August 14-17, 2004.

Bruno, R., Conti, M., and Gregori, E. "WLAN Technologies for Mobile Ad Hoc Networks," in *Proceedings of the 34th Hawaii International Conference on System Sciences*, Los Alamitos, CA: IEEE Computer Society Press, 2001, p. 11.

Cannataro, M., and Pascuzzi, D. "A Component-Based Architecture for the Development and Deployment of WAP-Compliant Transactional Services," in *Proceedings of the 34th Hawaii International Conference on System*, Los Alamitos, CA: IEEE Computer Society Press, 2001.

Capra, L. "Engineering Human Trust in Mobile System Collaborations," in *Proceedings of the 12th ACM SIGSOFT: International Symposium on Foundations of Software Engineering*, New York: ACM Press, 2004, pp. 107-116.

Carneiro, G., Ruela, J., and Ricardo, M. "Cross-Layer Design in 4G Wireless Terminals," *IEEE Wireless Communications* (11:2), 2004, pp. 7-13.

Chen, J., Sivalingam, K. M., and Acharya, R. "Comparative Analysis of Wireless ATM Channel Access Protocols Supporting Multimedia Traffic," *Mobile Networks and Applications* (3:3), 1998, pp. 293-306.

Condos, C., James, A., Every, P., and Simpson, T. "Ten Usability Principles for the Development of Effective WAP and m-commerce Services," *Aslib Proceedings* (54:6), 2002, pp. 345-355.

Dahlberg, B., Ljungberg, F., and Sanneblad, J. "Proxy Lady," *Scandinavian Journal of Information Systems* (14:1), 2002, pp. 3-17.

Dahlbom, B., and Ljungberg, F. "Mobile Informatics," *Scandinavian Journal of Information Systems* (10:1-2), 1998, pp. 227-234.

Davies, N., Cheverst, K., Friday, A., and Mitchell, K. "Future Wireless Applications for a Networked City: Services for Visitors and Residents," *IEEE Wireless Communications* (9:1), 2002, pp. 8-16.

Dogac, A., and Tumer, A. "Issues in Mobile Electronic Commerce," *Journal of Database Management* (13:1), 2002, pp. 36-42.

Drosos, C., Metafas, D., and Papadopoulos, G. "A UML-Based Methodology for the System Design of a Wireless LAN Prototype," in *Proceedings of the 7th IEEE International Symposium on Object-Oriented Real-Time Distributed Computing*, IEEE Computer Society, Vienna, Austria, 2004, pp. 45-51.

Esbjörnsson, M. "Work in Motion: Interpretation of Defects along the Roads," in *Proceedings of the 24th Conference on Information Systems Research in Scandinavia*, S. Bjørnestad, R. E. Moe, A. I. Mørch, and A. L. Opdahl (Eds.), Bergen, Norway, August 11-14, 2001, pp. 413-426.

Fife, L. D., and Gruenwald, L. "Research Issues for Data Communication in Mobile Ad Hoc Network Database Systems," *SIGMOD Record* (32:2), 2003, pp. 42-47.

Fogelgren-Pedersen, A. "Factors Promoting the Adoption of the Mobile Internet," in *Proceedings of the 25th Conference on Information Systems Research in Scandinavia*, K. Bødker, M. K. Pedersen, J. Nørbjerg, J. Simonsen, and M. T. Vendelø (Eds.), Bautahöj, Denmark, August 10-13, 2002.

Forsberg, K. "Task-in-Content: Supporting Mobile News Journalism," in *Proceedings of the 25th Conference on Information Systems Research in Scandinavia*, K. Bødker, M. K. Pedersen, J. Nørbjerg, J. Simonsen, and M. T. Vendelø (Eds.), Bautahöj, Denmark, August 10-13, 2002.

Gallis, H., Kasbo, J. P., and Herstad, J. "The Multidevice Paradigm in Knowmobile" Does One Size Fit All?," in *Proceedings of the 24th Conference on Information Systems Research in Scandinavia*, S. Bjørnestad, R. E. Moe, A. I. Mørch, and A. L. Opdahl (Eds.), Bergen, Norway, August 11-14, 2001, pp. 491-504.

Gao, X., Wu, G., and Miki, T. "End-to-End QoS Provisioning in Mobile Heterogeneous Networks," *IEEE Wireless Communications* (11:3), 2004, pp. 24-34.

Gupta, V., and Montenegro, G. "Secure and Mobile Networking," *Mobile Networks and Applications* (3:4), 1998, pp. 381-390.

Gustavsson, P., Lundin, J., and Nuldén, U. "Mobile Scenarios: Supporting Collaborative Learning among Mobile People," in *Proceedings of the 24th Conference on Information Systems Research in Scandinavia*, S. Bjørnestad, R. E. Moe, A. I. Mørch, and A. L. Opdahl (Eds.),, Bergen, Norway, August 11-14, 2001, pp. 59-72.

Haaker, T., Bouwman, H., and Faber, E. "Customer and Network Value of Mobile Services: Balancing Requirements and Strategic Interests," in *Proceedings of the 25th International Conference on Information Systems*, R. Agarwal, L. Kirsch, and J. I. DeGross (Eds.), Washington, DC, December 12-15, 2004, pp. 1-14.

Han, S. "A Framework for Understanding Adoption and Diffusion Processes for Mobile Commerce Products and Services and its Potential Implications for Planning Industry Foresight," in *Proceedings of the 25th Conference on Information Systems Research in Scandinavia*, K. Bødker, M. K. Pedersen, J. Nørbjerg, J. Simonsen, and M. T. Vendelø (Eds.), Bautahöj, Denmark, August 10-13, 2002.

Hang, L., Hairuo, M., Magda, E., and Sanjay, G. "Error Control Schemes for Networks: An Overview," *Mobile Networks and Applications* (2:2), 1997, pp. 167-182.

Hardless, C., Lundin, J., and Nuldén, U. "Mobile Competence Development for Nomads," in *Proceedings of the 34th Hawaii International Conference on Systems Sciences*, Los Alamitos, CA: IEEE Computer Society Press, 2001, p. 1048.

Hsieh, H., and Sivakumar, R. "On Using Peer-to-Peer Communication in Cellular Wireless Data Networks," *IEEE Transactions on Mobile Computing* (3:1), 2004, pp. 57-72.

Hu, M., and Zhang, J. "Opportunistic Multi-Access: Multiuser Diversity, Relay-Aided Opportunistic Scheduling, and Traffic-Aided Smooth Admission Control," *Mobile Networks and Applications* (9:4), 2004, pp. 435-444.

Huang, V., and Zhuang, W. "QoS-Oriented Packet Scheduling for Wireless Multimedia CDMA Communications," *IEEE Transactions on Mobile Computing* (3:1), 2004, pp. 73-85.

Ioanna, C., Damsgaard, J., and Knutsen, L. "Investigating Mobile Services Adoption and Diffusion in the Danish Market," in *Proceedings of the 27th Conference on Information Systems Research in Scandinavia*, P. Flensburg and C. Ihlström (Eds.), Falkenberg, Sweden, August 14-17, 2004.

Iraqi, Y., Boutaba, R., and Leon-Garci, A. "QoS Control in Wireless ATM," *Mobile Networks and Applications* (5:2), 2000, pp. 137-145.

Jiang, H., and Zhuang, W. "Quality-of-Service Provisioning in Future 4G Cellular Networks," *IEEE Wireless Communications* (11:2), 2004, pp. 48-54.

Jing, J., Helal, A. S., and Elmargarmid, A. "Client-Server Computing in Mobile Environments," *ACM Computing Surveys* (31:2), 1999, pp. 117-157.

Karimi, H. A., and Krishnamurthy, P. "Real-Time Routing in Mobile Networks Using GPS and GSI Techniques," in *Proceedings of the 34th Annual Hawaii International Conference on System Sciences*, Los Alamitos, CA: IEEE Computer Society, 2001, p. 11.

Kim, S., Cho, H., Hahm, H., Lee, S., and Lee, M. S. "Interoperability between UMTS and CDMA2000 Networks," *IEEE Wireless Communications* (10:1), 2003, pp. 22-28.

Kjeldskov, J., and Graham, C. "A Review of Mobile HCI Research Methods," in *Proceedings of the 5th International Mobile HCI Conference*, L. Chittaro (Ed.), Udine, Italy, September 8-11, 2003, pp. 317-335.

Kjeldskov, J., Skov, M. B., Als, B. S., and Høegh, R. T. "Is it Worth the Hassle? Exploring the Added Value of Evaluating the Usability of Context-Aware Mobile Systems in the Field," in *Proceedings of the 6th International Mobile HCI Conference*, M. D. S. Brewster (Ed.), Galsgow, September 13-16, 2004, pp. 51-73.

Krogstie, J., Lyytinen, K., Opdahl, A. L., Pernici, B., Siau, K., and Smolander, K. "Research Areas and Challenges for Mobile Information Systems," *International Journal of Mobile Communications* (2:3), 2004, pp. 220-234.

Køien, G. M. "An Introduction to Access Security in UMTS," *IEEE Wireless Communications* (11:1), 2004, pp. 8-18.

Langeheinrich, M. "Privacy by Design: Principles of Privacy Aware Ubiquitous Systems," in *Proceedings of the 3ʳᵈ International Conference on Ubiquitous Computing*, Atlanta, Georgia, 2001, pp. 273-291.

Lindgren, A., Almquist, A., and Schelen, O. "Quality of Service Schemes for IEEE 802.11 Wireless LANs: An Evaluation," *Mobile Networks and Applications* (8:3), 2003, pp. 223-235.

Lindroth, T. "Action, Place and Nomadic Behavior—A Study Towards Enhanced Situated Computing," in *Proceedings of the 25ᵗʰ Conference on Information Systems Research in Scandinavia*, K. Bødker, M. K. Pedersen, J. Nørbjerg, J. Simonsen, and M. T. Vendelø (Eds.), Bautahöj, Denmark, August 10-13, 2002.

Lindroth, T., Nilsson, S., and Rasmussen, P. "Mobile Usability: Rigor Meets Relevance When Usability Goes Mobile," in *Proceedings of the 24ᵗʰ Conference on Information Systems Research in Scandinavia*, S. Bjørnestad, R. E. Moe, A. I. Mørch, and A. L. Opdahl (Eds.), Bergen, Norway, August 11-14, 2001, pp. 641-654.

Ling, R. "'We Will Be Reached': The Use of Mobile Telephony Among Norwegian Youth," *Information Technology and People* (13:2), 2000, pp. 102-120.

Lipic, V., and Osmanovic, A. "The Power of mPeople—Mobile Customers: What Do They Really Want," in *Proceedings of the 24ᵗʰ Conference on Information Systems Research in Scandinavia*, S. Bjørnestad, R. E. Moe, A. I. Mørch, and A. L. Opdahl (Eds.), Bergen, Norway, August 11-14, 2001, 24, 2001, pp. 305-318.

Lu, W. W., Walke, B. H., and Shen, X. "4G Mobile Communications: Toward an Open Wireless Architecture," *IEEE Wireless Communications* (11:2), 2004, pp. 4-6.

Lundin, J., and Magnusson, M. "Sharing Best Practices among Mobile Workers," in *Proceedings of the 24ᵗʰ Conference on Information Systems Research in Scandinavia*, S. Bjørnestad, R. E. Moe, A. I. Mørch, and A. L. Opdahl (Eds.), Bergen, Norway, August 11-14, 2001.

Lundin, J., and Nuldén, U. "Supporting Workplace Learning for Police Officers Finding Guidance for Design in a Mobile Work Practice," in *Proceedings of the 27ᵗʰ Information Systems Research Seminar in Scandinavia*, P. Flensburg and C. Ihlström (Eds.), Falkenberg, Sweden, August 14-17, 2004.

Mahadevan, I., and Sivalingam, K. "Architecture and Experimental Framework for Supporting QoS in Wireless Networks Using Differentiated Services," *Mobile Networks and Applications* (6:4), 2001, pp. 385-395.

March, S., Hevner, A., and Ram, S. "Research Commentary: An Agenda for Information Technology Research in Heterogeneous and Distributed Environments," *Information Systems Research* (11:4), 2000, pp. 327-347.

Messeter, J., Brandt, E., Halse, J., and Johansson, M. "Contextualizing Mobile IT," in *Proceedings of the Conference on Designing Interactive Systems*, New York: ACM Press, 2004, pp. 27-36.

Metafas, D., Karathanasis, H. C., and Blionas, S. V. "Industrial Approach in Design Methodologies for Mobile Communication Systems," in *Proceedings of the 7ᵗʰ IEEE International Workshop on Rapid System Prototyping*, Thessaloniki, Greece, June 19-21, 1996, pp. 122-126.

Mishra, A., Nadkarni, K., Patcha, A., and Tech, V. "Intrusion Detection in Wireless Ad Hoc Networks," *IEEE Wireless Communications* (11:1), 2004, pp. 48-60.

Mohapatra, P., Li, J., and Gui, C. "QoS in Mobile Ad Hoc Networks," *IEEE Wireless Communications* (10:3), 2003, pp. 44-52.

More, E., and McGrath, M. "Working Cooperatively in an Age of Deregulation: Strategic Alliances in Australia's Telecommunication Sector," *The Journal of Management Development* (18:3), 1999, pp. 227-254.

Naruse, K. "The Survey of the Mobile Internet, Usage, Awareness, Study for M-Commerce," in *Proceedings of the 2003 Symposium on Applications and the Internet Workshops*, Orlando, FL, 2003, pp. 127-130.

Niebert, N., Schieder, A., Abrahamowicz, H., Malmgren, G., Sachs, J., Horn, U., Prehofer, C., and Karl, H. "Ambient Networks: An Architecture For Communication Networks Beyond 3G," *IEEE Wireless Communications* (11:3), 2004, pp. 14-22.

Nilsson, V. "Method for Researching Different Abilities by Mobility," in *Proceedings of the 24th Conference on Information Systems Research in Scandinavia*, S. Bjørnestad, R. E. Moe, A. I. Mørch, and A. L. Opdahl (Eds.), Bergen, Norway, August 11-14, 2001, 24, 2001, pp. 669-680.

Olla, P., and Atkinson, C. "Developing a Wireless Reference Model for Interpreting Complexity in Wireless Projects," *Industrial Management & Data Systems* (104:3), 2004, pp. 262-272.

Olla, P., and Patel, N. V. "A Value Chain Model for Mobile Data Service Providers," *Telecommunications Policy* (26:9), 2002, pp. 551-571.

Olsson, C. M. "Exploring the Impact of a Context-Aware Application for In-Car Use," in *Proceedings of the 25th International Conference on Information Systems*, R. Agarwal, L. Kirsch, and J. I. DeGross (Eds.), Washington, DC, December 12-15, 2004, pp. 129-140.

Östergren, M. "Implications of Speed Trap Services for Designing Roadside-Location-Dependent Messengers," in *Proceedings of the 27th Conference on Information Systems Research in Scandinavia*, P. Flensburg and C. Ihlström (Eds.), Falkenberg, Sweden, August 14-17, 2004.

Pareto, L., and Snis, U. L. "Work-Integrated Mobile Technology: Towards a Patient-Oriented Workplace in Health Care Settings," in *Proceedings of the 27th Information Systems Research Seminar in Scandinavia*, P. Flensburg and C. Ihlström (Eds.), Falkenberg, Sweden, August 14-17, 2004.

Park, S. H., Ganz, A., and Ganz, Z. "Security Protocol for IEEE 802.11 Wireless Local Area Network," *Mobile Networks and Applications* (3:3), 1998, pp. 237-246.

Pedersen, P. E., and Ling, R. "Modifying Adoption Research for Mobile Internet Service Adoption: Cross-Disciplinary Interactions," in *Proceedings of the 36th Hawaii International Conference on System Sciences*, Los Alamitos, CA: IEEE Computer Society Press, 2003.

Pedersen, P. E., and Methlie, L. B. "Exploring the Relationship between Mobile Data Services, Business Models and End-User Adoption," paper presented at the 4th IFIP Conference on e-Commerce, e-Business, and e-Government, Toulouse, France, August 22-27, 2004, pp. 1-29.

Phillips, C. E., Ting, T. C., and Demurjian, S. A. "Information Sharing and Security in Dynamic Coalitions," in *Proceedings of the 7th ACM Symposium on Access Control Model sand Technologies*, Monterey, CA, 2002, pp. 87-96.

Pica, D. "Location in Mobile Informatics: The Concept of 'Nomadic Reality' in Design," in *Proceedings of the 25th Conference on Information Systems Research in Scandinavia*, K. Bødker, M. K. Pedersen, J. Nørbjerg, J. Simonsen, and M. T. Vendelø (Eds.), Bautahöj, Denmark, August 10-13, 2002.

Pierre, S. "Mobile Computing and Ubiquitous Networking: Concepts, Technologies and Challenges," *Telematics and Informatics* (18), 2001, pp. 109-131.

Pitoura, E., and Bhargava, B. "Building Information Systems for Mobile Environments," in *Proceedings of the 3rd International Conference on Information and Knowledge Management*, Gaithersburg, MD, November 29-December 2, 1994, pp. 371-378.

Ravi, S., Raghunathan, A., Kocher, P., and Hattangady, S. "Security in Embedded Systems: Design Challenges," *ACM Transactions on Embedded Computing Systems* (3:3), 2004, pp. 461-491.

Raatikainen, K., Christensen, H. B., and Nakajima, T. "Application Requirements for Middleware for Mobile and Pervasive Systems," *Mobile Computing and Communications Review* (6:4), 2002, pp. 16-24.

Sabat, H. K. "The Evolving Mobile Wireless Value Chain and Market Structure," *Telecommunications Policy* (26), 2002, pp. 505-535.

Sanneblad, J. "BluePortal: A Framework for Mobile Ad Hoc Network Applications," in *Proceedings of the 24ᵗʰ Conference on Information Systems Research in Scandinavia*, S. Bjørnestad, R. E. Moe, A. I. Mørch, and A. L. Opdahl (Eds.), Bergen, Norway, August 11-14, 2001, pp. 569-582.

Sauer, J. "Development of Mobile Applications Based on the Tools & Materials Approach," in *Proceedings of the 27ᵗʰ Information Systems Research Seminar in Scandinavia*, P. Flensburg and C. Ihlström (Eds.), Falkenberg, Sweden, August 14-17, 2004.

Schoeman, M., and Cloete, E. "Architectural Components for the Efficient Design of Mobile Agent Systems," in *Proceedings of the 2003 Annual Research Conference of the South African Institute of Computer Scientists and Information Technologists on Enablement through Technology*, Fourways, South Africa, 2003, pp. 48-58.

Schwiderski-Grosche, S., and Knospe, H. "Secure Mobile Commerce," *Electronics and Communication Engineering Journal* (14:5), 2002, 228-238.

Senn, J. "The Emergence of M-Commerce," *IEEE Computer* (33:12), 2000, pp. 148-150.

Shih, G., and Shim, S. S. Y. "A Service Management Framework for M-Commerce Applications," *Mobile Networks and Applications* (7), 2002, pp. 199-212.

Siau, K., Lim, E., and Shen, Z. "Mobile Commerce: Promises, Challenges, and Research Agenda," *Journal of Database Management* (12:3), 2001, pp. 4-13.

Sklavos, N., Moldovyan, N. A., and Koufopavlou, O. "High Speed Networking Security: Design and Implementation of Two New DDP-Based Ciphers," *Mobile Networks and Applications* (10:2), 2005, pp. 219-231.

Smith, G. *The Object-Z Specification Language*, Boston: Kluwer Academic Publishers, 2000.

Smith, G. "A Formal Framework for Modeling and Analyzing Mobile Systems," in *Proceedings of the 27ᵗʰ Australiasian Computer Science Conference*, Dunedin, New Zealand, 2004, pp. 193-202.

Smith-Berndtsson, D., and Åström, J. "Is There a Need for Mobile Services? Understanding the Everyday Lives of 'Ordinary' Users with Cars," in *Proceedings of the 24ᵗʰ Conference on Information Systems Research in Scandinavia*, S. Bjørnestad, R. E. Moe, A. I. Mørch, and A. L. Opdahl (Eds.), Bergen, Norway, August 11-14, 2001, pp. 385-395.

Straub, T., and Heinemann, A. "An Anonymous Bonus Point System for Mobile Commerce Based on Word-of-Mouth Recommendation," in *Proceedings of the 19ᵗʰ Annual ACM Symposium on Applied Computing*, Nicosia, Cyprus, March 14-17, 2004, pp. 766-773

Tang, J., Terziyan, V., and Veijalainen, J. "Distributed PIN Verification Scheme for Improving Security of Mobile Devices," *Mobile Networks and Applications* (8:2), 2003, pp. 159-175.

Tang, J., and Veijalainen, J. "Using Agents to Improve Security and Convenience in Mobile E-Commerce," in *Proceedings of the 34ᵗʰ Hawaii International Conference on System Sciences*, Los Alamitos, CA: IEEE Computer Society Press, 2001.

Thorstensten, B., Syversen, T., Bjørnvold, T., and Walseth, T. "Electronic Shepherd: A Low-Cost, Low-Bandwidth, Wireless Network System," in *Proceedings of the 2ⁿᵈ International Conference on Mobile Systems, Applications, and Services*, Boston, MA, 2004, pp. 245-255.

Tsalgatidou, A., and Pitoura, E. "Business Models and Transactions in Mobile Electronic Commerce: Requirements and Properties," *Computer Networks* (37), 2001, pp. 221-236.

Van de Kar, E., Maitland, C. F., de Montalvo, U. W., and Bouwman, H. "Design Guidelines for Mobile Information and Entertainment Services," in *Proceedings of the 5ᵗʰ International Conference on Electronic Commerce*, New York: ACM Press, 2003.

Varshney, U., and Vetter, R. "Mobile Commerce: Framework, Applications and Networking Support," *Mobile Networks and Applications* (7:3), 2002, pp. 185-198.

Wang, Y., and Pang, X. "Security and Robustness Enhanced Route Structures for Mobile Agents," *Mobile Networks and Applications* (8:4), 2003, pp. 413-423.

Webster, J., and Watson, R. T. "Analyzing the Past to Prepare for the Future: Writing a Literature Review," *MIS Quarterly* (26:2), 2002, pp. xiii-xxii.

Wei, H., and Gitlin, R. "Two-Hop-Relay Architecture For Next-Generation WWAN/WLAN Integration," *IEEE Wireless Communications* (11:2), 2004, pp. 24-30.

Weilenman, A. "Mobile Methodologies: Experiences from Studies of Mobile Technologies-in-Use," in *Proceedings of the 24ᵗʰ Conference on Information Systems Research in Scandinavia*, S. Bjørnestad, R. E. Moe, A. I. Mørch, and A. L. Opdahl (Eds.), Bergen, Norway, August 11-14, 2001, pp. 243-256.

Weippl, E., and Essmayr, W. "Personal Trusted Devices for Web Services: Revisiting Multilevel Security," *Mobile Networks and Applications* (8:2), 2003, pp. 151-157.

Wu, H., and Chuang, P. "Dynamic QoS Allocation for Multimedia Ad Hoc Wireless Networks," *Mobile Networks and Applications* (6:4), 2001, pp. 377-384.

Xu, H., and Teo, H. "Alleviating Consumers' Privacy Concerns in Location-Based Services: A Psychological Control Perspective," in *Proceedings of the 25ᵗʰ International Conference on Information Systems*, R. Agarwal, L. Kirsch, and J. I. DeGross (Eds.), Washington, DC, December 12-15, 2004, pp. 793-806.

Yang, H., Ye, F., Luo, H., Lu, S., and Zhang, L. "Security in Mobile Ad Hoc Networks: Challenges and Solutions," *IEEE Wireless Communications* (11:1), 2004, pp. 38-47.

Yen, D. C., and Chou, D. C. "Wireless Communications: Applications and Managerial Issues," *Industrial Management & Data Systems* (100:9), 2000, pp. 436-443.

Yu, O. T. W. "End-to-End Adaptive QoS Provisioning Over GPRS Wireless Mobile Network," *Mobile Networks and Applications* (8:3), 2003, pp. 255-67.

ABOUT THE AUTHORS

Jens Henrik Hosbond is a Ph.D. student in Information Systems at the Department of Computer Science at Aalborg University. His research focuses on the emerging discourse of mobile systems development. He is currently working with a characterization of mobile systems development with respect to its constituting elements and how it is similar or different from traditional systems development. Jens can be reached at joenne@cs.aau.dk.

Peter Axel Nielsen is an associate professor in Information Systems at the Department of Computer Science at Aalborg University. For the past several years, he has been engaged in understanding information systems development practice and the use of methodologies. His research interests include analysis and design techniques, object-orientation, and software process improvement. He is coauthor of a book on object-oriented analysis and design and a book on software process improvement. Peter can be reached at pan@cs.aau.dk.

18 DESIGNING CONTEXT-AWARE INTERACTION: An Action Research Study

Carl Magnus Olsson
Ola Henfridsson
Viktoria Institute
Göteborg, Sweden

Abstract   *Context-aware computing is an important research theme of ubiquitous computing. One of the most debated issues regarding context-aware applications is the extent to which such applications can capture the complexity of social context. This debate has been fueled by the fact that many of the documented context-aware applications convey a relatively simplistic view of context. The typical separation between human activity and context is problematic as context is not something simply in which interaction occurs.*

This paper applies and evaluates the plausibility of Dourish's (2001a, 2001b, 2004) interactional context view for designing context-aware applications that transcend the mainstream design agenda in context-aware computing. On the basis of a canonical action research study, we develop and test design principles for context-aware applications that convey an interactional view of context. Recognizing the car not only as an excellent example of a ubiquitous information environment, but also as an interesting and complex use setting already commonplace in the modern community, we have implemented and assessed a car infotainment application to provide us with a firm illustration of what such a context-aware application might be.

Keywords   Action research, design-oriented research, context-aware computing, interactional view of context, ubiquitous information environments

1   INTRODUCTION

Over the years, a key research theme in ubiquitous computing has been context-aware computing. This research theme has been directed at exploring applications with the capacity to support users by aligning implicit human activity with computing services (Abowd and Mynatt 2000). Embedded in dedicated computing environments, such capacity relies on models of user environments that can be dynamically applied, developed, and modified as a response to changing circumstances (Lyytinen and Yoo 2002a).

Given its centrality to context-aware computing, the notion of context has been much debated (see Abowd and Mynatt 2000; Dourish 2004; Schmidt et al. 1999). One pressing issue is the extent to which context-aware applications can capture the complexity of social context. The majority of documented context-aware applications only use identity and location in their attempts to capture user environment changes (Abowd and Mynatt 2000). As an example, the seminal Active Badge system (Want et al. 1992) uses identity and location for triggering automatic doors, automatic telephone forwarding, and customized computer displays (Weiser 1991). Even though evaluations of the Active Badge system document promising results, it has been argued that more complex social situations would require context-aware applications that draw on notions of context that transcend attempts to approximate context with location (see Schmidt et al. 1999).

The scarcity of contextual cues when modeling human interaction may risk reducing the usefulness of context-aware applications. Even though many problems can be traced to technical issues including wireless networking, processing capability, storage capacity, and displays (Want et al. 2002), the omission of social aspects of context-awareness is a considerable problem (Dourish 2001a, 2001b). In fact, application-centered context-aware computing research has typically assumed context to be a form of information that is delineable, stable, and separable from activity (Dourish 2004). In particular, the separation between human activity and context is problematic since context is "not something merely 'in which' interaction occurs" (Giddens 1984, p. 71). Addressing this problem, Dourish (2004) suggests an interactional view where context is understood as something relational, dynamic, occasioned, and arisen from human activity. This view not only embeds a richer notion of human interaction but also enables a balanced take on the socio-technical challenges associated with ubiquitous computing (see Lyytinen and Yoo 2002b).

Lately, design-oriented information systems research has been recognized as a valuable way of developing insights applicable to new classes of information systems (Hevner et al. 2004, Markus et al. 2002). In particular in combination with the action research method, it provides a plausible approach to assessing promising conceptual work in authentic milieus (Lindgren et al. 2004). In an attempt to investigate human interaction support provided by context-aware computing applications, we therefore conducted an action research study (Baskerville and Wood-Harper 1996) with the objective of developing and testing design principles for context-aware applications that convey an interactional view of context. Recognizing the car not only as an excellent example of ubiquitous computing but also as a complex use setting strongly integrated in our everyday lives (Walker et al. 2001), this effort was taken in the context of car infotainment systems.

In collaboration with a car manufacturer and an automotive systems integrator, we developed a prototype application called CABdriver Space for evaluating the plausibility of the interactional view of context (Dourish 2001a, 2001b, 2004) in an authentic setting. CABdriver Space is a hand-held context-aware computer game intended to stimulate in-car interaction for both enjoyment and safety purposes. In using a significant amount of car-related contextual information and involving both passengers and driver, the car infotainment context provides an interesting setting for exploring contextuality in context-aware computing. Our previous work on the CABdriver concept has provided methodological insights for innovative prototype evaluation (Olsson and Russo 2004) as well as a first exploration of the interactional impacts of CABdriver with regard to the feasibility and usefulness of the application concept in cars (Olsson 2004).

2   DESIGNING INTERACTION THROUGH CONTEXT-AWARE APPLICATIONS

The increasing miniaturization and connectivity of mobile devices have enabled a wider diffusion of mobile services in people's everyday life. Triggered by drivers such as convergence, mass-scale availability, and mobility, this diffusion opens up a wide array of new research issues associated with the development and use of ubiquitous computing services (Jessup and Robey 2002; Lyytinen and Yoo 2002b). As highlighted by Lyytinen and Yoo (2002a), one such issue is to integrate large-scale mobile services with models of specific user environments that can be dynamically applied, developed, and modified as a response to changing circumstances.

However, the current understanding of user environments in context-aware computing is relatively underdeveloped (Abowd and Mynatt 2000; Dourish 2001a, 2001b). Context is frequently assumed to be a form of information that is delineable, stable, and separable from activity (Dourish 2004). In this regard, most context-aware applications use identity and location as sole indicators of contextual changes (Abowd and Mynatt 2000; Schmidt et al 1999). Theoretical and methodological approaches are therefore needed that can cater for the assembly of social and technological elements characterizing ubiquitous computing environments (Lyytinen and Yoo 2002b).

While the relationship between technical and social elements in information systems indeed has been highlighted over the years (see, for example, Orlikowski 1992; Walsham 1996), design-oriented research targeting new classes of information systems typically benefit from domain-specific theoretical frameworks (Walls et al 1992). In the case of context-aware applications, Dourish (2004) presents such a theoretical framework which views context as an interactional problem. Drawing on phenomenology, this framework is an attempt to provide a basis for designing context-aware interaction. In doing this, it outlines four interrelated assumptions that can work as vehicles for informing such design (Dourish 2004, p. 22). The first assumption posits that "contextuality is a relational property that holds between objects or activities." In other words, context is not external to the activities unfolding in particular instances. Second, this means that "the scope of contextual features is defined dynamically." Context is shaped through ongoing action, rather than predefined irrespective of what takes place in time and space. Third, context is, therefore, "an occasioned property, relevant to particular settings, particular instances of action and particular parties to that action," and, fourth, it "arises from the activity."

Dourish's work represents a promising research direction for the design of context-aware applications. However, much work is still needed to evaluate this direction in authentic settings. As highlighted by Abowd and Mynatt (2000), the delicate balance between prediction of the usefulness of novel technologies and observation of authentic use makes evaluation of ubiquitous computing research difficult. Indeed, the current wave of nomadic and ubiquitous computing environments challenges information systems researchers to adopt new research methodologies (Lyytinen and Yoo 2002b). In this vein, we designed an action research study for exploring the interactional view of context for designing a context-aware computer game intended to stimulate in-car interaction for both enjoyment and safety purposes.

3   RESEARCH METHODOLOGY

3.1   Research Design

The study reported in this paper was conducted as part of an action research project called "Mobile Services for In-Car User Value." The overall goal of this project was to explore different design challenges faced by car manufacturers that increasingly aim to support automotive commuters' everyday use of consumer electronics such as cell phones, mp3-players, PDAs, and smart phones. While one subproject targeted cell phone use and the issue of multi-contextuality (see Henfridsson and Lindgren 2005), the subproject presented here concerned PDAs and context-aware gaming.

Conducted between July 2002 and June 2004, the project was a lengthy collaborative study between the Viktoria Institute (research institute) and two firms operating in the automotive industry: Saab Automobile (car manufacturer) and Mecel (automotive systems integrator). Concurring with Robey and Markus' (1998) recommendation that practitioner sponsorship should be pursued to help overcome the commonly perceived rigor and relevance trade-off, the project was funded by the Swedish research agency VINNOVA together with the participating organizations.

Our action research followed the canonical action research method (Davison et al. 2004, Susman and Evered 1978) and thus corresponded to the five traditional phases: diagnosing, action planning, action taking, evaluating, and specifying learning. The *diagnosing* phase included collaborative (researchers and practitioners) workshop sessions and project meetings intended to identify core challenges in the car infotainment area. Documented through written notes and project minutes, these sessions and meetings focused on how the current automotive trend approaches interaction in cars (elaborated on in Olsson 2004) and how to design car infotainment that draws on the mobile setting of car traveling. This directed us to literature on context-aware computing and the notion of context. The diagnosing phase was followed by an *action planning* phase to specify actions that would allow us to test how an interactional view of context would affect design adapted to our specific setting. In collaboration with the practitioners, we developed three design principles that operationalized this theoretical framework into a design direction (see, for example, Walls et al 1992) intended to produce a meaningful context-aware application to assess from an automotive industry perspective. In the *action taking* phase, we developed a prototype, CABdriver Space, that embedded our design principles. In this regard, the prototype acted as research instrument for testing the plausibility of the design principles. Then, we recruited five families for evaluating the prototype over two months in their everyday life. The data collected and analyzed in the *evaluating* phase were later assessed jointly by researchers and practitioners for *specifying learning* with regard to both research and practice.

3.2 Data Collection

Concurring with the typical action research project, our data collection involved multiple data sources including project and workshop sessions, document review, lead user studies, open-ended questionnaires, and qualitative interviews (see Germonprez and Mathiassen 2004). Throughout the entire project, a total of 23 project meeting and workshop sessions were held and documented. These sessions were characterized by numerous discussion and decision points covering the infotainment concept, empirical studies, prototype development, and project deliverables.

As part of the two-month evaluation phase, semi-structured qualitative interviews (Patton 2002) were conducted with five families who had their cars modified for the evaluation of the CABdriver Space prototype. Because the prototype required a specific version of the Saab 9-3's infotainment platform, not commonly available to the public, the families could only be selected from a (fairly large) number of drivers from Saab Automobile. In order to avoid paying the price for making simplistic prototypes (Grudin 2001), we were forced to limit the selection of respondents in this way. However, it must be emphasized that none of the family members were associated with our project and were all known to provide precise and constructive feedback from previous in-house testing of other services.

Data was collected at two points of the evaluation period. Qualitative interviews were conducted half-way through the study. Consisting of both a joint family interview and individual interviews with each parent of the five families, these recorded and partly transcribed interview sessions lasted 150 to 210 minutes. During the family interviews, questions were formulated to encourage all family members to answer and they were specifically focused on tracing scenario descriptions of experiences from using the prototype. Questions ranged from appropriation questions (e.g., types of use and misuse, attitudes, conflict management, participation, changes in behavior, experimental use) to questions relating to their views on traveling by car with and without CABdriver, their expectations of what long-term use of CABdriver would mean to them, the future of the application concept, and their views on participating in the study. In covering similar questions, the individual interviews were conducted to trace individual differences between parents (because of their age, children were not interviewed individually).

The second data collection point consisted of an open-ended questionnaire designed on the basis of the interview round. It consisted of 27 questions corresponding to themes that emerged in analysis of the interview study. This questionnaire was answered in writing—one questionnaire per family—and followed up on how CABdriver had been appropriated, their perception on travel by car during this time, the long-term feasibility of the concept, possible future directions to consider implementing, and their feelings about being a part of the study. The questions were open-ended and again designed to stimulate participants to describe examples from the use to support their opinions.

4   DESIGNING INTERACTION IN THE
CAR INFOTAINMENT CONTEXT

4.1 Diagnosing

On the basis of collaborative workshop sessions with the industry partners, we started our action research by exploring the emerging area of car infotainment and its possibilities and limitations vis-à-vis Saab Automobile's technical platforms and infotainment strategy. Given Saab Automobile's targeted market segment of "modern individualists who reject the mainstream," the action research group decided early on to explore a car infotainment direction that breaks with tradition. This was important to our automotive partner as they felt the automotive industry has long struggled with few significant innovations over the last decade—a result of the strict in-house proto-typing and testing traditionally done. Saab Automobile strongly believed the industry as a whole had reduced external input that could have been used to foster new ideas to virtually none. The application was intended to utilize the information resources available from the in-car computing environment in order to benefit from the mobility aspects associated with car traveling. This breaks with the current trend for infotainment applications (including the rapidly growing introduction of gaming platforms such as Sony Playstation 2) in cars. These typically have no links to what goes on in or around the car. This intent also coincided well with our research agenda directed at inves-tigating how to design meaningful interaction through context-aware applications.

In the attempt to explore the plausibility of a context-aware car infotainment concept, the action research group decided that testing it in an authentic setting would be a cumbersome but worthwhile direction. Given this ambition, we would need to develop a prototype that would work as a design test of Dourish's interactional context view.

4.2 Action Planning

We then set out to develop a set of design principles that would cater for Dourish's (2004) interactional context view. We focused our efforts on formulating this descriptive theory into a design direction intended to produce more meaningful context-aware applications (see Walls et al 1992). Contrary to the context view held in mainstream context-aware computing literature, a core assumption in the interactional context view is that context arises from activity (Dourish 2004). With this in mind, we developed the following design principles:

- *The principle of relational context* specifies that the context-aware application should support users' understanding of context through linking human activity (e.g., driver activity) with actions taken by the application. This principle corresponds to Dourish's (2004, p. 22) context assumption saying "contextuality is a relational property that holds between objects or activities."

- *The principle of occasioned relevance* specifies that the actions taken by context-aware applications should be triggered by occasions unfolding in the course of activity (e.g., driving) that are deemed relevant by the involved actors (e.g., driver). This principle corresponds to Dourish's (2004, p. 22) context assumption saying that "context is an occasioned property" rather than something that is stable.

- *The principle of dynamic contextual scope* specifies that the context-aware application should be able to determine dynamically the scope of contextual features that are relevant to process at a given occurrence of context-triggered action. This principle corresponds to Dourish's (2004, p. 22) context assumption saying that "the scope of contextual features is defined dynamically."

We realize that development of design principles from something which has a phenomenological foundation is somewhat problematic. From a phenomenological perspective, we want to avoid treating context in an instrumental way, but at the same time we need guidance when we make our design choices during development. Thus, at some point, any designer will have to take a stand and say "this is my intention" and try to implement in accordance with that. In our case, these intentions have been consciously guided by the design principles set out. The same applies to the design of our evaluation, as we also wanted to assess in what way these guiding principles were enacted at use time and what unintentional consequences the design brought. It is in the nature of design that, inevitably, choices have to be made, regardless if they may later be found to bring unintended consequences (hopefully together with what was intended).

4.3 CABdriver Space: Action Taking

CABdriver Space is a car infotainment prototype that is intended to provide entertainment experiences linked to travel by car. Saab Automobile supplied Saab 9-3 hardware and hardware modifications needed for CABdriver Space to be developed, as well as enabled the communication between hardware and infotainment system where this was not already available. Necessary adaptations to the operating system of the infotainment center, primarily the implementation of an improved IP stack, but also integration of the Bluetooth access point on the infotainment system, were handled by Mecel. Together, all three partners defined the data transfer protocol (using TCP/IP as the carrier) to be used when communicating from the infotainment system to a PDA running Pocket PC, on which the Viktoria Institute developed the game. Together, this platform communicated data from the car, including from car support systems (e.g., traction control system, electronic stability program, anti-brake locking), current speed, fuel consumption, GPS position, RDS-TMC (radio wave traffic messages), and temperature to the PDA. The PDA in turn matched the position of the car with a geographical database to provide information such as gas stations, restaurants, parking spaces, speed limits, and road network.

In our desire to test Dourish's interactional context view in a design setting, we were instrumental in designing CABdriver Space so that it stimulated interaction between player and driver in a way that is adapted to the sensitive setting of a car. The player and her interaction with the driver are thus an important part of the prototype, which also further explains the name: Context-Aware Backseat Driver. CABdriver Space does not become meaningful (or indeed context-aware) unless the player and driver are able to associate the information affecting the game with the real world and use it to adapt their behavior accordingly. Screenshots and further explanations of CABdriver Space are provided in the Appendix.

Embedded in CABdriver Space are the three design principles we defined: relational context, occasioned relevance, and dynamic contextual scope. First, the game embeds the *relational context* principle by stimulating certain forms of interaction between passenger, driver, and application. The prototype is focused on object-activity, object-object, and activity-object relations, all striving to promote interaction adapted to the specific use setting. Examples of such design choices were 1:1 relations between turn signal and stress level (object-activity), momentary fuel consumption and the regeneration ability in the game (object-object), and excessive speeding and triggering of police mines (activity-object relation, greatly increasing the difficulty of the game). However, designing for the emergence of a specific meaning upon use is never an easy task. Given that context arises in action (Dourish 2004), context-aware applications that rely on this assumption have to come to terms with the fact that specific activity-activity relations are only enacted between humans during use and may not, at design time, be implemented in other ways than suggestions of certain behavior.

Second, the game embeds the *occasioned relevance* principle by coupling game events with occasions unfolding in the course of driving/traveling that are deemed relevant by the involved actors. For instance, CABdriver Space is designed to be significantly harder to play in the case of aggressive driving. This creates user incentives to influence the driver to drive more carefully. However, the learning is not unidirectional only (i.e., the passenger learning to understand the driver), but is also going in the opposite direction. In other words, the intent of the game is also to support the driver in linking her driving behavior to passenger responses. This bidirectional learning is intended to support the driver and passenger to jointly define the relevance of the context-triggered actions taken by the application. In order to enable such support, however, it is central that such triggers are in a satisfactory way coupled with occurrences in the course of driving.

Finally, the game embeds the *dynamic contextual scope* principle by assigning the actors the role of adapting the scope of contextual information used vis-à-vis the current situation. For instance, with CABdriver Space, the passenger has an important role in adapting her interaction with the driver to current driving conditions. Given that artifacts are unable to assign meaning to many complex driving situations, the passenger's ability to create accurate mental models—as well as to interpret the driver's mental model—becomes a key factor in order for the passenger to adapt the scope of contextual information to be shared with the driver. Using the driver workload parameter (in a Saab 9-3, the current driver workload depends on acceleration and braking, recent use of turn signal, electronic stability program activity, anti-spin control activity, and so on), CABdriver Space displays driver workload at all times as a small traffic light in the upper right corner of the screen. As illustrated in the Appendix, high driver workload makes the game more challenging to play, which in turn intends to make the player more focused on the game.

4.4 Evaluating

The CABdriver space prototype was evaluated over a two month period (November 2003 to January 2004). The evaluation included five cars and five Swedish families. At a meeting at Saab Automobile's head office in Trollhättan, Sweden, the families were introduced to the rationale behind our prototype design and evaluation strategy. We explained that they were expected to use CABdriver in their everyday driving as they themselves saw fit. In our desire for realistic evaluation conditions, Saab Automobile modified the hardware of the five cars involved, Mecel updated the infotainment center operating system, and each family was provided a PDA on which the Viktoria Institute had installed CABdriver Space.

The first design principle, relational context, appears to have had a significant impact on the participants. At design time, our desire was to inscribe certain behavior (safe and cautious driving through interaction between player and driver) into the relational aspects between activity-object, object-object, and object-activity. These appear to have largely played out as intended, creating activity-activity relations at use time, through the interaction our context-aware application was designed to stimulate.

> The family appreciated feeling that they better understood each other as well as the car and surrounding through the context-aware application....We prefer that something is dependant of the surroundings and the driving. You are influenced in a favorable way....Initially, the missions themselves were most appreciated by the players, but later to be able to affect driving and navigation was most rewarding. For the driver, it was most liked because your driving could affect the difficulty of the game. I have become a wiser, more aware driver. (Jan, Family 2)

Nevertheless, not only the intended consequences have been observed. One unintended consequence comes from the duality that some design choices may bring with them. In our case, this was the relation we put between use of turn signal and driver workload. As we purposely designed the game to become harder when driver workload went up, participants soon figured out that if they did not use their turn signal (when judged safe), they did not transmit a higher driver workload to the game and therefore actively helped the player rather than make it harder for them (an issue further discussed later in the evaluation).

As driver, you want to see how fast these inputs, like acceleration, affect regeneration [in the game]....You feel that you are a bit like God. (Thomas, Family 5)

Go easy on the gas, use turn signal selectively, [and] do not speed. (Family 5)

Related to the turn signal implementation issue, drivers and players clearly reported how interaction initiated by the player was not always adhered to strictly in the fashion the player desired. On some occasions, players demanded a particular response from the driver—a response not necessarily adapted to the traffic situation.

The player has asked the driver not to brake, for instance when driving in the city, which can become annoying for the driver after a while. You try not to brake, in order to avoid the nagging, which in turn creates dangerous traffic situations. (Per, Family 3)

Quit using the turn signal or the big monster will come! (Thomas, Family 5, about Fredrik, his frequent passenger)

Either you mess with him and use your turn signal extra, or you change lanes without using it. (Thomas, Family 5, describing his response to Fredrik)

This indicates that the contextual scope is dynamically defined (design principle three). The scope of which factors are relevant is quite different in one situation (e.g., stimulating smoother driving) while in another deemed less relevant to adapt to (e.g., it may be difficult to avoid hard braking in city driving). In other words, the scope has occasioned relevance (design principle two).

While we were not unaware that the particular scenario of smooth driving in city traffic may become an issue to the participants, we had hoped this would be settled by preemptive interaction from the driver, warning the player of what was ahead and explaining why this had to be so when she could not adapt a smoother style of driving. After all, during the three weeks the action research development team spent driving a Saab 9-3 to test the functionality and balance the application prior to the evaluation, we became aware of this possible issue, but after some training, we managed to negotiate rush-hour traffic without running into the problem discussed here. Although we managed to negotiate rush-hour traffic, the implementation may still incur a step that is too large to take for some drivers. In particular, this may be relevant for drivers that perceive much of the enjoyment in driving to lie in challenging conditions (Walker et al 2001), just as the father of Family 4 reflected on about his own driving. This is, therefore, an important design issue to resolve in order to avoid having the intended interaction lose its meaning as the difficulty level of the game becomes too high, thereby greatly affecting the ability of the application to support context-awareness.

Interaction has lessened [due to the difficulty level] and the children use it more like as a stand-alone game now [ignoring the option to interact] compared to when we started. The marble game on the PDA is a tough competitor. (Family 4)

In a sense, even this loss of meaning, promoting competition from context-unaware applications, illustrates how important the specific relevance of a particular scope in a given situation is for an application to promote an interactional view on context-awareness during use.

5   DISCUSSION

Context-aware computing is one important research theme of ubiquitous computing (Abowd and Mynatt 2000). In this theme, the notion of context has frequently been debated (e.g., Dourish 2004, Schmidt et al. 1999). Commonly, this debate comes from the relatively simplistic view of context that many of the documented context-aware applications convey. In these, context tends to be treated as a form of information that is delineable, stable, and separable from activity, and thus tends to disassociate human activity and context (Dourish 2004). This becomes problematic as context is "not something merely 'in which' interaction occurs" (Giddens 1984, p. 71).

This paper addresses the notion of context by applying and evaluating the plausibility of Dourish's interactional context view for designing context-aware applications. On the basis of a canonical action research study, we have developed and tested design principles for context-aware applications that convey such an interactional view of context. This research agenda resonated well with that of our industrial partners and formed the common ground for the collaboration. The design principles developed were (1) *relational context*, (2) *occasioned relevance*, and (3) *dynamic contextual scope*.

In our two month evaluation in the everyday life of five Swedish families, we discovered that the CABdriver Space prototype—and our design principles embedded in it—was generally appreciated by our evaluators. For instance, the prototype's stimulation of interaction between driver, passengers, and application contributed to an increased contextual understanding of the driving situation on behalf of both drivers and passengers. By embracing the theoretical assumption that context arises from activity, the magnitude of meaningful interaction triggered by the prototype contributed to our respondents' more reflective and sound driving. This indicates the general plausibility of the interactional context view for informing the design of context-aware applications.

Our research also indicates that applications that draw on this context view can produce unintended consequences. For instance, the evaluation showed that our attempt to trigger adapted behavior to the driving situation by linking the driver workload metric (supplied by the car) to the game plan was ambiguous. Even though the turn signal (as one of the parameters in this metric) typically indicates a busy driver, the relation between an object (the turn signal) and activity (turning) does not always mean that the driver actually perceives a higher workload. In fact, our respondents described how they on some occasions deliberately neglected to use the turn signal as they did not want to transmit a high workload to the game. This shows how contextuality arises not only in the course of action, but also how it depends on the specific relationship between objects and activities (design principle one). Furthermore, this illustrates well how the scope of relevant contextual features is dynamically defined (design principle three): in one instance, very relevant (such as rush hour traffic), while in another (simple lane change on a lonely highway), it is perceived as less important (design principle two).

On a general level, our research confirms Lyytinen and Yoo's (2002b) observation that it is increasingly difficult to distinguish between human and nonhuman actors in ubiquitous information environments. Context-aware applications perfectly exemplify the role of machine agency in human interaction. In fact, designing context-aware applications is largely about designing context-aware interaction, meaning that designers cannot oversee the contextual understanding needed for assessing the consequences of their design products. Given the scarcity of authentic evaluations in application-oriented context-aware computing research, our action research suggests a valuable way forward in handling the delicate balance between prediction of usefulness of novel technologies and observation of realistic use (see Abowd and Mynatt 2000). Drawing on a socially informed theoretical framework, it does so by offering a novel technology that is tested without the constraints and limitations of an experimental setting.

On a practical level, our action research contributed to Saab Automobile's dwelling with their car infotainment strategy and the state of innovation in the automotive industry as a whole. By participating in this project, Saab gained experience valuable for taking their attempts to break with the mainstream car infotainment agenda further. As the infotainment product manager was one of our key action research members, this learning is likely to have a strong organizational basis at Saab—useful for future releases of car infotainment concepts and services.

6   CONCLUSION

In this paper, we set out to evaluate the plausibility of an interactional view of context (Dourish 2001a, 2001b, 2004) by collaboratively developing a prototype application using an action research approach that is implemented through three design principles we defined: (1) *relational context*, (2) *occasioned relevance*, and (3) *dynamic contextual scope*. The contribution of this effort is to address the relative scarcity of contextual cues used when modeling and evaluating human interaction together with technology—an important issue within the rapidly growing theme of ubiquitous information environments in IS research. In particular, when combined with lab-like and other artificial evaluation settings, this scarcity may seriously affect the understanding and development of applications supporting context-awareness, a key area in ubiquitous computing (Abowd and Mynatt 2000).

Using the (hardware and software modified) Saab 9-3s of five families, our evaluation of CABdriver Space in everyday situations shows how the magnitude of meaningful interaction triggered by the prototype contributed to our respondents' more reflective driving. This confirms the plausibility of the interactional context view. Despite this, our results still call for more sophisticated theoretical frameworks that can capture the socio-technical complexity of designing context-aware interaction. We believe that the inherent machine agency component of context-aware applications needs more attention in addressing the notion of context as it emerges during use in ubiquitous information environments.

REFERENCES

Abowd, G. D., and Mynatt, E. D. "Charting Past, Present, and Future Research in Ubiquitous Computing," *ACM Transactions on Computer-Human Interaction* (7:1), 2000, pp. 29-58.

Baskerville, R. L., and Wood-Harper, A. T. "A Critical Perspective on Action Research as a Method for Information Systems Research," *Journal of Information Technology*, 11, 1996, pp. 235-246.

Davison, R. M., Martinsons, M. G., and Kock, N. "Principles of Canonical Action Research," *Information Systems Journal* (14), 2004, pp. 65-86.

DeSanctis, G., and Scott Poole, M. "Capturing the Complexity in Advanced Technology Use: Adaptive Structuration Theory," *Organization Science* (5:2), 1994, pp. 121-147.

Dourish, P. "Seeking a Foundation for Context-Aware Computing," *Human-Computer Interaction* (16:2-4), 2001, pp. 229-241.

Dourish, P. "What We Talk About When We Talk About Context," *Personal and Ubiquitous Computing* (8), 2004, pp. 19-30.

Dourish, P. *Where the Action Is: the Foundations of Embodied Interaction*, Cambridge, MA: MIT Press, 2001b.

Giddens, A. *The Constitution of Society—Outline of the Theory of Structuration*, Cambridge, UK: Polity Press, Cambridge, 1984.

Germonprez, M., and Mathiassen, L. "The Role of Conventional Research Methods in Information Systems Research," in *Information Systems Research: Relevant Theory and Informed Practice*, B. Kaplan, D. P. Truex III, D. Wastell and A. T. Wood-Harper, and J. I. DeGross (Eds.), Boston: Kluwer, 2004, pp. 335-352.

Grudin, J. "Desituating Action: Digital Representation of Context," *Human-Computer Interaction* (16), 2001, pp. 269-286.

Henfridsson, O., and Lindgren, R. "Multi-Contextuality in Ubiquitous Computing: Investigating the Car Case through Action Research," *Information and Organization* (15:3), 2005.

Hevner, A. R., March, S.T., Park, J., and Ram, S. "Design Science in Information Systems Research," *MIS Quarterly* (28:1), 2004, pp. 75-105.

Jessup, L. M., and Robey, D. "The Relevance of Social Issues in Ubiquitous Computing Environments," *Communications of the ACM* (45:12), 2002, pp. 88-91.

Lindgren, R., Henfridsson, O., and Schultze, U. "Design Principles for Competence Management Systems: A Synthesis of an Action Research Study," *MIS Quarterly* (28:3), 2004, pp. 435-472.

Lyytinen, K., and Yoo, Y. "Issues and Challenges in Ubiquitous Computing," *Communications of the ACM* (45:12), 2002a, pp. 63-65.

Lyytinen, K., and Yoo, Y. "Research Commentary: The Next Wave of Nomadic Computing," *Information Systems Research* (13:4), 2002b, pp. 377-388.

Markus, M. L., Majchrzak, A., and Gasser, L. "A Design Theory for Systems That Support Emergent Knowledge Processes," *MIS Quarterly* (26:3), 2002, pp. 179-212.

Olsson, C. M. "Exploring the Impact of a Context-Aware Application for In-Car Use," in *Proceedings of 25th International Conference on Information Systems*, R. Agarwal, L. Kirsch, and J. I. DeGross (Eds.), 2004, pp. 11-21.

Olsson, C. M., and Russo, N. "Applying Adaptive Structuration Theory to the Study of Context-Aware Applications," *Information Systems Research: Relevant Theory and Informed Practice*, B. Kaplan, D. P. Truex III, D. Wastell and A. T. Wood-Harper, and J. I. DeGross (Eds.), Boston: Kluwer, 2004, pp. 735-741.

Orlikowski, W. J. "The Duality of Technology: Rethinking the Concept of Technology in Organizations," *Organization Science* (3:3), 1992, pp. 398-427.

Patton, M. Q. *Qualitative Research and Evaluation Methods* (3rd ed.), London: Sage Publications, 2002.

Robey, D., and Markus, M. L. "Beyond Rigor and Relevance: Producing Consumable Research about Information Systems," *Information Resources Management Journal* (11:1), 1998, pp. 7-15.

Schmidt, A., Beigl, M., and Gellersen, H.-W. "There is More to Context than Location," *Computers and Graphics* (23:6), 1999, pp. 893-901.

Susman, G., and Evered, R. "An Assessment of the Scientific Merits of Action Research," *Administrative Science Quarterly* (23), 1978, pp. 582-603.

Walls, J. H., Widmeyer, G. R., and El Sawy, O. A. "Building an Information Systems Design Theory for Vigilant EIS," *Information Systems Research* (3:1), 1992, pp 36-59.

Walker, G. H., Stanton, N. A., and Young, M. S. "Where is Computing Driving Cars?," *International Journal of Human-Computer Interaction* (13:2), 2001, pp. 203-229.

Walsham, G. "Actor-Network Theory and IS Research: Current Status and Future Prospects," in *Information Technology and Changes in Organizational Work*, W. Orlikowski, G. Walsham, M. R. Jones and J. I. DeGross (Eds.), London: Chapman and Hall, 1996, pp. 466-480.

Want, R., Hopper, A., Falcão, V., and Gibbons, J. "The Active Badge Location System," *ACM Transactions on Information Systems* (10:1), 1992, pp. 91-102.

Want, R., Pering, T., Borriello, G., and Farkas, K. I. "Disappearing Hardware," *IEEE Pervasive Computing* (1:1), 2002, pp. 36-47.

Weiser, M. "The Computer for the 21st Century," *Scientific American*, September 1991, pp. 94-104.

ABOUT THE AUTHORS

Carl Magnus Olsson is a Ph.D. student at the University of Limerick, Ireland. He conducted the research reported here in the Telematics Group of the Viktoria Institute, Sweden, and holds a guest researcher position at the Operations Management and Information Systems Department of Northern Illinois University, USA. He was a participant in the ICIS Doctoral Consortium in Seattle, 2003, and his publications within ubiquitous information environments include conference papers at IFIP WG 8.2, IFIP WG 8.6 and ICIS. Carl can be reached by e-mail at cmo@viktoria.se.

Ola Henfridsson manages the Telematics Group at the Viktoria Institute, Göteborg, Sweden. He is also an assistant professor in Informatics at the School of Information Science, Computer and Electrical Engineering, Halmstad University. Dr. Henfridsson holds a Ph.D. degree in Informatics from Umeå University, Sweden, and is a member of the editorial board of the *Scandinavian Journal of Information Systems*. Dr. Henfridsson has published his research in journals such as *Information Technology and People*, *Information and Organization*, and *MIS Quarterly*. He can be reached by e-mail at ola@viktoria.se.

APPENDIX

The game itself can be described as a relatively straightforward shoot-em-up with added tactical elements. The screenshot on the left shows the radar and the road network around the car. A parking space can be seen about 150 meters behind where the car is right now. The scale is shown above the radar (500 meters radius is chosen here). By clicking the parking space, the player can initiate missions after reading about them, their level of difficulty, and rewards if completed.

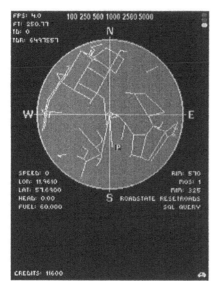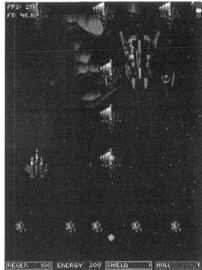

The screenshot on the right is from a mission as it is being played. The mid-left ship is the player, the big space-ship is the driver workload monster indicating an occupied driver, the T-shaped formation of ships are enemy spaceships and the string of round balls are the result of an excessive speeding violation. Fortunately, the driver is currently driving environmentally sound (low fuel consumption) as is indicated by the full regeneration bar in the bottom left corner. This also affects the recuperation of energy spent (second from left, bottom) when the player moves her ship, shoots, and needs to recharge her shield (third from left, bottom) after getting hit by the enemy. The bottom right bar shows how much is left of the hull—once it reaches zero, the mission fails.

19 APPROACHING INFORMATION INFRASTRUCTURE AS AN ECOLOGY OF UBIQUITOUS SOCIOTECHNICAL RELATIONS

Panos Constantinides
Michael Barrett
The Judge Institute of Management
University of Cambridge
Cambridge, UK

Abstract   *In this paper, we seek to understand the ecology of ubiquitous sociotechnical relations involved in the development and use of information and communication technologies. We draw on some examples from an empirical case study on the development and use of a regional healthcare information technology network to illustrate our conceptualization of this information infrastructure as an ecology. We conclude with some implications for theory and practice.*

Keywords   Information infrastructure, ecology, sociotechnical analysis, interpretive case studies

1   INTRODUCTION

The development and use of information and communication technologies (ICTs) takes place in an organizational context and is usually affected by the existing human and technological base or infrastructure. ICT projects may also be affected by surrounding environmental factors such as local political reforms or global changes that are beyond the control of project managers. More recently, researchers from diverse fields have coined the term information infrastructure to explain the complexity of factors and multiplicity of outcomes involved in large-scale ICT projects (e.g., Bowker and Star 1999; Ciborra et al. 2001; Hanseth and Monteiro 1997; Star and Ruhleder 1996). The underlying argument of this literature is that new technology is never developed from scratch but rather "wrestles with the 'inertia of the installed base' and inherits strengths and limitations from that base" (Star and Ruhleder 1996, p. 113). In other words, new technologies emerge on an already existing ecology of ubiquitous sociotechnical relations.

In this paper, we seek to go beyond existing knowledge by un-blurring the different layers of this ecology and contributing to a richer understanding of information infra-structure. To this effort, we draw on some of the theoretical developments of Latour (1999) and Peirce (1931-1958). Peirce's work will help inform our understanding of the process by which meanings are developed and transformed by an individual or between members of a community, as well as the ways in which knowledge becomes grounded in practice. Latour's ideas will help inform our understanding of the relationship between the social world and the world of technological artifacts. This theoretical mix of ideas will help us to distinguish between seven unique but interdependent layers of information infrastructure and the negotiations that take place between them. We illustrate these theoretical developments by drawing on a longitudinal, interpretive case study on the development and use of a regional healthcare IT network in Crete.

2   UNDERSTANDING INFORMATION INFRASTRUCTURE

We start the discussion by representing and organizing existing knowledge on information infrastructure according to the two most frequently referenced bodies of research. The first body of research gravitates toward the tendency of business schools to employ a positivistic epistemological stance, combined with the functionalist influence of computer engineers, while seeking to develop management agendas for the maximization of strategic business–IT alignment (Henderson and Venkatraman 1993; Weill and Broadbent 1998). The second body of research is "less immediately concerned with modeling and prescriptions" (Ciborra et al. 2001, p. 21) and more interested in an interpretive understanding of information infrastructure, while immersing itself in the multilevel context of sociotechnical processes (Bowker and Star 1999; Ciborra et al. 2001). We next discuss these diverse bodies of research in more detail while seeking to uncover some key themes to understanding the concept of information infrastructure.

2.1 Management Agendas Toward Strategic Business–IT Alignment

The first body of research views information infrastructure as the fundamental component of a firm's IT investment portfolio, which aims at maximizing business value by implementing "a number of as-yet-unspecified business strategies...more rapidly" (Weill and Broadbent 1998, p. 101). Based on this general view, the proponents of this body of research seek to define the *reach* and *range* of information infrastructure

(Duncan 1995), its *reusability* or *modularity* (Chung et al. 2003; Duncan 1995), and the *intangible resources* that it requires, such as human knowledge and skills, commitment, and competencies (Chung et al. 2003; Henderson and Venkatraman 1993; Weill and Broadbent 1998).

Based on these concepts, the key proponents of this body of research propose two approaches to managing a firm's information infrastructure, namely, management-by-maxim and management-by-deals (Weill and Broadbent 1998). On the one hand, the maxims approach refers to the development of firm-wide enforceable initiatives such as constructs for measuring the flexibility of information infrastructures (Byrd and Turner 2000; Duncan 1995), as well as a series of leadership principles for managing the emergence of new technologies (Weill and Broadbent 1998). On the other hand, the deal-making approach refers to political power issues and an uneven establishment of information infrastructure. Although the deal-making approach is present in approximately 40 out of the 80 cases examined by Weill and Broadbent (1998), the authors seem to lean in favor of the maxims approach. However, extensive review of top managers' opinions related to the actual management of information infrastructures points out that new technologies evolve in the interplay between multiple and contradictory forces, including unplanned systems requirements emerging from the lack of IT knowledge and the skills of the users (Chung et al. 2003; Duncan 1995). Thus, even though this first body of research has offered some valuable insights for our understanding of information infrastructure, we suggest that this conceptualization does not go far enough in accounting for the ongoing negotiations and interplay between sociotechnical relationships associated with the development and use of new technologies in organizations.

2.2 Interpretive Explanations of the Multilevel Context of Information Infrastructure

In their criticism of functionalist accounts of information infrastructure, some researchers argue that alignment is "heterogeneous, meaning that there is an open-ended array of 'things' that need to be aligned, including work routines, incentive structures, training, information-systems modules, and organizational roles" (Monteiro 2001, p. 72). Thus, alignment is an ongoing sociotechnical process and information infrastructure is a *heterogeneous* collage of different layers of technological components, people, institutions, and so on (Hanseth 2001; Hanseth and Monteiro 1997). In this view, technological artifacts have an equal role to play in the process of change (alignment to new goals). Specifically, by employing the theoretical lens of actor-network theory (ANT), researchers in the interpretive tradition are found to pay particular attention to the inscriptions carried in the features and functions of technological artifacts, which correspond to the efforts of the more dominant groups to implement specific programs of action. Based on this view, an information infrastructure becomes an actor by enforcing programs of action on its users, i.e., the roles to be played by each participant in the overall network (Monteiro 2001). For example, in an interpretive case study on the development of a customer relationship management (CRM) infrastructure at IBM, Ciborra and Failla (2001) argue how, by building the main steps of CRM on Lotus

Notes, IBM was able to "freeze the CRM discipline in silicon" (p. 117). The growing use of Lotus Notes by IBM employees increased the scope and depth of control of CRM processes by "'enforcing' globally behaviors on how to run the business" (Ciborra and Failla 2001, p. 118). Of course, the inscribed programs of action may not succeed because the actual use of IT may deviate from those; users may use the system in ways unanticipated by designers; they may follow an anti-program of action (Latour 1991). To this realization, more recent research employing the ANT terminology has been more careful in accounting for multiple views and multiple aspects of actor-network formation (Ellingsen and Monteiro 2003; Rolland and Monteiro 2002). However, ANT studies have been criticized for privileging the viewpoint of the designer or the manager, whose ability to inscribe certain behaviors on technological artifacts is deemed critical for the expansion and sustainability of a given actor-network (Bowker and Star 1999; Haraway 1988; Star and Griesemer 1989).

In an attempt to address these limitations, some researchers in the interpretive tradition have instead immersed themselves in an exploration of multiple viewpoints while acknowledging that several outcomes are simultaneously being negotiated by different groups and individuals (Bowker and Star 1999; Star and Griesemer 1989; Star and Ruhleder 1996). This group of researchers argue that first, an information infra-structure, just like any other technological artifact, is *learned as part of membership* in a community, and second, that an information infrastructure both *shapes and is shaped by the conventions of a given community*. In this respect and in contrast to ANT's focus on inscriptions of programs of action in artifacts aspiring to favored obligatory passage points (Latour 1991), this group of researchers argue that there is an indefinite number of ways in which entrepreneurs from different participating communities may create alternative passage points or outcomes in their own world (Star and Griesemer 1989). For example, after studying the development of a large collaborative system codesigned with a scientific community, Star and Ruhleder (1996) found that, despite good user prototype feedback and participation in the system development, there were unforeseen, complex challenges to usage involving infrastructural and organizational relationships. These challenges were born from such silent elements as feeling shame, fear, and rage, or from lying (to the point of claiming to use the system and not using it, or using one system to show the evaluators and then switching back to familiar technology in their routine work) (Star and Ruhleder 1996). These are the kinds of politics in action to which we should be paying attention (Bowker and Star 1999). The study of politics in action entails an understanding of the relationship of people with participant communities of practices, as well as an understanding of the ways in which artifacts and material arrangements become taken for granted in those communities (Bowker and Star 1999). Such an understanding aims at allowing for multiple voices to be heard, while also opening up possibilities to "disembed the narratives" contained in new technology development and use, and unearth the deeper social structures embedded in the broader organizational context (Star 2002, p. 110).

2.3 Summary of Key Themes

A first theme emerging from this brief review of the literature refers to the importance of moving away from functionalist, managerial views, which tend to treat information infrastructure as just another resource to be steered by upper management so as to achieve a maximum alignment to the business objectives of the given organization. We need to approach information infrastructure as an ever-evolving sociotechnical ecology of people, institutions, artifacts, and practices. To understand the different layers of the information infrastructure ecology, we need to acknowledge both the intentions and meanings of different groups and individuals, but also the dynamic role of technological artifacts in mediating those meanings and intentions.

A second theme refers to the importance of paying attention to the multiplicity of outcomes being negotiated by diverse groups and individuals in their work and social contexts at different points in time and space. While examining the intentions and meanings of the more dominant groups (e.g., senior managers) may help us understand how new technologies are conceptualized and developed, we will only be able to understand their implementation, use and scale-up or collapse if we disembed the underlying sociotechnical relations involved in the broader ecology.

The next section will attempt to go beyond these themes and contribute to a richer understanding of information infrastructure.

3   APPROACHING INFORMATION INFRASTRUCTURE AS AN ECOLOGY OF UBIQUITOUS SOCIOTECHNICAL RELATIONS

In this section, we draw on some of the theoretical developments of Latour (1999) and Peirce (1931-1958) to understand information infrastructure as an already existing ecology of ubiquitous sociotechnical relations and their respective crossovers. The term *crossover* is borrowed from Latour (1999, p. 194) to refer to the "exchange of properties among humans and nonhumans" in the process of their interaction to achieve different goals. Figure 1 outlines the discussion that will follow.

3.1 Individuals

We start our discussion with the abstract relations of individuals with their surroundings and the way in which ideas become conceptualized before being materialized and grounded in practice. This is linked to Peirce's (Vol. 2, § 300) ideas of a semiotically constituted world, whereby individuals experience their surroundings as *signs* standing for specific *meanings* to refer to specific *objects* (e.g., actions, events, artifacts). This interpretive process between signs–meanings–objects continues until a *habit* is created or transformed in the mind of interpreting individuals (Peirce 1931-58, Vol. 5, § 476). For Peirce, *habit* refers to a kind of disposition or rule of conduct, guiding our thoughts and actions about a given object, event, and so on (Vol. 7, § 468-523). Thus, what Peirce is suggesting here is that all knowing is a process and habits are created or transformed through inferences of past experiences.

To better illustrate this interpretive process consider the following example. In an empirical case study on the development and use of a regional healthcare IT network in

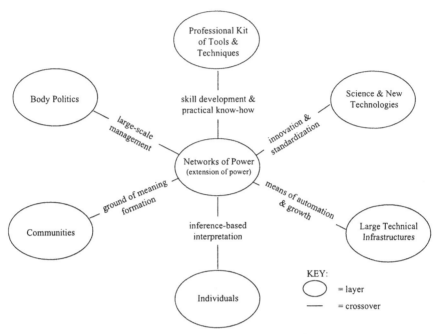

Figure 1. Information Infrastructure as an Ecology of
Ubiquitous Sociotechnical Relations

Crete, we had the chance to observe a group of cardiologists using a telemedicine
system to provide consultation to general practitioners (GPs) for patients with cardiac
problems. The system offered an alternative to the practice of calling cardiologists on
the phone and/or transferring patients with possible cardiac problems from primary
healthcare centers to the hospital where the cardiologists work. The system added on
the capabilities of simple phone calls by enabling the exchange of patient data such as
electrocardiographs between GPs and cardiologists and minimized unnecessary patient
transfers to the hospital. Even though the system offered these benefits, the actual practice of consultation rested on the cardiologists' inferences of past experience and
knowledge and the information provided by the GPs. Furthermore, the practice of
providing a final diagnosis rested on the physical examination of the patient by the
cardiologist. As a cardiologist explained,

> *For me to give a diagnosis I have to see the patient's X-ray, also have a look
> at his ECG [electrocardiograph] and compare them, perform an ultra sound
> examination on him, etc., and then decide what is wrong with him....You start
> with the initial suspicion and you eliminate possibilities as you go along, by
> doing more tests and examining more things.*

Thus, linkages between existing meanings (e.g., meanings about cardiac conditions), new information (e.g., medical signs about the patient), and new actions (e.g., the

physical examination of the patient), are established only through a process of inference-based interpretation.

3.2 Professional Kit of Tools and Techniques

This interpretive process is mediated by a series of tools and techniques, which individuals use to achieve certain objectives (Latour 1999). In the above example, the GPs employed an ECG device to generate an ECG of the patient, the telemedicine system to send the ECG to the cardiologist, and so on. This professional kit of tools and techniques is filtered until it becomes part of the individual's habits. Certainly, although some tools and techniques will survive the filtering, others will be discarded for not being able to fulfill the purpose of the individual's existing habits. Still others may be kept for other purposes based on other habits. In this respect, although tools and techniques may be devised and shifted (accommodated to fit certain objectives) by different individuals, their meaning will be completely independent of their use. For example, in the Crete case study, the telemedicine system, by itself, represented no action and consequently no meaning; in the hands of an initial group of self-motivated cardiologists and GPs, the telemedicine system provided a means with which to make sense of and produce diagnoses for patients with cardiac problems; in the hands of a group of GPs, who were later integrated to the network of participating physicians, the telemedicine system represented a poor alternative to existing practices because in the case of an emergency "it will be too slow of a response… so, the use of the system is not very practical," as one GP noted. Thus, different individuals will choose to interpret the same set of tools and techniques differently at different times; some will focus on the advantages and others will focus on the disadvantages, others still will completely ignore newly introduced tools and techniques and refuse to let go of their existing, more familiar kit and know-how. This refers to the pliability of tools. Tools only gain some durability within a given context under the agreement of a community. As Latour (1999) notes, tools and techniques represent the extension of skills rehearsed in the realm of social interaction.

3.3 Communities

A community is formed at the point when a shared inquiry eventually points toward a common set of meanings, agreed upon by all participants in the inquiry (Peirce 1931-1958, Vol. 5, § 407). Once formed, a community represents the realm of social interaction whereby community members ground their interpretations of their surroundings into common habits. A community, thus, establishes an association between the process of knowing in an individual's mind and the agreed-upon practices of a collective whole. Still, a community will not always consist of the same individuals and, thus, even though some members may remain, the community's common habits are bound to change and with it will change the kit of existing tools and techniques. For example, in the Crete case study, the telemedicine system was initially embraced by one GP at a rural primary healthcare center and three cardiologists at a district hospital, forming an initial community of collaborators. However, when six more primary healthcare centers were integrated into the network, the community's common habits were seriously challenged by new interpretations and new members. The new members not only challenged existing meanings about the technology, but also challenged the practicality of its use. These ideas point to Peirce's notion of a "true continuum...whose possibilities of determination no multitude of individuals can exhaust" (Vol. 6, § 170). In a true continuum the possibility of reaching new meanings about a given reality is potentially unlimited. Thus, as interpretations drift, communities also continuously drift.

3.4 Large Technical Infrastructures

The conservation and growth of community ties depends on the ability of the community to "naturalize" (Bowker and Star 1999) its professional kits into large technological infrastructures. These infrastructures accumulate the professional kits of different communities with the goal to automate activities, ensure the distribution of resources, and provide a common substructure upon which more tools and techniques can grow. Like professional kits, these infrastructures become transparent in practice, taken for granted; they sink into the background only to become visible again when they break down or when they become used in a completely different way from the originally intended use (Star and Ruhleder 1996). For example, in the Crete case study, CreteTech, the private institute behind the efforts to create a regional healthcare IT network in Crete, not only developed and implemented the aforementioned telemedicine system, but also a series of other tools such as an electronic patient record system and a primary healthcare center information system. These tools were initially implemented selectively at three primary healthcare centers and a district hospital, which were thought to be more technology receptive. After some initial success, CreteTech, with the agreement of the initial group of participating physicians, proceeded with the implementation of the aforementioned systems to the rest of the regional healthcare centers in Crete in an effort to scale up the pilot. For some time, the regional healthcare IT network became transparent in use, until it started to break down, unused even by the initial group of users. The reasons behind this breakdown are not only connected to the capabilities and functions of the introduced technologies, but also intimately dependent on the presence or lack of a body politic.

3.5 Body Politic

A body politic refers to a *body*, the ecology of individuals, professional kits, communities, and infrastructures, and a *politic*, the framework of formal and informal rules and resources needed for managing the body. Thus, the politic represents the body's ground of meaning formation, which is less easy to mold than the ground of a given community, but which provides a common means for sense making among diverse communities. For example, in our empirical case study, the development and implementation of the regional healthcare IT network was a project initiated by

CreteTech with the support of some key stakeholders in the region of Crete. The success of this pilot project was recognized at the 2003 European eHealth awards when it received an honorable mention for its technologically advanced design. Despite this, however, neither the government nor any other agency supported the project. As an engineer at CreteTech explained,

> *The overall effort was a pilot project, but unlike other government and private projects it wasn't expected to be used on a routine basis. Doctors or other users weren't obliged to use it; they could either use it or not. Since we are not part of the Ministry of Health we don't have the authority to demand the use of the system and there wasn't such an issue anyway since this was an R&D project.*

In other words, the pilot project never received the formal support of the national and regional body politics. In consequence, CreteTech lacked the necessary authority to effectively manage and scale up the project throughout the region of Crete, something that ultimately led to the breakdown of the healthcare IT network.

3.6 Science and New Technology

Apart from professional kits and large technical infrastructures that provide a means for automation and growth for a given community or body politic, there is also science and the emergence of new technologies including such specialized equipment as medical imaging scanners. Such scientific objects may bring about dramatic transformation to the other layers of the information infrastructure ecology, often without the intention of a particular body politic or community. However, there is another important function attributable to this layer: standardization. Standardization is often not only a response to the need of making things commonly accessible, but more usually a response to new inventions and ways of integrating those to an existing infrastructure. This can be observed in the efforts to introduce a series of technological standards to respond to the emerging need of developing healthcare information infrastructures (Hanseth and Monteiro 1997).

In the Crete case study, although the healthcare IT network has collapsed, CreteTech's efforts to introduce such international standards as the Health Level 7 in the work practices of physicians in the region have continued apace. The regional health authorities of Crete have recently announced an open competition for the development of a regional healthcare IT network that incorporates many of the standards introduced by CreteTech during the pilot project. In this sense, the dynamic crossovers between the different sociotechnical layers, including CreteTech's commitment to state-of-the-art research and development projects, as well as the strong interest of a number of key healthcare professionals in the region to use new ICTs in their work practices, have brought about unexpected transformation in the existing ecology. After a long process of dynamic sociotechnical crossovers, the regional ecology of Crete is now more receptive to technological developments. However, this dynamic transformation will be negotiated in networks of power.

3.7 Networks of Power

The term *networks of power* is borrowed from Latour (1999) and refers to hybrids of humans and nonhumans and how both can equally mobilize (spread and extend) each other's strength and durability (i.e., how nonhumans can become standards and how humans can build enduring power relationships). In this sense, in the information infrastructure ecology, networks of power are ubiquitous (i.e., existing in all layers between key individuals and bodies politic, as well as their professional kits and infrastructures).

In the Crete case study, the CreteTech team initially managed to mobilize their efforts from the bottom up by gaining the support of a group of physicians. However, this network of power was later mediated by an intellectual property rights dispute between the director of CreteTech and a key official at the regional health authority over the development of electronic patient records in the region. As this example illustrates, the struggle for power is equally mediated from the bottom up as it is from the top down. Thus, networks of power sit in the center of the information infrastructure ecology, accumulating strength or succumbing to the weaknesses of the other layers.

4   IMPLICATIONS FOR THEORY AND PRACTICE

In this paper, we sought to go beyond existing knowledge and further our conceptual understanding of information infrastructure by unearthing its heterogeneous character. In so doing, we have realized information infrastructure as an already existing ecology of ubiquitous sociotechnical relations and their respective crossovers.

A key implication for theory refers to the need to take into account both the intentions and meanings of different groups and individuals, but also the role of technological artifacts in mediating those meanings and intentions. By drawing on Latour's (1999) collective of humans and nonhumans, as well as on some of Peirce's (1931-58) key theoretical developments, we have provided some useful analytical tools for theorizing change and development in the different layers of the information infrastructure ecology as wrought by the introduction of new ICTs. These conceptual developments have not only created possibilities for explicitly theorizing each of the layers of the information infrastructure ecology, but also understanding the multiplicity of outcomes being negotiated between human agents and their choice of artifacts at different points in time and space.

The importance of these conceptual developments is highly relevant for researchers and practitioners alike. In fact, a key implication for practice is the need to approach the development and use of new ICTs as an ongoing process of negotiation between human agents and their choice of artifacts. This process can only be understood through a clear description of the existing ecology of ubiquitous sociotechnical relations in which new technological artifacts are developed and used, including existing power relationships, relevant standards and their implications, participant bodies politic and their structural arrangements, existing infrastructures and artifacts and their mediating role, participant communities and their grounds of meaning formation, and key individuals and their interpretations. Only after analyzing the subtle mechanism of the dynamic crossovers between the different layers in the information infrastructure ecology can we begin to inform our management practices. In this sense and by accepting Latour's (1999, p. 214) suggestion that "humanity rests in the crossover," Figure 1 extends the theoretical contribution to issues of management and practice. Employing this figure as an epistemological starting point, we may not only inform the ways of theorizing information infrastructure, but also the ways of managing the crossovers between its different layers.

REFERENCES

Bowker, G., and Star, S. L. *Sorting Things Out—Classification and its Consequences*, Cambridge, MA: MIT Press, 1999.

Byrd, T. A., and Turner, D. E. "Measuring the Flexibility of Information Technology Infrastructure: Exploratory Analysis of a Construct," *Journal of Management Information Systems* (17:1), 2000, pp. 167-208.

Chung, S. H., Rainer, K. R., Jr., and Lewis, B. R. "The Impact of Information Technology Infrastructure Flexibility on Strategic Alignment and Application Implementations," *Communications of the AIS* (11:11), 2003, pp. 134-163.

Ciborra, C. U., Braa, K., Cordella, A., Dahlbom, B., Failla, A., Hanseth, O., Hepso, V., Ljungberg, J., Monteiro, E., and Simon, K. A. *From Control to Drift: the Dynamics of Corporate Information Infrastructures*, Oxford: Oxford University Press, 2001.

Ciborra, C. U., and Failla, A. "Infrastructure as a Process: The Case of CRM in IBM," in *From Control to Drift: The Dynamics of Corporate Information Infrastructures*, C. U. Ciborra, K. Braa, A. Cordella, B. Dahlbom, A. Failla, O. Hanseth, V. Hespo, J. Ljungberg, E. Monteiro, and K. A. Simon (Eds.), Oxford: Oxford University Press, 2001, pp. 105-124.

Duncan, N. B. "Capturing Flexibility of Information Technology Infrastructure: A Study of Resource Characteristics and Their Measure," *Journal of Management Information Systems* (12:2), 1995, pp. 37-57.

Ellingsen, G., and Monteiro, E. "A Patchwork Planet: Integration and Cooperation in Hospitals," *Computer Supported Cooperative* Work (12), 2003, pp. 71-95.

Hanseth, O. "The Economics of Standards," in *From Control to Drift: the Dynamics of Corporate Information Infrastructures*, C. U. Ciborra, K. Braa, A. Cordella, B. Dahlbom, A. Failla, O. Hanseth, V. Hespo, J. Ljungberg, E. Monteiro, and K. A. Simon (Eds.), Oxford: Oxford University Press, 2001, 56-70.

Hanseth, O., and Monteiro, E. "Inscribing Behavior in Information Infrastructure Standards," *Accounting, Management and Information Technology* (7:4), 1997, pp. 183-211.

Haraway, D. "Situated Knowledge: The Science Question in Feminism and the Privilege of Partial Perspective," *Feminist* Studies (14), 1988, pp. 575-599.

Henderson, J. C., and Venkatraman, N. "Strategic Alignment: Leveraging Information Technology for Transforming Organizations," *IBM Systems Journal* (38:2-3), 1993, pp. 472-484.

Latour, B. *Pandora's Hope: Essays on the Reality of Science Studies*, Cambridge, MA: Harvard University Press, 1999.

Latour, B. "Technology is Society Made Durable," in *A Sociology of Monsters: Essays on Power, Technology and Domination*, J. Law (Ed.), London: Routledge Press, 1991, pp. 103-131.

Monteiro, E. "Actor-Network Theory and Information Infrastructure," in *From Control to Drift: the Dynamics of Corporate Information Infrastructures*, C. U. Ciborra, K. Braa, A. Cordella, B. Dahlbom, A. Failla, O. Hanseth, V. Hespo, J. Ljungberg, E. Monteiro, and K. A. Simon (Eds.), Oxford: Oxford University Press, 2001, pp. 71-83

Peirce, C. S. *Collected Papers of Charles Sanders Peirce*, Volumes I–VI edited by C. Hartshorne and P. Weiss, Cambridge, MA: Harvard University Press, 1931-1935; Volumes VII and VIII edited by A.W. Burks, Cambridge, MA: Harvard University Press, 1958.

Rolland, K. H., and Monteiro, E. "Balancing the Local and the Global in Infrastructural Information Systems," *The Information Society* (18), 2002, pp. 87-100.

Star, S. L. "Infrastructure and Ethnographic Practice: Working on the Fringes," *Scandinavian Journal of Information Systems* (14:2), 2002, pp. 107-122.

Star, S. L., and Griesemer, J. R. "Institutional Ecology, 'Translations' and Boundary Objects: Amateurs and Professionals in Berkeley's Museum of Vertebrate Zoology, 1907-39, *Social Studies of Science* (19:3), 1989, pp. 387-420.

Star, S. L., and Ruhleder, K. "Steps Toward an Ecology of Infrastructure: Design and Access for Large Information Spaces," *Information Systems Research* (7:1), 1996, pp. 111-134.

Weill, P., and Broadbent, M. *Leveraging the New Infrastructure: How Market Leaders Capitalize on Information*, Boston: Harvard Business School Press, 1998.

ABOUT THE AUTHORS

Panos Constantinides has been a member of the Ph.D. program at the Judge Institute of Management Studies at the University of Cambridge since October 2001. Panos has recently assumed responsibilities as a Research Associate for the Cambridge-MIT Institute working with Michael Barrett of the Judge Institute of Management Studies. His research interests are in the area of information infrastructure with a particular interest in healthcare. Panos can be reached at pc262@cam.ac.uk.

Michael Barrett is a member of the faculty in Information Systems at the Judge Institute of Management, Cambridge University, where he is also Director of the MPhil. program in Management. His research interests are in the area of information systems innovation and organization change with a particular interest in global knowledge management. His work is of an interdisciplinary nature, and he has published in a wide number of journals including *Information Systems Research*, *Academy of Management Journal*, and *Accounting, Organizations, and Society*. Michael has worked previously in consulting with Oracle Canada Corporation and Colgate Palmolive Ja Ltd. He continues to research and provide executive development programs with a number of organizations including IBM, HP, BT, and the World Health Organization.

20 THE SLIGHT SURPRISE OF INTEGRATION

Gunnar Ellingsen
Department of Telemedicine
University of Tromosø
Tromsø, Norway

Eric Monteiro
Department of Computer and Information Science
Norwegian University of Science and Technology
Trondheim, Norway

Abstract   *Western hospitals of some size are characterized by a proliferation of nonintegrated information systems, resulting in considerable frustration both among users and information technology personnel. Consequently there have been many integration efforts. Such efforts typically include some or all of the four principle classes of hospital-based systems: electronic patient records, laboratory systems, radiology systems and patient administrative systems. In this study, we trace the implementation process during most of 2004 at the University Hospital of North Norway, where these systems were part of a larger replacement project. We analyze the images and visions of order and perfection serving as a foundation for the decision to replace the existing IT portfolio. Furthermore, we analyze the manner and form in which unintended consequences of the integrated solutions appear and, finally, how the very act of integration may indeed produce rather than curb disorder. As a result, a lack of integration of any reasonably complex information system is an immanent feature.*

Keywords   Hospital information systems, EPR, integration, order perfection

1   INTRODUCTION

– Perfectionism would be dangerous.
John Law

The health care sector in general, and Western hospitals in particular, are characterized by a proliferation of information systems. More likely than not, a hospital of some size will harbor a seemingly unmanageable collection of different information systems, including specialized ones designed by entrepreneurial users for local needs. A symptomatic expression of this is the observation that many information technology departments in hospitals often do not know—but resort to crude estimates— which information systems are really in operation. In contrast with the promises of ubiquitous information environments, the availability of computational power and services at all times in all places (Buderi 2001), the acute challenges for users of information systems in hospitals are directly related to the lack of integration.

Hospitals are thus fertile breeding grounds for considerable frustration and dissatisfaction. For these reasons, hospitals provide a particularly fruitful site to explore efforts of integration of information systems, a challenge highly relevant to larger public and business organizations. Traditional approaches to integration in IS are dominated by technical solutions (Liu et al., 2001; Tsiknakis et al., 2002). Our perspective, strongly influenced by recent work (Berg 1998; Ellingsen and Monteiro 2003; Procter et al. 2003), recognizes the technical problem of integration as deeply embedded in organizational issues of collaboration and coordination.

Empirically, we trace the implementation process during most of 2004 at the University Hospital of North Norway (UNN), where an existing electronic patient record (EPR) system (by Siemens called DocuLive EPR) was replaced with another (called Dips). EPR systems form one out of four major classes of information systems in hospitals. The other three are laboratory systems, radiology systems (RIS/PACS), and patient administrative systems (PAS). The (lack of) integration between these four core applications was an influential element in the whole replacement process. Our analysis focuses on three aspects of integration.

First, the replacement of the old EPR took many by surprise. It was the result of 8 hard-fought years with a considerable acquired installed base of investment and political prestige. It was a joint effort of all the five university hospitals in Norway, which coincide with five largest hospitals in the country. The decision to replace it was accordingly difficult to reach. In our analysis, we point out how images of an "integrated" alternative acted as an influential rhetorical thrust here. An integrated solution mobilizes strong images and visions of order and perfection, functioning as attractive promises of a brighter future (Swanson and Ramiller 1997). We are concerned with developing a closer understanding of the mechanisms at play and what roles these take in negotiations.

Second, well into the implementation process, the merits of the new solution started to fade. Not altogether surprisingly, the integrated solution—attractive for its seductive simplicity—turned out not to be so straightforward. Unforeseen problems and implications arose, threatening to undermine the entire project. We analyze the manner and form in which these unintended consequences of the integrated solution appear (Berg 1998; Latour 1999), specifically the way disorder was relocated rather than eliminated.

Third, as argued by some scholars, the implications of tighter and better integration, intended to increase order and perfection, may in fact turn out to have exactly the opposite effects (Berg and Timmermans 2000; Hanseth et al. 2004; Law 2003). The very act of integration may indeed produce rather than curb disorder. This suggests a highly nonintuitive, deeply disturbing understanding of integration with potentially wide-reaching, yet under-specified, analytical and practical implications well worth exploring. It portrays a lack of integration of any reasonably complex genealogy of information systems as an *immanent* feature.

2 CONCEPTUALIZING INTEGRATION IN INFORMATION SYSTEMS

The integration of healthcare software systems has remained one of the most prominent issues in healthcare software development (Kuhn and Giuse 2001; Mykkänen 2003, p. 173; Xu et al. 2000, p. 157). Boochever (2004:16), for instance, underscores that "system integration would provide the platform for improved workflow, patient throughput and patient safety, as well as decreased cost." Integration is expected to automate the medical processes, such as patient admission, transfer and discharge, ordering of laboratory and radiological examinations or medication, and automatic or on-demand (solicited or unsolicited) receipt of results (Tsiknakis et al. 2002, p. 11). Basically, this includes the four principal classes of hospital-based systems—the EPRs, the laboratory systems, the radiology systems (RIS/PACS), and the patient administrative systems (PAS).

An integrated solution is supposed to give the physicians easy access to data from multiple information sources (Friedman 2001, p. 1529; Tsiknakis et al. 2002, p. 6; Winsten 2000), thus providing a complete picture of the patient's/client's medical history. The multiple information sources are accessed seamlessly from a single point of end-user interaction (Boochever 2004, p. 16). This avoids the physician having to perform redundant activities, such as specifying the patient identifying information over and over again (Ginneken 2002, p. 101). Accordingly, a completely integrated IT solution is a clear goal: "A scalable I-EHR [integrated electronic health record] would provide the means to access all available clinical information, at a corporate, regional, national or even international level" (Tsiknakis et al. 2002, p. 5). The care plan describing what will be performed or what has been performed during the patient's stay clearly benefits clearly from the integration of the patient's laboratory tests, radiology examinations, and treatments (Liu et al. 2001, p. 194).

Despite the high aspiration of an integrated solution, Berg (1998, p. 294) fairly accurately characterizes the situation when he maintains that "fully integrated [EPR]...is hard to find." One cause is that many software products have been built and acquired from heterogeneous sources during a long period of time, and the systems have differences in implementation technologies and architectures (Mykkänen et al. 2003, p. 173).

Accordingly, it does not come as a surprise that there have been many different strategies and approaches to integration (Hasselbring 2000). These may be seen as an expression of the enormous challenges and difficulties with integration. The integration mechanisms include technical solutions like federated database systems, World Wide Web (Grimson et al. 1998, p. 124), ERP-systems (Grimson et al. 2000), components (Clayton et al. 2003, p. 2), and Internet portals. Common models and architectures are also suggested (Bernstein et al. 2005).

Taking one step back from this crude outline, the historical pattern is relatively clear: full integration of information systems in hospitals remains a dream. If this is so, how should we move from here? It seems to us there are two alternative routes. The first amounts to maintaining the ambition and trying out new (technical) mechanisms for integration. As indicated above, this is a well-known strategy with a considerable number of existing suggestions and, surely, quite a few to come. The other alternative, largely unexplored within IS (for an exception, see Hanseth et al. 2004), is more radical. Inspired by recent developments in science studies, it provocatively challenges the root assumption of "full integration," namely the possibility of an all-embracing solution. Such a solution implies strong assumptions of an underlying order and perfection as everything has to fit together. This alternative approach to integration questions the very *ambition* of integration embedded in full integration: What if the lack of success with integration in hospitals is neither accidental nor transient? What if efforts of producing order always simultaneously produces the opposite? As Berg and Timmermans (2000) point out,

> These orders do not emerge out of (and thereby replace) a preexisting disorder. Rather, with the production of an order, a corresponding disorder comes into being....The order and its disorder, we argue, are engaged in a spiraling relationship—they need and embody each other (pp. 36-37).

> The two orders [referred to, i.e., two alternative clinical treatments] we have described *produce the very disorder they attempt to eradicate* (p. 45).

Law (2003) makes a similar point, but pushes further by underscoring the ultimately dysfunctional nature of preserving the ambition of full integration with the implied completeness and perfection.

> So what's the argument here? The answer is: it's an argument about *imperfec-tion*....That there are always many imperfections. And to make perfection in one place (assuming such a thing was possible) would be to risk much greater imperfection in other locations....The argument is that entropy is chronic..... Some parts of the system *will* dissolve...For a manager accepting imperfection is not a failing. It is an advantage. Indeed a necessity. Perfectionism would be dangerous (p. 11).

Finally, Latour (1999), in his expositions more recent than the ones that tend to be the most-cited within the IS research community, in a similar manner underlines how ambitions and intentions are never realized.

> That action is slightly overtaken by what it acts upon; that it drifts through translation; that an experiment is an event which offers slightly more than its inputs (p. 298).

> There is a drift, a slippage, a displacement, which, depending on the case, may be tiny or infinitely large (p. 88).

Summing up, we discuss and explore analytical and practical implications for integration when information systems are recognized as immanently heterogeneous.

3 METHOD

The case study was conducted at the University Hospital of North Norway (UNN). UNN has approximately 4,000 employees, including 400 physicians and 900 nurses. The hospital has 600 beds of which 450 are somatic and 150 psychiatric.

The study belongs to an interpretive research approach (Klein and Myers 1999; Walsham 1993) and includes participant observations, interviews, document analysis, and informal discussions. The data collection was conducted by the first author the results are presented in Table 1.

We endeavored to take the different sources of field data into consideration in the interpretation process. The method included relatively detailed case write-ups for the sites involved (see, for instance, Eisenhardt 1989, p. 540) followed by an examination of our data for potential analytical themes. Whenever something interesting seemed to emerge from the data (Schultze 2000, p. 25), we tried to categorize the data according to these themes in order to make good overviews based on the perspectives chosen.

Table 1. Data Collection Results

Participant Observations	Participation in 60 project meetings in the Dips project from its initial stages (January 2004) and onward. This has also resulted in a 60 transcribed documents.
	The project members participating in these meetings were IT consultants, physicians, secretaries, bio-engineers, and nurses. Their number varied from 5 to 16.
Informal Talks	50 notes based on informal talks with participants of the Dips project and users.
Interviews	10 open-ended interviews with a tape recorder of users of whom 8 where physicians.
Document Archive	400 e-mails sent to the Dips project and the project document archive consisting of several 100 documents.

4   CASE OUTLINE

The University Hospital of North Norway (UNN) has for almost 8 years parti-cipated in the national and longstanding Medakis project (1996–2003). This project started out as an ambitious, collaborative project between the five Norwegian university hospitals and the vendor Siemens with considerable financial and political backing from the health authorities. The overall goal was to develop a common, all-encompassing EPR for these hospitals, covering the needs of all of the different health professions in different hospital departments (Ellingsen and Monteiro 2003). Despite falling signifi-cantly short of these expectations, the DocuLive EPR has been in operational, increasingly wide-spread, use in the five university hospitals for several years.

The key role of EPRs in Norwegian health care is reiterated regularly in health policy programs (SHD 1996, 2001). This, however, has not been sufficient to coordi-nate an integrated and uniform health care. A sweeping health reform in 2002 shifted the ownership of the Norwegian hospitals from the counties over to the government in an attempt to curb expenditures and poor exploitation of existing resources. The former five health regions were replaced by five regional health enterprises with substantial autonomy, each comprising one of the former university hospitals and several local hospitals.

The Regional Health Enterprise Northern Norway (here referred to as Health Region North), in a surprising decision in December 2003, exercised its newly gained autonomy to break out of the long-term Medakis collaborative effort. As the large university hospital, UNN, was the only hospital in the northern health region running DocuLive EPR, Health Region North decided to replace this system with what the 10 other (smaller) hospitals in the region had, namely, systems from the vendor Dips. The vendor Dips is one of three vendors in the Norwegian hospital-based EPR market. Dips covers about 30 percent of the market through its installations at mostly smaller hospitals (Lærum et al. 2001). The Dips EPR module comes integrated with a radiology module, laboratory module, PAS module, and a psychiatry module.

Health Region North supported the project with 10 million NOK. Beyond that, UNN was assumed to provide the necessary personnel resources. In January 2004, UNN established a Dips implementation group consisting of personnel from UNN and Dips. The initial plans aimed at replacing the EPR and the PAS module by November the same year. The laboratory module was pushed back to a later stage mostly due to lack of resources on the vendor's part. The project decided not to replace the existing RIS module with the RIS module from Dips. The existing RIS module was developed locally at UNN and was considered the better choice.

The pre-project ending in March 2004 identified no major obstacles to the implementation, but concluded that the process amounted to a mere substitution, not requiring user involvement, which should be finished in 3, not 6, months. A key challenge was to ensure that Dips was integrated into the existing, extensive portfolio of information systems, many of which were integrated with the old PAS module.

The project did implement Dips within the three months (by June 2004) and was largely considered a success by the project group. The speedy processes paid the toll with a lack of user training, though, as only half of the physician were put through training sessions. Concerns were also raised when it was discovered that Dips lacked some functionality, especially relating to the text editor, signature routines, and administrative routines.

Implementing the Dips laboratory modules was considered crucial for a completely integrated solution. For the Clinical Chemistry, Immunology, and Clinical Pharmacology laboratories, this was an unquestionable argument. Nevertheless, the laboratories were concerned about the new functionality in Dips. The laboratory of Clinical Chemistry had over a period of several years developed its own system which "frankly speaking, we are quite satisfied with," as one expressed it. Since Dips implementation in the summer of 2004, a considerable amount of resources both from Dips and UNN has been poured into developing a laboratory module that could satisfy the different laboratories.

5 ANALYSIS

We structure our analysis of integration into three parts focusing on the imagery of "perfect" integration, how simplification in one place is created by reintroducing additional work for others, and how the endeavor to achieve complete integration is self-defeating.

5.1 Imagining an Integrated Future

The perceived messiness of the nonintegrated initial situation made the imagined future with Dips extremely attractive. In line with Law (2003), the rhetorical thrust of a completely orderly and all-encompassing solution was massive as "We want Dips...then we get everything we need." Figure 1 illustrates the situation.

The existing partly nonintegrated IT portfolio

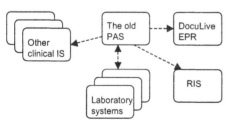

The dotted arrows indicate integration of patient information (date of birth, personal identity number, name, address, etc). The direction of the arrows indicates which way this information flows.

The envisioned integrated Dips portfolio

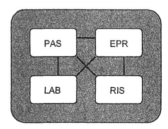

Figure 1. The Existing and the Envisioned IT Portfolio

Initially, UNN was the only hospital out of 11 in the health region running DocuLive EPR and not Dips. To change this was argued to be common-sense, obvious, thus black-boxing the issue into an invincible argument (Latour 1999). In the words of top IT management in Health Region North, "There are 11 hospitals in this region and 10 running Dips. Therefore it is obvious that UNN should run Dips." The resulting centralization implied that upgrades, user requests, and general database management could be streamlined. Health Region North thus expected significant reduction in expenditures.

Furthermore, the users at UNN (especially the physicians), were dissatisfied with their existing IT portfolio. In daily work, they depended on having access to x-ray descriptions, laboratory results, and the EPR. A lack of mutual integration of their existing PAS, EPR, and laboratory systems made this situation difficult. As one a physician phrased it,

I don't have the laboratory results; I don't have the x-ray description. Instead I have three different logon codes that I have to use on three different systems [DocuLive, Laboratory, and RIS] and I have to leave and enter the different systems in turn.

The users perceived DocuLive EPR as largely a standalone application. In contrast, Dips could presumably offer a complete package including (RIS, PAS, EPR, laboratory system, and psychiatry). The vendor Dips promotes their Dips-modules as a complete and integrated solution.

The Dips solution is based on a common architecture, integrated modules and a common logon-procedure across the different modules.

The Dips modules resided in the same database, implying that some registers in the database are shared between the modules. The modules are developed in the same programming language Delphi, thus offering a coherent user interface. However, taking full advantage of the Dips functionality presupposes that all of these modules are used as a package.

In sum, the replacement of DoucLive EPR with Dips drew on strong visions of a sanitizing or hygienic effort to purge UNN of its perceived mess (Berg and Timmermans 2000; Law 2003).

5.2 Relocating, Not Eliminating, Disorder

For sure, the integrated Dips solution improved the access for physicians to clinical information from different sources. It was accordingly perceived as more orderly by most physicians. But as argued by Berg and Timmermans (2000), creating order in one place simultaneously creates disorder in other places. Disorder is relocated and transformed, not eradicated. More specifically, creating order for some creates disorder for others, which spawn work-arounds to amend. The overall level of order and disorder, however, appears to be largely constant. We present three illustrations.

First, it is the responsibility of the secretaries to update the paper-based patient records. Whenever new information is entered into Dips EPR, print-outs to the paper version are necessary. In DocuLive, the content was sorted by time of document production, making it feasible to print out only the last document. In Dips EPR, however, sorting is by time of consultation. This implied that often a new document was inserted in the middle of many other documents due to various delays. As a result, all of the documents following the new one had to be printed out in order to maintain continuity in the paper record. This was a laborious process that made it more difficult to keep the paper-based record up-to-date.

The printouts in Dips EPR generate more and more chaos. Many documents are already printed out. Then suddenly a new document is produced with consultation date back in time. This document is then inserted [automatically] 15 to 20 documents before the last document (e-mail from a secretary to the project group).

Second, from the outset it was evident that the Dips lab solution and the Dips RIS were not as functional as the existing solution. While the project decided not to replace their locally developed RIS, it was decided to replace the existing laboratory systems. Most of the laboratories agreed, following the largest, the Clinical Chemistry laboratory. A user at this laboratory argued that their reason for participation was that

We take the additional burden to ease the work for the physicians in the clinic.

After implementing the laboratory module, the laboratories experienced that the routines were more cumbersome than before and they had to hire additional people to manage them. They also had to participate in extensive efforts in further developing the functionality in Dips.

The Microbiology Laboratory was not prepared to undertake the additional work of implementing and using Dips. Here, the users felt that the laboratory module needed significant development in order to make it acceptable.

Dips has altogether nothing that is suitable for us…the problem for everybody that makes laboratory systems is that the vendor starts out where the production is most intensive, and that is clinical chemistry. But clinical chemistry has an incredibly simple data structure (Head physician, Micro-biology Laboratory)

This implied among other things that the developers had given little attention to clinical information, material, and location, and finally the grouping, analysis, and assessments of these things. Consequently, the laboratory refused to implement Dips.

Third, even the primary beneficiaries of an integrated solution (the physicians) had to pay a price. They had to accept that the EPR functionality in Dips was poorer than in their old DocuLive EPR. The editor in the EPR was not well-known as was Microsoft Word in DocuLive EPR. The Dips editor lacked simple editor functionality (e.g., a medical dictionary). In addition, the signature routines in Dips EPR turned out to be less flexible. It was not possible to cancel a signature. Despite being able to countersign documents, the countersignature did not appear on the letters. Moreover, when a head physician responsible for countersigning made changes to the content, the initial author did not get any notification. The authoring physician could not sign a document whenever other users had opened it. Sometimes this resulted in "man-hunts" for the physician who had opened it and, if unsuccessful, the IT help desk had to free the document in order to enable it to be signed.

5.3 The Dysfunctional Quest for Perfection

The introduction of Dips was, as outlined earlier, initially motivated by strong images of order, purification, and efficiency. The IT management at UNN argued that this was "just a simple system replacement of the existing PAS and EPR." However, by viewing it as such a simplification, the very efforts of introducing order are in themselves likely to generate disorder as predicted by Berg and Timmermans (2000), Hanseth et al. (2004), and Law (2003). We provide a few illustrations.

At the core of this was the dramatically underestimated effort of replacing the large installed base of information systems. The Dips project experienced difficulty in obtaining a complete overview of the status of these integrations. As the project leader for the technical team put it,

> *All those smaller systems imply a chaotic situation. And we don't know who has made the integration, what is integrated and how things are integrated. Moreover we don't know how much [of this functionality] is actually in use.*

Therefore, half-way into the implementation it was discovered that completely replacing PAS was extremely risky as many of the existing systems would stop working because they especially depended on functionality provided by the PAS system (searching records, reimbursement functionality, different codes, reports, etc.). As an alternative strategy, the old PAS was kept "alive" alongside with the PAS module in Dips. In this way, all of the other systems could be left untouched (see Figure 2). However, this strategy required integration between the old PAS and Dips PAS in order to maintain the existing information flow and the possibility of uniquely identifying the patients across systems. As a result, the IT department developed a gateway program running on a computer that monitored changes in the Dips PAS. Whenever new patients were inserted into Dips or other changes were made on patient information, this was synchronized with the old PAS.

This caused some additional work for the users of the old IT portfolio. For instance, when a user wanted to create a new sample in one of the laboratory systems, she had to connect the sample to a particular patient. Whenever the patient did not exist in the laboratory system, which regularly was the case, she had to

1. Logon to the Dips system and insert the patient.
2. Wait until the gateway machine had synchronized this information with the old PAS. This process approximately took 3 to 4 minutes
3. The user could then find the patient in the laboratory system (through its integration with the old PAS.

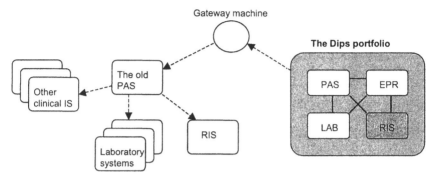

Figure 2. The Gateway Machine

This procedure implied an increased complexity. Users of the old IT portfolio, depending on the gateway machine, also had to use Dips on a daily basis with the only purpose being to insert new patients.

A smooth information flow between the old IT portfolio and Dips was extremely dependent on an up-and-running gateway machine. However, sometimes the gateway machine was down or it failed to synchronize patients (for instance, filled-in data fields were lacking). Therefore, the gateway machine and its associated transactions had to be monitored by IT personnel. In cases of failed synchronisation, the users had to insert new patients in their old IT portfolio anyway. In such cases, the IT personnel had to make the synchronisation manually.

A further complication was how the personal identity number for patients was processed. This number is given to Norwegian citizens some months after their birth, implying that foreigners and newborns don't have this number (or it for other reasons is missing). When these persons had to be registered in the IT portfolio at UNN, an emergency identity number had to be produced. Dips and the old PAS had different rules for producing such a number, implying that the gateway machine had to make a conversion. This implied that the same patient could exist in both the old IT portfolio and in Dips with a different personal identity number, generating uncertainty whether this was the same patient. As a result, yet another program was made, which at the same time accessed both the old PAS and Dips in order to guarantee that the patient was the same.

A fundamental argument for Health Region North was that a standardized Dips solution for every hospital in the region (preferably placed in one location) would make it easier to support Dips. The IT chief in Health Region North underscored this strategy by stating "then every change can be made in one place only." However, after implementing Dips, the IT department at UNN experienced that when parts of the Dips system had to be upgraded, the whole system was influenced. This resulted in the whole system regularly being unavailable for the users. For instance, upgrading the laboratory module implied that the Dips PAS and the Dips EPR module became unavailable for users also. Together with a need for a frequent upgrade policy, this enforced a problem.

When a new version appears from the vendor once a week, it creates a lot of work for us. It is not just like obtaining the file from Dips and then believing that it is ready for use. We have to make a new installation package each time and this new version must be distributed to 2800 PCs (IT consultant, UNN).

6   CONCLUSION

In contrast with more traditional descriptions of integration in IS, we have presented a case where integration efforts, despite good intentions, spawned additional work (work-arounds). Worse still, we have also pointed out examples of self-defeating effects in the sense that integration generates *in*creased levels of disorder. It is, as discussed earlier, always possible to regard these non-intended effects as transient, hinging on particular circumstances in the case narrative. Indeed, some of our illustrations (e.g., the gateway machine) have been partly replaced; some non-intended effects have been amended.

It would, however, seriously underestimate our account to conclude that this puts the project in particular and integration efforts more generally back on track. The gist of our position is that the disorder generated by integration efforts is *immanent*. When specific instances of this disorder are eliminated, new ones are simultaneously produced, possibly relocated.

This perspective on integration should not be misconstrued as an abstract, purely analytic point. More importantly, it has quite real implications for design, practitioners, and managers. At UNN, the integration efforts were aimed at establishing a more orderly collection of information systems, but more pressing, through this, to support more cost-effective work routines. Initial estimates suggested that expenditures would be reduced with 8.5 million NOK a year (UNN intranet news, published August 10, 2004). As the repercussions of the project unfolded, in strictly economical terms, the integration has been self-defeating, since later estimates suggest that the Dips portfolio will increase the expenditures with 4.5 million NOK a year.

ACKNOWLEDGMENTS

This research has been partially supported by the Norwegian Centre for Electronic Patient Record Systems (www.nsep.no).

REFERENCES

Berg, M. "Medical Work and the Computer Based Patient Record: A Sociological Perspective," *Methods of Information in Medicine* (38), 1998, pp. 294-301.

Berg, M., and Timmermans, S. "Orders and Their Others: On the Constitution of Universalities in Medical Work," *Configurations* (8), 2000, pp. 31-61.

Bernstein, K, Bruun-Rasmussen, M., Vingtoft, S., Andersen, S. K., and Nøhr, C. "Modeling and Implementing Electronic Health Records in Denmark," *International Journal of Medical Informatics*, 2004.

Boochever S. S. "HIS/RIS/PACS Integration: Getting to the Gold Standard," *Radiology Management* (26:3), May-June 2004, pp. 16-24

Buderi, R. "Computing Goes Everywhere," *Technology Review.Com*, January/February 2001 (available online at http://www.technologyreview.com/articles/01/01/buderi0101.asp).

Clayton, P. D., Narus, S. P., Huff, S. M., Pryor, T. A., Haug, P. J., Larkin, T., Matney, S., Evans, R. S., Rocha, B. H., Bowes, W. A., III, Holston, F. T., and Gundersen, M. L. "Building a Comprehensive Clinical Information System from Components: The Approach at Inter-mountain Health Care," *Methods of Information in Medicine* (42), 2003, pp. 1-7.

Eisenhardt, K. M. "Building Theories from Case Study Research," *Academy of Management Review* (14:4), 1989, pp. 532-550.

Ellingsen, G., and Monteiro, E. "A Patchwork Planet: Integration and Cooperation in Hospitals," *Computer Supported Cooperative Work* (12:1), 2003, pp. 71-95.

Friedman, B. A. "The Total Laboratory Solution: A New Laboratory E-Business Model Based on a Vertical Laboratory Meta-Network," *Clinical Chemistry* (47:8), 2001, pp. 1526-1535.

Ginneken, A. M. "The Computerized Patient Record: Balancing Effort and Benefit," *International Journal of Medical Informatics* (65), 2002,pp. 97-119.

Grimson, J., Grimson, W., Berry, D., Stephen, G., Felton, E., Kalra, D., Toussaint, P., and Weier, O. W. "A CORBA-Based Integration of Distributed Electronic Healthcare Records Using the Synapses Approach," *IEEE Transactions on Information Technology in Biomedicine* (2:3), 1998, pp. 124-138.

Grimson, J., Grimson, W., and Hasselbring, W. "The SI Challenge in Health Care," *Communications of the ACM* (43), 2000, pp. 48-55.

Hanseth, O., Jacucci, E., Grisot, M., and Aanestad, M. "Reflexive Standardization: Side-Effects and Complexity in Standard-Making," unpublished manuscript, 2004.

Hartswood, M., Procter, R., Rouncefield, M., and Slack, R. "Making a Case in Medical Work: Implications for the Electronic Medical Record," *Computer Supported Cooperative Work* (12:3), 2003, pp. 241-266.

Hasselbring, W. "Information System Integration," *Communications of the ACM* (43:6), 2000, pp. 32-38.

Klein, H., and Myers, M. "A Set of Principles for Conducting and Evaluating Interpretive Field Studies in Information Systems," *MIS Quarterly* (23:1), 1999, pp. 67-94.

Kuhn, K. A., and Giuse, D. A. "From Hospital Information Systems to Health Information Systems: Problems, Challenges, Perspectives," *Methods of Information in Medicine* (4), 2001, pp. 275-287.

Latour, B. *Pandora's Hope: Essays on the Reality of Science Studies*, Cambridge, MA: Harvard University Press, 1999.

Law, J. "Ladbroke Grove, or How to Think About Failing Systems," Centre for Science Studies, Lancaster University, December 2003 (available online at http://www.comp.lancs.ac.uk/sociology/papers/law-ladbroke-grove-failing-systems.pdf).

Liu, C. T., Long, A. G., Li, Y. C., Tsai, K. C., and Kuo, H. S. "Sharing Patient Care Rrecords Over the World Wide Web," *International Journal of Medical Informatics* (61), 2001, pp. 189-205.

Lærum, H., Ellingsen, G., and Faxvaag, A. "Doctor's Use of Electronic Medical Records Systems in Hospitals: Cross Sectional Survey," *British Medical Journal* (323:7325), 2001, pp. 1344-1348.

Mykkänen, J., Porrasmaa, J., Rannanheimo, J,. and Korpela, M. "A Process for Specifying Integration for Multi-Tier Applications in Healthcare," *International Journal of Medical Informatics* (70), 2003, pp. 173-182.

SHD. " Governmental Action Programme 2001-2003: Electronic Interaction in the Health and Social Sector 'say @," 2001 (available online at http://odin.dep.no/archive/shdvedlegg/ 01/04/Sitek046.doc).

SHD. "More Health for Each BIT: Information Technology as a Means for an Improved Health Service—Action Plan 1997-2000," Ministry of Health and Social Affairs, Norway, 1996.

Schultze, U. "Confessional Account of an Ethnography About Knowledge Work," *MIS Quarterly* (24:1), 2000, pp. 3-41.

Swanson, E. B., and Ramiller, N. C. "The Organizing Vision in Information Systems Innovation," *Organization Science* (8:5), 1997, pp. 458-474.

Tsiknakis, M., Katehakis, D. G., and Orphanoudakis, S. C. "An Open, Component-Based Information Infrastructure for Integrated Health Information Networks," *International Journal of Medical Informatics* (68), 2002, pp. 3-26.

Xu, Y., Sauquet, D., Zapletal, E., Lemaitre, D., and Degoulet, P. "Integration of Medical Applications: The 'Mediator Service' of the SynEx Platform," *International Journal of Medical Informatics* (58-59), 2000, pp. 157-166.

Walsham, G. *Interpreting Information Systems in Organizations*, Chichester, UK: John Wiley, 1993.

Winsten D.,and McMahan, J. "Integrating Your Radiology Information System in a Complex Computing Environment," *Radiology Management* (22:4), July-August 2000, pp. 26-28.

ABOUT THE AUTHORS

Gunnar Ellingsen is affiliated to the newly established study-program on E-health and Telemedicine at the University of Tromsø, Norway. Before completing his PhD in 2003, he has worked several years as an IT consultant at the University Hospital of North Norway. His research interests centres on the design and use of electronic patient records in hospitals. He has published articles in Information and Organization, Journal of Computer Supported Cooperative Work, Methods of Information in Medicine, Scandinavian Journal of Information Systems, International Journal of IT Standards & Standardization Research and British Medical Journal. Gunnar can be reached at gunnar.ellingsen@unn.no

Eric Monteiro is professor at the Department of Computer and Information Systems at Norwegian University of Science and Technology. He is broadly interested in organizational transformations and ICT in general, and issues of standardization and globalization in particular. His publication outlets include *MIS Quarterly, Journal of CSCW, Science, Technology & Human Values, Information and Organization, Methods of Information in Medicine, The Information Society*, and *Scandinavian Journal of Information Systems*. Eric can be reached at eric.monteiro@idi.ntnu.no.

Part 5

Innovation and Diffusion of Ubiquitous Information Environments

21 SCALING THE WALL: Factors Influencing the Conditions for Market Entry in the Mobile Data Market

Annemijn F. van Gorp
Carleen F. Maitland
Brian H. Cameron
School of Information Sciences and Technology
The Pennsylvania State University
University Park, PA U.S.A.

Abstract   *Advances in mobile technology have created a fertile ground for the development of new and innovative information and entertainment services. However, the road from development to commercialization of these services is one that is currently under construction. In this research, we seek to understand the relationships between developers of information services and the powerful mobile network operators that dominate the industry, which in turn shed light on the forces shaping the diversity of information sources on the mobile Internet. To understand these relationships, we have undertaken a research project in which we follow the attempts of a small firm to commercialize their information service in the United States. The project combines knowledge of industry structures with the first-hand market entry experience of a small firm. Results derived from the application of an institutional economics theoretical lens indicate that informal institutions, technology, and market power have combined to create the context for mobile services provision, which can be characterized as a highly fragmented market. This market fragmentation, together with technology, market power, and informal institutions, defines the choices application developers must make and indirectly determines the developers who will and will not be able to enter the market.*

Keywords   Mobile application provision, J2ME, BREW, business model, market structure

1   INTRODUCTION

Internet technologies make possible the sharing of information between widely diverse sources and audiences. With the fixed Internet, the provision of this information is undertaken on both commercial and noncommercial bases. For some information suppliers, the choice to provide information on a noncommercial basis is a result of underdeveloped payment systems. On the mobile Internet, the operator's control of the network infrastructure and ownership of the customer relationship resolves this payment dilemma as long as the information provider is willing to conform to the technical and administrative requirements of these powerful players. Thus, through control and ownership, operators are potentially in a position to influence the information made available to consumers.

In this research, we seek to understand the relationships between providers of information services and the powerful mobile network operators that dominate the industry, as well as the subsequent effects of these relationships on diversity of information sources. At the outset of the mobile Internet industry, there was speculation of two likely outcomes. One outcome would be a mobile Internet industry where the network operators would maintain their dominance and serve as gatekeepers for mobile Internet content. The second outcome would be an industry where powerful content providers would turn the network operators into "bit pipes," limited to merely trans-mitting a wide variety of content. In the current early stages of industry development in the United States it appears the first outcome has taken hold. Mobile operators or intermediaries serve as gatekeepers for the information that is available to mobile Internet users. This leads to the following questions: How have such developments on the distributors' side influenced the conditions for market entry for application developers? How do firms who want to make content and applications available to mobile consumers operate in this environment? What are the resultant incentives and disincentives for market entry?

To understand the forces at work, we employ an institutional economics theoretical framework and combine knowledge of industry structures with information gained from observing the market entry experience of a small firm. The goal of this exercise is first to confirm the hypothesized role played by technology and firm strategies and, if justified, to more clearly understand the interactions between the factors. These findings will provide a more clear understanding of the implications of the current environment in the U.S. mobile industry for information diversity.

2   INSTITUTIONS AND TECHNOLOGICAL CHANGE

In the field of new institutional economics, institutions are considered the humanly derived constraints that shape human interaction and have been compared to the rules of a game (North 1990). As with game playing rules, institutions are both formal and informal and shape the behavior of individuals as well as the strategies employed by teams (organizations). Applied to firms and markets, institutional theory has been used to describe the interaction between formal institutions, such as laws and regulations, and informal institutions, such as norms of particular contexts, in shaping firm behavior and strategies (e.g., Alston et al. 1996). The number of studies performed on informal institutions is relatively small and they are primarily concerned with economic development. Among the few that focus on the firm, the emphasis is on entrepreneurship: they examine the role of informal institutions in enforcing property rights when formal institutions are vague (Peng 2004), and the presence and absence of the influence of social norms and relationships in entrepreneurial activity (Frederking 2004). In a departure from these studies, which consider the broad gap between national legal structures (formal institutions) and social norms (informal activities), we cover a middle ground. This middle ground consists of the area where national legal frameworks do not apply; however, powerful firms have created the rules for market entry, which we consider informal institutions.

A significant force in the mobile industry influencing informal institutions is technology. As discussed by Arthur (1989) and David (1985), technological change is path dependent and, particularly with network technologies, lock-in can occur. Thus, the set of mobile technologies that exists today is the result of related events and technology choices made in the past. Furthermore, lock-in can serve as a significant source of power for a firm. Indeed, as noted by North (1990), competition among technologies is based more on the traits of the firms representing the technologies than on the technologies themselves.

In addition to technology, the study of firm behavior must also consider firm-specific factors (De Vlaam and Maitland 2003; Oliver 1991). Firm-specific factors of interest here are the ownership and use of resource asymmetries, particularly in relation to access to network infrastructure, information, and consumers. As explained by Barney (1986), in strategic factor markets, firms acquire resources that are used to implement strategies in product markets. However, the only way, other than blind luck, to obtain competitive advantage from these resources is to have more accurate expectations (information) about their value to the firm. However, if the new resource is rare, inimitable, and non-substitutable, this will influence the firm's strategy in obtaining the resource (Makadok and Barney 2001). This insight has implications for the relationship between developers and mobile operators, who in providing access to customers offer a fairly rare and inimitable resource. Furthermore, these concepts also provide a basis for comparing our results with those from other markets.

To understand the costs and benefits to market entry faced by developers we propose to link the concepts of technology, strategy, institutions, and the conditions for market entry in the following way (see Figure 1). First, we propose that technologies of the mobile industry influence the strategies pursued by mobile industry distributors, which include operators as well as intermediaries, as regards managing consumer applications and content. This relationship is symbiotic and hence the influence is bi-directional. The technology and strategy combine to create the rules of the game that are the informal institutions. The informal institutions, in turn, create a part of the market entry context for developers.[1]

---

[1] The arrows in Figure 1 are meant to indicate influence only and do not imply causality.

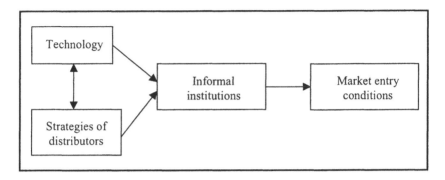

Figure 1. Conceptual Model

We begin with a general description of mobile Internet technologies and distribution strategies, followed by a description of the informal institutions faced by developers and the resultant conditions of market entry. The paper concludes with analysis and discussion of the role that technology and the strategies of powerful distributors play in defining the informal institutions of the market and their implications for the diversity of types of firms, and hence content, represented on the mobile Internet.

3   TECHNOLOGICAL BACKGROUND OF THE MOBILE INTERNET AND DISTRIBUTION STRATEGIES

To understand the strategic choices of operators and application developers, it is first necessary to understand the context within which they operate. We first provide an overview and background on the mobile Internet industry before we continue with a discussion about the technologies and the strategies by various players that together are shaping the industry.

3.1 Technologies in the U.S. Market

The U.S. market for mobile services is dominated by five national operators: Verizon Wireless, Cingular/AT&T Wireless, Sprint, Nextel, and T-Mobile. Cingular, with its recent acquisition of AT&T Wireless, is the current market leader with 47 million customers. It is followed by, respectively, Verizon Wireless (42 million), Sprint PCS (22 million), T-Mobile (16 million), and finally Nextel (15 million).[2]

---

[2]From "Largest Mobile Telephone Companies" (http://en.wikipedia.org/wiki/Largest_ mobile_phone_companies).

For the past four years, all of the operators[3] have been busy managing the transition from the comparatively simple business of offering voice services to the rather complicated business of mobile data services provision. For these operators, mobile data provision includes both managing significant infrastructure upgrades as well as managing the provision of content and applications. These changes have presented a market entry opportunity for stand-alone content and application providers that provide services to end-users on either a commercial or noncommercial basis.

3.1.1   The Mobile Internet

Before continuing this discussion, we first need to define the term *mobile Internet.* Mobile Internet actually refers to two types of data networks: *intra*net as well as true *Inter*net. First, all mobile operators provide their own proprietary data services, which typically entail services such as ringtones, instant messaging, games, news services, e-mail, and other applications. We may perceive such service offerings as large intranets (a.k.a. the "walled garden"), as only the particular operator's customers may access these services.

The majority of operators provide browsing capabilities as well. To this extent, end-users may browse to sites hosted on servers outside the operator's domain (intranet). These sites are typically based on WAP (wireless access protocol), a standard that is supported by the majority of phones nowadays and which enables the display of text on mobile phones. We might call these true mobile Internet services, as anyone with a WAP-supported phone may access these sites, while at the same time anyone may host a WAP page on a server. Mobile users may browse to the WAP page or may find it by using, for example, Google's mobile search engine. However, one issue coming into play is that operators may inactivate browsing functions on mobile phones, or that they may require subscription to their proprietary services via which end users then access browsing functions. For example, Cingular Wireless provides free browsing services where the end user just pays per KB download, while Verizon Wireless requires paid subscription to its GetItNow portal via which end-users then access the browsing function. On top of the GetItNow subscription, they need to pay for downloading time as well. Thus, operators, through their subscription services, are still largely in control of whether, and how, customers may access these mobile Internet services.

Besides operators' control through subscription services, another constraining factor in further development of the true mobile Internet concerns the lack of widely accepted, independent payment mechanisms. In the current dominant model, end users pay the operator for all services, and the operator in turn pays the content or application provider. This means that for all commercial purposes, the content or application provider is required to offer services via operators' proprietary intranets.

---

[3]Here we focus on the dominant national operators. There are approximately 100 additional small operators but they have yet to provide an additional outlet for content and applications.

3.1.2   Wireless Platforms

The development of the mobile Internet will also depend on the underlying technologies. While technologies such as wireless access protocol (WAP), short message service (SMS), and the related multimedia message service (MMS) are available on nearly all handsets, the dominant technology for more advanced applications has yet to be decided. The two contenders are Java 2 Platform, Micro Edition (J2ME) and Binary Runtime Environment for Wireless (BREW). These competing technologies allow for the development of more advanced applications, enabling color display, sound, interactivity, etc. BREW is a proprietary platform developed by QUALCOMM, while J2ME, which is an optimized Java runtime environment, is an open standard. Mobile devices supporting J2ME are unable to execute BREW applications. However, devices supporting BREW are able to execute J2ME applications with special software. Nevertheless, this is a development only recently introduced and not pervasively marketed as yet. Formerly, BREW-capable phones were only able to execute BREW in itself.

While BREW's use by developers has been limited, J2ME has experienced widespread use, due in part to the prevalence of Java, an open standard, as a development tool for a variety of desktop and server applications. The widespread availability of J2ME applications has created more choice and often better prices (sometimes even free) for end-users. With experienced Java programmers around every corner, developing in BREW incurs greater costs in adjusting to the platform. However, these negative consequences for BREW development have led to the introduction of software, making BREW more easily compatible with J2ME.[4] However, operating in both environments is not as simple as merely translating the software as each technology is associated with different operators or intermediaries, each with their own processes and procedures and business models. Thus, the choice of platform technology is a complicated one, best made early in the development cycle.

The lack of uniform standards in technology makes access to mobile services more complicated: (operator specific) devices typically support only a few platforms, and thus limit the end-user's access to only content and application services based on those particular platforms. While J2ME and BREW are inherently distinct programming platforms, and developers may want to value them in terms of costs of development tools, access to information, speed of execution, power of available APIs, etc., debates with proponents for both standards indicate they provide rather similar capabilities.

---

[4]For example, BREW2Bridge entered the market in 2003, allowing developers to download tools that let them build BREW applications by using Microsoft Visual Studio .NET or J2ME, thus helping developers avoid rewriting applications for various operator or handset specific requirements. Additionally, BREW2Bridge enables the running and testing of J2ME applications on BREW-enabled platforms. However, the developer needs a BREW-enabled Java virtual machine (JVM) to run the tool, as without the JVM one is unable to run the J2ME application in the BREW emulator or download the J2ME application to the phone. These tools are all available for download at the QUALCOMM/BREW Web site. Furthermore, Emertec's Geode and IBM's J9 allow for BREW-compatible JVMs. However, they are not yet available for purchase.

Nevertheless, a study by Zelos Group Inc in June 2004 predicts that 90 percent of a projected 100 million mobile devices between now and 2009 will contain either BREW or Java (J2ME), with Java remaining the dominant platform. Furthermore, regardless of Java's projected dominance, Zelos Group points out that Java's openness is actually limiting its evolution, because of lengthy community consensus building processes. The proprietary standard of BREW may, therefore, allow for easier technological advance. This is in line with a more often heard argument that, in mobile space, proprietary solutions have been more effective in creating markets for content, data, and billing. While we cannot look into the future, such debates point out that while technological characteristics are important, it is also important to recognize the link between the technologies and the business models of the organizations who champion them.

3.2 Distributors' Mobile Strategies

Along with these platform technology choices, the provision of mobile content and applications will be greatly influenced by the business strategies pursued by operators as well as intermediaries (content aggregators that bring developers and operators together). A business model may be identified as the organization of product, service, and information flows, as well as the sources of revenues and benefits for both suppliers and customers (Timmers 1998). Furthermore, while not explicitly considered in many business model studies, a business model is seen as being inextricably linked to new technologies (Hawkins 2002). In the mobile industry, business models are largely driven by operators who organize networks of service providers to fill the roles required to offer complex services (Maitland et al. 2005). The networks differ in the way roles are distributed throughout the network and, in particular, in the degree that operators choose to outsource or internally manage content and quality control. These strategies have important implications for application developers and content providers in their market entry attempts. Table 1 provides a short overview of these characteristics, which are discussed below.

3.2.1 Content Control

The degree to which operators manage content internally differs greatly. To this extent, the relationships with developers are of great importance. Relations with developers are by all operators maintained through so-called developer zones, which is a virtual community platform (on the Internet) through which developers commercialize their applications. All contact regarding the full commercialization process between potential developers and operator or intermediary occurs through these developer zones. These provide, among others, information on programming requirements, discussion forums for information exchange among developers themselves and between developer and operator or intermediary, services for uploading applications, etc.

Some operators, namely AT&T Wireless, Cingular (partly), Verizon Wireless (only for WAP based services), and T-Mobile, manage their own developer zones, and therefore a direct relationship with developers. This means that operators are in full control

Table 1. Operator's Mobile Strategies

Operator	Name Service/ Virtual Store	BREW/ J2ME	Developer Zones: In-house/ Outsourced	Testing: In-house/ Outsourced
Cingular	MEdia Net	J2ME	• In-house developer zone: Cingular Wireless Developer Program • Outsourced: Cell-mania developer zone for Cingular	• CWDP: N/A • Cellmania: developers testing themselves
AT&T Wireless	mMode	J2ME	In-house: devCentral	• WAP: developers testing through AT&T's WAP gateway • J2ME: Outsourced to VeriTest
Verizon Wireless	GetItNow	BREW	• In-house (WAP): The Zôn • Outsourced (BREW): QUALCOMM	• WAP (The Zôn): N/A • BREW (QUALCOMM): NSTL
Sprint PCS	Sprint PCS Vision	J2ME	• Partly in-house: Sprint Application Developers' Pro-gram (registration only) • Partly outsourced: Formerly to Handango, cur-rently searching for new solution	N/A
T-Mobile	T-Zones	J2ME	In-house: T-Mobile Developer Center	N/A
Nextel		J2ME	Outsourced: Cellmania (specific developer zone for Nextel)	N/A

of what services will become available and in which manner (e.g., software specifications, revenue streams, etc.). However, Verizon Wireless (applications in BREW
format), Cingular (partly), Sprint PCS (partly), and Nextel have outsourced the management of their developer zones to other organizations. For BREW, as a proprietary
standard, services may only be developed for, and distributed by, its patent holder,
QUALCOMM. Therefore, for Verizon Wireless' BREW applications, developer
relationships are inherently maintained by QUALCOMM. Rather similar intermediaries
for J2ME development exist, however they do not have strict business models related
to technology such as BREW. Operators may outsource any part of their operations
voluntarily. For example, Cingular and Nextel have developer zones managed by
Cellmania. Sprint PCS has recently ceased its cooperation with Handango, which used
to be the primary aggregator and manager for all of its J2ME applications. Additionally,
Sprint PCS maintained its own developer zone by which it maintained contact with
developers. Sprint PCS is now searching for a new partner.

The parties to which developer zones are outsourced gain great influence on which
applications to accept. QUALCOMM, for example, aggregates all of the applications
from which the operator then may choose. Additionally, the operator will negotiate with
the developers, and thus still has influence on the relationship, however not specifically
on which applications are accepted in the first instance. While Cellmania has developer
zones specifically targeted toward a particular operator (i.e., Cingular and Nextel), it is
not clear whether it also performs all negotiations, or whether the operator still takes
responsibility for this part of the process.

In addition to the potential outsourcing of developer relations, the majority of
operators have agreements with so-called publishers and other third parties providing
application directories as well. For example, Handango cooperates with all large
operators except for Nextel. These publishers make agreements with developers and
maintain their applications, as well as guide them through the negotiation process with
operators. For operators, publishers provide easy access to thousands of applications
from which to choose without having to deal with the complete commercialization
process through which developers need to go. These relations are generally maintained
in addition to the operators' own (or outsourced) developer zone relationships.

Finally, a last potential source of cooperation for operators constitutes the so-called
application directory services as provided by third parties. For example, mFinder and
J2ME mFinder, provided by Cellmania, are large directories containing thousands of
applications. After initial agreements between operator and third party provider to
establish access to such directories, operators' customers enter the directories—
completely owned and managed by a third party—remotely to find applications of their
choice. In this case, no further agreements between operator and application provider
exist at all. Here the operator loses complete control over services provision aside from
the potential influence on directory providers' business strategies.

3.2.2 Quality Control: Testing Programs

In addition to content control and related business models, the testing of
applications can be perceived as an important part of the process of commercialization

of applications. While typically strict requirements are already set for software creation itself, additional testing takes place before applications are accepted in virtual stores. This is performed as perceived necessary by operators or intermediaries. Different testing procedures are in place. First, after testing an application on the developer's own workstation, the developer may have to upload it to the intermediary or operator of choice with which certain agreements have been reached. The latter then either outsources the testing, or performs the testing in-house. Also, in some cases, developers test their applications themselves, using specific directions as provided on the respective developer zones. A third possibility is the requirement for a developer to obtain a testing certificate from a specified software testing company. In this case, the operator is not at all involved in the testing procedure, except for setting requirements. Major software testing companies are NSTL and VeriTest, who serve respectively QUALCOMM and AT&T Wireless. In the case of QUALCOMM, developers just need to show their certificate. They pay the testing fee themselves.

Outsourced testing will lead to high quality levels and reliability: applications are generally tested on a host of devices as well as to networks, and thus assure great interoperability. If a developer has to do the testing personally, typically only one device may be available. Professional testing, however, does add to the costs of commercializing applications. It is unclear how these costs are precisely covered, but often we found that developers have to pay for the testing in order to become part of an operator's alliance network. These few hundred dollars extra costs make it more difficult for especially smaller developers to commercialize their applications. However, it ensures that end users will receive reliable services.

3.3 Interaction: Technology and Distributors' Strategies

The discussion above shows that technology and business model may be highly intertwined. Dependent on the application platform—BREW or J2ME—particular business models may develop. As was already touched upon, BREW means more than just a technological standard. It is both a standard and business model, owned and patented by QUALCOMM. This has limited BREW-based services to only be developed for and distributed by QUALCOMM.

In the United States, Verizon Wireless is the only operator using the BREW standard and business model, whereas all other major operators employ applications based on the open-standard J2ME. As a result, a smaller variety of BREW applications is available, and in the United States only accessible by Verizon Wireless' customers. Verizon Wireless, therefore, has been able to develop a very close relationship with QUALCOMM. This means that Verizon Wireless has great control over development of BREW as a standard, and the way BREW applications are brought to the market.

On the contrary, J2ME does not determine a specific business model. Moreover, the degree of control over technology by the operators using J2ME is significantly smaller, as it is an open standard. Regardless, we can see that the market has led to certain outcomes of service offerings. First, as we have seen, use of proprietary data services (referred to earlier as intranets) remains common across all operators, whether operators employ BREW or J2ME. The main difference lies in the fact that, on the wider (mobile) Internet, many J2ME applications are available to download independent of any operator. While end users may find these by themselves through search engines or browsing, large directories as provided by Cellmania (J2ME mFinder), for example, seem to be the most common modes for access. With these directories being the result of closed data networks and proprietary information services, the providers of these directories have taken on an important role in the market. In many cases they have been able to take control over operators' virtual stores or wireless portals (the customer's entry point to the mobile Internet). This is much like the case of Verizon Wireless' GetItNow portal being powered by BREW, even though the latter is a requirement coming along with the BREW business model. In more detail, if we look at J2ME application provision, we see that Cellmania powers the Nextel Store as well as Cingular's Wireless Software Store, while Handango formerly took care of Sprint PCS Vision. This implies that these third parties are taking over the operator's control of available content and applications, to some extent, as well as gaining more influence on quality assurance, as developers typically submit their applications to these third parties.

These developments lead to a couple of insights. First, while BREW technology has created a relatively strictly controlled market for application development, J2ME development remains very open. Second, in relation to business model development, we find that the BREW standard has allowed for greater quality assurance, as very specific testing procedures are in place. While for J2ME this part remains open to the operator or intermediary, no uniform quality standard has been set. While it does not necessarily mean lower quality, it has led to a lower level of control over quality.

4 INFORMAL INSTITUTIONS AND MARKET ENTRY CONDITIONS

The mobile Internet market entry conditions for application and content developers will be shaped by general economic factors, such as the availability of venture capital and labor market conditions, as well as factors specific to the mobile industry itself. Here we are concerned with the latter, and consider these factors to include both the informal institutions or rules as well as some more general market conditions that are the result of technologies and strategies pursued by distributors.

4.1 Informal Institutions in the Mobile Internet Industry

The interdependence of technology and strategies of distributors creates a variety of rules that influence all aspects of the application and content developers' market entry decisions. The rules are grouped into two classes that vary in terms of their implications for the role of the distributor in the business of the developer.

In the first class of rules, the distributor has significant influence. One rule in this class is whether or not *approval* for a product/service concept is required. Whether or not this rule applies depends on a developer's choice of distributor. Furthermore, approval may go beyond the distributor's product concept to include an assessment of the developer's financial standing. A second rule is whether or not the developer will have to use third-party testing, which in turn specifies the testing organization and reduces a developer's control over costs and time to market.

In the second class of rules, there are less severe control implications. One such rule is the requirement to meet technical specifications for an application as defined by the distributor. These specifications typically include requirements for self-testing, as well as terms and conditions for access to reduced cost *testing subscriptions* that allow developers to test applications on several phone models. A second rule is agreeing to the terms and conditions of the revenue sharing agreement, which are usually specified by the distributors. A third set of rules developed by distributors governs access to technical and business process assistance. These rules are typically codified and enforced in the developer zones. While some distributors make support freely available, others create special categories of support which developers can buy into.

While these rules demonstrate the results of the interaction of technology and strategies pursued by distributors, they are certainly not an exhaustive list. Neither are they the sole determinant of market entry conditions. Below we discuss how these rules and the industry characteristics resulting from technologies and strategies combine to create a partial picture of the market entry conditions.

4.2 Market Entry Conditions

Market entry conditions are of interest because they influence entrepreneurs' decisions of whether to enter a market or put their resources to other uses. In this case, we are interested in the market entry conditions encountered by developers as compared to those firms who have made content and applications available on the fixed Internet. For the mobile Internet, we have found that the implications of technology and business strategy can be characterized as five effects, which we describe here.

The first effect is related to the concept of the strategic factor market. As compared to other industries (for example, retail outlets), developers have a fairly limited number of distributors through whom they can gain access to customers. Furthermore, circumventing these distributors by approaching customers directly, which is possible due to the Internet technology, results in great challenges for managing payments.

The second effect concerns the fragmentation of platform technologies and how they limit developers' access to particular market segments. In choosing a platform technology, the developer chooses the market segment served by the operators supporting that technology.

The third effect is the result of agreements between operators and intermediaries. Agreements between operators and intermediaries include those concerned with operating developer zones as well as managing content control. In addition to specifying the terms and conditions of access to these services by developers, developers are also affected by the stability (or lack thereof) in the intermediary/operator relationship.

The fourth and fifth effects are trade-offs. Developers encounter the fourth effect in their decision to purchase access to customers directly through an operator or through an intermediary. In this decision, developers face a trade-off between being close to customers, which is typically achieved through an operator, versus ease of the commercialization process, which typically faces fewer barriers with an intermediary. A similar trade-off is experienced in the area of quality control. Whereas aligning with a distributor with strict quality control requirements creates greater costs, it also establishes higher quality of all offerings and can attract more customers.

These market conditions, in combination with the rules faced by developers, will influence their decisions on when or whether or not to enter the market. What we see is that the market conditions include a fragmented industry with competing technologies and mechanisms that challenge the ability of developers to maintain control over the process of commercialization. These conditions may make entry for *de novo* entrants, new firms unaffiliated with existing firms, difficult. These conditions can be compared with the relatively easy market entry conditions faced by entrepreneurs wanting to place content and applications on the fixed Internet. However, while the processes for delivering content and applications for these firms may have been and continue to be much simpler, the ability to collect payment has presented its problems.

5 CONCLUSIONS

As the discussion of informal institutions and conditions for application developers' market entry highlights, the market for mobile data services has been shaped to a large extent by a complex interaction between technology and distributors' strategies. In this research, we set out to answer a set of questions related to the development of the industry and its implications for the provision of applications and content in the mobile Internet.

Developments in the market on the distributors' side have provided for a relatively small number of national operators to gain significant market power, which has enabled operators to influence the development of the industry's informal institutional context. Distributors' significant control over content and quality has set the rules of the game for developers' commercialization of application services. The multiple platform technologies have created a fragmented market for application and content. In this situation, application developers must choose simultaneously a platform technology and a distributor with whom to align. The choice of distributor will also determine the rules the application developer must follow to enter the market. These rules, similar to the informal institutions discussed by Peng (2004) and Frederking (2004) create costs and benefits for market entry. Thus, this research contributes to the literature on informal institutions by extending the conceptualization of informal institutions from norms and social ties to further include the rules and regulations created by powerful firms.

While developers wield some power in being able to choose among different institutional contexts by choosing operators, and hence presumably may influence unfavorable rules through defection, the large number of application developers and their relatively low market power leaves them as *takers* rather than *makers* of the institutional context. Even as the intermediaries might begin to challenge the market power of the operators, it is unclear the extent to which they will be able to follow through. Trends of consolidation among the operators—Cingular's recent acquisition of AT&T Wireless as well as the likely future merger between Sprint PCS and Nextel—favor a further consolidation of power in this realm.

Naturally the power structure created by a small number of national operators versus a large number of developers, has both positive and negative consequences. The ability of operators to create an institutional context that enhances quality and inter-operability through strict testing requirements has benefits for testing firms as well as for consumers. However, it also implies stricter control on availability of specific information services by the operators. Additionally, we may argue that the terms and conditions for market entry will influence the types of firms that can incur the costs created by the institutional environment. Trends in this institutional environment suggest that established firms with sound financial histories will be welcome, while start-ups may find market entry more difficult. This, combined with the fragmented nature of the industry which provides incentives for developers to make multiple offerings, suggests that the industry may evolve to include a few developers and content providers that provide a large share of the applications and content for the mobile Internet. We can only ask ourselves if, in such an environment, fixed Internet inno-vations such as blogs could emerge. Additionally, we may ask what consequences these current market developments have on service for consumers in underrepresented groups, such as minorities and rural users. It could very well be possible that larger firms will be forced to develop for the average user, thereby affecting the diversity of services.

ACKNOWLEDGMENTS

This research was made possible, in part, by a grant from AT&T Wireless. The authors wish to thank Lloyd Holder and Glenn Greenblatt of NSTL Inc. for valuable insights into the evolution of the mobile industry.

REFERENCES

Alston, L. J., Eggertsson, T., and North. D. (Eds.). *Empirical Studies in Institutional Change*, Cambridge, UK: Cambridge University press, 1996.
Arthur, W. B. "Competing Technologies, Increasing Returns and Lock-in by Historical Events," *The Economic Journal* (99:394), 1996, pp. 116-131.
Barney, J. B. "Strategic Factor Markets: Expectations, Luck, and Business Strategy," *Management Science* (32:10), 1986, pp. 1231-1241.
David, P. "Clio and the Economics of QWERTY in Economic History: A Necessary Though Not Sufficient Condition for an Economist," *The American Economic Review* (75:2), 1985, pp. 332-337.
De Vlaam, H., and Maitland, C. F. "Competitive Mobile Access in Europe: Comparing Market and Policy Perspectives," *Communications & Strategies* (50), 2003, pp. 69-96.
Frederking, L. C. "A Cross-National Study of Culture, Organization and Entrepreneurship in Three Neighborhoods," *Entrepreneurship and Regional Development* (16:3), 2004, pp. 197-215.
Hawkins, R. "Do Business Models Matter?," position paper presented to the International BITA B4U Workshop, Business Models for Innovative Mobile Services, Delft, The Netherlands, November 15-16, 2002.
Maitland, C. F., Van de Kar, E. A. M., Wehn de Montalvo, U., and Bouwman, H. "Mobile Information and Entertainment Services: Business Models and Service Networks," *International Journal of Management and Decision Making* (6:1), 2005, pp. 47-64.

Makadok, R., and Barney, J. B. "Strategic Factor Market Intelligence: An Application of Information Economics to Strategy Formulation and Competitor Intelligence," *Management Science* (47:12), 2001, pp. 1621-1638.

North, D. C. *Institutions, Institutional Change and Economic Performance*, Cambridge, UK: Cambridge University Press, 1990.

Oliver, C. "Strategic Responses to Institutional Processes," *The Academy of Management Review* (16:1), 1991, pp. 145-179.

Peng, Y. "Kinship Networks and Entrepreneurs in China's Transitional Economy," *The American Journal of Sociology* (109:5), 2004, pp. 1045-1075.

Timmers, P. "Business Models for Electronic Markets," *Electronic Markets* (8:2), 1998, pp. 3-8.

ABOUT THE AUTHORS

Annemijn van Gorp is a Ph.D. candidate in the School of Information Sciences and Technology at the Pennsylvania State University. She has a M.Sc. degree in Systems Engineering, Policy Analysis and Management from Delft University of Technology in the Netherlands. Annemijn's research interests include the effect of market structure, competition, and policy on the provision of both fixed and wireless broadband Internet access services, as well as the changing roles of national, regional and international institutions in the provision of telecommunications services. Annemijn can be reached at avangorp@ist.psu.edu.

Carleen Maitland is an assistant professor in the School of Information Sciences and Technology at the Pennsylvania State University. She received a doctorate in 2001 from Delft University of Technology in the Netherlands, where she was an assistant professor prior to joining Penn State. She also holds M.S. (Stanford University) and B.S. (Worcester Polytechnic Institute) degrees in engineering and served as a Peace Corps Volunteer in Malawi, southern Africa. Carleen's research interests include the effects of new mobile and wireless technologies on organizations and industry structure, as well as the role of national policies in bringing about these effects. She has published in journals such as *Telecommunications Policy*, *Information Economics and Policy*, and *Communications and Strategies*. Carleen can be reached at cmaitland@ist.psu.edu.

Brian H. Cameron is an assistant professor of Information Sciences and Technology at the Pennsylvania State University. Prior to joining Penn State, he was Director of Information Technology for WorldStor, Inc., a storage service provider (SSP) in Fairfax, VA. As director of IT, Brian was responsible for designing and building the company's national IT infrastructure. He designed and managed the implementation of the corporate network infrastructure and also managed the implementation of a $3.5 million ERP/CRM system. He has also held a variety of technical and managerial positions with IBM and Penn State. Brian has his Ph.D. and MBA from Penn State. His primary research and consulting interests include enterprise systems integration, storage networking, emerging wireless technologies, and the use of simulations and gaming in education. He has designed and taught a variety of courses on topics that include networking, systems integration, storage networking, project management, and IT consulting. Brian can be reached at bcameron@ist.psu.edu.

22 AN INTERNATIONAL MOBILE SECURITY STANDARD DISPUTE: From the Actor–Network Perspective

Shirley Chan
University of Hong Kong
Hong Kong

Heejin Lee
University of Melbourne
Melbourne, Australia

Sangjo Oh
Dongyang Technical College
Seoul, Korea

Abstract   *In 2004 there was a trade and technology dispute of significance between China and the United States surrounding a mobile security standard called WAPI (Wireless LAN Authentication and Privacy Infrastructure). Using the remarkable size of its domestic market as a lever, China is challenging some existing or being-shaped standards to set its own standards not only within its own territory but also potentially in the world markets. WAPI is another example in a series of these attempts. Using the actor-network theory, we investigate the process of mobile standards setting in the international context where superpowers like China and the United States compete.*

Keywords   Standards, actor-network theory, China, WAPI, WiFi

1   INTRODUCTION

In 2004 there was a trade dispute of significance between China and the United States. The Chinese government announced in November 2003 that its own wireless security protocol known as WAPI (Wireless LAN Authentication and Privacy

Infrastructure) would be put in effect from December 1, 2003. While the 802.11 WiFi[1] standard developed by the Institute of Electrical and Electronics Engineers (IEEE) was the internationally used, common security protocol for wireless equipment (Lemon 2004), China wanted to set up WAPI as a standard for domestic markets (Hoo 2004; Kanellos 2004). WAPI is not compatible with international standards, and does not work well with chips based on WiFi (Fordahl 2004). Mandatory compliance with the WAPI standard is to be required for both domestically produced and imported equipment such as Centrino notebooks, PDAs, and other wireless devices (Suttmeier and Yao 2004).

China gave the WAPI algorithms to 24 Chinese companies only—some of which are potential competitors with foreign firms (Suttmeier and Yao 2004). Western chip-makers are required to pay these Chinese companies a per-chip royalty for WAPI and/or cooperate with them on development (Kanellos 2004) if they want to market their products in China. For the foreign/Western chipmakers, it means that they may have to provide technical product specifications to potential competitors. The foreign chipmakers responded with dissatisfaction and resistance. These foreign companies might have to staff local facilities if they want to participate in the market as the WAPI technology cannot leave the country (Kanellos 2004). Complying with the WAPI standard would increase their manufacturing costs as they have to make a special type of device for China and another type for the rest of the world (Reuters 2004 as cited in Suttimeier and Yao 2004).

More importantly, this appears to be a violation of the national treatment commitment under the TBT (Technical Barriers to Trade) provisions of the World Trade Organization (Suttmeier and Yao 2004). Chipmakers, especially in the United States, went to their governments for intervention, and the incident developed to the extent that the U.S. Secretary of State, Collin Powell, and other high-level senior officials got involved. The Chinese government finally conceded that the WAPI implementation was to be delayed indefinitely.[2]

This recent controversy over WAPI has attracted much attention from various stakeholders including the U.S. and Chinese governments, wireless product manu-facturers, technology professional bodies (e.g., IEEE), and other international regulatory bodies. However, there has been little attention from academic communities.

In this paper, we examine the development of the dispute through the lens of actor-network theory. Our goal is to understand the patterns of interaction and the dynamics among the stakeholders surrounding standards setting. With respect to the data collection method, this study is based on documentary data containing mostly media

---

[1]WiFi is the short-form for *wireless fidelity* referring to any type of 802.11 network, whether 802.11b, 802.11a, dual-band, etc. (Http://www.webopedia.com/TERM/W/Wi_Fi.html). The term is promulgated by the WiFi Alliance, founded in 1999 as an international association (industry consortium) to certify interoperability of wireless local area network products based on the IEEE 802.11 specification. Currently the WiFi Alliance has over 200 member companies from around the world, and over 1,500 products have received WiFi® certification since certification began in March 2000 (www.WiFi.org).

[2]Perkins Coie, China Legal Highlights, June 2004 (http://www.perkinscoie.com/content/ren/updates/china/june2004.htm).

data and some archival data (McCulloch 2004). We searched not only English-language sources, but also Chinese-language sources. The Chinese-language sources were searched by the first-named author who is bilingual in English and Chinese.

The remainder of the paper is organized as follows. The following section presents the actor-network theory, followed by a brief description of the method used. Then the case under study is described in a wider context of China's accession to the WTO and the technical background of WAPI. In section four, we examine the WAPI dispute through the ANT lens and discuss various implications. The concluding section presents contributions and limitations of the paper and suggests a direction for future research.

2 ACTOR–NETWORK THEORY

Actor-network theory was developed in the sociology of science and technology (Callon 1986a, 1986b, 1987; Callon and Latour 1981). It originates in a belief that "the study of technology itself can be transformed into a sociological tool of analysis" (Callon 1987, p. 83). Engineers who design, develop, and diffuse a technical artifact embody (*inscribe* by the ANT terminology) into the artifact how it is used, their intention, and their vision of the society and the world which the artifact best fits. In this sense, they become sociologists, or, using Callon's word, *engineer-sociologists*. The technical aspects of the engineer's work are profoundly social. Therefore, it is impossible to distinguish between the technical and the social during the process of innovation. When we accept that the technical is social, an artifact, on which engineers inscribe the social they want to see and realize, becomes an entity, or in ANT terminology, an actor with the same nature and characteristics of a human actor. The distinctiveness of ANT is that it does not distinguish between human and nonhuman actors.

ANT helps us to describe how actors form alliances and involve other actors and use nonhuman actors (artifacts) to strengthen such alliances and to secure their interests. This process is called *translation*, defined as "the methods by which an actor enrolls others" (Callon 1986b, p. xvii). Translation, when an actor-network is created, consists of four processes (Callon 1986a): *problematization* (the focal actor defines interests that others may share and establishes itself as indispensable and as the obligatory passage point through which all of the actors that make up an actor-network must pass), *interessement* (the focal actor convinces other actors), *enrolment* (other actors accept the interests as defined by the focal actor), and *mobilization* (the focal actor uses a set of methods to ensure that the other actors act according to their agreement and would not betray). To translate is to oblige an actor to consent to the passage defined by the focal actor (Callon 1986b). Translation is not always successful, but often fails and halts at any stage. Callon (1986a) stated that each entity enlisted by the problematization could choose to submit to being integrated into the initial plan or, inversely, refuse the transaction.

It is recognized that ANT has a potential for understanding the complex social interactions associated with information technology (Walsham 1997). Since the pioneering works of Hanseth and Monteiro (1997) and Walsham and Sahay (1999), ANT has been gaining attention from a section of the Information Systems research community and increasingly popular as a powerful tool "to help us overcome the current poor understanding of the information technology (IT) artifact" (Hanseth et al. 2004). Hanseth and Monteiro investigate how standards in a health information infrastructure in Norway inscribe behavior among related actors, and suggest that the notion of inscriptions is a promising vehicle for understanding the complexity of information infrastructure and standardization processes. Walsham and Sahay analyzed the unsuccessful implementation of GIS for district-administration in India. Their finding was that the GIS initiatives failed to create and maintain a stable actor-network with aligned interests. ANT has theoretical advocates for its utility in studying the complex networks embedded in, or impacting on, various IS implementations involving technological innovation (Tatnall and Gilding 1999) and in generating detailed and contextual empirical knowledge about IS (Doolin and Lowe 2002). ANT has since been applied in various IS studies (see the special issue of *Information Technology & People* (17:2), 2004).

Two studies are introduced here because they deal with standards from the ANT perspective. Fomin and Keil (2000) reviewed economic literature on standard setting and alliance formation as well as the social network theories, including, but not limited to ,ANT, to come up with a socio-economic theory of standardization. Yang et al. (2003) analyzed the role of standards and their impact on the diffusion of broadband mobile services in Korea.

In this paper, we investigate through the lens of ANT how the WAPI controversy between China and the United States evolved. ANT is employed to understand the dynamics of international competition surrounding technological standard settings in the globalized context of technology development.

3   THE CASE DESCRIPTION

Before we describe how the WAPI case evolved, we present the background: China's accession to the WTO and the technical origins of the WAPI standard.

3.1 China's Accession to the WTO and Standards

China joined the WTO in 2001. After China joined the WTO, Chinese domestic industries faced more challenges from globalization and foreign competition (Suttmeier and Yao 2004). Under the WTO principle of free international trade,[3] such traditional instruments of industrial or economic protection as tariffs would be limited by WTO obligations (Suttmeier and Yao 2004). WTO obligations limit traditional means of trade protectionism such as barriers or quotas. Standards are an effective means to protect and promote national industry within the WTO framework (Suttmeier and Yao 2004). China's post-WTO technology policy, therefore, emphasized the importance of standards (Standardization Administrative Commission of China 2001 as cited in Suttmeier and Yao 2004). Standards are China's deck of cards (Chen 2004).

---

[3]See the World Trade Organization's site, "The WTO...In Brief," at http://www.wto.org/english/thewto_e/whatis_e/inbrief_e/inbr00_e.htm.

National technology standards are an increasingly important item on China's development and foreign relations agenda. It is not surprising that the Chinese Standardization Administrative Commission conducted a major research project, "China's Technology Standards Strategy Development," and in September 2004 published its final report as a consultation draft setting out China's technology standards implementation plan from 2005 to 2020 among other issues (Standardization Administrative Commission of China 2004).

3.2 The Technical Background of WAPI

Although many claim that the wireless network standard proposed by China is proprietary, this claim is only partially true. It is similar in many ways, or even seems to be identical, to IEEE's 802.11 wireless networking standard (Wireless Fidelity or WiFi). There is only one difference. That is, it uses a different security protocol, called WAPI (Wireless LAN Authentication and Privacy Infrastructure Protocol), which is the symmetric encryption algorithm used between a wireless device and the access point after both of them have been authenticated (Zhu 2004). WAPI is not part of the 802.11 standard, which relies on WEP (Wired Equivalent Privacy) (Zhu 2004).

WEP is an encryption scheme introduced in IEEE 802.11a and 802.11b (September 1999). It is included in subsequent standards such as 802.11g. As the name implies, it is intended to make wireless networks as resistant to snooping and intrusion as wired networks. The standards make encryption with a 64-bit key a mandatory capability and 128-bit encryption an option (Geier 2004). Almost all vendors provided both 64- and 128-bit WEP encryption in their subsequent products. However, it was soon found that WEP could be easily cracked by intercepting and analyzing a sufficiently large amount of encrypted traffic. Used wisely and in conjunction with other measures, WEP can keep a low-traffic network quite secure, but is unsuitable for high-traffic corporate wireless LANs, where an attacker can quickly collect enough packets to extract the keys. Since WEP was found to have a security hole, vulnerable to the external attacks, efforts have been made to fix the problem, two of which are noteworthy: WPA and IEEE 802.11i.

In October 2002, the WiFi Alliance announced WPA (WiFi Protected Access), replacing WEP. It was a response to the delayed development by IEEE of a new security centric protocol 802.11i. When WPA was introduced, a task group of IEEE was still in the middle of developing 802.11i. Related firms needed a quicker solution, even though it might have restricted functionality. As the WiFi Alliance had been working closely with IEEE, it was determined that the interim standard WPA should be designed for forward-compatibility to become a subset of 802.11i.

The long-awaited wireless LAN security standard 802.11i was finally ratified in June 2004. IEEE 802.11i is an amendment to the 802.11 standard specifying security mechanisms for wireless networks. The WiFi Alliance refers to the new standard as WPA2.

China claimed that WAPI was developed to shore up the security of wireless networks. WAPI was announced in 2003, after the industry consortium WiFi Alliance approved the interim standard WPA. WPA is a standard agreed on by the members of the consortium. It was not an international standard ratified by international standardization bodies like IEEE, of which 802 committees have been responsible for the standardization of LAN technologies and protocols for decades, although the WiFi Alliance and IEEE worked closely in this regard.

4 DISCUSSION: ANALYZING OR INTERPRETING THE CASE THROUGH THE ANT LENS

The key theoretical tenet of ANT is *translation*. This section discusses, analyzes, and interprets the case of the WAPI dispute between China and the United States through the stages of translation.

4.1 China as the Focal Actor Translation: Problematization

Callon (1986a) stated that there are four moments of translation. The first one is *problematization*, during which the focal actor seeks to become indispensable to other actors by defining the nature and the latter's problems and then suggesting that these would be resolved if the actors negotiated the "obligatory passage point." The CSAC, representing the Chinese government, spotted the security holes in the WiFi standards. They problematized this and proposed a solution (WAPI), at least within its own territory. WAPI was created as an actor and became an obligatory passage point through which all the actors who want to participate in the China market must pass.

The first step in this problematization is the "interdefinition of the actors" (Callon 1986a). The WAPI dispute was very much about the Chinese government wanting the international (predominantly American) community to adopt and comply with WAPI as an internationally accepted mobile security standard. It appears that the focal actor was the Chinese government as represented by the CSAC. Having WAPI as the internationally recognized mobile security standard would require the alliance from three other main actors in this scenario: the U.S. government, the world (or non-Chinese, although mostly American) IT business community represented by the WiFi Alliance, and international bodies such as IEEE 802 Local and Metropolitan Area Networks Standards Committee.

Callon (1986a) mentioned that the second step in the problematization would involve the definition of the obligatory passage point (OPP) in relation to the focal actor making itself indispensable to the other actors and defining the latter's interests and problems. CSAC, representing the Chinese government, defined the interests of the other actors as follows. For the U.S. government, the interests would be protecting and expanding the American national and business interests (Fang et al. 2004). With respect to the American IT business community, their interests would be tapping into the vast commercial potential of the world's largest telecommunication market—China (Chang et al. 2005). Regarding international bodies, the interests would be maintaining international mobile security standards (Fang et al. 2004).

4.2 WAPI as the Obligatory Passage Point

China's immense market potential had made the Chinese government more confident in using its economic might as a bargaining chip in shaping international technology standards (Standardization Administrative Commission of China 2004). Equipped with such sheer confidence and given that China is the world's largest telecommunication market (Chang et al. 2005), China's official statements and media reports emphasized "market" as the main or almost the sole criterion in determining a country's power in setting international technology standards. During a meeting of the Chinese officials in July 2003 with respect to WLAN national standards, they reached a consensus: "Standards form the foundation stone of the information industry, and that market is the pillar of standards" (Fang et al. 2004). Some experienced technology professionals also commented, "Why can't we use the huge market to make Chinese standards as international standards?" (Fang et al. 2004). In the CSAC's consultation report (Standardization Administrative Commission of China 2004), the Commission commented that the foundation on which China could realize its Chinese technology standards strategy (part of the strategy would be to make Chinese standards the international standards) is the continual growth of the Chinese national economy.

In light of the Chinese perception of the market as the main or even sole criterion in granting China the power in setting international technology standards as explained above, it appeared that CSAC thought it could make WAPI the OPP for various other actors that would need to accept WAPI in order to realize their respective interests. Accepting WAPI would mean paving the way for American business corporations to have more participation in the Chinese telecommunications industry and this would realize the U.S. government's interests in expanding American business activities. Accepting WAPI and working with those 24 Chinese companies having the WAPI algorithms would be a way to cultivate good relationships with Chinese IT industry (critically important to doing business in a country such as China, where relationships can prevail over rules in many situations) and would realize the interests of American IT businesses in reaping commercial benefits in the huge China telecommunications market. Recognizing WAPI as an international mobile security standard would show that international bodies appreciated the importance of the market in shaping international technology standards, and that these bodies realized the importance of carrying out their duty of maintaining international standards, often reflected by the interests of industry members.

4.3 Unsuccessful Interessement: United States Protesting China

The actions by which the focal actor attempts to impose and stabilize the identity of the other actors, defined during problematization, is called *interessement* (Callon 1986a). If successful, interessement confirms (more or less completely) the validity of the problematization and the alliance that it implies (Callon 1986a). When CSAC announced in May 2003 the promulgation of the WAPI standards and then in November

2003 the implementation of the same (Fang et al. 2004), one could contend that it was an action of interessement. This is because regulations have legal binding force, and the potential acceptance of the legal force by various other actors would suggest their confirmation that WAPI is the OPP addressing the problems or realizing the interests of various actors that China defined for them.

Subsequent events showed that CSAC as the focal actor failed to make WAPI the OPP for the other actors and was unsuccessful in the interessement process. Callon (1986a) stated that each entity enlisted by the problematization could choose to submit to being integrated into the initial plan or, inversely, refuse the transaction. As mentioned earlier in the WAPI background information, opposition to accepting WAPI as an international mobile security standard from all of the other actors (U.S. government, American IT businesses, and international bodies) was so intense that the Chinese government announced, in April 2004, an indefinite postponement of the WAPI implementation.[4]

It appeared that CSAC failed because it had overlooked factors other than market in determining the power of a country in setting international technology standards. These other factors include *international influence* and *international behavior*. The WAPI background information shows that the WiFi Alliance successfully elicited support from the U.S. government and the international community in taking action to protest the Chinese government's decision on mandatory WAPI implementation and advocate using WiFi as the universally applicable mobile security standard. This is because while China is a growing major power, the U.S. is more influential in international relations.

Callon (1986a) also mentions that if other actors choose to refuse the transaction defined for them by the focal actor and do not submit to the latter during interessement, they can define their identity, goals, orientations, motivations, or interests in another manner. This is exactly what the other actor, the WiFi Alliance, chose to do. During its course of opposing China's WAPI decision, the WiFi Alliance redefined the various actors' identity and interests by initiating another actor-network with itself as the focal actor and the other actors (the U.S. government, the international regulatory bodies, and CSAC representing the Chinese government) and making them all passing through the obligatory passage point of WiFi.

4.4 Competing Actor Networks: WAPI Versus WiFi Standards, an Unfinished War

Standards are classified into three types by the processes by which they are established: formal, *de facto*, and *de jure* standards (Hanseth and Monteiro 1997; Hanseth et al. 1996; Schmidt and Werle 1992). *De facto* standards are established through market mechanisms; there are no regulating, institutional arrangements

---

[4]See Perkins Coie "China Legal Highlights" at http://www.perkinscoie.com/content/ren/updates/china/january2004.htm and http://www.perkinscoie.com/content/ren/updates/china/june2004.htm.

influencing the process. *De facto* standards are often developed by industrial consortia or vendors (Hanseth and Monteiro 1997; Weiss and Cargill 1992). *De jure* standards are imposed by law. Formal standards are worked out by standardization bodies which are often voluntary standardization organizations like IEEE.

The CSAC spotted security concerns regarding WiFi. They identified these concerns as an opportunity to establish WAPI as an alternative standard in China in the first instance. They problematized WiFi and tried to set up WAPI as a *de jure* **standard** in the territory of China.

In response to China's WAPI, the WiFi Alliance built an actor-network to protect WiFi. The Alliance was closely working with IEEE, a voluntary standardization organization, which had a working group for mobile security standards. They were in the process of producing a formal standard for mobile security. The Alliance was developing its own standard, compatible with IEEE 802.11. Defied by the Chinese WAPI, the WiFi Alliance approached the IEEE. Because the WiFi market did not grow enough for a standard to be established as a *de facto* standard, they needed a formal approach. The Alliance mobilized all of the actors favorable to WiFi by convincing them that WiFi would be in their interests, and WAPI would be a threat to their interests. In the end, China announced the indefinite delay of WAPI implementation.

It appears that China failed or was defeated in this dispute. However, translation is a never-completed process (Callon 1986a). According to one Chinese article (Digil63 2004), the U.S. government promised the Chinese government that WAPI would be reviewed by IEEE. This means that WAPI may be included in IEEE related regulations and recognized as an international standard. Furthermore, the recent decision to discuss WAPI by the ISO (International Organization for Standardization) indicates that this standard war will continue. Figure 1 presents the two competing actor networks. It shows how in each of the WAPI and WiFi actor-networks, various actors were entangled in a complex web of alliances in the context of the ANT theoretical principles of problematization, interessement, enrolment, and mobilization.

5   Conclusion

Standard setting involves a variety of stakeholders. There are multiple interests at stake, particularly when they are concerned with international standards. Standards embody interests of nations, industries, and organizations. In the case of WAPI, China attempted to capitalize on its market size and increasingly capable technical community to set up a national (ultimately aiming to be international) standard that reflects its national interests.

In this paper, we have presented an international case as to how China's increasing market power stimulated its desire to have more say in mobile security standardization, thereby challenging the traditional landscape of international technology standards setting. We examined the dispute surrounding China's attempt to set its own mobile security standard (WAPI). The process and dynamics between stakeholders in standards setting are more complex at the international level. To understand the complexity of standard setting, we used the perspective of ANT.

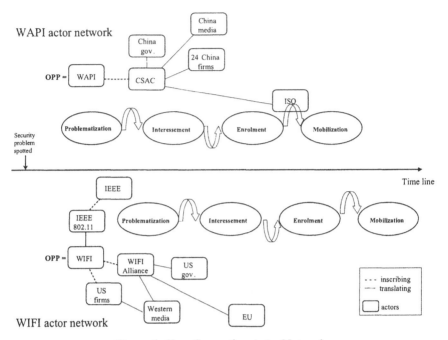

Figure 1. Two Competing Actor Networks

Translation is a never-completed process. As seen in the recent development (the decision to discuss WAPI by the ISO), the WAPI actor network is continuously developing, competing against other related actor networks. Therefore, to be able to understand the process of standard setting, further research is required which follows the development over a longer period of time. WAPI is just one instance in which China endeavored to set its own technological standards different from, if not totally incompatible with, international standards. Other instances include EVD (Enhanced Versatile Disc), IGRS (Intelligent Grouping and Resources Sharing), AVS (Audio, Video Coding Standard), and TD-SCDMA (Time Division Synchronous Code Division Multiple Access) standards (Suttmeier and Yao 2004). All of these attempts offer opportunities to investigate the process of standards setting.

REFERENCES

Callon, M. "Some Elements of a Sociology of Translation: Domestication of the Scallops and the Fishermen of St Brieuc Bay," in *Power, Action and Belief*, J. Law (Ed.), London: Routledge and Kegan Paul, 1986a, pp. 197- 233.

Callon, M. "The Sociology of an Actor Network: The Case of the Electric Vehicle," in *Mapping the Dynamics of Science and Technology: Sociology of Science in the Real World*, M. Callon, J. Law, and A. Rip (Eds.), London: Macmillan, 1986b, pp. 19-34.

Callon, M. "Society in the Making: The Study of Technology as a Tool for Sociological Analysis," in *The Social Construction of Technological Systems*, W. E. Bijker, T. P. Hughes, and T. Pinch (Eds.), London: The MIT Press, 1987.

Callon, M., and Latour, B. "Unscrewing the big Leviathan," in *Advances in Social Theory and Methodology*, K. Knorr-Cetina and A. V. Cicourel (Eds.), London: Routledge & Kegan Paul, 1981, pp. 277-303

Chang, J., Fang, X., and Yen, D. C. "China's Telecommunication Market for International Investors: Opportunities, Challenges and Strategies," *Technology in Society* (27:1), 2005, pp. 105-121.

Chen, K. "China Will Keep Pursuing Digital Standards," *Wall Street Journal,* April 23, 2004, p. B1

Digi163. "National WAPI Wireless Technology Rules May be Included into IEEE Regulations," (in Chinese), 2004 (available online at http://www.DiGi163.com/2004/4-25/84810.html; (accessed October 29, 2004)

Doolin, B., and Lowe, A. "The Reveal Is to Critique: Actor-Network Theory and Critical Information Systems Research," *Journal of Information Technology* (17), 2002, pp. 69-78.

Fang, H. D., Pan, H. H., and Fu, Z. "The Many Pressures of WAPI Standard: Can China Take Them?" (in Chinese), 2004 (available online at http://price.zol.com.cn/article/2004/0428/95632.shtml; accessed October 30, 2004).

Fomin, V., and Keil, T. "Standardization: Bridging the Gap Between Economic and Social Theory," in *Proceedings of the 21ˢᵗ International Conference on Information Systems*, W. J. Orlikowski, S. Ang, P. Weill, H. C. Krcmar, and J. I. DeGross (Eds.), Brisbane, Australia, 2000, pp. 206-217.

Fordahl, M. "Intel Won't Comply with Chinese Wireless Standards," *Information Week*, March 11, 2004 (available online at http://www.informationweek.com/story/showArticle.jhtml?articleID=18311987; accessed October 30, 2004).

Geier, J. "802.11 WEP: Concepts and Vulnerability," Internet.Com Tutorials, June 20, 2002 (available online at http://www.WiFiplanet.com/tutorials/article.php/1368661; accessed December 1, 2004).

Hanseth, O., Aanestad, M., and Berg, M. "Actor-network Theory and Information Systems: What's So Special?," *Information Technology and People* (17:2), 2004, pp. 116-122.

Hanseth, O., and Monteiro, E. "Inscribing Behavior in Information Infrastructure Standards," *Accounting, Management, and Information Technology* (7:4), 1997, pp. 183-211.

Hanseth, O., Monteiro, E., and Hatling, M. "Developing Information Infrastructure: The Tension between Standardization and Flexibility, *Science, Technology, and Human Values* (21:4), 1996, pp. 407-426.

Hoo, S. "China Seeks to Develop its Own High-Tech Standards," *Information Week*, May 24, 2004 (available online at http://www.informationweek.com/story/showArticle.jhtml?articleID=20900553; (accessed October 27, 2004).

Kanellos, M. "Divide between U.S. Tech Firms, China—A Great Wall?," News.Com, March 19, 2004 (available online at http://news.com.com/Divide+between+U.S.+tech+firms,+China--a+great+wall/2100-1006_3-5175837.html; accessed April 25, 2005).

Lemon, S. "Despite Shelving WAPI, China Stands Firm on Chip Tax," InfoWorld.com, April 22, 2004 (available online at http://www.infoworld.com/article/04/04/22/HNshelvingwapi_1.html; accessed April 25, 2005).

McCulloch, G. *Documentary Research in Education, History and the Social Sciences*, London: Routledge Falmer, 2004.

Reuters. "US Has No Plan for WTO Case on China WiFi Rules," February 19, 2004, cited in . R. Suttmeier and X. Yao, "China's Post-WTO Technology Policy: Standards, Software and the Changing Nature of Techno-Nationalism," *The National Bureau of Asian Research: Special Report*, Number 7, May 2004.

Schmidt, S. K., and Werle, R. "The Development of Compatibility Standards in Tele-communications: Conceptual Framework and Theoretical Perspective," in *New Technology at the Outset: Social Forces in the Shaping of Technological Innovations*, M. Dierkes and U. Hoffman (Ed.), New York: Campus Verlag, 1992, pp. 301-326.

Standardization Administrative Commission of China. "Using Standardization to Protect and Promote Development of China's National Industry" (in Chinese; available online at http://www.sac.gov.cn/articles/1351.htm; accessed November 23, 2001).

Standardization Administrative Commission of China. "China's Technology Standards Development Strategy Research: Final Report (Consultation Draft)" (in Chinese; available online at http://www.sac.gov.cn/news/general/4136_1.doc; accessed October 30, 2004).

Suttmeier, R., and Yao, X. "China's Post-WTO Technology Policy: Standards, Software and the Changing Nature of Techno-Nationalism," *The National Bureau of Asian Research: Special Report,* Number 7, May 2004.

Tatnall, A., and Gilding, A. "Actor-Network Theory and Information Systems Research." in *Proceedings of the 10ᵗʰ Australasian Conference on Information Systems*, B. Hope and P. Yoong (Eds.), School of Communication and Information Management, Victoria University of Wellington, Wellington, New Zealand, 1999, pp. 955-966.

Walsham, G. "Actor-Network Theory and IS Research: Current Status and Future Prospects," in *Information Systems and Qualitative Research*, A. S. Lee, J. Liebenau, and J. I. DeGross (Eds.), London: Chapman & Hall, 1997, pp. 466-480.

Walsham, G., and Sahay, S. "GIS for District-Level Administration in India: Problems and Opportunities," *MIS Quarterly* (23:1), 1999, pp. 39-65.

Weiss, M., and Cargill, C. "Consortia in the Standards Development Process," *Journal of the American Society for Information Science* (43:8), 1992, pp. 559-565.

Yang, H., Yoo, Y., Lyytinen, K., and Ahn, J. "Diffusion of Broadband Mobile Services in Korea: The Role of Standards and its Impact on Diffusion of Complex Technology System," unpublished paper, 2003 (available online at http://weatherhead.cwru.edu/pervasive/Paper/UBE%202003%20-%20Yoo.pdf; accessed January 11, 2005).

Zhu, D. "Wireless Authentication and Privacy Infrastructure Protocol (WAPI) Specification," Sun Tzu International, LLC, 2004(available online at http://www.suntzureport.com/wapi/wapi.pdf; accessed January 11, 2005).

ABOUT THE AUTHORS

Shirley Chan started her career as a lawyer specializing in information technology law and moved into information management. She is a senior research associate at the University of Hong Kong Business School and a management consultant to a company within the Swire Group, Cathay Pacific's major shareholder. She graduated from Hong Kong, Harvard, and Victoria Universities, and has published in various international business journals. Shirley can be reached at shirley.chan@lycos.com.

Heejin Lee is a senior lecturer in the Department of Information Systems at the University of Melbourne. He earned his doctorate from the London School of Economics. His research interests include broadband and mobile Internet, time/space and IT, and IT/IS in developing countries. He has published several papers on broadband and temporal aspects of IT in leading international journals. Heejin can be reached at heejin@unimelb.edu.au.

Sangjo Oh is an associate professor of Electronic Commerce, Dongyang Technical College, Korea. He earned his master and doctoral degrees from Seoul National University. His research interests are on the role of social constructs in the implementation, diffusion, and success of e-Business and e-Government. Sangjo can be reached at secase@dongyang.ac.kr.

23   ORDINARY INNOVATION OF MOBILE SERVICES

Steinar Kristoffersen
Petter Nielsen
Jennifer Blechar
Ole Hanseth
University of Oslo
Oslo, Norway

Abstract　　*The anabolic growth of dot.com—with third-generation network license auctions as the grand finale—implied a series of large investments in mobile technology. Without new products and services utilizing this infrastructure (m-services), however, these investments may never be recouped, and today there is no sure sign of demand for these new nomadic applications in the market. This paper shows how actors in the m-services value network coordinate their efforts to bring such applications to the marketplace. It shows their risk averse and locally optimizing strategies, which theoretically are very different from the current fascination in Information Systems with **disruptive** innovation. This paper illustrates the need for a theory of ordinary innovation in nomadic and ubiquitous computing.*

1   INTRODUCTION

The adoption of mobile services seems to be fading in the Scandinavian countries. This is not due to a lack of interest in mobile devices, however. Although some markets are almost completely saturated with respect to mobile phones (96 percent ownership in Norway[1]), there is still growth in hardware sales. For example, Norway and Sweden, currently among the most mature markets in this respect, saw a 25 percent increase in sales last year alone.

---

[1]First half of the year 2004, as reported by the Norwegian Postal and Telecommunication Authority.

Network traffic is also increasing, with Sweden, Norway, and Denmark showing a 10 to 20 percent growth in mobile-originated voice traffic time. However, the operators' revenue in Sweden decreased by 2 percent,[2] probably due to increased competition. According to analysts, new services will be required in order to secure growth and justify investments in next-generation mobile telephony[3] (Vincent 2001).

Next-generation mobile telephony is very much a product of the expansive business conjunctures toward the end of the 1990s.[4] This period was characterized by its orientation toward radical innovation and technologies (typically Internet-based), which would (it was claimed) radically change the industrial landscape which they entered.[5] For instance, one of the companies which we are currently studying was at one point devoted to developing "a revolutionary system that provides the user with easily understandable travel assistance before and during a journey." Its ambitions included

- Stunning use of 2D and 3D
- Cutting-edge technology and methodology
- Unique visualization
- Multi-resolution image representation

This type of rhetoric was not conflated by the burst of the dot.com bubble, however. The aim of most projects back then was to create radically new functionality on top of an infrastructure (the Internet) that had taken on almost mythological proportions, and of which it was though no one could really envisage its limitations. This line of attack it seems, has become reified as the definition of *innovation* as such. Indeed, many programs offering innovation studies and training in entrepreneurship are preoccupied with the idea of a start-up, unique ideas, and the hard work of a dedicated, enthusiastic team.[6]

Within academia as well, and perhaps most coherently building on the framework of disruptive innovation as proposed by Christensen (1997), there has been lot of interest for this category of innovative processes. In this perspective, *disruptive* technologies are described as creating entirely new markets through new technology. This technology might initially be underperforming compared to *sustaining* technologies which are meeting the needs of the biggest, most profitable customers. However, it serves the need of a fringe segment of customers who would otherwise not be able to enjoy this functionality (it might, for example, simply be cheaper or offer less mainstream, but still critical functionality for some). When technology development catches up with customer requirements (and, simplistically, Moore's law implicates that it will), then it is too late for the incumbent to become competitive: The industrial landscape has changed.

---

[2]See http://www.digi.no/php/art.php?id=114473.

[3]See http://www.digi.no/php/art.php?id=113043.

[4]See http://wirelessreview.com/mag/wireless_grief_dotcom_era/.

[5]Insofar as we know, there have not been any systematic studies of the dot.com rhetoric as such. However, many good examples exist (see http://www.funkybusiness.com/funky/).

[6]See http://www.grunderskolen.no, for example, or http://www.hbs.edu/entrepreneurship/bplan/findteam.html, where the business plan contest is a particularly good illustration.

In some of this literature, not only does it become apparent that disruptive innovation is a laudable objective, inasmuch as the alternative outcome is extinction (Christensen 1997), but it is also one for which normative or at least methodological steps can be taken (Christensen and Overdorf 2000; Cosier and Hughes 2001; Kostoff et al. 2004; Thomond et al. 2003).

Although we are not, in this paper, going to argue strongly against the perspective outlined above, we wish to present an empirical framework that as a supplement can help us better understand, on a more detailed level, the transformations in the tele-communications market as they unfold over time as well as on a day-to-day basis.

Currently, mobile services show modest uptake and high price sensitivity. However, such services are embedded in a complex and not completely open infra-structure; there is fundamentally a high threshold for content providers wanting to come out into the marketplace with new services. They need access agreements with operators. They need a mechanism for billing,, and the medium itself is not used widely enough for it to be useful as a marketing platform; content providers have to market their products in other (and more expensive) channels such as magazines in order for consumers to become aware of the services. Additionally, consumers are still quite demanding and competition is tough. For service providers and developers, therefore, the risk is high. This is a situation in which actors have to coordinate their work finely and with a perspective of reducing risk, or they might end up in bankruptcy.

One of the biggest challenges in this emerging industry is to develop efficient and reasonable value chains. Making and managing value chains can be seen as coordina-ting business models and practices. Therefore, this paper will explore the ways in which coordination, which we find of primary importance, takes place between actors in the mobile service network in Norway. Three case studies, representing a content provider, a content aggregator, and the network operators, will be presented and discussed.

The next section of this paper will briefly discuss existing theories used in the mobile telecommunications arena. This will be followed by an overview of the three cases. The results of the case studies will then be presented through the discussion followed by the conclusion.

2 RELATED RESEARCH

There have been a number of studies carried out on m-business from various perspectives over the last several years. Telecommunications was (and is) an integral component of the promise of exponential growth of industrial activity and wealth that was made by the "new economy." Clearly, these promises were overly optimistic, but even though developments in this sector have fallen somewhat short of expectations, we are still witnessing a tremendous technological advancement in wireless networks and mobile technologies. Thus, this area has generated renewed interest in the research field.

Some of this recent research is oriented toward analyzing industrial developments in the telecommunications industry and the emerging business relationships on a macro-level. For example, Lyytinen and King (2002) describe an innovation framework for the wireless industry. Their model of the *innovation system*, the *market*, and the *regulatory regime* has been adopted in studies of the mobile arena in different regions (see Yang et al. 2003; Fomin et al. 2004). Although this model is useful in pointing to essential interactions and relationships, in our cases we found an opportunity of delving into the same aspects on a more detailed, observable level.

Other work has been carried out within the same general tradition, but at a lower level of detail. For instance, Camponovo and Pigneur (2002) and Mylonopoulos et al. et al. (2002) focus specifically on an exploration of the various actors involved in the m-business arena to provide insight into changing roles and relationships in this market. While work such as this has been useful to provide general guidance to the structure and composition of the mobile services arena, most contributions are primarily conceptual, rather than empirical. We believe that empirical contributions are warranted as well, and that they are indeed a necessary prelude to developing a coherent theory of this emerging domain.

3   MOBILE SERVICES IN NORWAY

We now turn to our cases: The Norwegian mobile network operators' (NetCom and Telenor) *CPA* (content provider access) platform, *MultimediaContent.com*'s[7] mobile content distribution, and *mPay's* mobile payment solution. Briefly, the CPA is a set of services that gives content providers access to the SMSC[8]-based infrastructure of the telecommunications network, as well as the billing services that make it possible (in a cost-effectiveness perspective, at least) to charge users for low-cost services. MultimediaContent.com is a content aggregator. Primarily, the services that they provide are

- managing suites of content (games, ring tones, logos) for mobile portals
- marketing to end-users as well as operators
- testing content for various handsets

mPay is both a content provider and a payment solution, providing a content service allowing users to pay for parking using their mobile phones and (in the future) a mobile payment solution service to content owners/aggregators. A simple view of our cases, then, is that they include a content provider (mPay), a content aggregator (MultimediaContent.com), and the operators (Telenor and NetCom).

Data was collected from our cases through a variety of qualitative methods. Related to the implementation and operation of CPA, a total of 39 formal interviews were conducted with managers, designers, and system developers in a total of 23 different organizations. Interviews were recorded and fully transcribed and included the network operators as well as the largest aggregators and content providers. The field site selected was thus not one organization, but rather a business sector with a range of actors which together provide the necessary resources, competencies and components to make up the

---

[7]Names have been changed for anonymity.
[8]Short message service center.

platform. For the mPay case, several in-depth interviews were conducted with the founder and an employee in the organization. These were recorded and partially transcribed. Other informal discussions also took place and the data presented in this paper related to this case was reviewed and confirmed by the founder of the organization. For MultimediaContent.com, data was collected in semi-structured interviews with three managers, plus document studies facilitated by a project database covering the period from 1999 up to present activities.

The technical infrastructure upon which this value chain is configured is SMS-based. Customers request content using SMS, and receive (to their handset) a SMS or a push-WAP message. The handset deals with the message either by displaying content directly, or fetching it across GPRS from a URL embedded in the message. The crux of the wider business infrastructure will have to be found at the interplay and coordination of and between such actors, and we will present that next.

3.1 The CPA Platform

In 1997, the two Norwegian mobile phone network operators (NetCom and Telenor) launched platforms for exclusive content and utility-based SMS services for their respective mobile subscribers. Both attempts, however, suffered from only being a part of a "value adding services" offering and thus receiving limited internal resources either for investments in technology or investing in content. While these platforms generated very limited traffic, the network operators came to understand that external third parties, had the initiative, time, and resources to develop new service concepts. In addition, they appeared to be better equipped to know which services would be accepted by the market; how to market and price them correctly; and able to associate their brand with a wider variety of services than the network operators. Actors such as media windows, including newspapers, magazines, and TV broadcasters, also demonstrated their ability to provide relatively inexpensive marketing space for their own SMS services. At the same time, these external actors were pushing for market-wide access to subscribers.

To meet this situation, the mobile phone network operators launched the public content provider access (CPA) platform in 1999. While internal initiatives were taken by the network operators, proactive external actors played an important role in pushing the operators to introduce the platform. Their role in propelling the development of the platform has continued with application houses bringing together the network operators to develop service concepts such as interactive TV shows. The CPA platform enables external content providers to provide SMS services in a transparent manner, and charge subscribers for those services through the basic SMS structure (currently 0.15€ to 8€). Thus, the operators did not choose to compete on *differentiation* of services exclusively provided in one of the networks (as they previously had), but, on the contrary, pursued an "open garden" approach to increase the size of the total market. The typical content provided over the CPA platform comprises yellow pages, ring tones and logos, TV interactivity (voting and chat), games, news, stock quotes, weather information, traffic information, horoscopes, jokes, etc. Today, this is the basis for an economically sustainable business with a total annual turnover of approx 1 billion NOK (125 million €) in 2004, a substantial growth from 600 million NOK in 2003.

Content acquisition is initiated by subscribers requesting content by sending an SMS (short message service) to certain short numbers (e.g., 1999). The SMS is processed by the message center (SMSC) of the network operator and forwarded to the respective content provider by the CPA platform. Content providers have agreements (with similar request numbers and rating classes) with both network operators, making the platforms and the network operators transparent for the subscribers. The content provider returns the content to the subscriber via the CPA platform, and the cost which the subscriber is to be charged (on the regular phone bill) is specified with a rating class. Based on this, a billing request is sent by the CPA platform to the billing system of the respective operator. The revenue generated is basically shared between the network operator and the content provider as per an agreed (and standardized) revenue-sharing model (respectively 30/70).

The technical implementations of the CPA platforms by the network operators have been simple (both implementations were originally based on the previous platforms with additional open interfaces), at least partly as a result of these services still being considered value adding. At the same time, because of the network operators' legacies of message centers and billing systems in addition to the competition among them, close coordination such as standardizing the CPA interfaces for content providers have not been feasible. These different interfaces are creating a higher entry cost for new content providers; however, both integrators and aggregators provide support. While the integrators provide applications that deliver one common interface for the platforms, the aggregators further provide access to a short number and handle the administrative interaction with the network operators.

In Table 1, a comprehensive picture of the value chain is drawn with roles and tasks. While the different roles appear as independent, several actors may play several roles. For example, large aggregators collecting content from several content producers as well as content providers commonly also act as content providers, application houses and integrators. Some media windows, such as media houses and TV broadcasters, typically capitalize on their content as well as their media window for marketing purposes.

Table 1. Roles and Tasks Within CPA

Roles	Tasks
Content producer	Content production
Content provider	Content production, service innovation
Aggregator	Service innovation, content aggregation
Application house	Service innovation
Integrator	Providing common interfaces to CPA platforms
Network operator	Transportation, billing
Media window	Marketing
Subscriber	Consume content services

Guidelines related to the services that can be provided, how they are marketed, and how the subscribers are treated have been important for avoiding behavior that may jeopardize the market created by the CPA platform. However, coordinated guidelines were not formalized and introduced until late 2004 (based on regulations and discussions with the Norwegian Competition Authority, the Consumer Ombudsman, and the Data Inspectorate). Up until then, the majority of content providers were cautious not to bring the platform too much attention from the media and the authorities. Provision of content services for fixed line phones in Norway are strictly regulated when it comes to content, for pricing as well as revenue sharing models. The risk of the introduction of a similar regulations for the CPA platform made content providers and network operators even more eager to avoid misuse and media attention.

The network operators' delegation of the responsibility of developing new service concepts and bringing them to the market to external actors has been successful in the sense of increased traffic and a much broader service offering. The CPA platform is not a detached platform provided by a network operator, but appears more like an assemblage of a range of different actors with their respective initiatives, investments, and technical components. On the one hand, the network operators have arranged a highly favorable revenue sharing model while still being in control of the value chain. At the same time, they are farming out the responsibility for further technical development to actors such as application houses, leaving *them* with marginal expenses. On the other hand, many smaller actors take responsibility for developing new services and service concepts. They receive limited revenues as, in the worst case, they must share with several other actors (content producers, content providers, aggregators, application houses, integrators, and media windows). Primarily having only a handful of employees, they are also usually opportunity-based in the sense that they are narrowly focused on developing trendy services and selling for the moment. They are thus neither very well equipped and nor primarily focused on introducing new service concepts. As long as CPA is the only alternative for providing this type of content services, the services will have to conform to its business model and the kind of services it supports.

3.2 Mobile Content Distribution

Multimedia.com is an independent provider of mobile games and marketing applications. They started out in 1993 as a small start-up with grand ambitions and only two owners, both of whom were employees. Today the company has around 120 shareholders. Early in the 1990s, the focus was on Internet technology, games, and direct (demographically based) marketing and animation. Eventually Multimedia.com turned toward the mobile market in 1998-1999 and started working on algorithms that made 3D-animation on mobile phones possible via very limited bandwidth. This culminated in several successful demonstrations in collaboration with Ericsson (at industry shows such as Telecom 1999, CeBit 2000, GSM 2000).

Unfortunately, the market for such applications never really came about, and the company has been struggling since 2000 with finding a value proposition that customers (mainly operators) would find attractive. They have ended up producing and deploying consumer-oriented content to mobile phones: logos, ring tones, and games. This activity mainly takes place in the subsidiary MultimediaContent.com Ltd, which has distribution agreements with several operators and "storefronts" on the Web worldwide. Over 100 content providers have entered into signed agreements with MultimediaContent.com and they have also signed an exclusive 5 year commercial agreement with one of the larger divisions of a Chinese operator to provide premium SMS and data services. MultimediaContent.com has developed a technology-independent platform for mobile content management, provisioning, and distribution, based on experiences from another subsidiary of Multimedia.com, DigitalMobility.com.

Distributing content to mobile terminals is based on SMS and WAP. SMS is the carrier for requests. WAP is the application protocol. The application server (which is, for all practical purposes, a virtual machine that makes its applications available on the Internet via an interface that wraps simple data types in XML) creates on request (received via an SMS gateway, for instance) a push access protocol (PAP) message which is then sent to the WAP push-enabled mobile telephone across SMS. The technical coordination, thus, is quite simple: The users send an SMS to the operator with the name of the item they want. The operator's CPA platform (or equivalent) recognizes the number, associates that with a content provider, and queries their MultimediaContent.com platform (or equivalent) for the URL for that particular item. The application server gets the URL and produces a PAP which it sends to the push proxy/mobile gateway. From there it goes to the user's phone, which fetches the content using WAP with SMS or GPRS as a bearer.

The technology involved is really simple, but the business is risky. No one knows in advance exactly which applications (ring tones, games, logos, etc.) will bring in enough money to defend development costs (and recover sunk costs for failed attempts). When the first-movers successfully established themselves in this business, the costs of development were lower; there was less competition and the consumers were not so demanding. Now, one must look at the coordination between actors in this setting from different angles, for example, as parts of a political and tactical positioning toward a more mature market. The parties need to do practical knowledge management since they are not at all self-contained with regards to the competencies required to implement an end-to-end service. They need to implement risk management (and risk sharing) strategies, since succeeding with a end-to-end service requires a much greater investment than what each party could afford individually (given that they do not know in advance what exactly will become a "hit" in the market). Therefore, coordination in the commercial aspects of this case is a lot more involved. *It does the work of orchestrating many small contributions into a larger offering that the market, in total, just might end up paying enough to justify the expense.* The roles of the various actors involved and their tasks are summarized in Table 2.

The roles presented in Table 2 overlap nicely with the requirements of consumer content for the impulsive, highly mobile customer: The storefronts market content by building a strong brand name; they subscribe to content from aggregators who take the responsibility of testing the content for all the handsets supported by an operator in an area. Developers need aggregators in order to handle internationalization and testing for them. Operators are "bit-pipe-carriers," plus they can do the billing effectively. Web hotels have an established role. It is probably not critical, but since most of these actors are small (typically 2 to 20 employees, which is already more than they can defend in terms of cash-flow), they would probably not be willing to try to handle hosting themselves for such small volumes of traffic.

Table 2. Roles and Tasks in Mobile Content Provisioning

Roles	Tasks
Game developer	Conceptualizing, implementing and carrying out programming projects which produce games, typically for the J2ME platform.
Content provider	Managing rights and technical adaptation of content for various platforms, such as ring tones, logos, etc.
Aggregator	MultimediaContent.com's role. The most important task is to compile a set of appealing services and introduce them to storefronts, i.e., Web portals. They also test content for the relevant mobile phones in the market. The aggregator pays the developers.
Storefront	This is the media window that the consumer sees, e.g., on the web, which brand and present a collection of content (from various or only one aggregator) in their market.
Network operator	The owner of the technical infrastructure makes sure that there is capacity and capabilities in the network to deal with the requests and the traffic. Moreover, in the mobile telecommunications industry, this is the "owner" of the customer and, thus, the role that can cost-effectively perform billing.
Web hotel	Stores the data. Any data. The telephone will fetch content here given the URL received.

To summarize, Multimedia.com started out trying to invent and introduce revolutionary and disruptive technologies. However, they seem to have ended up in a more modest "Kirznerian" role of an entrepreneur that promotes equilibrium within the existing system as they "discover gaps, increase the knowledge about the situation and reduce the general level of uncertainty" (Hultén and Mölleryd 2000). Multimedia.com's subsidiary MultimediaContent.com makes it possible for small developers to take great risks by introducing their content together with a critical mass of others into a market that has a limited albeit smoothly coordinated business model.

3.3 mPay

mPay is a mobile payment solution developed in 2001, owned by Scangit AS in Norway. Currently this organization offers primarily a parking payment service, and has service agreements with private and public parking organizations in Norway such as EuroPark, P-Compagniet, the city of Oslo, and other municipalities around the capital. The concept for this service is that customers are able to use their mobile phone in order to pay for or extend parking rather than using coins in the parking meter. The motivation for people to use the service is the convenience of not having to find coins and the ability to pay for the exact amount of parking used (no overpaying and no forgetting about the parking meter). While the mobile payment service is today offered only for parking, mPay hopes to expand their payment solution to other products and to other content providers in the future. Thus, mPay can be considered both a payment solution service and a content provider.

In order to use the mPay service, customers need to register via the Internet, entering their personal data including their credit card information for payment. This information is all stored by mPay. Once the customer is registered, they are able to use the service by sending an SMS message through their mobile phone. Payment for the services initiated by the customer is managed by mPay and performed in cooperation with major credit card banking institutions including Teller (formerly Visa Norway), Euroconex, and Nordea. Once the customer sends an SMS message to pay for the product (parking), the message is transferred through to mPay, who matches the message with the registered customer information. This customer information, including the billing information, is then transferred to the banking institution on a regular basis for payment for the service. Thus, mPay is essentially a payment solution service that acts as an intermediary between the customers, (potentially) other content providers, and the banking institutions, carrying none of the risk associated with the transaction.

mPay originated through cooperation with EMT, Estonia and, as a content provider for parking services, currently has only one main competitor in Norway: EasyPark. EasyPark was established in 1998 and is the current leader for mobile parking payment in Norway with approximately 12,500 customers. Both mPay and EasyPark afford customers the ability to pay for parking services through various means, including via major credit cards, such as Visa or MasterCard. While mobile payment for content via credit cards is not a unique situation in Norway and other services exist which also provide such capabilities, the mPay model is of interest as it offers the ability to establish payment for content via a channel not necessarily under the control of the network operators, as is the case for most services and models currently available in Norway. One of the few exceptions is the "electronic wallet" type of service such as Payex, which resembles the mPay model as it provides customers a payment option other than one closely associated with the mobile network operators. The main difference is that Payex primarily requires consumers to "fill up" their account prior to being able to purchase content whereas mPay debits or charges purchases directly to the credit or debit card as content is purchased.

As a payment solution service, mPay has become another actor in the overall m-services value chain and hopes to offer a new alternative to content providers often frustrated with the CPA model described above. However, as a new actor, the roles and responsibilities of the various players in the value chain have shifted slightly where some tasks previously managed by the mobile operators, such as managing customer information or billing, are now managed by mPay (see Table 3). Just as in the CPA case, actors in this value chain may play several roles. For example, with mPay providing payment for parking services, it is playing the role of a content provider as well as payment intermediary.

Once the consumer is registered for the mPay service, mPay manages this customer information and the billing for content consumed. Actual billing for this content is handled through regular Visa, MasterCard, etc. bills by the respective banking institutions as described above. Thus, one of the major changes in the mPay model versus the CPA model is the control of customer information and billing. In addition, because mPay essentially manages contact between customers, parking institutions

Table 3. Roles and Tasks in mPay

Roles	Tasks
Network operator	Provide infrastructure and network
Content owner	Own content, agree content availability to market
Content provider	Provide content services to market, manage agreements with content owners
mPay	Manage billing for content consumed; manage agreements with content providers and banking institutions. Manage all customer information
Banking institutions	Provide billing for content consumed, manage payments
Consumer	Consume content services, register as mPay customer

(content owners) and banking institutions, the key to the mPay service model rests primarily on coordination and agreements, many of which were established and are managed through informal networks by the founder of the service. These informal channels have been a key to the initiation of the mPay service and its original success in the market

4 DISCUSSION

We can now explore the activities and the interdependencies between the cases while also investigating possible simultaneity constraints and eventual outsourcing of responsibilities and work. This will, of course, be greatly simplified but perhaps it can point in the direction of general trends in this market or to areas in which a future theoretical framework could be used.

In each of the cases, the activities and goals of the actors converge at a general level and can be discussed in relation to the coordination of processes surrounding content acquisition and distribution. For example, in establishing the CPA model, the primary goal for the network operators seems to have been to provide a channel for content owners to sell and distribute content (and thus generate network traffic) without giving up control of the physical infrastructure or the customer relationships they currently have. Thus, the CPA model is a win-win for the network operators as it requires little effort on their part while they gain revenue in the form of revenue sharing from content sold, increased network traffic, and increased potential customer support. The mPay model, on the other hand, can be viewed as one competing solution to this CPA model as mPay hopes to establish a relationship with customers themselves and to manage billing information, etc. such that they can offer content providers another option for the billing of content. Finally, MultimediaContent.com is essentially a content aggregator with the objective of compiling a sufficiently interesting set of services into one packaged offering, and then make a profit from brokering these services.

Coordination of these activities takes place through standardized agreements and interfaces: The CPA is a "one-size-fits-all" contract with entrance costs that also serve as a threshold for small, independent content providers. Instead, operators want aggregators to deal with the content providers. The operators channel traffic through to the storefronts, which return input and the price to be charged, and accordingly initialize billing. Apart from that, operators (automatically) generate SMS and WAP push-messages through their infrastructure and all they see are SMS messages and URLs. Aggregators make sure that the content is tested and they take money from the storefronts, which they split between themselves and the content providers. Again, this is regulated by a standardized contract (in the MultimediaContent.com case). Similarly, mPay mediates a standard contract between the customer and the banking institution. Basically, they are virtual machines that imprint the voucher and send an electronic copy to the credit card company.

Looking at these three cases together, it becomes clear that a lot of the coordination work that is carried out aims at reducing risk and minimizing variable expenses for each of the actors. For example, mPay's role as an intermediary allows them to offer content without carrying any risk associated with the transaction, leaving this responsibility to the banking institutions. Similarly, the CPA model essentially alleviates the operators from any risk associated with unfavorable or illegal content by positioning this task with the content aggregators. At a general level, this is a strategy of optimizing locally, and it is not really representative of tremendously innovative or disruptive technologies. This is perhaps the single most interesting point that can be identified from our fieldwork: There are no disruptive technologies at play, and this is certainly something worth looking more keenly at in future research. For instance, Multimedia.com, as a typical dot.com company with highly disruptive ambition ended up (finally) being successful at making a modest profit from locally optimizing one existing step of the value network in telecom, rather than revolutionizing it.

What, then, is the effect of this local optimization? We think that the question should be turned around: *What is the reason that we see such local (rather than systemic) optimization?* Given that most of the current services offered today are rather lightweight and carefree entertainment services, which are bought by the customer in a spur-of-the-moment impulsive transaction, the cost of building, marketing, and billing is rather out of proportion with the actual price that one can expect the user to be willing to pay. Building an innovation infrastructure on top of which new businesses and truly innovative application ideas can be deployed is a tremendous challenge, which we will continue to address in our research. And while the network operators have created new business for content providers by implementing CPA platforms according to a open garden philosophy, the platforms implemented are only minor extensions of their existing infrastructure and the network operators' control over the value chain is far from being challenged and deconstructed into a value network.

Within these cases, the interdependencies are evident, much of it related to the outsourcing of various tasks and processes. For example, MultimediaContent.com outsources the hosting of content, either back to the storefront or to a Web hotel. This is not an ideological choice; instead, it is rather pragmatic. The mother company has a lot of competencies in this area but they are all located abroad, in a country with is limited and unreliable Internet capacity. Perhaps the most important resource in the emerging market of mobile services is the presentation of services in the context of marketing. In order for customers to impulsively buy indifferent content, such as ring tones, logos, and games, the marketing has to be aggressive and strong. Therefore, such a simple resource as the common short number (e.g., 1999) for services across operators is a valuable resource. For the content providers, access to the validated customer database and the factoring services of the operators or credit card companies is a valuable resource. The CPA provides the necessary mechanism for preparing and pushing the WAP messages with content or URLs to the handsets.

Coordination in this emerging industry seems to be mainly about managing loose interdependencies in a nonlinear value chain of actors. They are not concerned with traditional manufacturing challenges of optimizing their production lines, or even working together toward a common goal. Nor are they (as in the alternative dot.com-conception of the telecommunication industry) concerned with crafting an entirely new economy that will revolutionize large parts of society. The reality seems to be rather in the middle. Actors coordinate their efforts so that they can hedge their value propositions by creating critical mass and sharing risk related to development and marketing. Thus, they can secure a minimal cash-flow and, simply, keep going.

5   CONCLUSION

Over the past decade, we have seen tremendous growth in the telecommunications sector. However, growth has not been uniform. Vendors still see increasing sales of new devices. A lot of it is marketed by promises made about appealing new services that will be made possible by the next-generation technology. These promises, however, remain primarily unfulfilled. Starting to uncover why this is the case and putting ourselves in a position from which remedies may be proposed, we have analyzed one excerpt from the value chain of this industry. Although, at this stage, chiefly descriptive in nature, our research aims to create a constructive intellectual platform.

Our ambition is to move on with more in-depth studies of this field. It should be guided by a clearly defined knowledge interest, which in part has been inspired by the findings of this paper: Why do actors only *successfully* engage in *limited* exploitation of next-generation nomadic computing? Why are there such a limited number of new applications being developed and, to the extent that they are, why is the end-user adoption so modest? The contribution and development of theoretical frameworks play an important part in understanding this picture. Good analytical mechanisms may help us understand how the field is unfolding; they provide useful concepts and predict change. However, empirical studies such as those presented in this paper are a necessary platform for such work in the next instance.

REFERENCES

Camponovo, G., and Pigneur, Y. "Analyzing the Actor Game in m-Business," in *Proceedings of the First International Conference on Mobile Business*, N. A. Mylonopoulos (Ed.), Athens, Greece, 2002 (available online at http://www.mobiforum.org/proceedings/papers/01/1.1.pdf.

Christensen, C. M. *The Innovator's Dilemma: When New Technologies Cause Great Firms to Fail*, Boston: Harvard Business School Press, 1997.
Christensen, C. M., and Overdorf, M. "Meeting the Challenge of Disruptive Change," *Harvard Business Review*, March-April 2000, pp. 67-76.
Cosier, G., and Hughes, P. M. "The Problem with Disruption," *BT Technology Journal* (19:4), October 2001, pp. 9-14.
Fomin, V. V., Gao, P., and Damsgaard, J. "The Role of Standards and its Impact on the Diffusion of 3G Wireless Mobile Services," in *Proceedings of the European Academy for Standardization: 9th EURAS Workshop on Standardization*, F. Bousquet, Y. Buntzly, H. Coenen, and K. Jakobs (Eds.), Paris, May 13-14, 2004, pp. 97-104.
Hultén, S., and Mölleryd, B. "Entrepreneurs, Innovations and Market Processes in the Evolution of the Swedish Mobile Telecommunications Industry," paper presented at the Eighth International Joseph A. Schumpeter Society Conference, Manchester, UK, June 28-July 1, 2000.
Kostoff, R. N., Boylan, R., and Simons, G. R. "Disruptive Technology Roadmaps," *Technological Forecasting and Social Change* (71), 2004, pp. 141-159.
Lyytinen, K., and King, J. L. "Around the Cradle of the Wireless Revolution: The Emergence and Evolution of Cellular Telephony," *Telecommunications Policy* (26:2), 2002, pp. 97-100.
Mylonopoulos, N., Sideris, I., Fouskas, K., and Pateli, A. "Emerging Market Dynamics in the Mobile Services Industry," White Paper WHP-2002-01, MobiCom Consortium, 2002 (available online at http://www.mobiforum.org/cgi-bin/mobi/mobi.cgi).
Thomond, P., Herzberg, T., and Lettice, F. "Disruptive Innovation: Removing the Innovators' Dilemma. Knowledge," paper presented at the British Academy of Management Annual Conference, Harrogate, UK, September 2003.
Yang, H., Yoo, Y., Lyytinen, K., and Ahn, J-H. "Diffusion of Broadband Mobile Services in Korea: The Role of Standards and its Impact on Diffusion of Complex Technology System," paper presented at the Workshop on Ubiquitous Computing Environment, Cleveland, Ohio, October 24-26, 2003.
Vincent, G. "Learning from i-Mode," *IEEE Review* (47:6), 2001, pp. 13-18.

ABOUT THE AUTHORS

Steinar Kristoffersen is a post-doctoral research fellow with the Department of Informatics at the University of Oslo, holding a Ph.D. from Lancaster University, UK. He worked as a consultant in mobile applications development for 5 years before returning to do academic research. Before that, he was a research director at the Norwegian Computing Centre. His current areas of research include infrastructures, innovation and methods; architectures for mobile IT, computer-supported cooperative work (CSCW), and human-computer interaction (HCI). Steinar can be reached at steinkri@ifi.uio.no.

Petter Nielsen is a Ph.D. candidate at the Department of Informatics at the University of Oslo. His research interests are related to strategies for designing services for mobile devices. He is currently engaged in empirical research related to the emergence of new content services and telecommunication platforms, seen as a result of convergence between telecommunication and information technology, both locally and on a global scale. Petter can be reached at pnielsen@ifi.uio.no.

Jennifer Blechar holds an MSc in Analysis, Design and Management of Information Systems from the London School of Economics and Political Science, UK, and a BA in Mathematics from Bryn Mawr College, USA. She is currently a Ph.D. candidate and research fellow with the Department of Informatics at the University of Oslo, Norway, and has several years experience as a consultant within the telecommunications field. Her research interests involve the design, implementation and diffusion of high value content services in the mobile industry. Jennifer can be reached at jennifjb@ifi.uio.no.

Ole Hanseth (http://heim.ifi.uio.no/~oleha) is Professor at the Department of Informatics at the University of Oslo. He worked for a number of years within applied research and business until he moved back to academia in 1997. His main research interests are related to large scale information systems and infrastructures. Ole can be reached at oleha@ifi.uio.no.

24 THE UBIQUITY AND UTILITY OF RESISTANCE: Codesign and Personalization of Information Systems

Melanie Wilson
University of Manchester
Manchester Business School
Manchester, UK

Abstract   *In assessing the positive and negative connotations of ubiquity, this paper favors association with cohabitation and domestication of technology rather than colonization and domination. Unpredicted user responses to technology are often framed as resistance. Despite its ubiquity, resistance remains a neglected topic in information systems research, and belief in technology as "the one true way" of solving a problem means that it will often be demonized. Recognition of the powerful nature of IS elucidates sources of resistance: the policies governing the behavior and reactions of users to technology will impinge on the range of user activities deemed to be recalcitrant. This is especially important with the types of technology involved in ubiquitous information environments as they are often used outside of organizations for leisure and social activities. However, one cannot assume that newer mobile technologies deployed to achieve organizational goals will be adopted and used by employees with the degree of success that these technologies have enjoyed in voluntary environments. An alternative approach is advocated: resistance is perceived not as a threat, but as a site for personalization, and local adaptation; users' subversive acts can play a role in improving the technology; IS failure can be lessened and resistance may ultimately play a role in stabilizing a system. Finally, an argument is made for personalization through user-driven codesign as part of a strategy of utilizing resistance.*

Keywords   Resistance, acceptance, personalization, domestication, innofusion, critical, codesign

1   INTRODUCTION

Portable artifacts, wireless communication, and wallet-sized smart cards—new mobile information technology may herald an era of endless activity, devoid of the boundaries that previously protected the haven of detached time. With technology keeping indolence at bay, users remain permanently connected, easily detected, and inescapably contactable—never absent or idle. Readings of the progressive nature of such developments hinge on assumptions about the willingness of users to adopt the technologies and the way of life they inaugurate. Whatever the technical design of the environment for usage, the social and political context of a change situation constitute major factors in the successful implementation of technology. To improve future innovations, we need to learn the lessons of past implementations. The argument in this paper is that the codesign of ubiquitous socio-technical systems remains desirable, with those who carry out the work orchestrating adaptations. As shall be shown, this standpoint challenges the negativity of managerialist and technocratic discourse concerning resistance and acceptance.

The term *ubiquity* can imply the occupation and colonization of local environments by dominating powers. The notion of codesign then becomes a crucial consideration. This paper pursues the critical call that "the control of technology by those affected by it remains a desirable agenda" (Bauer 1995, p. 1). At the same time, by revealing the ubiquity of resistance, the reader is to be persuaded that noncompliance is an inevitable consideration for implementers. Correlating personalization with the adaptation of technology to local needs reveals the positive role and innovative potential of recalcitrance. The suggestion here is that this alternative view of resistance forms the basis of strategies for dealing with local reactions to new technology in ubiquitous information environments. This conclusion is reached by recognizing the prescriptions contained in imposed technology, and that such an imposition invites subversion. In all of this, user responses to new socio-technical ensembles need to be contextualized in terms of their mandatory or volitional environments.

To overcome the bias toward managerialism that infuses much of the writing on employee responses to innovation, a critical perspective is employed to rethink technology acceptance via an engagement with literature on resistance. The position of this paper builds on earlier alternative approaches to resistance (Hirschheim and Klein 1989; Hirschheim and Newman 1988; Markus 1983), while bringing in Waddell and Sohal's (1998) observation that "there is a strong case that suggests that resistance should not be approached adversarilly because it can play a useful role in an organizational change effort" (p. 544). Adopting a multidisciplinary approach, the view of user agency described herein recognizes the power relations in organizations where legitimacy of behavior is circumscribed by project sponsors.

The paper is structured as follows. First, existing critical literature on resistance to information systems, technology, and change is reviewed. Second, resistance is framed within a political comprehension of organizational realties. Third, an alternative rational view of resistance is described. Fourth, the creative aspects of resistance are delineated. In conclusion, the contribution to the conference themes and a critical agenda are described.

2 USER AND EMPLOYEE RESISTANCE TO TECHNOLOGY AND CHANGE

2.1 The Critical Information Systems Literature on Resistance

The influential Information Systems literature on resistance contains seeds of what has become identified as a critical approach. Often containing emancipatory aims, criticality entails a challenge to existing patterns of power and authority, critiquing technological determinism, highlighting the subjective nature of information, and demonstrating the existence of managerialist perspectives dominating approaches to IS (Howcroft and Trauth 2004). Within the set of writings that explicitly recognized the political and conflictual nature of systems development within organizations (for example, Franz and Robey 1984; Lyytinen 1987; Newman and Noble 1990), Markus' (1983) seminal paper, in particular, pointed to assumptions about resistance as a function of the political reality of organizations. The power plays involved in the acceptance process have been explored more recently by Cendon and Jarvenpaa (2001) and Doolin (2004), while Brown et al. (2002) suggest that power and political issues associated with implementation may be influential in driving resistance to new technology. On this theme, Munkvold (1999) offers us an account of users' rationale for resisting a new IS.

In directing attention to the perspective of the user, and thereby underscoring the marginalization of recalcitrant users, Hirschheim and Newman (1988) highlight the implicit managerialist approach to acceptance that still pervades treatment of non-acceptance. Hirschheim and Klein (1989) further this revelation of perspectives, reminding us that designers have their own world views which steer them toward identification of different problems and solutions. Lyytinen (1987) and Robey et al. (1993) provide studies of differences in perspectives between systems developers and potential users, thereby offering some explanation for the resistance phenomena. Markus and Bjørn-Andersen (1987), and Beath and Orlikowski (1994) have deconstructed the tensions that underlie the developer-user relationship. Marakas and Hornik (1996), meanwhile, examined the dissonance between stated support for a system and actual resistance to that system.

In relation to IFIP Working Group 8.2 conferences, of late there have been a variety of papers focusing on resistance (for example, Allen and Kern 2001; Sorensen et al. 2001; Tapia 2004; Whitley and Hosein 2001; Wilson 2002; Wilson and Howcroft 2000). This may be explained by the increasing recognition of the ubiquity of resistance.

2.2 The Ubiquity of Resistance in Organizations

Resistance to change is always possible (Trader-Leigh 2002) and constitutes the little-recognized but critically important contributor to the failure of change projects (Waddell and Sohal 1998). Organizational theory tells us that resistance is built into the nature of organizations, thanks to the inertia that permits greater reliability and predictability (Waddell and Sohal 1998). So, the tendency toward stability and away from risk means individuals will defend the status quo, thereby confronting change. In addition, people do not happily accept the domination of others: "There is a general tendency among those subject to power and control to resist by challenging the systems and rules imposed on them" (Doolin 2004, p. 352). This accounts for Schein's (1998) observation that resistance to change in organizations may be one of the most ubiquitous of organizational phenomena. In relation to IS on a global level, variance in technological development can be largely explained by the existence of resistance (Mokyr 1990), and even with strong closure around a technological framework, resistance trhives (McLaughlin et al. 1999)

2.3 Resistance: A Loaded Term

Despite the ubiquity of resistance in organizations and its influence on technological developments (Mokyr 1990), this multifaceted phenomenon (Ansof 1988) still remains a curious topic of study in a discipline where the very phenomena of study, information systems, instigate change and leave upheaval in their wake. Resistance is viewed as a structural or a personal deficit, irrational, morally bad, and ultimately futile (Bauer 1995). Zaltman and Duncan (1977, p. 63) define resistance as any conduct that serves to maintain the status quo in the face of pressure to alter the status quo. However, resistance is a loaded term. In the context of new technology, it is used in an accusatory fashion, serving mainly to blame those who resist, and often implying a managerial and technocratic bias (Bauer 1995).[1]

The treatment of resistance by those engaged in IS development or research inherits much from organizational theory and management research, where it has a history of receiving a very bad press (Waddell and Sohal 1998). Most commonly linked with negative employee attitudes or with counter-productive behaviors (e.g., Brown et al. 2002), resistance is also associated with the introduction of unanticipated delays and costs instabilities to the process of strategic change (Ansof 1988). The notion of utility in resistance remains overlooked (Waddell and Sohal 1998). Likewise, in technology and innovation studies, the term, resistance elicits contradictory connotations, loaded with a managerial and modernization bias (Bauer 1995). In addition, there is a tendency to focus only on so-called *technical* issues, at the expense of the social; yet political, social, economic, technical, and organizational factors are interwoven into ICT systems (Dutton et al. 1995).

From the perspective of IS professionals, it may well be that the IS group in an organization simply cannot understand the resistance on the part of the users (Brown et al. 2002). Bauer (1995, p. 13) argues that the managerial discourse inherent in the treatment of resistance proves that "rationality is claimed by the designer, and actions that challenge his or her proposal are 'resistance'"; those who employ the designer assume a Tayloristic "one best way." Overall, an attitude exists whereby all technological projects are seen as a legitimate tribute to great human achievements, ignoring the complementary stories that need to be told.

---

[1]Historically, and in stark contrast, *Resistance* stands for the clandestine (and morally praiseworthy) insurgence against an occupying, illegitimate power during World War II.

3   POWER AND RESISTANCE

To overcome the managerial bias surrounding the study of noncompliance, a critical approach undertakes an examination of the political context of technological deployment in order to explore how environmental and political factors impact technology acceptance attitudes and behaviors (Brown et al. 2002). This also permits an understanding of the forces that give rise to, define, and discipline resistance.

3.1 Interests, Scripts and Quiet Politics

Understanding resistance to IS innovation implies examination of the organizational distribution of power, not just factors inherent to the system (design features) and factors inherent to the person (subjective norm and perceived behavioral control) (Brown et al. 2002, p. 293). Organizational and economic interests are likely to be reflected in the particular configuration of an information system (Shaiken 1986) and so, in return, information systems are likely to support and enhance the interests of a minority who already are in more powerful situations (Hirschheim and Klein 1989; Markus and Bjørn-Andersen 1987). Within the context of power relations in organizations, IS play a crucial role in mediation, especially during times of change.

In addition, the control aspects of information systems have implications for issues of power and inequality in organizations (Knights and Murray 1997). When stabilized, an information system may become a powerful media through which daily routines of the organization are orchestrated. Information systems can change work practices, and inscribe a moral order (Bloomfield 1991). Technology is perceived as an intermediary, employed as a *change agent* to bring about behavior required by those sponsoring the development project—such as standardization (Berg and Bowker 1997; Hanseth et al. 1996). This implies that information systems incorporate particular assumptions and particular world views (Hirschheim and Klein 1989) rather than some objective set of facts about the organization. Information systems are implemented with the intended effect that operatives behave in accordance with their agenda or script (Wilson 2002). These "quiet politics" should be investigated to see how they arouse resistance and how they become embedded in information infrastructure, embodying particular values, policies and modes of practice (Bowker et al. 1995).

3.2 Legitimacy, Resistance, and Retribution

In contrast to the attention paid to the existence and exercise of power through the technology, acts of resistance by the non-legitimate, marginalized, and less-powerful actors have been largely disregarded (Wilson 2002). Yet resistance bears witness to conflict, can take many forms, and implies that power and domination are never total: they are processes, rather than permanently achievable states. We need also to consider the anticipated and actual consequences one may experience in response to acts of resistance. Resistance is a form of risky behavior (Bauer 1995). A person who violates norms and rules runs the risk of exclusion, punishment, and material sanctions.

Elsewhere, this reality has been related to dysfunctional organizational culture where a practice of "shoot the messenger" means that the politics of blame pervade. Given the hierarchical nature of most management structures, no one wants to be the harbinger of bad news and thus top management rarely directly receives news of slippage. This culture of non-reporting of doubts, flaws, and failures to senior management in organizations, argue Dutton et al. (1995), obfuscates the creation of a climate where organizational learning can take place and prevents remedial action from being taken. This would suggest the need for a different approach to dissent.

3.3 Acceptance, Mandatory and Volitional Contexts

To improve our understanding of technology acceptance, we need to scrutinize active policies toward usage. In recognizing the political realities of organizational life, we are concerned with distinguishing between mandatory and voluntary contexts, since the policies governing the behavior and reactions of users to the technology will impinge on the range of user activities deemed to be recalcitrant. This is especially important with the types of technology involved in ubiquitous information environments as they are used outside of organizations, often for leisure or social activities. However, one cannot assume that newer mobile technologies deployed to achieve organizational goals will be adopted and used by employees with the same degree of success that the same technologies have enjoyed in leisure or voluntary environments.

In the IS literature, user responses have typically been evaluated via user satisfaction, focusing on attitudes toward the outputs of a system and the IS group, rather than that of using the system (Brown et al. 2002). The major technique for measuring and understanding acceptance is the technology acceptance model (TAM), which has been used by a number of authors in IS (Adams et al. 1992; Agarwal and Prasad 1997; Davis 1989; Davis and Venkatesh 1996). According to TAM, other things being equal, the easier the system is to use, the more useful it will be. A more critical approach to the use of TAM is offered by Brown et al. (2002), who argue that the model is limited because of context: the research was conducted in environments in which adoption was *voluntary*. This is key, since, as we have seen, issues of power and resistance hinge on the notion of consent.[2]

As Brown et al. describe, the decision to implement a new IT architecture within a firm results in individual users having limited, if any, control over the implications of this decision. Users will eventually be offered limited choices in the software available and, therefore, will be forced to comply with the decisions of others. Given this context, the validity of the TAM is put in question when the behavior is mandatory: "A mandatory use environment is defined here as one in which users are required to use a specific technology of system *in order to keep and perform their jobs*" (Brown et al. 2002, p. 283). And despite the fact that people appear to use the technology, this does not mean that their attitude is not one of resentment, which may display itself elsewhere.

---

[2]Other research on acceptance has also suffered from such bias: the theory of reasoned action focuses entirely on volitional behavior.

It is possible to have an effective information system without positive attitudes or satisfaction on the part of users. But the negative attitudes will have potentially profound consequences in a mandatory situation. Mandated use can lead to users delaying or obstructing the implementation; resenting, underutilizing, or sabotaging the new system; or separating from the organization (Brown et al. 2002).

As Turner (1990) warns, the imposition of a system of control almost inevitably invites its subversion. The levels of prescriptions are also embodied in technologies: the more prescriptive they are, the more constraints on users' behavior, increasing subversive acts. Legitimate interaction is dictated by the script of the technology. Additionally, although there is a continuum of voluntariness, user *perceptions* of voluntariness will vary (Brown et al. 2002).

We can take the example of smart card technology to examine the significance of voluntary and mandatory environments for adoption/non-adoption issues. Smart cards are to be understood as personal, portable, flexible, secure tokens that form an integral part of a larger information infrastructure. They have a range of uses in voluntary arenas such, as supermarket shopping and access to transport systems. As such they are relatively noncontroversial (although there were more concerns during their earlier rollout). Contrast this to the UK government's plans for national identity cards operating on a similar technology, but resistance to the proposed technology seems inevitable. For the government, the technologies were a justifiable mandatory technology.[3] However, opponents argued that the proposals are flawed on political, technical, and financial grounds and constituted an ineffective response to the problems of security and fraud, while posing an unacceptable threat to civil liberties.[4]

Alternatively, users may be able to elect to use a technology or not—even in mandated environments (Brown et al. 2002).[5] The crucial issue is whether there are alternatives or not, and access to an earlier system or way of working may decrease the possibilities of stabilization (Wilson and Howcroft 2002). In both Munkvold's (1999) and Doolin's (2004) longitudinal studies, usage of the technology was never mandatory and choice was possible. Combined with earlier mistrust of implementers, the users chose the older substitute. The risk of non-stabilization may increase with time rather than decrease, depending on levels of support, as is seen in the cases of Munkvold and of Wilson and Howcroft (2002), where a spiral downward was created as early adopters rejected the technology. McLaughlin et al. (1999) recount the struggle to secure a central place for the new system in the work practices of the staff located outside the

---

[3]To enable the fight against crime and terror, prevention of fraud, a halt to illegal immigration, a stop identity theft, to move the UK into line with Europe with the government claiming that the innocent had nothing to fear (Home Office, www.homeoffice.gove.uk/comrace/identitycards).

[4]The latter has meant a challenge from the Judicial Court of Human Rights, questioning issues concerning storage of information, the entry of information otherwise available, obtaining information from documents not designated for this purpose, the entry on the register by compulsion, issues of disclosure of information, and issues of authorization for collection and disclosure of information (Home Office, www.homeoffice.gove.uk/comrace/identitycards).

[5]The exception being broad-scope systems such as ERP systems, where employees do not have a decision regarding use.

center, who associated the earlier system with autonomy at the local departmental level. These power issues relate also to the tension between global systems and local user needs.

4   RATIONAL VIEW OF RESISTANCE TO CHANGE AND TECHNOLOGY

The negative perspective and adversarial approach that dominates treatment of resistance have little theoretical support (Waddell and Sohal 1998). From a user perspective, there is likely to be some rationale for resistance, including imperfect technology whose flaws can be subsequently revealed by resistance. This is a functional view of resistance. Properly directed, resistance can improve design and ensure stability. Indeed, Mokyr (1990) observes that, to historians, resistance can act as a force that shapes technology. These issues are now explored.

4.1 Rationale for Resistance

Resistance is far more complex than previously thought (Munkvold 1999). It is a function of a variety of social factors, and can, contrary to managerial discourse, stem from a rational fear of detrimental effects to individual interests (Hirschheim and Newman 1988). At the same time, the nonrational factors are only nonrational from the perspective of another (Lyytinen 1987). Usually treated as sinister, even the negative political factors, such as favoritism and point-scoring, have a rationale of their own for the individuals concerned. Krovis (1993) argues that if changes are considered negative by organizational members, then there is likely to be resistance, which in turn will have ramifications on the success of the information system, and on the ability of the organization to deal with IS-related change.

With the increased penetration of computers in society comes increased reasons for resistance, yet the common-sense assumption that the object of resistance is technology should be challenged. Bauer (1995) suggests that causes relate to antecedents, which are often ignored due to concentration on the process of resistance and effects. In order to understand what is being resisted and why, research should investigate social, cultural, and organizational context, resistor's perspectives of (negative) effects. Resistance can be directed against technical devices because they are a symbolic focus of what infringes on people's livelihood—the traditional meaning of Luddism or machine breaking. In the case of IS, then, we should make a distinction between resistance to computers/computerization (hardware), resistance to types of applications (software), resistance to new work practices,[6] and resistance to the (political) consequences of the innovation.

---

[6]We may want to extend this to include the implications of ubiquitous information environments as this may mean an end to the boundaries between work and leisure (Wilson and Greenhill 2004).

Where supporters of a new system may see only irrationality, alternative justifi-cations underpinning acts of resistance include reduced autonomy, lack of involvement, lack of felt need, bonds to existing technologies, and adoption costs (Munkvold 1999, p. 265). The sizeable number of variables deemed to have direct relevance to resistance to change is significant in accounting for the ubiquity of resistance (Trader-Leigh 2002).

4.2 Resistance as Indicator of Alternatives

The questionable notions of progress and the technocratic discourse noted above can be challenged by acts of resistance. Resistance points out that it is a fallacy to believe change itself to be inherently good. We know that a design is necessarily bounded within constraints of space and time (Simon 1981), and so the notion of a single best solution—rationality writ large—is hardly justifiable since "under any constraint, different assumptions suggest different solutions and legitimate the 'resis-tance' to a single best design" (Bauer 1995, p. 13). Hence, resistance also encourages the search for alternative methods and outcomes (Waddell and Sohal 1998), a critical source of innovation and a testament to the fallacy of the "one best way."

4.3 Resistance as the Pain of Innovation

Resistance can also be seen as the acute pain of the innovation process (Bauer 1995), a signal, warning of things that should be examined (Waddell and Sohal 1998). It is naïve to assume that a change process that occurs only with minimal resistance must have been a good change and managed well; evidence of resistance can be a useful window into underlying tensions (Trader-Leigh 2002). Resistance can be used to secure a sustainable future—a tool to negotiate the change versus status quo boundary (Waddell and Sohal 1998). Resistance balances demands for change against the need for constancy and stability. On the creative front, resistance brings with it an influx of energy. Apathy is not a good response to change, whereas resistance can be harnessed: "With resistance and conflict comes the energy or motivation to seriously address the problem at hand" (Waddell and Sohal 1998, p. 545).

5 THE PRODUCTIVE ASPECTS OF RESISTANCE

5.1 Local Resistance to Adapt and Stabilize Standard Systems

Given the importance of the implementation stage, and the fact that local consequences are almost certainly likely to differ from consequences in distant places, an information system may well be stabilized in one location, yet destabilized upon implementation elsewhere. McLaughlin et al. (1999) concur with the open nature of the information system, noting that the systems they studied were reopened and reshaped, and that "attempts to close the lid will only be successful where managers recognize the distinction between standardized use and integration of the system, and local versions of its stabilization by different groups" (p. 224).

In relation to personalization, this paper seeks to underline the importance of context for interactions and responses by users to socio-technical ensembles by differentiating between mandatory and volitional environments. This is because personalization requires examination of organizational distribution of power (Brown et al. 2002). In particular, we emphasize that within work organizations, users will be more likely to experience a mandatory environment. However, the comments made could be extended to more user-driven innovations. Second, we argue that personalization may be improved by the adoption of a less confrontational stance toward subversive acts, incorporating such innovations as part of a user-driven codesign strategy where resistance is utilized.

Within large, distributed organizations, issues of personalization will overlap more strongly with localization, although elsewhere they may be treated as distinct phenomena. In such (mandatory) environments, the possibilities of personalization are related to *innofusion*: the adaptation of technology to suit local needs. This endorses a view of the innovative characteristic of recalcitrant behavior. McLaughlin et al. recognize the fundamental tension that managers have to resolve: the move to standardize the system on the one hand, and the need to respond to the requirement to localize the system on the other. Relating resistance to the regulation of users, local practices can be analyzed for their role in mediating regulatory control from central management. We might ask, how far can local practices be regarded as a form of resistance to new technologies? Yet this need not be framed negatively since "frequently, initial resistance by staff to new technology turns out to have facilitated the ultimate stabilization of a system" (McLaughlin et al. 1999, p. 222). Strong resistance to new procedures by users ensured modification of the system, accommodating most of the users' demands. Similarly, Munkvold (1999) sees implementation as a process of maturation. He implicitly acknowledges that in distributed organizations the resistance will be from the local, where IS successes will be enabled if adaptation at a local level is permitted.

Given the political nature of IS development in organizations and our critical emphasis on human agency and emancipation with regard to the issue of user resistance, this opens the door to ask questions about the right to control technological development. The first step in direct control is to ensure people obtain the technology they prefer. In more volitional environments, ubiquitous computing systems aspire to offer a more personalized (and presumably better) experience, in return for the disclosure of some personal information by the users of the systems. However, the personalized is limited to the menu of possibilities envisaged by the designers. It does not allow for the users to develop something more original and creative.

5.2 Codesign: Participation or Managing Resistance?

Resistance behavior continues to be an unmanaged process (Trader-Leigh 2002). Waddell and Sohal (1998) suggest a thoroughly positive approach, arguing for actively utilizing resistance to stabilize the change process. The difficulty of organizational change is exacerbated by the management of resistance, derived from a simple set of assumptions and misunderstandings of recalcitrance. This adversarial approach needs to be replaced with one that retains the possibility of benefitting from resistance. Techniques need to be extended to carefully manage change and to utilize resistance, with an emphasis on communication, feedback, and teamwork.

In the past, codesign has been on the model of participation and enrolment as a means to involve users in the development process. Participative approaches are advocated where resistance is expected to be high and it is intended to lower noncompliance by increasing the commitment to change (Waddell and Sohal 1998). The degree to which participation is an "authentic process" varies from the inspiring and genuine workers input enabled by the early Scandinavian School (see, for example, Nygaard 1992), through to tokenism and even authoritarianism (Howcroft and Wilson 2003b). Nevertheless, it is unlikely that without industrial action workers could insist on participation where management was averse to a more democratic work form. Hence the paradox of terms, such as "empowerment," since the control by management of the boundaries of power reveals that the participation process is itself controlled by management and, therefore, cannot lead to an equality of input (Howcroft and Wilson 2003a). In the main, participation is not quite the same as utilizing resistance. The behavior of users in repugning technology is likely to be framed in terms of their deficiencies in understanding the benefits (Munkvold 1999; Wilson 2002; Wilson and Howcroft 2000, 2002). Less authentic participative forms can end up being a one-way marketing process, including battering the users with information, and a misunderstanding of user needs (McLaughlin et al. 1999). "Though these techniques may be categorized as participative in form, they are far from participative in nature. They amount to little more than an exercise in salesmanship and clearly illustrate an adversarial management mindset" (Waddell and Sohal 1998, p. 546). Reporting mechanisms should perhaps allow users to establish how the technology is best suited to them and the way they carry out their work.

6 CONCLUSION

This paper contributes to the study of technology adoption and non-adoption by setting out to rethink our biased views toward resistance. It is thus critical in nature (Howcroft and Trauth 2004) with its underlying emancipatory aims: it seeks to emphasize that ubiquity does not equate to colonization but rather cohabitation. Further, it explicitly recognizes the political nature of organizations, intending to upset existing patterns of power and authority. It entails a critique of technological determinism, and highlights and challenges the managerialist perspective that pervades the treatment of resistance to date. In their stead, a more constructive language is offered in association with resistance, and the validity, usefulness, and indispensability of challenging new, yet untried solutions is suggested.

In offering a critical approach to the literature on resistance to technology and organizational change, the paper sought to remind the IS community of lessons we have yet to learn from past experience with IS development. It is hoped that this will inform the approach to new phenomena brought about the ubiquitous nature of new information environments. In rethinking technology acceptance, the paper have challenged many traditional assumptions about organizations, computing, and work insofar as they relate to resistance. It also touched on the issue of personalization from the perspective of codesign consisting of local modifications in a process of innofusion, replacing negative views about non-conformity and usage. The work now is to provide concrete examples of adoption and resistance, with users placed center stage and the account analyzed with the theoretical insights entailed in the paper.

REFERENCES

Adams, D. A., Nelson, R. R., and Todd, P. A. "Perceived Usefulness, Ease of Use, and Usage of Information Technology: A Replication," *MIS Quarterly*, (16:2), 1992, pp. 227-247.
Agarwal, R., and Prasad, J. "The Role of Innovation Characteristics and Perceived Voluntariness in the Acceptance of Information Technologies," *Decision Sciences*, (28:3), 1997, pp. 557-582.
Akrich, M. "The De-scription of Technical Objects," in *Shaping Technology/Building Society*, W. E. Bijker, and J. Law (Eds.), Cambridge, MA: MIT Press, 1992.
Allen, D., and Kern, T. "Enterprise Resource Planning Implementation: Stories of Power, Politics, and Resistance," in *New Directions in Information Systems Development*, B. Fitzgerald, N. Russo, and J. I. DeGross (Eds.), Boston: Kluwer Academic Publishers, 2001, pp. 149-162.
Ansof, I. *The New Corporate Strategy*, New York: John Wiley & Sons, 1988.
Bauer, M. (Ed.). *Resistance to New Technology*, Cambridge, UK: Cambridge University Press, 1995.
Beath, C. M., and Orlikowski, W. J. "The Contradictory Structure of Systems Development Methodologies: Deconstructing the IS-User Relationship in Information Engineering," *Information Systems Research* (5:4), 1994, pp. 350-377.
Berg, M. And Bowker, G. "The Multiple Bodies of the Medical Record: Towards a Sociology of an Artifact," *The Sociological Quarterly* (38:3), 1997, pp. 513-538.
Bloomfield, B. P. "The Role of Information Systems in the UK National Health Service: Action at a Distance and the Fetish of Calculation," *Social Studies of Science*, (21:4), 1991, pp. 701-734.
Bowker, G. C., Timmermans, S., and Star, S. L. "Infrastructure and Organizational Transformation: Classifying Nurses' Work," in *Information Technology and Changes in Organizational Work*, W. Orlikowski, G. Walsham, M. R. Jones, and J. I. DeGross (Eds.), London: Chapman and Hall, 1995, pp. 344-370.
Brown, A.A., Massey, A.P., Montoya-Weiss, M. M., and Burkman, J. R. "Do I Really Have To? User Acceptance of Mandated Ttechnology," *European Journal of Information Systems* (11), 2002, pp. 283-295.
Cendon, B. V., and Jarvenpaa, S. L. "The Development and Exercise of Power by Leaders of Support Units in Implementing Information Technology-Based Services," *Journal of Strategic Information Systems* (10) 2001, pp. 121-158.
Davis, F.D. "Perceived Usefulness, Perceived Ease of Use, and User Acceptance of Information Technology," *MIS Quarterly* (13:3), 1989, pp. 319-340.
Davis, F.D., and Venkatesh, V. "A Critical Assessment of Potential Measurement Biases in the Technology Acceptance Model: Three Experiments," *International Journal of Human-Computer Studies* (45), 1996, pp. 19-45.
Doolin, B. "Power and Resistance in the Implementation of a Medical Management Information System," *Information Systems Journal*, (14), 2004, pp. 343-362.

Dutton, W. H., MacKenzie, D., Shapiro, S., and Peltu, M. *Computer Power and Human Limits: Learning from IT and Telecommunications Disasters,* PICT Policy Research Paper No. 33, Edinburgh University, UK, 1995.

Franz, C. R., and Robey, D. "An Investigation of User-Led Systems Design: Rational and Political Perspectives," *Communications of the ACM* (27:12), 1984, pp. 1202-1209

Hanseth, O., Monteiro, E., and Hatling, M. "Developing Information Infrastructure: The Tension between Standardization and Flexibility," *Science, Technology and Human Values* (21), 1996, pp. 407-426.

Hirschheim, R. A., and Klein, H. K. "Four Paradigms of Information Systems Development," *Communications of the ACM* (32:10), 1989, pp. 1199-1216.

Hirschheim, R. A., and Newman, M. "Information Systems and User Resistance: Theory and Practice," *Computer Journal* (31:5), 1988, pp. 398-408.

Howcroft, D., and Trauth, E. "The Choice of Critical Information Systems Research," in *Relevant Theory and Informed Practice,* B. Kaplan, D. Truex, D. Wastell, A. T. Wood-Harper, and J. I. DeGross (Eds.), Boston: Kluwer Academic Publishers, 2004, pp. 195-211.

Howcroft, D., and Wilson, M. "Paradoxes of Participatory Design: The Janus Role of the Systems Developer," *Information and Organizations* (13:1), 2003a, pp. 1-24.

Howcroft, D., and Wilson, M. "Participation: 'Bounded Freedom' or the Hidden Constraints on User Involvement," *New Technology, Work and Employment* (18:1), 2003b, pp.2-19.

Knights, D., and Murray, F. "Markets, Managers, and Nessages: Managing Information Systems in Financial Sservices," in *Information Technology in Organizations: Strategies, Networks, and Integration,* B. P. Bloomfield, R. Coombs, D. Knights, and D. Littler (Eds.), Oxford, UK: Oxford University Press, 1997.

Krovis, R. "Identifying the Causes of Resistance to IS Implementation," *Information and Management* (25), 1993, pp. 327-335.

Lyytinen, K. "Different Perspectives on Information Systems: Problems and Solutions," *ACM Computing Surveys* (19:1), 1987, pp. 5-46.

Marakas, G. M., and Hornik, S. "Passive Resistance Misuse: Overt Support and Covert Recalcitrance in IS Implementation," *European Journal of Information Systems* (5), 1996, pp. 208-219.

Markus, M. L. "Power, Politics and MIS Implementation," *Communications of the ACM* (26: 6), 1983, pp. 430-444.

Markus, L., and Bjørn-Andersen, N. "Power Over Users: Its Exercise by Systems Professionals," *Communications of the ACM* (30:6), June 1987, pp. 498-504.

McLaughlin, J., Rosen, P., Skinner, D., and Webster, A. *Valuing Technology: Organizations, Culture and Change,* London: Routledge, 1999.

Mokyr, J. *The Lever of Riches: Technological Creativity and Economic Progress,* New York: Oxford University Press Inc., 1990.

Munkvold, B. E. "Challenges of IT Implementation for Supporting Collaboration in Distributed Organizations," *European Journal of Information Systems* (8), 1998, pp. 260-272.

Nygaard, K. "How Many Choices Do We Make? How Many Are Difficult?" in *Proceedings of the Software Development and Reality Construction Conference,* C. Floyd, H. Züllighoven, R. Budde, and R. Keil-Slawik (Eds.), Berlin: Springer-Verlag, 1992, pp. 52-59.

Newman, M., and Noble, F. "User Involvement as an Interaction Process," *Information Systems Research* (1:1), 1990, pp. 89-113.

Robey, D., Smith, L., and Vijayasaaarathy, L. R. "Perceptions of Conflict and Success in Information Systems Development projects," *Journal of Management Information Systems* (10:1), 1993, pp. 123-139.

Sauer, C. *Why Information Systems Fail: A Case Study Approach,* Oxfordshire, UK: Alfred Waller, 1993.

Schein, E. *Organizational Psychology,* London: Prentice Hall, 1998.

Shaiken, H. *Work Transformed: Automation and Labor in the Computer Age*, New York: Lexington Books, 1986.

Simon, H. A. *Administrative Behavior* (4th ed.), New York: Simon and Schuster, 1997.

Sorensen, C., Whitley, E. A., Madon, S., Klyachko, D., Hosein, I., and Johnstone, J. "Cultivating Recalcitrance in Information Systems Research," in *New Directions in Information Systems Development*, B. Fitzgerald, N. Russo, and J. I. DeGross (Eds.), Boston: Kluwer Academic Publishers, 2001, pp. 297-316.

Tapia, A. H. "Resistance or Deviance? A High-Tech Workplace During the Bursting of the Dot-Com Bubble," in *Relevant Theory and Informed Practice,* B. Kaplan, D. Truex, D. Wastell A. T. Wood-Harper, and J. I. DeGross (Eds.), Boston: Kluwer Academic Publishers, 2004, pp. 577-596.

Trader-Leigh, K. E. "Case Study: Identifying Resistance in Managing Change," *Journal of Organizational Change* (15:2), 2002, pp. 138-155.

Turner, G. *British Cultural Studies* (2nd ed.), London: Routledge, 1990.

Waddell, D., and Sohal, A. S. "Resistance: A Constructive Tool for Change Management," *Management Decision* (36:8), 1998, pp. 543-548.

Whitley, E. A., and Hosein I. "Doing Politics Around Electronic Commerce: Opposing the Regulation of Investigatory Powers Bill" in *New Directions in Information Systems Development*, B. Fitzgerald, N. Russo, and J. I. DeGross (Eds.), Boston: Kluwer Academic Publishers, 2001, pp. 415-438.

Wilson, M. "Rhetorics of Enrolment and Acts of Resistance: Information Technology as Text," in *Global and Organizational Discourse about Information Technology,* E. H. Wynn, E. A. Whitley, M. D. Myers, and J. I. DeGross, Boston: Kluwer Academic Publishers, Massachusetts, 2002, pp. 225-248.

Wilson, M., and Howcroft, D. "The Role of Gender in User Resistance and IS Failure," in *The Social and Organizational Perspective on Research and Practice in Information Technology*, R. Baskerville, J. Stage, and J. I. DeGross (Eds.), Boston: Kluwer Academic Publishers, 2000, pp. 453-471.

Wilson, M., and Greenhill, A. "Gender and Teleworking Identities in the Risk Society: A Research Agenda," *New Technology, Work and Employment* (19:3), 2004, pp. 207-221.

Wilson, M., and Howcroft, D. "Re-conceptualizing Failure: Social Shaping Meets IS Research," *European Journal of Information Systems* (11:4), 2002, pp. 236-250.

Zaltman, G., and Duncan, R. *Strategies for Planned Change*, Toronto: Wiley, 1977.

ABOUT THE AUTHOR

Melanie Wilson is a senior lecturer in Management Information Systems at the Manchester Business School, University of Manchester, UK. Her current research interests include critical approaches to information systems; resistance, adoption, and failure of information systems; gender and information technology; and at-home telework. Her publications can be found in *Information and Organization, Journal of Strategic Information Systems, Information Technology and People, European Journal of Information Systems, Journal of Information Technology,* and *New Technology, Work and Employment.* A trained linguist, she also has industrial experience in the export manufacturing sector. Melanie can be reached at Melanie.Wilson@manchester. ac.uk.

Part 6

Position Papers

25   CRACKBERRIES: The Social Implications of Ubiquitous Wireless E-Mail Devices

Melissa A. Mazmanian
Wanda J. Orlikowski
JoAnne Yates
Sloan School of Management
Massachusetts Institute of Technology
Cambridge, MA U.S.A.

1   RESEARCH FOCUS

Mobile communication technologies provide a variety of opportunities for new forms of human interaction. Technologies such as e-mail, cell phones, and wireless e-mail devices, often seen as overcoming spatial and temporal boundaries, have become standard features of contemporary organizational life. From the perspective of information professionals, these tools appear to wield direct influence on the daily experience of managing work, stress, and life. It is easy, however, to forget that such technologies are not used in a vacuum. Individuals make sense of communication technologies and decide when and how to use them in light of particular social, spatial, and temporal contexts. In this process, they take into account the characteristics of their tools, current social expectations, institutional norms, current and historical understandings of technology, and the everyday tasks in which they are engaged. The resulting patterns of use and their consequences (labeled "technologies-in-practice" by Orlikowski 2000) reflect the interaction of these multiple elements over time, affecting both the individuals interacting with the tools as well as the contexts within which their use is situated.

Focusing on the process of sensemaking and norm formation that accompanies the use of a new technology, this research explores how information professionals use wireless e-mail devices (WEDs)[1] in their daily lives. As communication technologies

---

[1] Of these devices, BlackBerry, a product of Research in Motion (RIM), currently holds dominant market share and popular attention. On November 17, 2004, RIM announced it had reached 2 million users (http://www.rim.net/news/press/2004/pr-17_11_2004-01.shtml).

become increasingly mobile, the ability for people to stay connected expands into new temporal and physical settings. As individuals negotiate this potential, they find their use of WEDs challenging taken-for-granted expectations of connectivity, responsiveness, pacing, and etiquette. We are interested in understanding how individuals negotiate numerous and often conflicting organizational expectations, personal goals, and properties of a technology when enacting their technologies-in-practice. Further, we are investigating the implications of such use for both individual experiences and broader organizational structures.

2   CONCEPTUAL GROUNDING

Communication technologies appear to encourage new perceptions of time. According to scholars, individuals in modern society no longer experience time as the linear phenomenon instantiated during the industrial revolution (Zerubavel 1982) but rather as a relative, multiple, and dynamic experience. While reflecting nuanced distinctions, terms such as *polychronic* (Bluedorn et al. 1999; Cotte and Ratneshwar 1999; Schein 1985; Slocombe 1999), the *illusion of simultaneity* (Cooper 2001; Nowotny 1992), *network time* (Hassan 2003), or *timeless time* (Castells 1996) all highlight our current struggle to conceptualize how time is experienced in an age characterized by accelerated pace, ungrounded space, and expanded connectivity. While communication technologies do not cause these changes, people's engagement with the functionality of such technologies interacts with social and organizational expectations and engenders changes in the pace, space, boundaries and stress of work (Gripenberg 2004; Isaacs et al. 2002; Rennecker 2003; Sawyer and Southwick 2002). Given this dynamic, the mobile and asynchronous properties of WEDs may encourage individuals to experience these tools as both mediating and intensifying the experience of simultaneity, speed, and connectivity in the workplace.

While not specifically looking at the effects of communication technologies, scholars have found that the intensity and accelerated pace of information-driven organizations result in the sensation of a constant time famine that directly affects stress (Perlow 1999) and strain (Adams and Jex 1999; Teuchmann et al. 1999). Given the amount of scholarly attention focused on shifting experiences of time and space in the information age, it is surprising that relatively few studies have focused on how individuals actually incorporate mobile communication technologies into their daily lives. We thus know little about such questions as how individuals actually experience polychronicity,[2] how communication technologies affect this dynamic, whether wireless devices increase or decrease perceived control over time famine, and potential implications of these changes.

Focusing a broad societal lens on technology, some scholars have explored similar questions by analyzing cell phone use in public spaces. Conceiving of cell phone use as a new category of communication that is mobile and constantly connected, a number

---

[2]Polychronicity is defined as the preference either to simultaneously engage in multiple tasks or to treat interruptions as equal to planned activities (Cote and Ratneshwar 1999, p. 184).

of studies have examined individual experiences of connectivity as well as the social consequences of private conversations invading public space (Brown 2001; Cooper 2001; Katz and Aakhus 2002; Meyrowitz 1985). Research in this stream posits that by normalizing expectations of availability and eradicating markers of physical context, use of cell phones encourages both self-monitoring and the informal monitoring of others (Cooper 2001; Green 2001). Focusing on the relationship between individuals and their jobs, we build on this work in two ways. First, we focus on the recursive relationship between social expectations that shape individual action and the actions that shape and redefine organizational expectations. Second, we aim to flesh out how specific properties of WEDs enable and constrain both the patterns of use and subjective experiences of such use.

Wireless e-mail devices share many properties with cell phones, but unlike the cell phone, WEDs today are text-based, asynchronous, and silent.[3] Because they lack the audible obtrusiveness of cell phones, some see wireless e-mail devices as appropriate for use during face-to-face interaction. As individuals use wireless e-mail devices in new situations, groups are forced to renegotiate norms of interpersonal interaction. Furthermore, the asynchronous nature of e-mail opens the door for new patterns of communication. Some popular narratives have cast mobile devices such as cell phones as organizational electronic leashes that harness people to organizations at all moments of their lives. The properties of WEDs are such that they may similarly be viewed as a more unobtrusive, although perhaps more insidious, monitoring device.

Finally, the introduction of WEDs into diverse interpersonal situations raises new issues. Tools such as wireless e-mail devices are used more and more in the physical presence of others, and yet no current work explores how such use may affect such interactions. The silent, mobile, and unobtrusive properties of WEDs facilitate use in face-to-face situations where individuals would be unlikely to talk on the phone or interact with a computer. How does the concept of social presence translate in situations where individuals are dividing their attention between face-to-face and virtual interaction? And, given this possibility for fractured presence, how do people negotiate physical and virtual interactions when the use of mobile communication technologies enters public spaces?

3   DATA

We are currently engaged in a field study examining the use of WEDs among mobile information professionals[4] and their spouses. Focusing primarily on 2 research sites, we have conducted 69 semi-structured interviews to date, with 27 interviews at a

---

[3]While use of SMS (short message service) or text messaging via cell phones is popular in other parts of the world, it has not yet taken off in the United States, and is not perceived (at least by the professionals we talked to) to be comparable to wireless e-mail devices.

[4]The label *mobile information professionals* was defined by RIM as their initial target group. Information-based industries include law, venture capital, investment banking and consulting. Adoption of wireless e-mail devices among this group is extensive.

small venture capital firm (including all 27 employees), 22 interviews at a mid-sized law firm (270 lawyers), and 8 interviews with spouses of these professionals. During the initial investigation for this research, we also conducted 12 additional interviews with assorted investment and venture capital professionals. Our principle sites were chosen as the basis of comparison for reasons of similarity (clear internal hierarchy, reliance on information, resource richness, and prevalence of travel) and difference (task, size, and power position with client).

Lasting from 30 minutes to 2 hours, interviews have focused on the adoption and use of the wireless e-mail devices: organizational context and expectations, organizational work practices and communication patterns, framing of the device, emergence and evolution of group norms associated with its use, incorporation of the device into everyday activities, experience of use while traveling, perceptions of connectivity, efficiency and productivity associated with its use, emotional responses (including stress) to use of the device, and work/family issues related to use. We are currently in the process of coding our initial interviews and have begun conducting follow-on interviews which involve examining a 24 to 48 hour period of messages sent and received by participants on their wireless e-mail devices.

4   PRELIMINARY FINDINGS

In our preliminary qualitative analysis of the interviews, we find that people differentiate wireless e-mail devices from other communication technologies in terms of patterns, norms, and experience of use. Furthermore, we find that the technologies-in-practice enacted with WEDs may be encouraging new interpersonal and organizational dynamics. Across the board, participants report constant and sustained interaction with their devices, at all hours and locations of their day. This interaction is informed by personal choices, perceived organizational expectations of constant availability, and work norms regarding appropriate use.

Most salient, and in contrast to the synchronous, point-to-point experience of talking on a cell phone, WEDs appear to allow users to watch and monitor conditions at work constantly and from a distance. In general, individuals experience carrying a WED as facilitating their ability to "stay in the loop" while controlling their terms of communication and catching problems early so as to avoid flare-ups. Rather than seeing this technology as an electronic leash, participants associate use of WEDs with stress relief and increased control over their work. In general, they experience WEDs as allowing them *to monitor*, rather than *to be monitored*.

Paradoxically, users also describe increasing expectations of responsiveness in themselves and others; for example, they report that they expect others to have read their messages within a matter of hours. They also sense increasing pressure to be constantly connected, available, and responsive. However, they view this increased pace and pressure as independent of their own use of WEDs. So far, our preliminary results do not suggest significant differences in these experiences along the lines of gender, hierarchy, or work/family situation, although we continue to investigate how these factors interact with user experience of WEDs.

The sense of constant attention to WEDs (monitoring and interacting) appears to challenge group norms of behavior concerning where and how individuals are connected. While many feel that the relative silence and asynchronous nature of WEDs makes their own use of them in social situations less rude than use of cell phones and other audible mobile devices, individuals also report strong reactions to the inappropriate use of WEDs by others. Spouses, in particular, do not feel that the mobility provided by the device is valuable if the attention of their spouse is directed at the tool rather than toward the family. Use of WEDs during face-to-face meetings is common, but perceived differently by various members of an organization. Individuals note their desire to interact with the device during face-to-face situations, while acknowledging that such use diverts their attention from the immediate context. Both within and across the two organizations, we find overall agreement that the use of WEDs in face-to-face meetings is rude. Yet, we find little evidence that individuals share these opinions with each other or agree about the relationship between etiquette and actual use. We will continue to examine the effects of WEDs on interpersonal relations and organizational effectiveness, and plan to build exploratory theory about the social implications for individuals and organizations of the use of these devices.

ACKNOWLEDGMENTS

This research is supported by a grant from the National Science Foundation under award number IIS-0085725.

REFERENCES

Adams, G. A., and Jex, S. M. "Relationships between Time Management, Control, Work-Family Conflict, and Strain," *Journal of Occupational Health Psychology* (4:1), 1999, pp. 72-77.

Bluedorn, A. C., Kalliath, T. J., Strube, M. J., and Martin, G. D. "Polychronicity and the Inventory of Polychronic Values (IPV): The Development of an Instrument to Measure a Fundamental Dimension of Organizational Culture," *Journal of Managerial Psychology* (14:3/4), 1999, pp. 205-231.

Brown, B. "Studying the Use of Mobile Technology," Chapter 1 in *Wireless World: Social and Interactional Aspects of the Mobile Age*, B. Brown, N. Green, and R. Harper (Eds.), London: Springer, 2001, pp. 3-14.

Castells, M. *The Rise of the Network Society*, Oxford, UK: Blackwell Publishers Ltd., 1996.

Cooper, G. "The Mutable Mobile: Social Theory in the Wireless World," Chapter 2 in *Wireless World: Social and Interactional Aspects of the Mobile Age*, B. Brown, N. Green, and R. Harper (Eds.), London: Springer, 2001, pp. 19-31.

Cotte, J., and Ratneshwar, S. "Juggling and Hopping: What Does it Mean to Work Polychronically?," *Journal of Managerial Psychology* (14:3/4), 1999, pp. 184-205.

Green, N. "Who's Watching Whom? Monitering and Accountability in Mobile Relations," Chapter 3 in *Wireless World: Social and Interactional Aspects of the Mobile Age*, B. Brown, N. Green, and R. Harper (Eds.), London: Springer, 2001, pp. 32-44.

Gripenberg, P. "Virtualizing the Office: Micro-Level Impacts and Driving Forces of Increased ICT Use," *Information Society and the Workplace*, T. Heiskanen and J. Hearne (Eds.), London: Routledge Taylor & Francis Group, 2004, pp. 103-125.

Hassan, R. "Network Time and the New Knowledge Epoch," *Time & Society* (12:2/3), 2003, pp. 225-241.

Isaacs, E., Walendowski, A., Whittaker, S., Schlano, D., and Kamm, C. "The Character, Functions, and Styles of Instant Messaging in the Workplace," Conference on Computer Supported Cooperative Work, New York: ACM Press, 2002, pp. 11-20.

Katz, J. E., and Aakhus, M. A. "Conclusion: Making Meaning of Mobiles—A Theory of Apparatgeist," Chapter 19 in *Perpetual Contact*, J. E. Katz and M. A. Aakhus (Eds.), Cambridge, UK: Cambridge University Press, 2002, pp. 301-318.

Meyrowitz, J. *No Sense of Place: The Impact of Electronic Media on Social Behavior*, New York: Oxford University Press, 1985.

Nowotny, H. "Time and Social Theory: Towards a Social Theory of Time," *Time & Society* (1:3), 1992, pp. 421-454.

Orlikowski, W. "Using Technology and Constituting Structures: A Practice Lens for Studying Technology in Organizations," *Organization Science* (11:4), 2000, pp. 404-428.

Perlow, L. A. "The Time Famine: Toward a Sociology of Work Time," *Administration Science Quarterly* (44:1), 1999, pp. 57-81.

Rennecker, J. "Anticipating the Unanticipated Consequences of Instant Messaging (IM) for Individual Productivity," *Sprouts: Working Papers on Information Environments, Systems and Organizations* (3:3), 2003, Article 7.

Sawyer, S., and Southwick, R. "Temporal Issues in Information and Communication Technology-Enabled Organizational Change: Evidence From and Enterprise Systems Implementation," *The Information Society* (18), 2002, pp. 263-280.

Schein, E. H. *Organizational Culture and Leadership*, San Francisco: Jossey-Bass, 1985.

Slocombe, T. E. "Applying the Theory of Reasoned Action to the Analysis of an Individual's Polychronicity," *Journal of Managerial Psychology* (14:3/4), 1999, pp. 313-323.

Teuchmann, K., Totterdell, P., and Parker, S. K. "Rushed, Unhappy, and Drained: An Experience Sampling Study of Relations between Time Pressure, Perceived Control, Mood, and Emotional Exhaustion in a Group of Accountants," *Journal of Occupational Health Psychology* (4:1), 1999, pp. 37-54.

Zerubavel, E. "The Standardization of Time: A Sociohistorical Perspective," *The American Journal of Sociology* (88:1), 1982, pp. 1-23.

ABOUT THE AUTHORS

Melissa Mazmanian is a doctoral student in the Organization Studies Group at the Sloan School of Management, Massachusetts Institute of Technology. Her research focuses on the experience of information technologies as used in practice. She examines the role of organizations in shaping micro behaviors of technological use, the effect of such behaviors in shaping organizational structure, communication, and practice, and the individual experience of integrating new technologies into everyday life. In 2002, Melissa received a Master's in Information Economics, Management and Policy from the University of Michigan. She can be reached at melmaz@ MIT.EDU.

Wanda J. Orlikowski is a professor of Information Technologies and Organization Studies at the Sloan School of Management and the Eaton-Peabody Chair of Communication Sciences at the Massachusetts Institute of Technology. She received a Ph.D. from the Stern School of Business at New York University. Her primary research interests focus on the recursive relationship between organizations and information technology, with particular emphasis on organizing structures, cultures, work practices, and change. She can be reached at wanda@ MIT.EDU.

JoAnne Yates is Sloan Distinguished Professor of Management at the Sloan School of Management, Massachusetts Institute of Technology. JoAnne examines communication and information as they shape and are shaped by technologies, ideologies, and work practices over time, both in today's organizations and in organizations historically. In her contemporary work, JoAnne studies communication and work practices around electronic communication media in organizations, focusing on genres and on temporal and communication practices. She has published on these topics in *Administrative Science Quarterly, Organization Science,* and elsewhere. She can be reached at jyates@MIT.EDU.

26 BUILDING A UBIQUITOUS ARTIFACT THAT INTEGRATES PROBLEM-SOLVING AND LEARNING PROCESSES TO SUPPORT CREATIVITY

Mikko Ahonen
Hypermedia Laboratory
University of Tampere
Tampere, Finland

This ongoing Ph.D. research work started with observations of shortcomings in the innovation and knowledge management processes in two companies, one Finnish and the other American. An extensive creativity and innovation literature survey was conducted. Problems were identified in three areas: idea evaluation (Amabile 1998), systematic idea development to the innovation phase (Drucker 1985), and community participation in individual idea suggestions (Hargadon 2003). A specific model, the technology brokering model (Hargadon and Sutton 1997) was chosen. From this starting point, a mobile prototype was built, evaluated, and gradually improved using a design science research framework (Hevner et al. 2004; Järvinen 2004) and action research methods. The utility of the prototype is evaluated in three case organizations. This paper focuses on describing the mobile and ubiquitous computing related challenges in this prototype building process.

Earlier work relates to the research of mobility, mobile architectures, user interfaces, and mobile learning (Ahonen et al. 2004; Syvänen et al. 2003), most recently in the global MOBIlearn project.[1] Within this research work, a mobile artifact is built to support learning, problem-solving, and creativity processes. According to Goodyear (2000), such an artifact and related tools should support individual construction of meaning and personal *learnplace* creation. From the perspective of the current research, the notion of learnplaces points, first, to ubiquitous computing environments and, second, to the informal learning area. However, due to the constantly changing context

---

[1]For information on the MOBIlearn project, visit http://www.mobilearn.org.

in mobile work and mobile learning, this learnplace creation is a complex task, both technically and organizationally.

Livingstone (2000) defines informal learning as the activities that happen outside the curricula and aim at understanding, knowledge building, and skills acquisition. The supporting informal learning is, however, difficult. Livingstone (p. 54) sees major challenges in recognizing incidentally initiated learning and irregularly timed learning. Within the creative problem solving cycle, these learning processes are closely related to understanding a problem and a mess-finding phase (Treffinger and Isaksen 1992). The two learning types mentioned by Livingstone set requirements for tools; these tools need to be available immediately when needed and latency is not always tolerated. In the current research case, the tool must support *ad hoc* idea input and related data gathering in text, picture, and sound formats. This multimedia (including SMS and MMS messages) integration need evolved from previous case studies. Therefore, within the current research case, the client-server architecture and related prototype are chosen (independent mobile java (J2ME) client with database and application logic support on the server). Additionally, a portal framework (like Jetspeed) is planned to support different task models of smart phones and PCs. This portal framework with workflow support is also expected to enable autonomous, agent-type functionality through Web services. One challenge with idea processes is notification of users when a certain task is accomplished or a certain piece of information is available. For this purpose, work-flow and messaging platform support is needed.

This approach, focusing primarily on offline and asynchronous activities, is partially contradictory to the common access hype of anyplace, anytime, anywhere. The view of Perry et al. (2001) is that such hype misrepresents the reality of the difficulties faced by mobile workers. When thinking about the design science utility viewpoint, certain requirements are set by the cost and time saving needs. The monetary costs of com-munication when mobile, combined with the lower bandwidth, higher latency, and reduced availability, effectively require that important data be stored locally on the mobile machine (Ratner et al. 2001). In addition to cost and time saving needs, rhythm plays an important role in communication. Churchill and Wakeford (2002) see that the "experience of mobility is embedded in an experience of temporality which includes mutually negotiated rhythms of contact, availability and accessibility." This notion about rhythm has caused inspection of the communication processes around ideas. Perspective-making and perspective-taking are being considered. As stated by Boland and Tenkasi (1995, p. 369), "Making a strong perspective and having the capacity to take another perspective into account are the means by which more complexified knowledge and improved possibilities for product or process innovation are archived." By explaining the idea better to others and by integrating the viewpoints of others, it may be possible to avoid a common caveat in the innovation process: "Even in the trenches of new-product development, we reward people for coming up with new ideas and, in the process, create 'not invented here' cultures that refuse to pursue ideas they didn't come up with themselves" (Hargadon 2003, p. 12).

In conclusion, the design science research framework used in this research is fundamentally a problem-solving paradigm. It seeks to create an innovation that defines the ideas, practices, technical capabilities, and products through which the analysis, design, implementation, management, and use of information systems can be effectively and efficiently accomplished (Hevner et al. 2004). The research needs to be constructed with both scientific rigor and user relevance in mind in order to create a functional architecture and a tool to support the creativity, learning, and idea processes described earlier.

REFERENCES

Ahonen, M., Syvänen, A., and Vainio, T. "Towards Pervasive and Adaptive Learning Environments," in *Proceedings of UAHCI 2005: 3rd International Conference on Universal Access in Human-Computer Interaction*, Las Vegas, NV, July 22-27, 2005 (forthcoming).

Amabile, T. "How to Kill Creativity," *Harvard Business Review*, September-October 1998, pp. 77-87.

Boland, R., and Tenkasi, R. V. "Perspective Making and Perspective Taking in Communities of Knowing," *Organization Science* (6:4), July-August 1995, pp. 350-372.

Churchill, E., and Wakeford, N. "Framing Mobile Collaborations and Mobile Technologies," in *Wireless World. Social and Interactional Aspects of the Mobile Age*, B. Brown, N. Green, and R. Harper (Eds.), London: Springer, 2002, pp. 154-179.

Drucker, P. *Innovation and Entrepreneurship*, Oxford, UK: Butterworth Heinemann, 1985.

Goodyear, P. M. "Environments for Lifelong Learning: Ergonomics, Architecture and Educational Design," in *Integrated and Holistic Perspectives on Learning, Instruction and Technology: Understanding Complexity*, J. M. Spector and T. M. Anderson (Eds.), Dordrecht: Kluwer Academic Publishers, 2000.

Hargadon, A. *How Breakthroughs Happen*, Cambridge, MA: Harvard Business School Press, 2004.

Hargadon, A., and Sutton, R. I. "Technology Brokering and Innovation in a Product Development Firm," *Administrative Science Quarterly* (42), 1997, pp. 716-749.

Hevner, A. R., March, S. T., Park, J., and Ram, S. "Design Science in Information Systems Research," *MIS Quarterly* (28:1), 2004, pp. 75-105.

Järvinen, P. *On Research Methods*, Tampere: Opinpajan kirja, 2004.

Livingstone, D. "Exploring the Icebergs of Adult Learning: Findings of the First Canadian Survey of Informal Learning Practices," NALL Working Paper #10-2000, Ontario Institute for Studies in Education, University of Toronto, 2000.

Syvänen, A., Nokelainen, P., Ahonen, M., and Turunen, H. "Approaches to Assessing Mobile Learning Components," in *Tenth European Conference for Research on Learning and Instruction Book of Abstracts*, L. Mason, S. Andreuzza, B. Arfé, and L. Del Favero (Eds.), 2003.

Perry, M., O'Hara, K., Sellen, A., Brown, B., and Harper, R. "Dealing with Mobility: Understanding Access Anytime, Anywhere," *ACM Transactions on Computer-Human Interaction* (8:4), December 2001, pp. 323-347.

Ratner, D., Reiher, P., and Popek, G. J. "Replication Requirements in Mobile Environments," *Mobile Networks and Applications* (6), 2001, pp. 525-533.

Treffinger, D. J., and Isaksen, S. G. *Creative Problem Solving: An Introduction*," Sarasota, FL: Center for Creative Learning, 1992.

ABOUT THE AUTHOR

Mikko Ahonen is an assistant professor at the University of Tampere, Finland. Mikko began his career in the 1980s in the software industry with a degree in computing. While studying for his MA (Ed. Sc.) in the 1990s, he did research in distance education and video conferencing. Mikko's business view comes from years spent at Sonera Juxto teleoperator service, where he was responsible for knowledge management R&D. Recently, Mikko's work is in the area of mobile learning research, primarily in the MOBIlearn project (www.mobilearn. org). Currently, he is devoting all of his time to creativity and innovation research in order to finalize his computer science thesis. He can be reached at mikko.ahonen.uta.fi.

27 EFFECTS OF WIRELESS MOBILE TECHNOLOGY ON EMPLOYEE WORK BEHAVIOR AND PRODUCTIVITY: An Intel Case Study[1]

Majorkumar Govindaraju
David Sward
Intel Corporation
Santa Clara, CA

Wireless mobility is impacting business and home users by changing the way we work and live (Lyytinen and Yoo 2002). Research studies have modeled the patterns of use in ubiquitous computing environments (Cousins and Robey 2003). Intel began migrating users from Intel® Pentium® II processor-based notebook bundles to Intel® Centrino™ mobile technology-based notebook bundles in 2003. To study how wireless-enabled laptops impact productivity and work behavior, Intel studied more than 100 Intel employees in different offices around the United States by providing them with the same Intel Centrino mobile technology notebook bundles used in our migration. We tested participants in Intel's Human Factors Engineering Usability labs, gathered data from weekly activity logs kept by study participants, evaluated responses to pre- and post-surveys, evaluated actual usage patterns from the records of wireless hotspot access service providers, and conducted one-on-one interviews with study participants. We observed a productivity gain of 37.3 percent between the two systems which confirmed our business decision to migrate to wireless technology. What surprised us, though, was the pace at which our participants' work behaviors changed during the study. The key findings of the study are summarized below.

Time Slicing. Time slicing refers to the worker's ability to slice time and convert smaller and smaller portions into valuable work time. On an older notebook, an extra few minutes wouldn't have been enough to allow an employee to plug in, start up the

---

system, connect to a remote network and do useful work. The new Intel Centrino mobile technology bundles, however, can quickly connect to the network, allowing the participant to check e-mail or perform a fast search on the Web between meetings. The ease of connection, wireless hotspot availability, and performance gains allowed participants to become productive in smaller units of time. Participants reported that they had a more positive sense of "being on top of their work," and were more responsive to team members, clients, and suppliers. One user said, "I had to wait during a child's appointment one evening. I went to a hotspot, pulled down my e-mail, and worked on an urgent issue. It was great to have the flexibility to do this so I didn't have to log on when I got home at 9:30 that evening."

Time Shifting. Time shifting refers to the worker's ability to distribute time around work and personal obligations and shift their work times as needed to reduce times of low or no productivity. As time slicing became second nature, workers in the study tended to become more adept at time shifting, or arranging their day to optimize effectiveness at work while managing personal obligations. Once wirelessly connected, these employees had an increasing number of places and times to effectively and productively connect to the corporate network. They could choose to work from new and different locations when those were more convenient than connecting from office or home. For example, they could more effectively manage commute time by using wireless hotspots. A user commented,

> I was able to meet [an] extremely tight planning deadline while on the road for the day meeting with a client. Without Intel Centrino [mobile technology], I would have either missed [the] deadline or would have not taken advantage of the opportunity to meet with the client, which had been in the works for about two months.

Ubiquitous Wireless Use and Better Work-Life Balance. Wireless connections, great battery life, and a thinner, lighter form factor led participants to carry and rely on their notebooks much more often. Participants have developed a growing affinity for their notebooks. A user said,

> I was attending my son's soccer tournament on Saturday, and work came up that needed to be finished. Luckily, I had my notebook in the trunk and was able to find a hotspot 5 minutes away. I connected and finished the work. Before I would have been forced to drive home (more than an hour each way), and would have missed most of the tournament.

We worried that participants might view the location flexibility they gained as a further encroachment of business time into personal time. However, they reported that increased mobility allowed them to flexibly and conveniently manage their work obligations and protect personal time more effectively. The added flexibility and convenience that allowed participants to manage work obligations helped them manage their personal time more effectively as well. A user commented, "I set up a wireless access point at home and I'm no longer trapped in the den. I can sit with family while I'm getting bits of work done."

Intel is deploying more wireless enabled systems across the company based on these encouraging results. Intel continues to extend the wireless proliferation by developing platform architectures using technologies such as 802.11 a/g and Wi-Max.

REFERENCES

Lyytinen, K., and Yoo, Y. "Research Commentary: The Next Wave of Nomadic Computing," *Information Systems Research* (13:4), 4, December 2002, pp. 377-388.

Cousins, K., and Robey, D. "Patterns of Use within Nomadic Computing Environments: An Agency Perspective on Access—Anytime, Anywhere," paper presented at the Workshop on Ubiquitous Computing Environments, Case Western Reserve University, October 2003.

ABOUT THE AUTHOR

Majorkumar Govindaraju is a Senior Human Factors Engineer at Intel Corporation. He is part of User Centered Design team within the Information Technology division in Intel and applies human factors methodologies for developing usable products. His previous work in Intel included projects aimed at finding the corporate business value of information technology products and solutions. Majorkumar has worked in the field of human factors engineering and ergonomics since 1993 and has written over 35 research publications and white papers. He obtained a Ph.D. in Industrial Engineering with emphasis in Human Factors from the University of Cincinnati. Majorkumar can be reached at majorkumar.govindaraju@intel.com.

David Sward is a Staff Human Factors Engineer at Intel Corporation, Chandler. David has established and managed cross-disciplinary teams that apply user-centered design to the development of Intel products and for services from Intel's Information Technology division. He is currently engaged with several companies, academic institutions, industry forums, and consulting firms to develop processes that measure the business value of information technology. David has worked in the field of human factors engineering since 1991 and is an adjunct faculty member in the Applied Psychology program at Arizona State University East, teaching classes in human factors engineering, human-computer interaction, and the usability engineering lifecycle. David can be reached at david.s.sward@intel.com.

Part 7

Panels

28 UBIQUITOUS COMPUTING FOR HEALTH AND MEDICINE

Chris Atkinson
Centre for Research in Systems in Information Systems
The University of Manchester
Manchester, U.K.

Bonnie Kaplan
Yale Center for Medical Informatics
Yale University
New Haven, CT U.S.A.

Kent Larson
School of Architecture and Planning
Massachusetts Institute of Technology
Cambridge, MA U.S.A.

Henrique M. G Martins
Judge Institute of Management
University of Cambridge
Cambridge, U.K.

Jay Lundell
Proactive Health Group
Intel Corporation
Hillsboro, OR U.S.A.

Martin Harris
Cleveland Clinic
Cleveland, OH U.S.A.

Ubiquitous information environments today generally include smart cell phones, GPSs, RFIDs, and sensors inside buildings. If accepted by users, wirelessly connected mobile ICT devices like handhelds/PDAs, tablet PCs, or laptop/notebook PCs can also be seen to constitute a platform for information systems ubiquity at the work place and beyond. The growth of these technologies is creating new business models and opportunities while changing our notions—and our places—of computing, communication, and work. Already the distinctions between home and work place, leisure and work, private and public are breaking down.

With the advent of new technologies, similar changes are occurring in health care delivery and the distinction between home and locus of health care. Ubiquitous computing in health care is paving the way in which these new technologies intersect with the institutional, social, and private spheres, blurring areas of public and private life, health and illness, work routines, professionalization, and organizational boundaries while contributing to changes in personal empowerment and identity. Ubiquitous medical devices make it possible to monitor patients in their work, domiciliary, and institutional settings as well as enabling peripatetic clinicians to access clinical information and services for treatment of the patient outside of clinical organizations. These also have the potential to lead to the reconfiguration of clinical practices and, to a certain extent, empower the patient, particularly elderly and disabled people. Home health care devices, for example, make it easier for them to live within their own home or chosen institutional environments. Ubiquitous computing also could change the relationship between primary and secondary care by enabling primary care providers to take a much more active role in the effective management of morbidity outside clinical environments.

Informatics in health care has, to date, focused on biomedical informatics, patient clinical record systems, telemedicine, order entry and results reporting, and health billing and administrative systems. These have been accessed primarily through static devices such as workstations, mainly located in hospitals, clinics, or doctors' offices. The advent of ubiquitous computing has opened up a new domain for health and medical informatics. In the process, old issues take on new aspects, and new issues arise that IS researchers need to appreciate—and learn how to address.

The panel will explore the nature of ubiquitous computing and its capacity to change care both at home and in geographically dispersed organizational settings. Panelists are drawn from academia, industry, and health care, with backgrounds in IS, architecture, medical informatics, and cognitive psychology. They will discuss the nature of ubiquitous computing in health and social care by examining ubiquitous computing in the home, the general practitioner's office, and the hospital in different countries. They also will describe a range of research approaches, from field work, to observation and modeling peripatetic care delivery, to experimental living spaces with embedded sensors. While focusing on health care, the panel will explore such general issues as

- How are ubiquitous computing devices used within domiciliary, work, and dispersed institutional settings?
- What might be the relationship between ubiquitous computing and professional roles; personal identities; community relationships; home, locus of health care, and work; and empowerment of individuals employing these new technologies?
- What future organizational models and clinical processes arise out of the availability of ubiquitous computing?

- What research epistemologies and methodologies are appropriate for the study of ubiquitous information systems?
- What are the appropriate methods and methodologies for the representation, development, and application of ubiquitous technologies and care environments?
- What can we learn about ubiquitous computing in health care that is relevant to other uses of these technologies?

Bonnie Kaplan, Yale Center for Medical Informatics, will moderate the session.

Chris Atkinson, Centre for Research in Systems in Information Systems, School of Informatics Systems, The University of Manchester, will report on current and future research and development that explores the use of ubiquitous and mobile devices in the diagnosis and monitoring of patients within their domicilary setting by primary care providers. The research and development is based on creating clusters of general practices within the UK's National Health Service. These clusters would pool their diagnostic technologies and specialist medical skills together. They would share ubiquitous patient monitoring technologies and access patient notes, teleconsultations, and clinical images through the NHSnet and telecommunications media. These, in turn, would be augmented with therapeutic care to chronically ill individuals using domiciliary ubiquitous devices and patient monitoring technologies.

Kent Larson, Director, Changing Places, Principle Research Scientist, School of Architecture and Planning, Massachusetts Institute of Technology, will discuss PlaceLab, a highly instrumented apartment-scale shared research facility where new technologies and design concepts can be tested and evaluated in the context of everyday living. The rich sensing infrastructure of the PlaceLab will be used to develop techniques to recognize patterns of sleep, eating, socializing, recreation, etc. Particularly for the elderly, changes in baseline activities of daily living are believed to be important early indicators of emerging health problems, often preceding indications from biometric monitoring. The unique data sets generated by the PlaceLab will aid in the development of activity pattern recognition tools. Techniques will be tested that support the effective human-computer interaction required for the proactive encouragement of healthy behaviors related to diet, exercise, medication adherence, etc.

Henrique M. G. Martins, Judge Institute of Management, University of Cambridge, will discuss hospital organizations, where ubiquitous computing is increasingly manifesting itself via initiatives to implement and deploy mobile information communication technology (MICT) devices like PDAs, tablet PCs, and mounted PCs on carts, with and without wireless support. The assumption is that such devices can enhance clinical work practices. Such, however, deserves to be analyzed, as well as the attitudes and practices of hospital organizations toward the usage of such devices by clinicians. Based on fieldwork data from the United States, United Kingdom, Portugal and Singapore, effects of mobile ICTs on clinical practice by individual doctors will be discussed. At the organizational level, a preliminary categorization of different strategies will be advanced together with illustrative examples from researched cases.

Jay Lundell, Senior Researcher, Proactive Health Group, Intel, will discuss Intel's Proactive Health Group, which explores the ways in which ubiquitous computing can support the daily health and wellness needs of people in their homes and everyday lives.

They use ethnography to discover the needs and challenges of older adults, particularly those struggling with cognitive decline. Jay will present some of Intel's pervasive sensing technologies and work deploying sensor networks to detect, track, and facilitate the social health of elders.

Martin Harris is the chief information officer and chairman of the Information Technology Division of the Cleveland Clinic Foundation in Cleveland, Ohio, a private, non-profit group practice that includes an academic medical center, outpatient services, a research institute, and an education foundation. He is also the executive director of e-Cleveland Clinic, a series of e-health clinical programs offered over the Internet.

29 SOCIO-TECHNICAL RESEARCH CHALLENGES IN UBIQUITOUS COMPUTING: The Case of Telematics

Ola Henfridsson
Viktoria Institute

John King
University of Michigan

Glenn Mercer
McKinsey Consulting

Dave Pavlich
Yellow Roadway

Walt Scacchi
University of California, Irvine

The modern automobile is an outstanding area of success for the diffusion of ubiquitous computing technologies (Walker et al. 2001; Want et al. 2002). The typical vehicle is equipped with a whole set of computer systems, controlling many of its taken-for-granted components such as the climate, engine, and transmission. Indeed, driving is an example of computer use that is weaved into the fabric of our everyday life (see Weiser 1991).

Telematics has lately emerged as a promising application area that combines vehicular computer systems and mobile network technologies for delivering value-adding services to both consumers and organizations. The services projected include fleet management, infotainment, remote diagnostics, vehicle management, and many more. While telematics is still in its infancy, industry analysts portray telematics as a fast-growing business domain for the coming years. Looking back at previous technology hypes, however, it can be assumed that the outcome of the current surge is dependent on the successful configuration and cultivation of business, organizational, and technological elements. In this regard, information systems researchers are well positioned for investigating the phenomena emerging with telematics.

The purpose of this panel is to explore a number of emerging telematic research issues with specific relevance for the field of information systems. Many of these issues are socio-technical in nature. This fact not only challenges IS researchers to apply their common stock of knowledge, but also to engage in developing novel theoretical and methodological approaches suitable for investigating the heterogeneous nature of telematics. Because telematic services typically rely on boundary-spanning mobility involving interconnected organizational and technological elements, the areas in which novel thinking is needed concur roughly with those of nomadic or ubiquitous information environments (see Lyytinen and Yoo 2002). Indeed, the development and use of telematic services often involve multiple user groups and interests, business actors and value propositions, as well as numerous coexisting open and proprietary technical standards utilized in different subsystems. Given this complexity, theoretical and methodological advancement can be necessary to understand how to conceptualize, design, and use ubiquitous applications and information systems for integrating the vehicle in the day-to-day practical problems of business, pleasure, and work.

We aim to stimulate discussion by presenting views on the following issues:

- Why is telematics an interesting application and challenging domain?
- How can we understand and analyze interactions between interconnected social and technical elements in telematic services?
- How can we deal with the methodological challenges involved in studying boundary-spanning mobility?
- How can the issue of multi-contextuality in ubiquitous computing be studied in the telematics context?
- What are the challenges in developing and designing large scale telematics infrastructures?
- What are the implications of telematics for transportation?

Each panelist will give a 10 minute presentation, raising particular issues and viewpoints engendered by their own experience of telematics research and practice. After the presentations, the audience will have an opportunity to discuss these and other viewpoints in what hopefully will be an interesting debate about challenges triggered by telematic applications and services.

Ola Henfridsson will discuss the multi-contextual nature of ubiquitous computing services. Ubiquitous computing envisions seamless access of mass-scale services over the multitude of contexts that users encounter in everyday mobility. However, to be successful, such computing must simultaneously be designed to provide transparent, integrated, and convenient support in localized use contexts. The issue of multi-contextuality makes the design of ubiquitous computing services and environments a challenging endeavor. In particular, the discussion will focus on the socio-technical challenges involved in designing systems support for mobile device use in cars. The discussion will work as a basis for exploring the potential role of ubiquitous computing support technology for mediating use patterns of general, multipurpose mobile devices in specific, resource-demanding use settings.

Glenn Mercer will discuss passenger car telematics in North America, as other panelists offer both a global perspective and insights into commercial vehicle telematics. As he sees it, the primary challenge facing telematics adoption—with all due respect for the wonders that the technology offers—is the weakness of the business case for it. We may indeed see telematics installations continue to rise in North America, but if this occurs only because car companies feel they must "give away" such installations gratis to consumers just to maintain competitive parity with rivals, then the technology must be declared a disappointment. We had hoped, in the early years of hype around this group of technologies, that there would have been a more attractive value proposition for drivers, so that they would pay for telematics systems at least in sufficient amounts to cover costs, if not to offer providers a profit. This has turned out—so far—not to be the case.

In speculating on the reasons for the low value drivers assign to telematics in North America, one can come up with several hypotheses:

- Market immaturity: perhaps too many people are just too unaware of what telematics can do for them (on the other hand, the United States has more telematics installations, via GM's OnStar, than the rest of the world combined).
- Regulatory issues: concerned about driver distraction, regulators and car companies have chosen telematics implementations that are safer but perhaps less attractive to customers than they otherwise might be, many navigation systems block route reprogramming unless the car is pulled to the side of the road and stopped, which is perhaps wise but certainly frustrating for the driver.
- Fundamental weakness in demand: the American grid pattern of road construction greatly erodes the value of navigation systems; rush-hour provision of traffic data from radio stations competes with onboard congestion updates; and ubiquitous cell phones (now being equipped with e-911) make some safety and security features of telematics redundant. Have we just not yet found the "killer app"?
- Competitive dynamics: does the sight of GM's OnStar system persistent failure to deliver profits (or even user renewal rates above 25 percent) dampen enthusiasm for other innovators to enter the market?

There may be other reasons for the lack of progress so far. Mr. Mercer would be very interested in input from attendees as to their hypotheses. He will also lay out a few thoughts on what developments might reinvigorate the telematics market for North American passenger vehicles.

Walt Scacchi is interested in discussing the interaction of different informatic or telematic regimes in venues like the personal automobile. Millions of new automobiles are being built and deployed worldwide each year, each as a mobile web of computing systems, sensors, control actuators, alarms, displays, and haptic interfaces, all dependent on vehicle power sources. This web is arrayed around applications addressing engine management and pollution control, safety and vehicle dynamics, driver dashboard (vehicle operating status) displays, and environmental and entertainment console. However, different organizational entities (design studios, automobile factories, car dealers, gasoline stations, and service centers) are associated with the design, manu-facturing, sales, operation, and maintenance of these automobiles. Somehow a common or integrated regime of computing hardware, software, and network technologies must be developed that spans and interlinks these disparate organizations, their information processing systems, and information workflow. Now add to this (1) many automobile commuters also bring along cell phones, media players and mobile computers, which can increasingly interface to one or more of the existing automobile applications or embedded systems, and (2) the emergence of so-called intelligent roadways and traffic flow management systems that monitor collective patterns of moving vehicles through government agencies (or their contractors). Finally, add to this the reality of widely deployed computing systems needing to be increasingly updated or patched, together with some users actively seeking to modify these systems to improve vehicle performance. We now come to see that the automobile is rapidly becoming one of the most ubiquitous, computing system-intensive venues of everyday life, yet it is perhaps one of the least studied. How and why we should engage in studies of the automobile as a socio-technical interaction network thus serves as a point of discussion.

REFERENCES

Lyytinen, K., and Yoo, Y. "Research Commentary: The Next Wave of Nomadic Computing," *Information Systems Research* (13:4) 2002, pp. 377-388.

Walker, G. H., Stanton, N. A., and Young, M. S. "Where is Computing Driving Cars?," *International Journal of Human-Computer Interaction* (13:2) 2001, pp. 203-229.

Want, R., Pering, T., Borriello, G., and Farkas, K. I. "Disappearing Hardware," *IEEE Pervasive Computing* (1:1) 2002, pp. 36-47.

Weiser, M. "The Computer for the 21st Century," *Scientific American*, September 1991, pp. 94-104.

30 COMMUNITY-BASED WIRELESS INITIATIVES: The Cooperation Challenge

Scott A. Shamp
University of Georgia
Athens, GA U.S.A.

Lev Gonick
Case Western Reserve University
Cleveland, OH U.S.A.

Sirkka L. Jarvenpaa
University of Texas at Austin
Austin, TX U.S.A.

Pouline Middleton
CrossRoads Copenhagen
Copenhagen, Denmark

Around the world, municipalities are exploring wireless as a way to improve their communities. Evangelists of community-based wireless are finding the technical challenges the easiest to master. Tougher challenges come in forging the partnerships, collaborations, and cooperative agreements necessary to make their community wireless initiatives a success. This panel will explore how three wireless initiatives in various stages of implementation are addressing the challenge of cooperation.

The OneCleveland initiative (http://www.onecleveland.org) will be represented by **Lev Gonick**, Chief Information Officer for Case Wester Reserve University. **Sirkka Jarvenpaa**, the James L. Bayless/ Rauscher Pierce Refsnes, Inc. Chair in Business Administration at the McCombs School of Business, University of Texas at Austin, will represent the Austin Wireless City project (http://www.austinwirelesscity.org/). **Pouline Middleton**, Managing Director of CrossRoads Copenhagen, will represent their project (http://www.crossroadscopenhagen.com/). **Scott Shamp**, Director of the New Media Institute at the University of Georgia, will represent the Wireless Athens Georgia Zone (http://www.athenscloud.com/), as well as serving as moderator for the panel.

Each panelist will briefly describe their wireless initiative and will highlight their strategies for fostering collaboration between government, business, service providers, educational institutions, and users.

31 UBIQUITOUS COMPUTING IN PRACTICE

Dick Braley
FedEx Services
Memphis, TN U.S.A.

Andy Fano
Accenture Technology Labs
Chicago, IL U.S.A.

Ora Lassila
Nokia Research Center
Boston, MA U.S.A.

John Light
Intel Research
Hillsboro, OR U.S.A.

Matt Germonprez
University of Wisconsin, Eau Claire
Eau Claire, WI U.S.A.
Case Western Reserve University
Cleveland, OH U.S.A.

Ubiquitous computing is intended to support new information environments, up to the minute sensory information, and context recognition. Companies around the world are implementing ubiquitous computing to support these needs in the form of short-range wireless systems for vehicle monitoring, sensor networks for complex systems management, and context aware devices for *ad hoc* networking. Participants of this panel illustrate how some of the world's leading companies are using ubiquitous computing. In addition, the participants raise questions about the impact of ubiquitous computing, intended and unintended, on both social and technical outcomes.

The FedEx Operating Companies provide a natural setting for the implementation and application of ubiquitous information environments because of their many service systems including a courier work force serving millions of customers worldwide, tens of thousands of trucks and delivery vans, sort facilities around the globe, and stations and customer service locations worldwide. FedEx is interested in how the philosophy and technology related to ubiquitous information environments can impact work environments, productivity enhancements, and customer satisfaction. The use of specific technologies such as Bluetooth, ZigBee, GPRS, CDMA, Software Defined Radios, "Smart Dust," and sensors by FedEx in ubiquitous information environments raises questions of how these specific technologies can help coordinate the afore-mentioned service systems and enhance the likelihood of success in implementing large-scale business solutions.

At Intel Research, wireless sensor networks are recognized as having the potential of revolutionizing how we see our world. These sensor networks are deployed over very large areas, without the expensive and often destructive installations that accompany centralized systems. They are in their infancy, so large-scale wireless sensor networks today might involve 65 sensor nodes covering an area of two acres. Ultimately, these networks may allow us to keep track of all the oceans, wilderness, farmland, and complex human-built systems to a level that allows them to be managed more efficiently and effectively. In the process of building several such networks, Intel has identified key technological and informational questions that must be resolved to enable more widespread use. One such deployment, in a Canadian vineyard, emphasizes three informational questions of how to determine the density of sensor nodes needed, what data should be collected, and how to make the information available to people so it can be most useful. Scaling these questions to thousands or millions of nodes makes compelling information technology questions.

Accenture Technology Labs developed the Accenture Remote Sensor Network prototype, a wireless mesh network of sensor nodes that can be spread across any area (from a factory to a forest floor), enabling organizations to gain unprecedented visibility and insight into product conditions and operations. To demonstrate how the network functions in a rugged, real-world environment, the Accenture Technology Labs' R&D team launched a field test with a vineyard in Northern California. The test involved embedding a network of wireless sensors across a 30 acre area to continuously sense humidity, wind, water, and soil and air temperature. Challenges the Accenture team overcame during testing included protecting the hardware from the elements and rodents, ensuring the reliability of the communication link, and, most importantly, building the right insight applications needed to make data useful for decision-making.

Nokia uses ubiquitous computing technology to better adapt to user tasks through automatic context recognition. The context can have many dimensions, such as a device's location, time of day, environment (outdoors, indoors, in the car, etc.), ambient noise level, and temperature. Context definitions, however, require complex knowledge representation to realistically model the real world. Mobile phones, in their smart-phone manifestations, are true ubiquitous computing devices, capable of communicating in an *ad hoc* fashion with other devices near and far. This communication, while potentially benefitting from context information, can also serve as a source of information for identifying the device's context. Semantic Web technologies offer a convenient yet powerful framework for supporting context-awareness, and are well suited to enhance interoperability. At Nokia, context recognition raises questions about what sophisticated approaches are required to support interoperability and *ad hoc* networking in ubiquitous computing environments.

Mark Weiser's vision of ubiquitous computing is becoming increasingly apparent in today's computing landscape. We must understand the technologies we are capable of working with, the processes and systems we expect these technologies to support, and the questions within this computing paradigm in order to engage in dialogue, research, and practice regarding ubiquitous computing. In this panel, panelists present technologies, systems, and questions that exist at some of the foremost companies using ubiquitous computing. We hope this will provide a forum for rich dialogue among practitioners and academics that will inform and shape our theories and practices with increasingly ubiquitous information environments.

Index of Contributors